AUSTRALIAN
Medicinal Plants

AUSTRALIAN Medicinal Plants

E.V. Lassak & T. McCarthy

This edition published 1997 by Reed
a part of Reed Books Australia
35 Cotham Road, Kew, Victoria 3101

Published 1990 by Mandarin
Reprinted 1992

First published in 1983 by
Methuen Australia
Reprinted 1984, 1985, 1987

Designed by Robin James

Copyright © Erich V. Lassak and Tara McCarthy 1983
© Paintings and drawings Betty Hinton 1983

All rights reserved. Without limiting the rights under copyright above, no part of this publication may be reproduced, stored in or introduced into a retrieval system, or transmitted in any form or by any means (electronic, mechanical, photocopying, recording or otherwise), without the prior written permission of both the copyright owner and the publisher.

Produced in China

National Library of Australia
cataloguing-in-publication data:
Lassak, E.V. (Erich V.).
Australian medicinal plants.

Bibliography.
Includes index.
ISBN 0 7301 0503 2.

1. Medicinal plants - Australia.
I. McCarthy, Tara. II. Title.

581.6340994

Contents

Caution
6
Preface
7
Authors' note
9
1 Introductory notes and observations
11
2 Narcotics and painkillers
21
3 Headaches, colds and fevers
45
4 Tonics
73
5 Antiseptics and bactericides
Treatment of wounds and inflammations
94
6 Skin disorders
123
7 Digestion and elimination
141
8 Miscellaneous cures
166
9 More myth than medicine?
181
10 The medicinal plant industry
193
Table of plant uses
209
Bibliography and references
221
Glossary
225
Index
230

Caution

THIS BOOK DESCRIBES Australian native medicinal plants and their *reported* uses. The authors do not endorse any plant or method of application found here as a prescription for any particular ailment. We strongly discourage experimentation by untrained persons in the collection and administration of native plants for medicinal purposes because, as can be seen in the text of this book, many plants can be dangerous taken internally or applied externally. Scientifically, their real effects have yet to be determined. The authors and publisher waive any responsibility for injuries to readers of this book resulting from the use of plants listed here.

Preface

THE LARGE VOLUME of information on Australian medicinal plants is fragmented. Apart from J.H. Maiden's chapter on this subject in his book *The Useful Native Plants of Australia,* published in 1889, most of the remaining information is contained in various technical articles scattered through a multitude of scientific journals, governmental reports, brief references in books, and the like and is on the whole not easy to obtain. Botanical nomenclature has in many cases been modified owing to progress made in the past 150 years in the taxonomy of our native flora. One of the aims of this book was, therefore, to collect as much as possible of the information available and to amend plant species names in accordance with present day knowledge, thus making it a suitable point of departure for any future research in this area.

Even though this work attempts to be as complete as possible the authors are aware of gaps. For example, a small number of plants has been omitted if serious doubts existed as to their identity or uses. Introduced plants, as far as possible, have not been included; even though there could be some that may have been introduced so early in the history of the Colony as to make their status doubtful. Furthermore, records of plant utilization being presently gathered by scholars of Australian Aboriginal culture, and until now unpublished, have, apart from the odd exception, not been included.

It has been said that 'drugs are poisons in sub-lethal doses'. Though this is undoubtedly the case with the great majority of drugs, specific references to a species' poison-plant potential have been usually omitted. The reader is referred to S.L. Everist's excellent book *Poisonous Plants of Australia* published in 1974. Likewise, references to food potential and food value have not been included, and the reader is directed to the recent book of A.B. & J.W. Cribb, *Wild Food in Australia.*

The aim of this book is to present to the interested public the potential of our native flora, to spur on and point the way to further work in this neglected field, and thus to extend the pioneering efforts of Dr J. Bancroft, his son Dr T.L. Bancroft, Dr J. Lauterer, and the eminent Baron F. von Mueller during the last century and continued for a time after the Second World War by the Australian Phytochemical Survey.

The subdivision of this book into chapters, such as Tonics, Narcotics and painkillers, Digestion and elimination, has been arrived at by grouping together broad areas of reported uses rather than by a consideration of underlying causes. The authors realize that a headache, for example, may be due to a number of different causes: high blood pressure, tension, indigestion, a variety of infectious diseases, or even a brain tumour. However, those who originally utilized the cures did not, on the whole, distinguish between causes either; thus it is felt that the method used is justifiable although it does cause overlaps between chapters.

Since most plants had more than one area of application a Table of plant species and of their uses has been included as an appendix as a means of rapid cross-referencing.

Individual plant descriptions (included at the end of each chapter where they are most relevant) are not botanically diagnostic, but have been included in order to help the reader familiarize himself with the general appearance of the plant. For the benefit of the non-botanist they have been rendered, as far as possible, in everyday English, and a glossary is included at the end of the book.

Remarks as to active constituents are meant only as a rough guide, since in many cases the activity has not been fully substantiated. A more thorough search of the chemical literature may provide additional information and the authors, therefore, beg the reader's forgiveness for any omissions.

References are where possible to books or major reviews rather than to individual technical papers (even though exceptions occur), and have been dictated by considerations of space.

Authors' note

IT IS WITH GREAT PLEASURE and gratitude that we wish to acknowledge help without which the writing of this book would not have been possible:

Dr R. Boden, Director, National Botanic Gardens and Herbarium, Canberra, Dr L.A.S. Johnson, Director, Royal Botanical Gardens and National Herbarium of N.S.W., Sydney, Dr R.W. Johnson, Director, Queensland Herbarium, Indooroopilly and members of their respective staffs for most helpful discussions, botanical assistance as well as permission to reproduce numerous photographic slides. Included here are slides taken by J.M. Baldwin, C. Green, M. Fagg, M. Olsen, I. Ravenscroft, A.N. Rodd and R.T. Walker. We thank also Mr and Mrs W. Hinton for several slides of northern Queensland plants, Mrs T. Berry, Miss D. Levitt, Drs R.B. Longmore, J.T. Pinhey and L.J. Webb, Messrs G. Althofer, Director, Lake Burrendong Arboretum, A. Barr, H. Hunt, P. Latz, R. Mendham, D. Smyth, F. Towney, P. Trezise and their friends for giving freely of their time for discussions and recounting of their experiences, Messrs G.R. Davis and J. Hillier for allowing us to include photographs of their respective field operations, and our families for patience, help and constant encouragement. One of us (E.V.L.) wishes particularly to thank his wife for her assistance in getting the manuscript finished on time.

To our parents, partners and friends with profound thanks for their help and forbearance.

CHAPTER ONE

Introductory notes and observations

Eucalyptus globulus

AUSTRALIAN MEDICINAL PLANTS fall broadly into four categories:
  (a) those which have been used by the Aborigines,
  (b) those used by European settlers (and in some rare cases by other migrant groups),
  (c) plants which, though native to Australia, have been used exclusively overseas where they also occur in the native state, and finally
  (d) plants not used as such, but whose pharmacologically active components could be extracted and used by the pharmaceutical industry.

Some overlap exists, particularly between the first two categories. Some plants have been used by settlers and Aborigines alike; in some cases it is not clear whether the settlers borrowed a cure from the Aborigines or the other way round. Dulcie Levitt, who spent twenty-five years as a missionary on Groote Eylandt, suspects that the local Aborigines used the essential oil rich leaves of certain paperbark melaleucas for treating colds only after noticing missionaries using eucalyptus oil in similar circumstances.[1] Both oils are rich in 1,8-cineole and exhibit, therefore, a very similar odour.

Whilst the use of plant remedies by the early white settlers is on the whole well documented, most Aboriginal uses have been transmitted from one generation to the next and finally to us entirely by word of mouth. This immediately presents certain problems, for example:
  (a) were the preparation of the remedy and the method of treatment correctly reported,
  (b) was the plant species properly identified,
  (c) did mistakes or inaccuracies creep in during reporting, such as through language difficulties?

It is interesting to note that many entries in Roth's list[2] of plants used medicinally by north Queensland Aborigines were not obtained from direct contact but are based on reports of others. For example:

> *Excoecaria parvifolia,* F.v.M.—for pains and sickness. The natives use the bark mashed up in water in a wooden trough, and heated with stones from a fire close by. The wash is applied externally to all parts of the body, rubbing it on. Cloncurry, Mitchell Rivers (E. Palmer).
>
> *Calamus caryotoides,* Mart.—On the Bloomfield River, the young shoots, when eaten, are believed to cure headache (R. Hislop).
>
> *Ficus scabra,* G. Forst [*Ficus coronata* is the species actually referred to]—The milky juice of the young shoots is employed by the natives medicinally, and is represented by Murrells, from personal experience, to be very efficacious in healing wounds. After the application of the milky juice ... the scraped root-bark of the Grewia ... is used as a poultice to the wound. Cleveland Bay (A. Thozet, quoted by E. Gregory).

The method of preparation of the remedy is extremely important and, as Dulcie Levitt[1] observes, 'it is so easy to think you know what they are doing and you don't'. Miss Levitt admits she thought the preparation of 'cocky apple' *(Planchonia careya)* bark for an antiseptic simply meant shredding it into a container with water. In actual fact

> what they did was to chop the bark off the tree (most trees have a hard outside bark and a thinner inside bark), and it is usually the thinner inside bark that

is used. They peel the inside bark, which in this case was red, away from the hard grey outside bark, fold it up, twisted it and hammered it on a stone and then shredded it with their fingers and then put it in the container of water.

In another instance Miss Levitt observed the crushed *green* berries of an unfortunately unidentified species) being rubbed on the body against tinea, whereas open sores were treated only with the ripe *white* berries. Green, or even partly green, berries were discarded in the latter case. This precision is often lacking in some older reports on Aboriginal plant use.

The precise identification of the plant is another problem. Both Dulcie Levitt and Peter Latz (a botanist and ecologist with the Arid Zone Research Institute of the Northern Territory) assure us that the Aborigines are very good botanists and probably do not make many mistakes. Miss Levitt reports, for instance, that in northern Australia only certain barks were used for their antiseptic qualities, and stresses that not just any bark was used. Apart from any reservations one may have about infallibility in general, errors could have been introduced by a person insufficiently versed in Aboriginal name usage who may have made the wrong connection between an Aboriginal name and its botanical equivalent. 'Adikalyikba' is applied on Groote Eylandt to two crinum lilies, *Crinum asiaticum* and *C. uniflorum;* both have characteristic big onion-like bulbs at the base. The same name, 'adikalyikba', was also applied to certain toadstools with round white tops. 'Pituri', though chiefly applied to a narcotic preparation from *Duboisia hopwoodii,* was occasionally applied to certain species of *Nicotiana* with similar narcotic properties. The same common names could thus be applied to different species with either some superficial similarity in appearance, or similar pharmacological effects.

Another source of serious error has been described by J.H. Maiden as follows: 'Aboriginals are sometimes so very willing to give names of plants to the traveller, that rather than disappoint him, they will prepare a few for the occasion.'[3]

According to Ethel Shaw explanations were often incomplete, if forthcoming at all:

> Sometimes the old man got very tired of so much questioning by the students of Aboriginal customs. One old man went off to bed one day after a long talk with an inquirer, saying he was 'too sick'. He remained 'sick' until the visitor left the station, when he speedily recovered. 'What was the matter with you, Dick?' someone asked. 'Oh, that fellow, he ask too many questions, he make me sick' was the reply.[4]

The problem of obtaining accurate information is a major one. The two examples just mentioned highlight some of the difficulties that arise when two very different cultures meet. Often they are exacerbated when the parties are either unwilling or incapable of adjustment to the sensibilities of the other. Dulcie Levitt tells us that the

> Aborigines take a long time to get to know a person and they don't really trust a stranger, because in the old days, a stranger was quite often an enemy. Therefore, it takes them about two years to even begin to get to know you. Although

they will tell you some things, there are a lot of things they won't tell you. They certainly won't tell anything to people who tend to laugh at any of their beliefs. You have to be very, very careful even if they tell you something that sounds absolutely preposterous. Don't show surprise or disgust or even disbelief. Don't query it.[1]

The problem is further compounded by the fact that only a handful of people are left who have extensive knowledge of Aboriginal herbal medicine. And, while men know all the plants, Peter Latz[5] tells us that it is the women who know the finer details of their respective uses. A lot of the information on medicinal plants must have been already irrevocably lost, particularly in the more densely populated and industrialized south-eastern states of Australia, and more is being lost every year as the older generation of Aborigines diminishes in number. The assumption that the Tasmanian Aborigines had no knowledge of herbal medicine, except for the use of the 'pigface', a species of *Carpobrotus* as a purgative[6] is unlikely to be entirely correct and may simply reflect our lack of knowledge of them owing to their early extinction.

Percy Trezise, artist, bush pilot, author and the man who helped establish the reserve 'Quinkan Country' on Cape York Peninsula reports[7] that, with only a few exceptions, the northern Queensland Aborigines already rely heavily on western medicine. Amongst these exceptions, where knowledge of traditional medicine is still alive, he includes the settlements at Aurukun, Edward River and on Mornington Island.

Scientists from the CSIRO have been involved since 1979 in the Cape York Ecology Transect Project (CAYET), which will include comments on Aboriginal medicinal plant use. Also in 1979, the Department of Primary Production and the Department of Health (including the Arid Zone Research Institute, Alice Springs) in the Northern Territory decided on a study of Aboriginal medicine, and they hope to produce in due course an Aboriginal pharmacopoeia.

It has been suggested that the Aborigines were originally a relatively healthy people and thus needed little medication. Occasional digestive upsets causing diarrhoea were adequately treated with numerous readily available astringents (such as eucalypt kinos); fevers were treated with a large variety of plants, amongst which the bark of *Alstonia constricta* stands out as particularly effective. Toothaches, relatively common among the elderly, owing to the wearing down of their teeth after a life-long diet of fibrous and tough food, were relieved by chewing the leaves of the common 'wilga' *(Geijera parviflora),* whereas cavities in teeth were filled with resins such as that of *Euodia vitiflora.* There were herbal remedies for wounds xand sores, colds and rheumatism, in fact for almost any common condition.

It was not until the arrival of the first white settlers that infectious diseases, such as our common measles, chicken pox, and mumps, and the more serious tuberculosis, venereal diseases (syphilis and gonorrhoea), as well as tetanus, were introduced causing terrible havoc amongst the native population unused to them, and thus without any resistance at all.

The Europeans' arrival influenced Aboriginal pharmacy in one important way. In the past plant material had been extracted in cold water or at best in warm water, by placing the container with the mixture (usually a bailer shell) near a fire or on hot stones. The introduction of metal pots allowed extraction with boiling water, an innovation readily appreciated and seized upon by the Aborigines.

The question of how much the settlers learned from the native population is not easy to answer. It appears from some reports that the new arrivals were on the whole unwilling to try Aboriginal treatments, preferring to try plants which reminded them in some way of those they had known in Britain and other European countries, as well as elsewhere (for example India and China). The language barrier, claimed by some as having prevented communication, is not, in the authors' opinion, an entirely satisfactory explanation. An ulcer or gaping wound do not require much communicating to get the message across that treatment is required.

One of the first, if not the first, plants used medicinally by the British immigrants was the 'Sydney peppermint' *(Eucalyptus piperita)*. The odour of its crushed leaves is vaguely pepperminty and probably reminded them of their own English peppermint *(Mentha piperita)*. Its volatile oil, obtained by steam-distillation of the foliage, was reputed to cure 'cholicky' complaints, and was the first plant product sent from Australia to England. As it happens the chemical composition of the two oils is very different. Menthol and menthone, the two major constituents of *Mentha piperita* oil are absent from *Eucalyptus piperita* leaf oil, whereas piperitone, the main component of the latter oil, is present in peppermint oil in trace amounts only. It was simply a happy accident of Nature that the two oils had similar medicinal qualities, and it was fortunate that *Eucalyptus piperita* oil was taken in small amounts only since it is somewhat more toxic than peppermint oil. But all this was discovered much later.

The question of who was first to discover the usefulness of *Eucalyptus piperita* caused some controversy since the honour was claimed by both John White, Surgeon-General to the Colony, and Denis Considen, Surgeon of the First Fleet (and assistant to White). White was generally credited with the discovery, until, well over a hundred years later, J.H. Maiden declared he felt Considen probably deserved the credit.[8] His view is based on a letter sent to Sir Joseph Banks by Considen in 1788 saying that he had sent a specimen of the oil to him and that 'if there is any merit in applying these and many other samples to the benefit of the poor wretches here, I certainly claim it, being the first who discovered and recommended them'. White, as Considen's superior, probably only acted officially in reporting the matter. Whatever the truth of who first guessed at and discovered the medicinal properties of *Eucalyptus piperita,* this initial promising result ushered in the next stage in the search for medicinally useful native plants.

Except for the fact that in many cases written records were kept, the early settlers' methods probably did not differ very much from those of the Aborigines. Plants were selected by comparison or reference to already known facts. So, for instance, the native mints *Mentha satureioides* and *Mentha diemenica* were substituted for the related European 'pennyroyal', *Mentha pulegium;* bitterness was associated with tonic and digestion-improving qualities, thus leading to the discovery and use of *Sebaea ovata, Alstonia constricta, Doryphora sassafras, Smilax glyciphylla* and many others.

The empirical approach prevailing at that time had many firm supporters, amongst them the naturalist T.W. Shepherd, who suggested that we should 'enquire into every circumstance where instinct or experience comes into play', as the following humorous, if somewhat longwinded anecdote quoted by Shepherd will show:

> Many years ago, we were on terms of friendship with a respectable old mastiff, who responded to the princely but familiar title of Tiger. This old fellow, whether a learned medico or not, ... had discovered an antidote to the poison peculiar to the Sydney 'Toad Fish' *(Tetraodon Hamiltonii)*. The old gentleman being somewhat epicurean in his tastes, and residing in the vicinity of one of the sandy beaches—so frequent on the shores of our beautiful harbour—was in the almost daily habit of wading amongst the briny wavelets in pursuit of the beforementioned, and well known, Plectognanthean Gymnodont, large numbers of which he captured and transferred to his assimilating laboratory with apparent satisfaction. As soon as his feast was concluded, he hastened to the neighbouring indigenous shrubbery, and there selected and partook of medicinal herbs which rendered the poison harmless. Our old friend followed his favourite pursuit for several years without appearing to suffer any ill consequences from his dangerous diet, nor did he relinquish his favourite sporting and banqueting enjoyments until grim old age 'held him fast'. Poor old Tiger! Might not this antidote, discovered by a dog, prove equally efficacious in relieving cases of poisoning by Toad fish which have often proved fatal to both children and grown persons.

Delightful as Shepherd's example of the experimental approach may be, there are gaping holes in the story. What a pity he did not mention *which* plants poor old Tiger ate. It is common for dogs to eat grass when they feel off colour, and apparently any grass will do. It is also possible that the poor old toad fish had met their match in Tiger's remarkable constitution. For all we know, the poison of the toad fish may not be nearly as toxic to dogs as it is to humans. The assumption, commonly applied in Europe by mushroom collectors, that fungi showing evidence of having been nibbled at or eaten by forest animals must be safe for human consumption is not a particularly scientific one. Koalas may ingest, for instance, comparatively large amounts of eucalyptus oil in their diet of eucalyptus leaves. The same amounts of eucalyptus oil would almost certainly kill a grown man. The simple explanation is that koalas generate sufficient amounts of glucuronic acid to be able to conjugate it to any oil ingested, thus allowing the water-soluble glucuronides of the various oil constituents to be eliminated in their urine. Man does not produce glucuronic acid in the same large amounts as the koala and thus cannot eliminate the oil sufficiently quickly.

Investigation, if it is to be of any value, has to be properly set out and completed. All variables have to be considered. Half-hearted hit-and-miss experiments may pose questions; they seldom lead to answers. If the experimenter neither turns green nor drops dead immediately he is only partially the wiser.

Interest in native medicinal plants seemed to wane between the First and

Second World Wars. This decline occurred for a number of reasons, amongst them the mushrooming of the pharmaceutical industry in Europe with concomitant sales pressures, the availability of very effective synthetic drugs such as 'aspirin' (acetylsalicylic acid) and the sulphonamides, improved means of transport, which not only shortened the time for drugs manufactured overseas to reach Australia, but which also increased their availability in outback areas, and last, but certainly not least, fashion.

Then, during the Second World War, the necessity of locating and developing new sources of plant drugs, particularly alkaloids, led to a resurgence of interest in the native flora, both from a chemical as well as from a pharmacological point of view. The effort, co-ordinated by the CSIRO and involving universities and government departments as well, became known in 1945 as the Australian Phytochemical Survey. During its entire existence, until the beginning of the 1970s, a prodigious number of plant species had been investigated, resulting in the isolation and structural elucidation of hundreds of new compounds. Whilst the chemical side of the operation expanded and kept flowing a constant stream of results, the pharmacological and biological testing lagged far behind, and, apart from some preliminary bacteriological screening and the like, produced little else. The author recalls his lack of success, in the late 1960s, in finding an institution willing to test the volatile oil of *Centipeda cunninghamii*, a plant reputed to be useful in the treatment of sandy blight, that is, purulent ophthalmia. The oil was finally sent to India to an institution interested in its properties.

Even though the Australian Phytochemical Survey did much to further our *chemical* knowledge of the Australian native flora, the final result in *economic* terms is far from impressive (for reasons that could be debated at some length but do not fall within the framework of this book). The only compounds produced on and off on a commercial scale in Australia (apart from cineole and essential oils in general) are hyoscine (an alkaloid), rutin (a flavonoid), and aesculin (a coumarin, the production of which is about to commence); the production of solasodine (a steroidal alkaloid from several species of *Solanum*) could become a viable proposition if the presently used raw materials for the production of cortisone became either unavailable or if their prices increased to such a level that solasodine could compete with them.

Finally, a few general remarks on botanical nomenclature and naming in general, as well as on chemical variability within species seem appropriate.

Andrew Ross, a medical practitioner in the New South Wales country town of Molong, wrote over a hundred years ago: 'The gum from the wattle tree, when dissolved in boiling milk, is now frequently used by many of the settlers in the interior for dysentery and diarrhoea; and it is said with very good results!'[9] Now, there are more than 700 species of *Acacia* (i.e. wattle) throughout the world. Some produce a lot of gum and some produce none. Some wattle gums, such as that of *Acacia decurrens*, are insoluble, whilst others, like that of *Acacia dealbata*, are very soluble in water. There are high molecular weight gums yielding viscous solutions, and there are low molecular weight wattle gums yielding relatively thin solutions. Which one did Dr Ross have in mind? This use of non-specific terminology has driven many a researcher up the proverbial wall.

One could add many more examples. The general term 'tea-tree' is even more confusing because if may refer to species of the genera *Leptospermum* and *Melaleuca*. 'Gum tree' in the Australian context refers to any tree producing a red or orange exudate of 'gum' and includes numerous species of *Eucalyptus* and *Angophora*. Many references to potentially useful plants have thus been robbed of all value simply because it is impossible to decide which precise plant species they refer to.

Likewise, the use of Aboriginal names may confuse matters; not so much because a certain plant may have many different names depending on how many different tribes used it, but rather because the white man's rendering of the sound he heard differed from person to person. The many spellings of the narcotic 'pituri' are such an example (see chapter 2). Another example of how the waters were muddied comes from J.H. Maiden commenting on a colleague's handwriting in describing the Aboriginal names for *Eremophila longifolia,* commonly known as 'emu bush'.

> 'Berrigan' is an Aboriginal name over a very wide area, but it is now a well established Australian vernacular ... It is the 'Kinyamurra' of the Mount Lyndhurst, South Australia, blacks (Max Koch). The late Dr A.W. Howitt gave me the name of 'Kunyamurra' as in use by the Aborigines of Killalpanina, Cooper's Creek, Lake Eyre, which seems very like Mr Koch's name, but as my dear friend Dr Howitt's handwriting was not of the same high quality as his scientific knowledge, the name should be confirmed.[10]

To complicate matters further, there are cases where the Aborigines have taken English words and changed them so as to be unrecognizable to whites when they boomeranged back under the guise of being genuine Aboriginal names. For example, it has been suggested that the term 'panaryle' of the Aborigines of Coranderrk Station in Victoria is a corruption of 'pennyroyal'.

Continuing research into the Australian flora, including revisions of groups of related species or of whole genera, may make name changes necessary. Some of the reasons are, for instance: a currently used name may become invalid if a previously published name comes to light and which, being the older one, takes precedence; varieties of one author may be elevated to species rank by another; a species may be switched from one genus to another; certain variable species may be split up into several new species upon closer inspection, etc.

S.T. Blake mentions in his revision of *Melaleuca leucadendron* that 'the name has been used in a very broad sense but correctly refers to one of a complex of ten species distinguished by hitherto overlooked characters in the sepals, indumentum, stamens and foliage correlated with differences in habit.'[11] He mentions, amongst other things, that the name *Melaleuca viridiflora* has been misapplied to *Melaleuca quinquenervia* (*Melaleuca viridiflora* is a quite separate species), a misapplication which still persists in some non-botanical circles, particularly outside Australia.

It is for these reasons that certain overseas plants, once erroneously thought to be native in Australia as well, and thus listed in some of the older references as Australian medicinal plants, have been omitted. A list of these is given for the sake of completeness:

Abutilon indicum—our species is *Abutilon albescens; Casearia esculenta*—our species is *Casearia multinervosa; Cordia myxa; Gratiola peruviana*—our species are *Gratiola pubescens* and *Gratiola latifolia; Hydrocharis morsus-ranae*—our species is *Hydrocharis dubia; Kyllinga brevifolia; Luzula campestris*—our species is *Luzula meridionalis; Melastoma malabathricum; Oxalis corniculata; Rostellularia procumbens* (also known as *Justicia procumbens*)—our species is *Rostellularia pogonanthera; Sesbania grandiflora; Syzygium jambolanum* (syn. *Eugenia jambolana*)—our species is *Syzygium moorei; Tephrosia purpurea*—the Australian species is mostly *Tephrosia brachyodon.*

It is a common mistake to think that all individuals of the same plant species must be chemically identical. This may stem from our contemporary view of the cultivated useful plants from Europe and elsewhere. Over thousands of years undesirable strains have been eliminated by continual culling, finally giving the impression of chemical similarity if not of complete constancy. For example, lavender grown commercially in southern France is all of the same type and yields on steam-distillation oils of almost constant composition; and all commercial peppermint oils from *Mentha piperita* contain between 50 and 55 per cent of menthol.

In Australia man had little or no time, or possibly inclination, to interfere with the natural selection of native plants. The Aborigines were not cultivators of the soil but nomads living by hunting and gathering.

In the 1920s the then Director and his Deputy of what is now the Museum of Applied Arts and Sciences in Sydney made an extraordinary discovery while on a botanical collecting trip in southern New South Wales. They stopped their car on a country road to inspect a stand of the broadleaved peppermint *(Eucalyptus dives)* and to their amazement found that the crushed foliage of one tree had the characteristic pepperminty odour normally associated with the species while the foliage of a neighbouring tree exhibited the scent of cineole. They had discovered the phenomenon of chemical variation within a species. They and their successors have shown that this is more the rule than the exception in the Australian flora.

Other well-known examples of chemical variation in essential-oil-bearing species include *Melaleuca quinquenervia* (one form of which is rich in 1,8-cineole and is used medicinally in New Caledonia, where it is known as 'Niaouli'), *Eucalyptus citriodora, Leptospermum petersonii,* and many, many others. Chemical variation is equally common in other native species. For instance, *Duboisia myoporoides* exists in forms rich in hyoscine (scopolamine) and anabasine, and in New Caledonia even in nicotine. Another pitfall is the variation in the amount of a medicinal component in a specific plant. The hyoscine content of *Duboisia myoporoides* leaves may vary from 0.3 to 2.5 per cent.

The Aborigines were aware of the phenomenon of chemical variation. Dulcie Levitt tells us that 'on Groote Eylandt there is a pea plant growing. It is not used on Groote Eylandt for anything, but it is used for medicine over ... on the mainland.'[1] She also mentions that the Aborigines will not eat the gum of *Erythrophleum chlorostachyum* ('Cooktown ironwood') growing on Groote Eylandt because it makes them ill, yet will eat it from trees growing on the Rose River, on the mainland opposite. The earlier mentioned case of the green berries of a particular plant being used for the treatment of tinea, whereas sores were treated with the ripe white berries, is another example of the Aborigines' realization that the active components in a plant were not constant.

It has been often suggested that different soil types are responsible for this variation. This is generally not so. Chemical composition is in most cases genetically determined. Since the seed from a given single parent is rarely genetically homogeneous, one would expect a great deal of variation in the progeny derived from it. In some of those cases where this does not appear to happen, it may simply mean that only those seeds predisposed to a particular type of soil germinated and grew into a healthy plant, whereas seeds predisposed to another type of soil failed to germinate.

It is easy to see that botanical knowledge has to be supplemented with some appreciation of the chemistry of the plant intended for use. Without this knowledge there will always be the increased danger of an extract or plant remedy either doing little good or being too strong and thus harmful.

CHAPTER TWO
Narcotics and painkillers

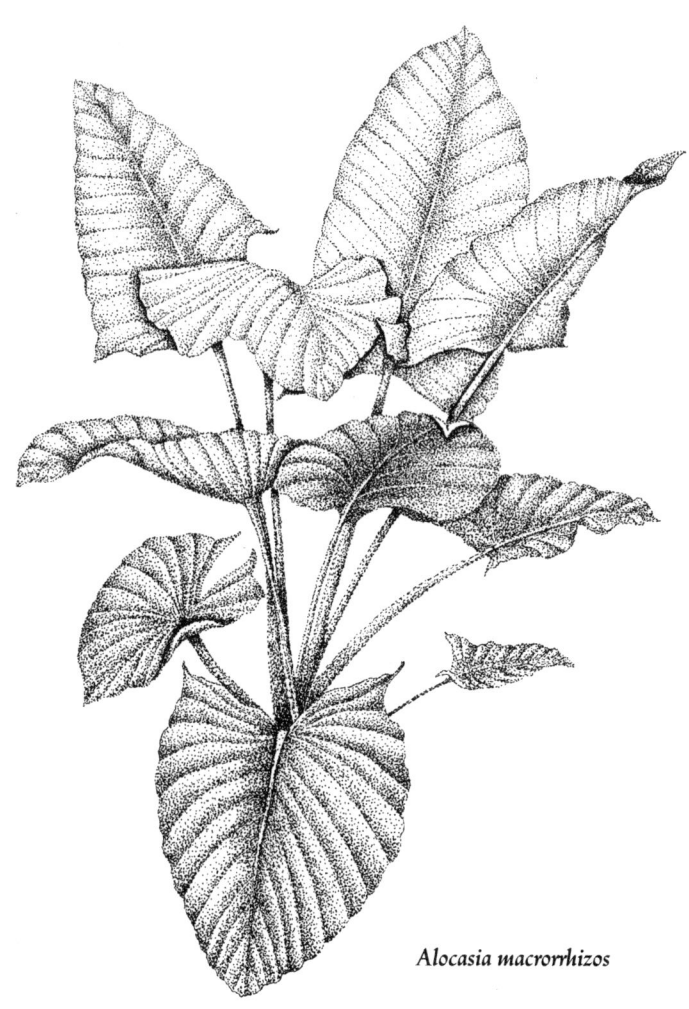

Alocasia macrorrhizos

AMONGST ALL NARCOTIC SUBSTANCES used by the Australian Aborigines, none surpassed 'pituri' in importance. Its fame led the north Queensland writer J.R. Chisholm to remark: 'What opium is to the Chinaman, what whisky is to the Scotchman, so is "pituri" to the western blackfellow. It is his very soul—without it he has no life almost.'[10]

The drug has been prepared from certain species of the family Solanaceae, in particular *Duboisia hopwoodii*, and, in certain areas of Central Australia, *Nicotiana excelsior* and *Nicotiana gossei*. The name 'pituri' was given to the drug by a small tribe that inhabited the sandhills country of the upper Mulligan River in western Queensland, near the boundary with the Northern Territory. The common use of this name throughout Central Australia has been attributed by T.H. Johnston and J.B. Cleland[12] to the influence of the white man. The spelling itself has been rendered in many different variations, for example, pedgery, bedgery, pitcheri, probably because of the difficulty in reproducing exactly the sounds of various unfamiliar Aboriginal languages, as well as owing to the interchangeability of 'p' and 'b', and 'd' and 't' observed by Roth in some of these languages in parts of western Queensland. Johnston and Cleland go on to suggest in their interesting articles on the history of this Aboriginal narcotic that 'pituri' should be reserved for the drug originally prepared in western Queensland from *Duboisia hopwoodii* and that the Aranda name 'ingulba' be used for the drug prepared from species of *Nicotiana*. The Luritja tribe's name for the drug, 'mingulba', is probably nothing more than a derivation of the latter.

The preparation of 'pituri' has been described by J.H. Maiden as follows:

> The drug is in the form of leaves, more or less powdered, mixed with finely broken twigs, forming altogether a brown herb. So fine is the powder, and so irritating, that the most careful examination of a specimen is attended with sneezing ... They gather the tops and leaves when the plant is in blossom, and hang them up to dry.[3]

A.W. Howitt, the leader of the rescue party that found King, the sole survivor of the ill-fated Burke and Wills expedition, made the following entry in his diary for 10 September, 1861: 'The native ... gave me a small ball of what seemed to be chewed grass as a token of friendship',[12] Later on the same day a member of Howitt's party was presented by the Aborigines 'with a small quantity of some dried plant from a bundle which one of them carried; it had a strong pungent taste and smell, and I am at a loss to conjecture its use unless a kind of tobacco.'[12] These two passages refer most certainly to 'pituri' in its prepared, chewed form, and to its condition prior to use, respectively.

'Pituri' was chewed by the Aborigines in much the same way, and probably for the same reasons, as tobacco by the Europeans. And just as in some societies a pipe is passed from one smoker to the next, so, according to an account left by Maiden, the chewing of 'pituri' took on at times the significance of a social event, 'a quid being passed from one native to another, and when they have had sufficient, one politely plasters it behind his ear.'[3]

The latter custom is not nearly so strange if one remembers the chewing gum mania of the early post-Second World War years when many a youngster preserved his precious lump of gum in exactly the same place—behind the ear!

Sometimes the drug was prepared by moistening the roasted dried leaves and stalks of *Duboisia hopwoodii* and rolling them in the ash of the bark, leaves, or twigs of certain species of *Acacia, Cassia, Eucalyptus,* before working them up into quids or rolls about 6 cm long and 1.5 cm in diameter. The quids were sometimes mixed with threads of native flax (a species of *Psoralea*) to make them stick together.[12]

The chief narcotic constituent of *Duboisia hopwoodii* (as well as of the two species of *Nicotiana, N. excelsior* and *N. gossei*) is the alkaloid nicotine, identified in the plant by A. Petit as early as 1879.[12] Some of the difficulties encountered by early researchers working on the chemical structure of 'piturine', the total alkaloidal extract of *Duboisia hopwoodii,* were due to 'piturine' being a mixture of nicotine and a second alkaloid, *nor*-nicotine. These two compounds are chemically closely related and may be very difficult to separate from one another.

Nicotine is a powerful poison affecting the nervous system. Symptoms of poisoning include nausea, diarrhoea, vomiting, mental confusion, twitching and convulsions. Free nicotine is readily absorbed through mucous membranes, but its salts (i.e. compounds resulting from its reaction with acids) are not. As with most alkaloids, nicotine usually occurs in plants bound to certain common organic acids, such as citric acid and malic acid. It may, therefore, be liberated from these salts by the action of alkalis such as are present in the ash of most plants, thus explaining the practice of mixing 'pituri' with ash prior to chewing. It is not quite clear whether the Aborigines discovered the enhancing effect of ash on the potency of the drug by themselves, or whether it was an innovation introduced by some of the early European immigrants. The basification of plant tissue with ammonia, lime, or magnesia, required for a complete and efficient recovery of alkaloids present, has been a standard procedure in the chemical industry for a very long time. For instance, the alkaloid caffeine may be solvent-extracted from ground tea leaves after mixing them with magnesia.

'Pituri' has also occasionally been smoked by the Aborigines. It appears, however, that this practice has been copied from tobacco-smoking Europeans.[12]

The initial effect of 'pituri' is that of a stimulant. Later, the user starts to feel a bit 'heavy' and finally sleepy. Dr Joseph Bancroft also found that its use caused severe headaches in Europeans.[10] Also, according to Dr Bancroft,

> The blacks about Eyre's Creek appeared to use it preparatory to undertaking any serious business, i.e. as a stimulant generally. As an example, one old man Mr. Gilmour and party fell in with, refused to have anything to say or do until he had chewed the pituri, after which he rose and harangued in grand style, ordering the explorers to leave the place. Mr. Wiltshire, however, states that it is not used for exciting their courage, or for bringing them up to fighting pitch, but to produce a 'voluptuous dreamy sensation'.[10]

Maiden again reported that

> In small quantities it has a powerful stimulating effect, assuaging hunger, and enabling long journeys to be made without fatigue, and with but little food. It is also used by the Aborigines to excite them before fighting.[3]

The explorer King, mentioned above, who lived for several months under very difficult circumstances with a tribe of Aborigines on Cooper's Creek near the present Queensland–South Australian border, occasionally 'obtained a chew of pituri which soon caused him to forget his hunger and the miseries of his position.'[12] As a matter of interest, the natives of eastern Africa, particularly of Ethiopia, chew the stimulant, alkaloid-rich leaves of *Khata edulis* to lessen the pangs of hunger and to combat fatigue.

Peter Latz mentions[5] that 'pituri' is still chewed in Central Australia even today, especially by the old people. Some five or six plant species are being used, but the ones most sought after, the ones considered to be strong and 'cheeky' generally, are also those containing the highest amounts of nicotine. Peter Latz also observes that chewing 'pituri' has little effect on him, presumably because he is a heavy smoker.

R. Helms, the naturalist of the Elder Expedition of 1891–92 was surprised that, although *Duboisia hopwoodii* was found from the Everard Ranges to the Barrow Ranges and throughout the Great Victoria Desert, it was not used by the Aborigines living there.[12] He assumed that its narcotic properties were unknown to them, that only the prepared drug was known outside the district where it was produced, and that those who obtained it by exchange were ignorant of its appearance in its natural state.

These views appear to be inconsistent with the evidence available. The Australian Aborigines were very capable experimenters in the field of plant use. For instance, they were aware of the narcotic properties of the botanically very different *Isotoma petraea* (family Lobeliaceae), which is also rich in nicotine, and used it for the same purposes as *Duboisia hopwoodii*;[13] and in the Everard Ranges themselves they utilized *Nicotiana excelsior*.[12] It seems odd, therefore, that they should have failed to recognize the potential usefulness of locally growing *Duboisia hopwoodii*, unless of course, it did not produce the desired effect. This latter possibility may be a more likely reason for the non-use of the plant. Could it be that the plants growing in the Everard Ranges contain altogether too small amounts of total alkaloid to have any real activity? or do they contain predominantly the much less potent *nor*-nicotine? The related *Duboisia myoporoides* exhibits very large variations in its alkaloid content.[14]

There are also reports that the Aborigines used the smoke of the burning leaves of *Duboisia hopwoodii* as an anaesthetic (probably owing to the drowsiness-inducing effect of nicotine) to lessen pain during certain operations.[12] An example of a frequently performed operation during which 'pituri' was used is the circumcision of boys during their initiation ceremonies.

Several other plants with mildly narcotic or painkilling properties may be worth mentioning. The 'wilga' *(Geijera parviflora)* has been reportedly used, in conjunction with other narcotic plants, to induce a sensation of drunkenness and drowsiness;[15] and an infusion of its leaves was suggested to J.H. Maiden by a forester at Dubbo in central New South Wales as a pain reliever. The infusion could be either drunk or applied as a lotion. Also, the leaf chewed to a pulp and placed in a hollow tooth was reputed to stop it from aching.[10] In view of the chemical variability of *G. parviflora,* these statements require thorough re-investigation.

A mysterious report in Roth's article on the use of the sap of the 'river mangrove' *(Aegiceras corniculatum)* in northern Queensland for earache specifies 'females only'![2] Is this simply a case of very early female chauvinism, or is there a rational basis for the discrimination? The plant contains a complex mixture of anthelmintic quinones, collectively named 'rapanone'.[16,17] Whether 'rapanone' has any analgesic or bactericidal properties is not known.

And whilst the analgesic principles in the two last named plants are not known, the painkilling properties of *Spilanthes grandiflora* may be due to spilanthol, a compound with local anaesthetic activity.[13] Other species of *Spilanthes,* used in South Africa for the relief of toothache, also contain spilanthol.

Acacia beauverdiana

FAMILY: Mimosaceae

VERNACULAR NAMES: 'Pukati'

DESCRIPTION: A shrub or small tree up to 6 m high. Its leaf-like phyllodes are flat, linear, about 6-10 cm long and 2-4 mm wide, with a hooked apex and numerous, very fine, parallel veins. Its golden flowers are borne in stalked, globular to slightly oblong heads less than 1 cm long. The calyx is shortly lobed and silky-hairy but the corolla is hairless. It flowers from early spring to summer.

HABITAT AND DISTRIBUTION: On coarse sands and sandy gravels in the semi-arid parts of south-west Western Australia, often in mallee.

MEDICINAL USES: The ash from the small top branches is mixed with equal parts of tobacco and chewed.[18]

ACTIVE COMPONENTS: Probably the alkali present in the ash; it releases the alkaloids from tobacco and thus enhances the narcotic effect of the drug.

Acacia cuthbertsonii

FAMILY: Mimosaceae

DESCRIPTION: A small shrub with a contorted, twisted trunk; up to 2.5 m high. It flowers from winter to spring, and its blossoms are yellow.

HABITAT AND DISTRIBUTION: Arid regions of Western Australia.

MEDICINAL USES: The Aborigines used the bark in conjunction with *Codonocarpus cotinifolius* for the relief of toothache and rheumatism.[18]

ACTIVE CONSTITUENTS: Not known.

Aegiceras corniculatum

(See colour plate facing page 32)

FAMILY: Myrsinaceae

SYNONYMS: *Aegiceras majus, Aegiceras fragrans.*

VERNACULAR NAMES: 'River mangrove'

DESCRIPTION: A tall shrub to small tree with alternate leaves. Leaves are leathery, very rounded near the apex, broad, 4–7 cm long and taper gradually into the stalk. Its deliciously scented flowers occur in bunches either at the end of branchlets or in upper leaf forks. The calyx has five white, stiff and very pointed lobes, about 5 mm long. The fruit is cylindrical or horn-shaped, opening in one or two lengthwise slits as the seed grows; it is 3–4 cm long. Leaves are often covered with salt crystals (except after rain).

HABITAT AND DISTRIBUTION: In coastal mangrove swamps, fringing tidal rivers and creeks as well as salt marshes. Extends further upstream, into merely brackish water, than mangroves of the genus *Avicennia*. New South Wales, Northern Territory, Queensland.

MEDICINAL USES: The Aborigines used a decoction of its leaves or the juice obtained by squeezing the leaves as eardrops for earache (curiously for females only).[2]

ACTIVE CONSTITUENTS: The leaves contain triterpenoid compounds. The bark contains isorhamnetin, syringic acid, and the anthelmintic substance 'rapanone'.[16] 'Rapanone' has been shown to consist of a mixture of several closely related quinones and is not a pure compound as originally thought.[17] Haemolytic saponins are present in the bark as well as in the fruits.[16] It is not known which of these compounds is responsible for the plant's analgesic properties.

Alocasia macrorrhizos

FAMILY: Araceae

SYNONYMS: *Colocasia macrorrhiza; Caladium macrorrhizon.*

VERNACULAR NAMES: 'Spoon lily', 'cunjevoi' of the Aborigines of southern Queensland, 'pitchu' and 'dhoo-ee' (Burnett River), 'hakkin' (Rockhampton), 'banganga' and 'nargan' (Cleveland Bay), 'koombi' (Tully), 'murgan' (Mt Cook), 'culgum'.

DESCRIPTION: A large, sometimes erect, but usually somewhat prostrate, hairless perennial herb with a thick rhizome. It may grow over 1 m tall and has fleshy, dark green, glossy leaves on a thick, rounded and spongy stalk, forming a rosette around the main stem. The leaf blade is 25 cm to 1 m long and 30–45 cm broad, broadly heart-shaped or deeply 2-lobed at the base and narrowed to a blunt tip. Leaf stalks are 25 cm to 1 m long and even longer. Its pale yellow to yellow-green flowers occur in highly scented spikes. The fruit is a small, red and oval-shaped berry, about 4–8 mm long.

The juice of the plant is very corrosive to mucous membranes.

HABITAT AND DISTRIBUTION: In rainforest and most forest areas, near creeks and in gullies in coastal Queensland and New South Wales as far south as Ulladulla.

MEDICINAL USES: In India used as an external stimulant and rubefacient.[3] Also used in muscular rheumatism, and in the treatment of sores, burns and ulcers.[19] The leaf juice is reputed to be useful for the relief of sunburn.[20] However, owing to its acrid nature, **extreme care should be exercised in keeping it away from the eyes and other sensitive tissues.**

It has been suggested that the milky juice from its rhizomes is useful for the relief of the pain caused by the stings of the 'giant stinging tree' *Dendrocnide excelsa,*

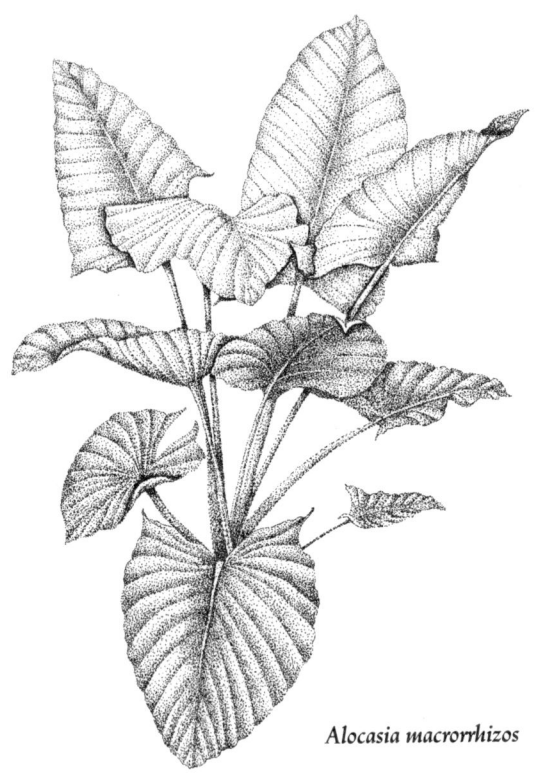

Alocasia macrorrhizos

previously referred to as *Laportea gigas*. This has been disputed by some people.[21]

ACTIVE CONSTITUENTS: Not known. The plant contains calcium oxalate[21] and cyanogenic glycosides in young leaves and stems.[22]

Alphitonia excelsa (See colour plate facing page 32)

FAMILY: Rhamnaceae

VERNACULAR NAMES: 'Red ash', 'mountain ash', 'leather jacket', 'Coopers' wood', 'white leaf', 'humbug' and 'murr-rung' (Illawarra district), 'nono-groyinandie' (Clarence River), 'culgera-culgera' (northern New South Wales) and 'mee-a-mee' and 'an-na' in Queensland.

DESCRIPTION: A tall tree with a grey bark and rusty hairy young branches and floral shoots. Its alternate leaves are leathery, broadly elliptical to narrow and tapered at both ends, blunt or pointed tipped, 7–12 cm long and with straight margins. They are usually white and hairy on the underside, sometimes rusty hairy. Clusters of small, 5-petalled flowers occur either in the forks of upper leaves or at the end of branchlets. Blackish berries, globular to egg-shaped and 6–10 mm in diameter occur in clusters.

HABITAT AND DISTRIBUTION: Widespread in or near rainforest; New South Wales, Queensland and Northern Territory.

MEDICINAL USES: The Aborigines used to apply leaves to sore eyes.[2] An infusion of the leaves in warm water was used for bathing in cases of headache,[20] and an infusion of the bark, root and wood was rubbed on the body as a liniment for body pains.[13,20] A bark and wood decoction was used as a gargle for toothache;[20] it was drunk as a tonic.[20] Young leaf tips were chewed for an upset stomach.[20]

ACTIVE CONSTITUENTS: Leaves contain triterpenoid saponins and the bark contains tannins. The wood contains alphitonin.[14] It is not known which of these (if any) compounds exhibit the analgesic and soothing properties mentioned.

Amorphophallus variabilis

FAMILY: Araceae

SYNONYMS: *Brachyspatha variabilis*

DESCRIPTION: A herb with a broad tuberous rhizome. Its leaves are deeply 3-lobed, each lobe being further subdivided; they arise at the base of the stems in a rosette-like fashion, leaf petioles are often 30 cm long. Leaf segments are very unequal, elongated elliptical, pointed and about 7–10 cm long, or egg-shaped and only about 2.5 cm long. Flower-bearing peduncles are over 30 cm long with large pointed leaf-like bracts at the base. The flowering portions of the fleshy spikes are about 5 cm long, the male parts being much longer than the female; the terminal appendage is narrow, cigar-or spindle-shaped and 25–30 cm long.

HABITAT AND DISTRIBUTION: Northern Territory; coastal areas.

MEDICINAL USES: Narcotic; the Aborigines used to smoke the leaves as a substitute for tobacco.[19]

ACTIVE CONSTITUENTS: Not known.

Barringtonia calyptrata

FAMILY: Lecythidaceae, sometimes separated as Barringtoniaceae

DESCRIPTION: A tree with very large alternate and blunt-tipped leaves; leaf margins are straight. The similar *Barringtonia asiatica* has wider leaves. Its cream-coloured flowers occur in long, drooping spike-like clusters with their calyxes tending to break off from the base like little caps. The fruit is narrow egg-shaped to elongated, 7.5–10 cm long and 2.5–4 cm broad.

HABITAT AND DISTRIBUTION: In light rainforest along the banks of streams as well as in more open forest in high rainfall areas of coastal northern Queensland.

MEDICINAL USES: A decoction of the leaves has been drunk by the Aborigines for fever and chest pains.[13]

ACTIVE CONSTITUENTS: Not known; the leaves contain saponins.[13]

Brucea javanica

FAMILY: Simaroubaceae

SYNONYMS: *Brucea sumatrana, Brucea amarissima*

DESCRIPTION: A shrub or tree with hairy young branches. Its compound leaves are 2.5–4 cm long and consist of five to eleven egg-shaped, tapered leaflets with pointed tips and coarsely toothed margins, 7.5 cm long, softly hairy. Its very small flowers are purple.

HABITAT AND DISTRIBUTION: Near the coast; Northern Territory.

MEDICINAL USES: The bitter seeds ('Macassar kernels') are used in Java to cure dysentery and in China for malaria.[23] Northern Queensland Aborigines used the leaves and roots as an analgesic.[13]

ACTIVE CONSTITUENTS: The seeds contain potentially anti-leucemic quassinoids.[24] The bruceins, very bitter tasting quassinoid esters, are present in the bark.[14]

Buchanania arborescens

FAMILY: Anacardiaceae

DESCRIPTION: A tree with shining leaves, equally green on both sides. Its white, 5-petalled flowers are very fragrant. The fruit is a bony 2-valved berry.

HABITAT AND DISTRIBUTION: Tropical and coastal areas of the Northern Territory and Queensland (Cape York Peninsula).

MEDICINAL USES: An infusion of the mashed inner bark and sapwood in water was used by the Aborigines as a mouthwash for toothache; an infusion prepared from roots was also used. The infusion should not be swallowed.[20]

ACTIVE CONSTITUENTS: Not known.

Buchanania obovata

FAMILY: Anacardiaceae

SYNONYMS: *Buchanania muelleri* var. *pilosus*, *Buchanania oblongifolia*.

VERNACULAR NAMES: 'Wild plum', 'mangkarrba'.

DESCRIPTION: A deciduous tree, up to 6 m high, with an open crown and a grey, scaly and fissured bark, red when cut and exuding a resinous sap. Its leaves are light, dull green and stiff. Flowers are yellowish and the fruit is a green plum-like berry.

HABITAT AND DISTRIBUTION: In open eucalypt forest in coastal areas of the Gulf of Carpentaria.

MEDICINAL USES: The Aborigines prepared a mouthwash by soaking the shredded inner bark and sapwood for three to four hours in water. After use the liquid was spat out and never swallowed. The infusion was also used as an eyewash (after careful removal of all solid matter) for sore eyes; there is even a report of temporary blindness having been cured by it. Cavities in aching teeth were plugged with soaked and shredded leaves and when the pain stopped the mouthwash was used to rinse out the mouth.[25]

ACTIVE CONSTITUENTS: Not known.

Callicarpa longifolia (See colour plate facing page 32)

FAMILY: Verbenaceae

VERNACULAR NAMES: 'Chukin' (Cairns)

DESCRIPTION: A woody shrub with somewhat reddish hairy young shoots, up to 3 m tall. Its opposite, oblong leaves are 10–15 cm long, dull green on both sides and hairy on the underside, with a long point and toothed margins. Its white hairy flowers occur in loose groups in leaf forks. The fruits are very small white to pale pink berries.

HABITAT AND DISTRIBUTION: It prefers wet tropical lowlands and swampy rainforest country of northern Queensland.

MEDICINAL USES: The bark has been chewed with lime as a substitute for betel leaf, probably as a narcotic.[19] Unspecified species of *Callicarpa* have been reported as being used as oral contraceptives and cures for colds.[13]

ACTIVE CONSTITUENTS: Not known.

Cassia artemisioides

FAMILY: Caesalpiniaceae

VERNACULAR NAMES: 'Silver cassia', 'blue bush cassia', 'parka'.

DESCRIPTION: A bushy shrub, up to 2.5 m high, covered with very fine hair giving it a greyish appearance. Its compound leaves consist of three to six pairs of narrowly cylindrical leaflets, more or less channelled above. Its flowers are orange-yellow. The pod is very flat and thin, 5–8 cm long and 8 mm broad. The seeds lie vertically in the pod. Flowers from summer to winter.

HABITAT AND DISTRIBUTION: From northern Western Australia through Central Australia to inland subtropical Queensland.

MEDICINAL USES: Its ash has been mixed by the Aborigines with native tobacco before chewing it.[18]

ACTIVE CONSTITUENTS: Probably the alkali present in the ash (it liberates the alkaloids contained in the tobacco).

Cerbera manghas

FAMILY: Apocynaceae

SYNONYMS: Has been confused with *Cerbera odollam;* as stated by Everist,[21] the two are not synonymous but very closely related species.

DESCRIPTION: A small tree exuding a milky sap when cut, with bright green more or less oblong leaves tapered at both ends, 10–30 cm long and 5–10 cm broad. Its large sweetly scented flowers are white with a yellowish throat and occur in dense clusters at the end of branchlets. Leaf-like bracts are 1–2.5 cm long, coloured and very deciduous. Fruits are single globular and fleshy berries up to 7.5 cm in diameter containing a single woody nut.

HABITAT AND DISTRIBUTION: Tropical coastal northern Australia.

MEDICINAL USES: The inside of the nuts is toxic but also has been reported to have narcotic properties. The bark is purgative; leaves are also used in Java as a laxative but may be rather too toxic for general use.[3] **The unripe fruit is very toxic.**

ACTIVE CONSTITUENTS: Cardiac glycosides, including cerberoside, thevobioside, deacetyltanghinin and neriifolin.[21]

Clerodendrum floribundum

FAMILY: Verbenaceae

VERNACULAR NAMES: 'Lollybush', 'thurkoo' (Cloncurry).

DESCRIPTION: A tall shrub or small tree with oval to narrow oval-shaped leaves tapered at both ends on 5–8 cm long petioles. Flowers occur in spikes in upper leaf forks. The corolla tube is about 3 cm long with long stamens. The fruit (with enlarged calyx) is dark or black.

HABITAT AND DISTRIBUTION: Widespread throughout all of northern Australia, along the coast as well as inland.

MEDICINAL USES: A wood decoction was used by the Aborigines for aches and pains.[20]

ACTIVE CONSTITUENTS: Not known.

Clerodendrum ovalifolium

FAMILY: Verbenaceae

SYNONYMS: Sometimes spelt *Clerodendron;* this applies to the other species of *Clerodendrum* mentioned in this book as well.

VERNACULAR NAMES: 'Ngula'

DESCRIPTION: A shrub, up to 3.5 m high with opposite, elliptical leaves. Its white flowers occur at the end of branchlets. The fruit is a deep purple and ripens in early winter.

HABITAT AND DISTRIBUTION: North-western districts of Western Australia.

MEDICINAL USES: The leaves were mixed with ashes and chewed by the Aborigines for their stimulant effect.[18]

ACTIVE CONSTITUENTS: Not known.

Crotalaria cunninghamii

FAMILY: Fabaceae

SYNONYMS: *Crotalaria sturtii*

VERNACULAR NAMES: 'Parrot pea', 'rattlepod', 'green bird flower', also the following Western Australian Aboriginal names 'murlun', 'piban', 'kunan', 'bilbun', 'galdjal', 'taliwanti' and 'taliyintiri'.

DESCRIPTION: A small shrub up to 1 m high, finely hairy, with round or slightly angular branches. Its leaves are egg-shaped or trifoliate, 2.5–8 cm long and densely hairy on both sides. Its yellowish green 'pea'-flowers are 3.5 cm long, sometimes longer. The seed pod is leathery, hairy and about 3.5 cm long. Flowers from late autumn to early spring.

HABITAT AND DISTRIBUTION: Confined to tropical northern Australia, from Western Australia to coastal tropical Queensland including Central Australia and northern South Australia.

MEDICINAL USES: The Aborigines were reported to use a decoction of the leaves to bathe sore eyes and to pour it over the head for headache. The method of preparation involved bruising the leaves, soaking them in water until it turned green, boiling the mixture and using it after cooling. The sap from bruised leaves was poured into ears for earache. The bark, boiled in water until it turned green, was used externally for swellings of the body and legs.[18,26]

ACTIVE CONSTITUENTS: Probably alkaloids.[18]

Dendrobium teretifolium *(See colour plate facing page 33)*

FAMILY: Orchidaceae

VERNACULAR NAMES: 'Pencil orchid'

DESCRIPTION: An epiphytic herb with creeping (never bulb-like) stems, up to 2 m long and branched. Its numerous leaves are stem-clasping, cylindrical and smooth, pendulous, 10–60 cm long. Its white or yellowish flowers occur in dense lateral spikes or grow out of the bases of leaves and are 5–6 cm in diameter. Flowers from winter to spring.

HABITAT AND DISTRIBUTION: Mainly near the coast on trees (chiefly *Casuarina*); Queensland and New South Wales.

MEDICINAL PROPERTIES: Bruised leaves are used in the South Pacific islands for severe headache and other pains.[27]

ACTIVE CONSTITUENTS: Not known.

Dodonaea lanceolata

FAMILY: Sapindaceae

VERNACULAR NAMES: 'Hopbush', 'pirrungu' (in Western Australia).

DESCRIPTION: An up to 2 m high shrub with alternate, narrow spear-shaped and almost veinless leaves. Leaf margins are straight. The petal-less flowers and young fruit are yellowish green. The fruit is a capsule with a winged appearance. Flowers from late autumn to spring.

HABITAT AND DISTRIBUTION: From northern Western Australia through Northern Territory to Queensland; widespread.

MEDICINAL USES: Western Australian Aborigines used to apply the bruised, cut up and boiled leaves, after slightly cooling them, to various parts of the body for the relief of pain, including snakebite.[18,20] A very much more diluted decoction of the leaves may be drunk for the same complaints;[18] at the same time leaves were tied under the belt to enhance the curative effect.[20]

ACTIVE CONSTITUENTS: Not known.

Dodonaea viscosa (See colour plate facing page 33)

FAMILY: Sapindaceae

SYNONYMS: *Dodonaea dioica, Dodonaea angustifolia.*

VERNACULAR NAMES: 'Sticky hopbush', 'giant hopbush', 'hopbush', 'watchupga', 'kirni', 'tecan'.

DESCRIPTION: A tall shrub, 3 m high or more with a thin reddish brown bark. Its alternate, narrow-elliptic or narrow-oblong leaves are 4–10 cm long and less than 1 cm broad; their margins may be toothed. Young leaves are sticky. The fruit, a 3-winged capsule is about 1 cm long and 1.4 cm wide; may be purplish in colour. The dried capsule is bitter and resembles hops. Flowers in early summer.

HABITAT AND DISTRIBUTION: Often in gullies and valleys; common in all eastern Australian states. Also in South Australia and Western Australia.

MEDICINAL USES: Used by the Aborigines as a pain killer: leaves were chewed, without swallowing the juice for toothache;[15] chewed leaves and juice were also used in the treatment of stonefish and stingray wounds (usually bound to the wound and left for several days).[15] A root decoction of the variety *laurina* was used externally for the healing of cuts and open wounds; the boiled roots or root juice gave relief from toothache.[20]

In India, a form of this bush was used as a febrifuge; in South Africa it was used to make a medicine for stomach disorders; in Peru, the leaves were reputedly chewed as stimulant.[19]

ACTIVE CONSTITUENTS: Not known; leaves contain a diterpenoid acid, various flavonoids, some 18 per cent tannin, and they are slightly cyanogenic.[14,28]

Aegiceras corniculatum (see page 26)

Callicarpa longifolia (see page 29)

Alphitonia excelsa (see page 27)

Dendrobium teretifolium (see page 31)

Dodonaea viscosa (see page 32)

Duboisia hopwoodii (see page 33)

Geijera parviflora (see page 36)

Duboisia hopwoodii *(See colour plate facing page 33)*
FAMILY: Solanaceae

VERNCULAR NAMES: 'Pituri' (often refers to the prepared drug as well); 'pitchiri', 'pitcheri', 'bedgery' and 'pedgery' are variant renderings by Europeans of 'pituri', also called 'emu plant', 'camel poison' and 'poison bush'.

DESCRIPTION: Usually a shrub, 3 m high or so, sometimes a small tree with a dark brown or purplish bark, smooth on young plants and on smaller branches but becoming yellow-brown and corky on older branches and trees. Its wood is lemon yellow with a vanilla-like odour when freshly cut. Leaves are alternate, variable in size and shape, often narrow and linear, but always much narrower than long; they are short-stalked, with straight margins, tapered at both ends, often with a recurved point and up to 15 cm long. Flowers occur in open groups at the end of branchlets, each consisting of a small green calyx and a broad bell-shaped white corolla with a purple striped tube and five lobes. The fruit is a black, up to 6 mm long, berry containing one or two seeds in a dark pulp.

HABITAT AND DISTRIBUTION: Confined to the more arid regions of Australia; prefers sandy and gravelly soils. Western New South Wales, Queensland, Central Australia to north-western coast of Western Australia.

MEDICINAL USES: Mainly as a stimulant and narcotic by the Aborigines. The dried and powdered leaves and twigs, often mixed with the ash of certain *Acacia* species, were chewed and sometimes smoked (like tobacco).[12,29]

ACTIVE CONSTITUENTS: The alkaloids nicotine and *nor*-nicotine. The total alkaloids present in fresh material may amount to 25 per cent (based on dry matter).[21]

Ehretia saligna
FAMILY: Boraginaceae

VERNACULAR NAMES: 'False cedar', 'coonta'.

DESCRIPTION: A small tree with alternate, up to 12 cm long, narrow leaves tapered at both ends on a rather thick petiole, and straight margins. Small flowers in irregularly branched groups at the end of branchlets. The fruit is globular, about 5-6 mm in diameter.

HABITAT AND DISTRIBUTION: Mainly on the islands of the Gulf of Carpentaria and in coastal northern Queensland.

MEDICINAL USES: A decoction prepared from the wood has been drunk by the Aborigines for aches and pains.[20]

ACTIVE CONSTITUENTS: Not known.

Eremophila fraseri
FAMILY: Myoporaceae

VERNACULAR NAMES: 'Turpentine bush', 'turpentine plant', 'wax bush', 'burro'.

DESCRIPTION: A shrub up to 3 m high with relatively large alternate, dark green leaves covered with a viscous, lacquer-like substance. The pillar-like outgrowths on its leaves are breathing pores. Its flowers are cream-coloured with white spots. Flowers from early winter to early spring.

HABITAT AND DISTRIBUTION: In the mulga country of Western Australia.

MEDICINAL USES: The Aborigines drank the decoction of the leaves for colds; the plant was also believed to cure toothache and rheumatism.[18]

ACTIVE CONSTITUENTS: Not known; the plant is reported to give a strongly positive test for alkaloids.[18] Leafy twigs contain a resin rich in diterpenoid acids. Leaves also contain a flavone and mannitol.[16]

Erythrina verspertilio

FAMILY: Fabaceae

VERNACULAR NAMES: 'Bat's wing coral tree', 'cork tree', 'grey corkwood', 'goomurrie', 'aranyi', 'kuntan', 'heilaman tree'.

DESCRIPTION: A deciduous tree up to 30 m high, armed with conical thorns. The bark is greyish brown and uneven, very green near the surface when cut. Branches, branchlets and sometimes leaf stalks are thorny. Leaves are alternate consisting of three 3-lobed leaflets with the lateral lobes spreading and curving outwards (resembling bat's wings). Orange-red to pale red flowers are curved and pendulous and occur both in leaf forks and at the end of branchlets; they are up to 4 cm long. Pods are tapered at both ends, 6–9 cm long and 1 cm broad and contain several red or yellow oval-shaped seeds, each about 8 mm long.

HABITAT AND DISTRIBUTION: In dry scrub (i.e. dry closed forest) or open forest and woodlands, both inland and in coastal districts of northern New South Wales, Queensland, Northern Territory and Central Australia.

MEDICINAL USES: A decoction of the leaves is reputed to act as a sedative.[19] The Aborigines soaked the bast and bark in water and applied it externally to sore eyes and for headache.[18]

ACTIVE CONSTITUENTS: Not known.

Eucalyptus terminalis

FAMILY: Myrtaceae

VERNACULAR NAMES: 'Mountain bloodwood', 'long fruited bloodwood', 'buna', 'bunara', 'kulcha'.

DESCRIPTION: A large tree with a greyish white short-flaky but persistent bark. Juvenile leaves are opposite, hairy and elliptical, 5–8 cm long; mature leaves are alternate, narrow, tapered at both ends, smooth and shining, 8–18 cm long. Leaf venation is fine, almost parallel. Flower clusters occur at the end of branchlets. Fruits are cylindrical to urn-shaped, thick, 20–30 mm by 11–14 mm. Leaves are almost completely without odour when crushed. Flowers from late autumn to early winter.

HABITAT AND DISTRIBUTION: On sandstone and ironstone ridges of the inland; Western Australia, South Australia, northern New South Wales and Queensland.

MEDICINAL USES: The Aborigines, as well as early settlers, drank a solution of the red kino for diarrhoea, as well as for chest and heart pains (perhaps due to indigestion).[18,26]

ACTIVE CONSTITUENTS: Tannins.[26]

NOTE: It should be noted that several species were called at some time *E. terminalis*. Consequently the uses stated may refer to a variety of species. For example a report mentioning the use of an aqueous solution of the kino of so-called *E. terminalis* as a mild laxative by the Aborigines of the Palmer River district of northern Queensland[2] should be viewed with some suspicion: not only does the use contradict the earlier stated application for the treatment of diarrhoea, but, more importantly, it cannot be what is now referred to as *E. terminalis* (may be *E. polycarpa*?).

Euodia vitiflora

FAMILY: Rutaceae

SYNONYMS: Often incorrectly spelt *Evodia*.

VERNACULAR NAMES: 'Toothache tree' (Cooktown)

DESCRIPTION: A shrub or tree up to 30 m high with a grey bark showing fine cracks or longitudinal fissures and tending to scaliness in older trees. Wood has a nauseating odour. Young shoots and flowering parts are rusty hairy. Its long-stalked leaves are opposite and are composed of three large leaflets (having the appearance of ordinary leaves). These leaflets are 10–20 cm long and 5–8 cm broad, elliptical, often drawn into a blunt point and glossy. Flowers occur in much-branched bunches in leaf forks; the four petals of each flower are hairy on both sides. Flowers in late spring.

HABITAT AND DISTRIBUTION: Northern coastal New South Wales to northern Queensland and adjacent tablelands.

MEDICINAL USES: The resinous exudate of the bark is placed in cavities in teeth to relieve pain. A bark decoction is rubbed on the body for pains.[13]

ACTIVE CONSTITUENTS: Not known; the resin is composed of a number of coumarins;[30] bark, leaves and branchlets give strongly positive tests for alkaloids.[31]

Evolvulus alsinoides

FAMILY: Convolvulaceae

VERNACULAR NAMES: 'Tropical speedwell'

DESCRIPTION: A perennial branching and silky herb, 15–30 cm tall with small, alternate, oblong leaves, 6–12 mm long, tapered at both ends and with undivided margins. In the variety *sericeus*, leaves are very white, with silky hairs. Its small white or blue flowers grow on slender stalks, one or two together. Petals are fused together giving the flower a wheel-like appearance.

HABITAT AND DISTRIBUTION: All states except Tasmania and Victoria, often in dryish grassland or open woodlands; the variety *sericeus* occurs in the tropical coastland regions of the Gulf of Carpentaria (including islands) and of northern Queensland.

MEDICINAL USES: Stalks, leaves and roots have been used as a remedy in dysentery and fever.[3] The variety *sericeus* has been used as a narcotic (substitute for pituri).[32]

ACTIVE CONSTITUENTS: Not known; however, the alkaloid evolvine has been isolated from the whole plant.[33]

Excoecaria parvifolia

FAMILY: Euphorbiaceae

SYNONYMS: Sometimes incorrectly spelt *Excaecaria*.

VERNACULAR NAMES: 'Guttapercha tree', 'jil-leer' (Cloncurry River).

DESCRIPTION: A small tree with alternate, narrow oblong and blunt-tipped leaves, 12–25 mm long and tapering into a short petiole. Flower spikes are in leaf forks and are 15–25 mm long. The fruit is a capsule. When wounded or cut, the tree exudes a corrosive milky sap **which causes temporary blindness.**

HABITAT AND DISTRIBUTION: Coast and hinterland of the Gulf of Carpentaria, and westward into the Northern Territory.

MEDICINAL USES: The Aborigines rubbed a heated infusion of the mashed bark into all parts of the body for pains and sickness.[2]

ACTIVE CONSTITUENTS: Not known.

Geijera parviflora (See colour plate facing page 33)

FAMILY: Rutaceae

SYNONYMS: *Geijera pendula*

VERNACULAR NAMES: 'Wilga', and less commonly 'Australian willow', 'dogbush', 'sheep bush ; 'gingerah' (Dubbo).

DESCRIPTION: A small tree, 6-9 m high and up to 30 cm in diameter. Its dense, dark green crown of pendulous branches, bearing alternate long (7-15 cm) and narrow (about 5 mm) leaves gives the tree a willow-like appearance and makes it one of our most valuable shade trees. Its bark is rough and dark-coloured near the butt and smooth and lighter coloured on the upper part and branches. It flowers in spring. The small flowers are arranged in open terminal clusters. The fruits are small, black, globular berries with a weak peppery taste.

HABITAT AND DISTRIBUTION: Dry inland; all states except Tasmania.

MEDICINAL USES: An infusion of the leaves has been used internally as well as externally as a lotion to alleviate pain. Chewed leaves were placed into cavities to stop toothache.[10]

Leaves, baked, powdered and smoked in conjunction with other narcotic plants induce drowsiness and drunkenness and have been used for ceremonial purposes.[15]

ACTIVE CONSTITUENTS: *Geijera parviflora* is chemically very variable. A form eaten by sheep contains the coumarin geiparvarin, whereas a form rejected by sheep contains another coumarin, dehydrogeijerin. The volatile oils present in the foliage are equally variable in their composition. Some are rich in the monoterpenoid alcohol linalool, others in phloracetophenone dimethyl ether.[14] None of the uses mentioned above has ever been related to the chemistry of the particular tree used; hence one can only guess that the coumarins and other compounds reported from the species possess medicinal activity.

Goodenia varia (See colour plate facing page 48)

FAMILY: Goodeniaceae

VERNACULAR NAMES: 'Sticky goodenia'

DESCRIPTION: A hairless small shrubby plant, either growing close to the ground or ascending, with 30-60 cm long stems. Leaves are stalked, thick, slightly and irregularly toothed, broadly elliptical or circular. The plant is sticky. Flowers are yellow; one to three occur together on short stalks. The calyx tube is short with narrow lobes, the corolla is hairless, about 1 cm long with the upper lobe deeply split. Flowers from late spring to late summer.

HABITAT AND DISTRIBUTION: Usually on clayey soils; north-western Victoria, South Australia, Western Australia and New South Wales.

MEDICINAL USES: Sedative; used by Aboriginal mothers to pacify their children on long and arduous trips.[15]

ACTIVE CONSTITUENTS: Not known.

Narcotics and painkillers

Grewia retusifolia

FAMILY: Tiliaceae

SYNONYMS: *Grewia polygama, Grewia helicterifolia.*

VERNACULAR NAMES: 'Dog's balls', 'dysentery plant', 'plain currant', 'dog nut', 'Jack's joy', 'emu berries'; 'karoom', 'ouraie', 'kooline', 'pam-mo', 'kou-nung' and 'mamurrinya' were used by Queensland Aborigines.

DESCRIPTION: A small straggling shrub with hairy, alternate, oblong to broadly spoon-shaped leaves, usually with toothed margins and three prominent veins. The fruit is 2-lobed, rather hard with a brownish skin, 10 mm in diameter, enclosing the seeds in a small amount of fibrous, acid-tasting pulp.

HABITAT AND DISTRIBUTION: Coastal tropical Queensland and Northern Territory.

MEDICINAL USES: The fruits, called 'jelly-boys' in Queensland, are said to be useful for diarrhoea and dysentery.[34] Dysentery and diarrhoea may also be treated by chewing the leaves or by drinking an infusion of the previously cooked (between hot stones) and mashed roots in water.[2,25] This root infusion was also used as an eyewash.[25] A root decoction has been used externally to treat boils and swollen limbs.[20] The Aborigines also applied the macerated leaves to aching teeth to stop the pain.[13]

ACTIVE CONSTITUENTS: Not known; the plant contains abundant mucilage.[19]

Isotoma petraea *(See colour plate facing page 49)*

FAMILY: Lobeliaceae

VERNACULAR NAMES: 'Rock isotome', 'wild tobacco', 'minekalpa', 'tundi-wari', 'pulbawari'.

DESCRIPTION: A small perennial herb with a hard rootstock and a few branched, erect and slender stems, 15–30 cm tall. Its alternately arranged leaves are broadly oblong and irregularly, but sharply toothed. Flowers are pale blue, 5-petalled and very conspicuous. The sap of the plant is very bitter and supposedly irritating to the eyes.

HABITAT AND DISTRIBUTION: In rock crevices, caves, and the like, often on granite in the dry interior of Australia.

MEDICINAL USES: The Aborigines chewed it in the same way as 'pituri' for its narcotic and stimulant effect.[13] The dried and powdered plant, mixed with equal parts of mulga tree ash *(Acacia aneura)* was used as a pain killer and for colds (much as we use aspirin); the ash undoubtedly served to release the alkaloids from the plant material.[18,26]

ACTIVE CONSTITUENTS: Alkaloids with nicotine-like action are present in the leaves; possibly lobeline.[31,35]

Melaleuca cajuputi

FAMILY: Myrtaceae

SYNONYMS: *Myrtus saligna, Melaleuca minor, Melaleuca trinervis, Melaleuca lancifolia, Melaleuca leucadendron* var. *lancifolia, Melaleuca leucadendron* var. *cajuputi,* and many others (see note on taxonomy of *Melaleuca* species under *Melaleuca quinquenervia*).

VERNACULAR NAMES: 'Swamp tea tree', 'paperbark tea tree' and many others which probably also apply to other similar Melaleucas.

DESCRIPTION: Sometimes a small shrub, but usually a tree up to 35 m high with a somewhat silvery crown; its smaller branches and twigs are slender but not drooping. Leaves are often hairy, tapered at both ends, 5–12 cm long and 1–4 cm wide; young shoots are densely silky hairy. Spikes up to 9 cm long, densely flowered. The flowers are white, greenish white or cream-coloured. Fruits are about 3 mm long and 3.5–4 mm wide. The species flowers between March and June and from August to December. The bark is papery, as in related Melaleucas, and does not help in its identification.

It may be distinguished from *M. quinquenervia* as follows: old leaves are closely dotted, rather thin in texture and reticulations are about as prominent as main veins. In *M. quinquenervia* old leaves are not conspicuously dotted, or are thin-textured and with more or less obscure reticulation.

HABITAT AND DISTRIBUTION: Like all Melaleucas related to *M. leucadendron*, it prefers well-watered or even swampy ground. In Queensland it often grows on coastal dunes. It also occurs in *Melaleuca dealbata* forests associated with *Melaleuca viridiflora;* in *Eucalyptus* forests.

Extends from northern Queensland to the Northern Territory and northern Western Australia. Also common in South-east Asia.

MEDICINAL USES: A cajuput-like paperbark growing in swamps on Groote Eylandt is used by local Aborigines for the treatment of aches and pains. Leaves are crushed in the hand and rubbed on. Sometimes young leaves and twigs are crushed and steeped in hot water; the liquid is used to bathe the affected area and the rest is poured over the head. Crushed leaves are sniffed to cure headache.[1]

Steam distillation of leaves and terminal branchlets yields the 'cajuput oil' of commerce (also spelt 'cajaput' or 'cajeput'). The oil is used internally for the treatment of coughs and colds, against stomach cramps, colic and asthma; the dose is one to five drops. It is used externally for the relief of neuralgia and rheumatism, often in the form of ointments and liniments. External application of a few drops on cotton wool for the relief of toothache and earache. L. Wundram's toothache drops are made of cajeput oil, rosemary oil, peppermint oil (one part of each) and absolute alcohol (half of one part).[36]

The oil is also reputed to have insect-repellent properties; it is a powerful antispasmodic and sudorific and is useful as an anthelmintic, particularly against roundworm.[3,11]

ACTIVE CONSTITUENTS: 1,8-cineole and alpha-terpineol present in the volatile essential oil (50 to 70 per cent and about 30 per cent respectively).[11]

Musa banksii

FAMILY: Musaceae

VERNACULAR NAMES: 'Native banana', 'morgogaba', 'boo-gar-oo'.

DESCRIPTION: A tree-like herb, 5–7 m high with large leaves, 2–3 m long. Flowers are clustered in the forks of large purplish leafy bracts; buds are large and conical at the apex of the flowering stalk. The whole flowering assembly is drooping. The fruit, a banana, is oblong, cylindrical and curved, 7–15 cm long and about 1 cm in diameter and contains a multitude of black seeds in only a very small amount of edible pulp.

HABITAT AND DISTRIBUTION: Rainforest; northern Queensland.

MEDICINAL USES: The sap is used as a cure for the sting of the stinging tree (species of *Dendrocnide*).[13]

ACTIVE CONSTITUENTS: Not known.

Nicotiana benthamiana

FAMILY: Solanaceae

SYNONYMS: Once wrongly included under *Nicotiana suaveolens*.

VERNACULAR NAMES: 'Muntju', 'tangungnu', 'tjuntiwari'.

DESCRIPTION: A vigorous plant with numerous erect leafy stems. Its alternate leaves are broadly egg-shaped, dull green and soft. Except at the top of the stems, where they are stalkless, its leaves have slender stalks. Flowers are whitish, with a long slender tube and five blunt lobes; fruits are capsules containing many pitted seeds.

HABITAT AND DISTRIBUTION: Prefers rocky granite outcrops of the arid regions of Australia; from north-western coast of Western Australia through Central Australia into north-western Queensland.

MEDICINAL USES: Mainly as a narcotic; leaves moistened by short chewing were rolled in the ashes of *Hakea* or *Acacia* species and the quid chewed.[37]

ACTIVE CONSTITUENTS: Contains about 0.3 per cent of the alkaloid *nor*-nicotine.[21]

Nicotiana cavicola

FAMILY: Solanaceae

VERNACULAR NAMES: 'Pinkaraangu', 'talara'.

DESCRIPTION: An erect annual herb with up to 50 cm high leafy stems. Its alternate leaves are broad with wavy margins. Leaf stalks are slender and winged but not stem-clasping. Its white flowers are about 2.5–4 cm long with five blunt spreading lobes. The calyx is sharply 5-toothed. Flowers in late spring.

HABITAT AND DISTRIBUTION: In shady places on granite outcrops in the dry regions of central Western Australia.

MEDICINAL USES: Stimulant; the dried and cured leaves were chewed by the Aborigines together with the ash of river gum.[18]

ACTIVE CONSTITUENTS: Not known, but probably alkaloids.

Nicotiana excelsior

FAMILY: Solanaceae

SYNONYMS: Once wrongly included under *Nicotiana suaveolens*.

VERNACULAR NAMES: 'Pulandu', 'balandu', 'pulantu', 'mingkulpa', 'piturr' and 'piturrba' (the last two undoubtedly corruptions of 'pituri').

DESCRIPTION: A strong leafy plant, almost devoid of hairs. Its alternate leaves are dull green, large and smooth with only a few spines on them; their stalks are produced downward. The tubular flower is whitish and large, with an obscurely lobed tip.

HABITAT AND DISTRIBUTION: On rocky ground and in gullies in the ranges of Central Australia.

MEDICINAL USES: Narcotic; mixed with ash and chewed (see other species of *Nicotiana* and *Duboisia* used for the same purpose).[38]

ACTIVE CONSTITUENTS: Leaves contain nicotine and *nor*-nicotine.[39]

Nicotiana gossei

FAMILY: Solanaceae

SYNONYMS: Once wrongly included under *Nicotiana suaveolens*.

VERNACULAR NAMES: 'Ingulba' (Finke River), 'mingulba'.

DESCRIPTION: A healthy green plant with soft, alternate leaves covered with soft but not sticky hairs. Leaves are large and broad, with a blunt tip; they narrow into the stem without a definite stalk. Flowers are white. The hairy flower tube is tipped by five broad and blunt lobes. The fruit is a capsule with numerous pitted seeds.

HABITAT AND DISTRIBUTION: An inland species found in the ranges of the southern Northern Territory and around the western Queensland border at the latitude of the tropic.

MEDICINAL USES: It has been used as a narcotic by the Aborigines, who chewed it in much the same way as 'pituri' with which it has been sometimes identified.[21]

ACTIVE CONSTITUENTS: Contains about 1.1 per cent nicotine.[21]

Pandanus spiralis

FAMILY: Pandanaceae

SYNONYMS: Confused by some authors with *Pandanus odoratissimus*, which is a separate species.

VERNACULAR NAMES: 'Mangkurrkwa'

DESCRIPTION: A slender tree, up to 9 m high with few branches and spirally tufted leaves, up to 2 m long at the end of branches. The fruiting body is orange, pendulous and somewhat globular, about 30 cm in diamater, bearing berries which are not pyramidal at the apex. Also, the tree has no aerial roots.

HABITAT AND DISTRIBUTION: In wet sandy places, swampy grasslands, near small water courses, but not near coastal dunes; tropical coastal regions of the Gulf of Carpentaria (Northern Territory and Western Australia only).

MEDICINAL USES: The inner core of the upper section of the trunk of young trees, not more than 3 m high, was eaten by the Aborigines for pains in the stomach and diarrhoea.[25]

ACTIVE CONSTITUENTS: Not known.

NOTE: Similar plants in Queensland are *Pandanus cookii* and *P. solms-laubachii*.

Petalostigma pubescens

FAMILY: Euphorbiaceae

SYNONYMS: Once included under *Petalostigma quadriloculare* and sometimes separated as var. *pubescens*.

VERNACULAR NAMES: 'Quinine tree', 'quinine berry'; several other common and Aboriginal names have been omitted here since it is not clear which species of *Petalostigma* they really belong to.

DESCRIPTION: A small tree up to 7.5 m high. Its alternate leaves are egg-shaped or shortly elliptic, 2-3 cm (rarely up to 5 cm) long, often blunt at the apex, shortly hairy and with straight margins (sometimes obscurely toothed with round tips). Yellow flowers occur in leaf forks. Flowering parts, as well as the globular or slightly elongated, yellow, orange or red fruits, are hairy. Fruits are up to 25 mm in diameter. Bark and fruits are bitter to the taste. This is a very variable species.

HABITAT AND DISTRIBUTION: Dry, sandy or rocky country of coastal areas of northern Western Australia, Northern Territory, Queensland and extreme north-eastern New South Wales.

MEDICINAL USES: The bark and fresh fruit have been used as a bitter tonic.[27] The bark has also been used in low intermittent fever in doses of 10 g three times a day,[27] whereas the fruit was reputedly useful in malaria.[19] A bark infusion has been used as an antidote for opium[19] and as an astringent.[40] An infusion of bark or fruit in water (one berry per mug) was used to relieve sore eyes: one drop was used.[18] This infusion was also used as an antiseptic wash.[26] Fruits held in the mouth were reputed to relieve toothache.[18,26] Fruits were also used as a vermifuge for horses.[19]

Fruits had to be used fresh since they apparently lost all activity after drying.

ACTIVE CONSTITUENTS: Not known; the bark apparently contains a volatile oil as well as a glycosidic bitter principle.[3]

NOTE: Until recently there appeared to exist some confusion in the taxonomy of *Petalostigma*. Many of the medicinal properties ascribed in older literature to *Petalostigma quadriloculare* may in fact belong to other species and in particular to *Petalostigma pubescens*, the most widely distributed species of this group. Consequently, all reported medicinal uses have been included here with the proviso that they may be shared as well by other species of *Petalostigma*. Only a thorough pharmacological study will sort out this question.

This may also explain Dr Bancroft's view that the bark of *P. quadriloculare* was physiologically inert.[27] It is quite possible, in view of the previously mentioned taxonomic uncertainties, that he in fact worked with an altogether different species, such as *P. triloculare*, occurring along the coast north of Brisbane (cf. entry on *P. quadriloculare*).

Petalostigma quadriloculare

FAMILY: Euphorbiaceae

SYNONYMS: *Petalostigma quadriloculare* var. *sericea*

VERNACULAR NAMES: 'Quinine bush', 'quinine berry' (the remarks under *P. pubescens* apply here too).

DESCRIPTION: A shrub less than 1 m high. Its alternate leaves are silky on the underside with shallowly round-toothed (or lobed) margins. Flowers are yellow in leaf forks. Anthers, ovary and capsule are quite hairless (unlike *P. pubescens*). Otherwise similar to *P. pubescens*. Often sends out vigorous unbranched shoots from rootstock after burning.

HABITAT AND DISTRIBUTION: Dry, sandy or rocky coastal areas of northern Western Australia, Northern Territory and northern Queensland.

MEDICINAL USES: As *Petalostigma pubescens* (see that entry).

ACTIVE CONSTITUENTS: Not known.

NOTE: See note at the end of *P. pubescens* entry mentioning some aspects of *Petalostigma* classification.

Polygonum barbatum

FAMILY: Polygonaceae

VERNACULAR NAMES: A 'smartweed'

DESCRIPTION: A herb with ascending stems, 60 cm to 1 m high. Its alternate, short-petioled leaves are tapered at both ends and are 7–15 cm long. The mid-rib carries a cover of hairs flatly pressed against the leaf. The sheath at the base of each leaf is hairy outside and bordered with long hairs. Flowers are on small, short-petioled spikes, 2.3–3.5 cm long and occur at the end of stems.

HABITAT AND DISTRIBUTION: Mainly near creeks of coastal Queensland.

MEDICINAL USES: In India an infusion of leaves is used for the alleviation of painful colic.[41] Seeds are carminative.[41] It has also been used as a diuretic[40] and an astringent.[19]

ACTIVE CONSTITUENTS: Not known.

Santalum obtusifolium

FAMILY: Santalaceae

DESCRIPTION: An erect shrub with a bluish green appearance, up to 2 m high. Its mostly opposite leaves are 2–5 cm long, narrow and tapered at both ends but with a rounded tip. They are dark green above, paler below, with their margins sometimes rolled under. Flowers occur in clusters in leaf forks. The fruit is a berry, about 7 mm in diameter, with a circular scar near its summit.

HABITAT AND DISTRIBUTION: Coastal areas and adjacent ranges of New South Wales.

MEDICINAL USES: A wood decoction has been drunk by the Aborigines for constipation and for aches and pains.[20]

ACTIVE CONSTITUENTS: Not known; leaves contain free proline, hydroxyproline and glutamic acid.[14]

Spilanthes grandiflora (See colour plate facing page 49)

FAMILY: Asteraceae

SYNONYMS: Has been wrongly referred to *Spilanthes acmella*.

DESCRIPTION: A prostrate loosely branched daisy, up to 60 cm in length. Its leaves are opposite, shortly stalked, egg-shaped and tapered at both ends, or sometimes linear; margins are undivided or with a few coarse teeth below the middle; 2.5–5 cm long with three prominent veins, hairless or with a few hairs. Flowers are yellow; the strap-like parts of the corolla are usually very short.

HABITAT AND DISTRIBUTION: Nearly always in coastal areas and near rivers; northern New South Wales, Queensland and Northern Territory.

MEDICINAL USES: The roots were chewed, but not swallowed for toothache; this treatment was introduced in Australia by Chinese immigrants.[13]

ACTIVE CONSTITUENTS: It may contain spilanthol, a local anaesthetic.[13]

Tinospora smilacina

FAMILY: Menispermaceae

VERNACULAR NAMES: 'Snakevine', 'yuwara', 'waramburr', 'urndarnda', 'wilgar', 'oondundo'.

DESCRIPTION: A woody creeping vine twisting around trees. A milky latex exudes from broken twigs. Its alternate leaves are fleshy and roughly heart-shaped with undivided margins. Its small green flowers occur in long spikes in leaf forks. The ripe fruit is a red oblong berry. Flowers from late autumn to early spring.

HABITAT AND DISTRIBUTION: The northern regions of Australia, and as far south as the far north-east of New South Wales.

MEDICINAL USES: Mainly as a painkiller; mashed stems are tightly wound around the head for headache and around limbs for rheumatism. Cut up stems are boiled and the strained stems wrapped around afflicted area for body pains; the liquid is used to bathe the aching parts. Also as a ligature for people spiked by stone fish to ease pain.[18] Wound around legs when suffering from leprosy to ease pain.[25] Used in cases of snakebite (induces vomiting).[18]

ACTIVE CONSTITUENTS: Bark gives positive tests for alkaloids;[42] otherwise not yet investigated.

Tribulus cistoides *(See colour plate facing page 49)*

FAMILY: Zygophyllaceae

DESCRIPTION: A trailing plant with densely hairy branches, extending up to 1 m along the ground. Leaves are opposite, compound, with one leaflet in each pair markedly smaller than the other; there are altogether seven to eight pairs of silky hairy leaflets in each leaf. Flowers are large and yellow, resembling buttercups. The fruit is a prickly burr.

HABITAT AND DISTRIBUTION: On sand dunes and near the coast of all northern parts of Australia.

MEDICINAL USES: The Aborigines use it to relieve toothache by keeping it between the gums and the cheek near the base of the aching tooth.[2]

ACTIVE CONSTITUENTS: Not known.

Ventilago viminalis

FAMILY: Rhamnaceae

VERNACULAR NAMES: 'Supplejack', 'supple Jack', 'vinetree', 'barndaragu'.

DESCRIPTION: A small tree, up to 6 m high with a dense leafy crown. It starts off being a woody climber, often with several stems twining around one another. Its bark is pale to dark brown. Its bright green leaves are alternate, 5-15 cm long and 6-12 mm broad, narrowed at the base into a short stalk and tapered above the middle into a blunt tip. Small creamy yellow flowers in open bunches. Pods are winged, about 2.5 cm long and 6 mm broad with a prominent midrib.

HABITAT AND DISTRIBUTION: Prefers arid to semi-arid regions of northern Australia, including western New South Wales.

MEDICINAL USES: The Aborigines mashed the roots and bark in water and used it for toothache, rheumatism and swellings, cuts and sores;[18] also as a hair restorative.[18] Its ashes were mixed with native tobacco to make it stronger.[20]

ACTIVE CONSTITUENTS: Bark contains triterpenes.[43] It also contains a number of anthraquinone derivatives such as chrysophanol, islandicin, ventimalin, viminalin, ventilagone and possibly helminthosporin.[14] Some of these may be responsible for the bactericidal properties of the bark.

Xylomelum scottianum

FAMILY: Proteaceae

SYNONYMS: Incorrectly referred to as *Xylomelum salicinum*.

DESCRIPTION: A small tree coated with minute white hairs. Its opposite leaves are oblong, tapering into the periole and bluntly tipped; somewhat sickle-shaped, pale green and bluish frosted on the underside, 10–20 cm long. Flowers occur in opposite, dense spikes, 3–5 cm long and are quite woolly. The large, narrow pear-shaped fruit is recurved at the end; it opens into two woody valves with flat seeds inside.

HABITAT AND DISTRIBUTION: Northern coastal Queensland.

MEDICINAL USES: An infusion of the leaves and bark has been drunk by the Aborigines for internal pains.[13]

ACTIVE CONSTITUENTS: Not known. The wood contains silicic acid.[16]

CHAPTER THREE

Headaches, colds and fevers

Eremophila maculata

THE LARGE NUMBER of Aboriginal remedies for the relief of the common cold and all its unpleasant side-effects, such as a congested nose, headache, sore throat, cough, various ill-defined body pains as well as mild fever, shows that this affliction was equally widespread here as elsewhere in the world. And considering the methods employed to deal with it, one may venture the guess that, just as elsewhere in the world, no cure had been found; some measure of relief, perhaps, but not much more than that.

Aromatic plants figure prominently amongst species used to treat colds and headaches and clear congested breathing passages. Often, leaves were simply crushed in the hand and sniffed, presumably in the belief that if a material had a powerful and pungent odour it ought to bring some relief. Several species of *Melaleuca* (*M. symphyocarpa,* a species related to *M. cajuputi, M. hypericifolia*), *Centipeda* (*C. cunninghamii, C. minima*), *Pterocaulon serrulatum, Mentha australis, Prostanthera cineolifera* (this last-named species may have been used first by the early settlers, rather than by the Aborigines), and many others have been used in this fashion. At other times leaf infusions or decoctions were drunk for colds and headaches: for instance *Melaleuca uncinata, Melaleuca quinquenervia, Stemodia grossa,* several species of *Eremophila* (*E. cuneifolia, E. freelingii, E. fraseri, E. longifolia*), *Cymbopogon procerus.*

The medicinal activity of several of these species may be directly traced to their cineole-rich leaf oils: 1,8-cineole, a common volatile component of numerous essential oils of, for example, *Melaleuca, Eucalyptus, Prostanthera* has the property of reducing the swelling of mucous membranes and of loosening phlegm, thus making breathing easier. It is so effective that is has become, the world over, a standard additive (in its pure state or in the form of a eucalyptus oil containing not less than 70 per cent cineole) to cough mixtures and elixirs, inhalants and even cough lollies. The author remembers having bought, some forty years ago in Czechoslovakia, pale green, eucalyptus-flavoured cough pastilles, called locally 'klokanky', that is 'kangaroo drops'. More recently he has noticed in the Paris underground, better known as 'Metro', posters of a koala in a gum tree advertising a similar product. Without any doubt eucalyptus oil is Australia's most important and best known contribution to medicine.

Although cineole-rich melaleucas have been used fairly extensively by the Aborigines of northern Australia for the relief of colds and headaches, no records appear to exist of a similar usage of eucalyptus leaves. In view of the widespread occurrence of this very large genus (both in number of species as well as individual trees) this seems rather surprising. And although eucalypts growing in the northern regions of Australia contain on the whole little volatile oil, so that their crushed leaves are almost odourless, one would have expected some reports of their use by the Aborigines of southern and south-eastern Australia where species containing high yields of cineole-rich oils abound, for example, *Eucalyptus leucoxylon, E. dives* (cineole form), *E. radiata* (cineole form) and many others. The absence of malodorous and irritating substances such as isovaleric aldehyde (a frequent component of certain eucalyptus oils) would make these species eminently suitable for sniffing purposes.

It is then that the Aboriginal people of the south were less susceptible to catching colds than their northern brothers? Most unlikely! It is more probable that the tribes of the south-eastern parts of the continent were obliterated by the encroachment of white settlement so early in Australia's history that no records were ever made of many of their customs and practices.

It is a popular practice, particularly amongst the older generation, to use a few drops of eucalyptus oil whenever the nose is congested, or at the onset of a cold. Some merely moisten their handkerchief with the oil and inhale the vapours, others will swallow a few drops, usually with a little sugar to improve or disguise the taste. Now, this latter practice may not be as harmless as it seems, if overdone of course, as the following anecdote will show.

A recent study of eucalyptus oil metabolism by the koala, carried out at the Museum of Applied Arts and Sciences in Sydney, has shown that the animal may ingest up to 10 g or so of 1,8-cineole per day without any adverse after-effect. The ingested leaf oil is conjugated with glucuronic acid present in the koala's blood and excreted in a water-soluble form in urine. Larger amounts of cineole would cause serious illness and even death. These findings were so exciting that they were freely publicized by way of lectures, articles and so on. And so it did not come as too much of a surprise when a gentleman rang up to add his personal experiences on this subject.

It appears that he had been in the habit, for about the past five years, of swallowing each day five to ten drops of eucalyptus oil to keep colds at bay and to 'make him feel good'. Later during those five years he started to feel discomfort and even pain in the region of his liver. On entering hospital for a check-up the matron apparently informed him that he suffered from cirrhosis of the liver and that, unless he stopped drinking immediately, his condition would further deteriorate. Now it so happened he was a tee-totaller and never so much as touched alcohol. The cause of his condition, as it turned out, was most likely the cineole he so regularly took 'to improve his health'!

Bark and leaf infusions or decoctions of certain species of *Eucalyptus* and *Acacia*, as well as eucalyptus kinos themselves, have been used to treat sore throats and coughs. The efficacy of these remedies is probably due to their astringent properties. Tannins present in these preparations (as will be mentioned in more detail in chapter 7) precipitate proteinaceous matter and thus will offer relief by stemming the secretion of excess fluid from the mucous membranes of the throat.

Amongst cures for rheumatism the leguminous plant *Tephrosia varians* (synonym: *Galactia varians*) deserves special mention. The medicinal properties of this plant growing at Coolgarra were praised by Mr Matthew Butler, J.P., in a letter to the famous botanist F.M. Bailey.

> On the 24th December, 1894, I was sent for to make the will of an old man who was, as he thought, dying of rheumatism. In a fit of abstraction he pulled up the root and ate it. Fancying it gave him relief, he pulled more, boiled it and drank the liquor. Within a week there was a marked change in him, and

now he is quite well and looks ten years younger. A miner, who has been suffering for over two years from a scrofulous infection took a decoction of this root for a fortnight, and his skin seems now perfectly clear, and he tells me he feels a new man. I had a slight touch of rheumatism in the leg and tried a decoction of the root, with the result that the pain has gone and the stiffness is wearing away.[45]

Dr Joseph Lauterer subjected the acrid-tasting roots to a preliminary chemical investigation from which he concluded that the resin (amounting to some 30 per cent of the weight of the dry root) was similar to guaiac resin, chemically as well as therapeutically, and might be recommended in rheumatism, skin diseases, scrofulosis and syphilis and may in some cases surpass guaiac (wood resin from *Guajacum officinale* and *G. sanctum* growing in the West Indies and northern South America) in quickness and certainty of effect.[45]

The bark of the giant stinging tree, *Dendrocnide excelsa* (formerly *Laportea gigas),* has also been used to cure rheumatism. A Mr. Crawford of Moona Plains in the Walcha district wrote the following letter concerning the medicinal properties of the tree to J.H. Maiden:

The bark is ... said to have been used by the blacks in the olden times for the cure of rheumatism, also for 'giggle giggle', a skin complaint, also for mange on their dogs. I can remember one man, said to have been cured of rheumatism, and said to have been so bad that he could only crawl round the room, supporting himself by the wall. The blacks took him in hand, stripped him, laid him out on a sheet of bark, rubbing him with the young leaves and bark of the *Laportea,* pounded up and boiled until it was of the consistency of treacle. It is said that they almost rubbed the man's skin off, but they cured the patient. I do not know whether you are aware of it, but the best cure for sting of the leaf is a piece of the bark (from a young plant is most convenient, chewed up and rubbed on the spot); it is as if you wiped the pain away with a cloth; it has the same effect used for sting of the large nettle found in the shrubs—a native nettle, I think.[46]

This native nettle is undoubtedly *Urtica incisa*.

The stinging tree does live up to its name, as many bushmen, foresters, bushwalkers and botanists can testify. Even leaves stored dry for half a century are known to retain their stinging power! Mr. George Althofer, naturalist and Director of the Lake Burrendong Arboretum, has described his experience with the plant:

I only just touched and it took at least five days to get rid of it. Every time I became hot it was agonising pain. I can quite understand people being driven mad by it. The pain! Just one or two hairs had stung me, and I think it was only dry hairs because I didn't actually handle them! They must have been blown onto me somehow or another.[47]

Various remedies for this excruciatingly painful sting have been suggested. Rubbing the sting with the leaves, stems or roots of cunjevoi *(Alocasia macrorrhizos)* has been one such remedy, but later reports say that this is either ineffectual or even heightens the pain.[3,46] Rubbing with Dettol has also been used with a varying degree of success. The wearing of protective

Goodenia varia (see page 36)

Isotoma petraea (see page 37)

Tribulus cistoides (see page 43)

Spilanthes grandiflora (see page 42)

Adiantum aethiopicum (see page 51)

Amyema quandang (see page 52)

Alyxia spicata (see page 52)

clothing to prevent contact and the use of anti-histamines have also been advocated.

Whilst most of the plant species listed in this book in connection with headaches, sore throat, colds and rheumatism have been used by the Australian Aborigines, about half of all plants listed as having febrifugal properties have been used exclusively elsewhere, particularly in India, where they also occur in the native state. It could well be that, apart from fevers accompanying colds and digestive upsets, and malaria in the north of Australia, infectious diseases were relatively unknown until the arrival of the first white settlers.

Clinical investigations conducted during the Second World War have shown, contrary to popular belief and some earlier records of clinical trials, that the total alkaloids of *Alstonia scholaris* ('dita bark') have no effect on malaria. Likewise, the bark alkaloids of *Alstonia constricta* have little antimalarial activity, even though they otherwise resemble, pharmacologically speaking, the alkaloids of the well known South American cinchona bark.

To conclude, a few comments on the reported insect repellency of cineole-rich essential oils seems appropriate. *Eucalyptus globulus* ('Tasmanian blue gum') has sometimes been called 'fever tree' or 'fever-prevention tree' since it was believed that malaria-spreading mosquitoes would soon leave houses where the oil was frequently used. Likewise, the absence of malaria in New Caledonia has been sometimes linked to the widespread occurrence of the cineole-rich form of *Melaleuca quinquenervia* on the island. An indication that this cannot be true is the fact that malaria existed until fairly recent times in the very north of Australia, where several species of *Melaleuca* rich in cineole abound. Tests have shown that all cineole-rich eucalyptus and melaleuca oils screened possessed, at best, extremely weak insect repellent properties, and that pure 1,8-cineole possessed none at all. The observation that a relatively high and constantly replenished concentration of eucalyptus oil vapour in the air will get rid of mosquitoes is undoubtedly related to the inherent toxicity of cineole (its so-called knockdown potential) to insects, rather than to any repellency.

Acacia bivenosa subspecies *wayi*

FAMILY: Mimosaceae

SYNONYMS: *Acacia ligulata, Acacia salicina* var. *wayi*.

VERNACULAR NAMES: 'Umbrella bush', 'small cooba', 'watarka'.

DESCRIPTION: A shrub up to 3 m high. Its leaf-like phyllodes are narrow, linear to oblong and are tapered at both ends with a recurved tip, rather thick and 4–9 cm long. Its flowers are a profusion of yellow-orange balls. The pod is hard, 5–10 cm long, constricted between individual seeds; it is always brittle between seeds. Flowers from late winter to early spring.

HABITAT AND DISTRIBUTION: Widespread on dry alkaline soils or coastal dunes; south-eastern Western Australia, South Australia and north-western Victoria.

MEDICINAL USES: Bark soaked in water or boiled in water and the decoction used as a cough medicine by the Aborigines.[18,20]

The ash has been used together with *Duboisia hopwoodii* for chewing.[18]

ACTIVE CONSTITUENTS: Not known; the ash is alkaline and helps release the alkaloids from *D. hopwoodii*.

Acacia holosericea

FAMILY: Mimosaceae

VERNACULAR NAMES: 'Liringgin'

DESCRIPTION: A small, bushy, silky-hairy or more commonly hairless tree up to 2.5 m high with 3-angled branchlets. Its leaf-like phyllodes are oval-oblong, 10–15 cm long and 2.5–8 cm broad and asymmetrical. Its yellow flowers occur in spikes 5 cm long. The legume is long and narrow, sometimes spirally twisted. Flowers from winter to end of spring.

HABITAT AND DISTRIBUTION: From northern Western Australia through the north of the Northern Territory into coastal tropical Queensland.

MEDICINAL USES: The aborigines used to soak the mashed roots in water and drink the infusion for laryngitis.[18]

ACTIVE CONSTITUENTS: Not known. The tree bark contains the alkaloid hordenine (about 1.2 per cent).[48] Hordenine has been used medicinally as a myocardial stimulant and in small doses as intestinal relaxant; in larger doses as intestinal stimulant.[49]

Acacia melanoxylon

FAMILY: Mimosaceae

VERNACULAR NAMES: 'Blackwood', 'black sally', 'hickory'; 'mootchong' and 'ja-jow-erong' in Victoria.

DESCRIPTIONS: A medium to fairly large tree, 6–30 m high. Young shoots are hairy. Phyllodes (petioles of leaf-like appearance) are thick, elliptic, sometimes slightly sickle-shaped, tapered at both ends, with usually four longitudinal veins, and 7–10 cm long and 1–2 cm wide. Pale yellow globular heads contain thirty to fifty flowers. Legume is curved or twisted, 8–10 cm long and 5–8 mm wide. Ribs on young branches are light-coloured. Flowers from late winter to late spring.

HABITAT AND DISTRIBUTION: In wet forests on good soil; widespread in Victoria; also in Tasmania, South Australia and New South Wales (in the Blue Mountains for example).

MEDICINAL USES: A hot infusion of the roasted bark was used by Victorian Aborigines to bathe rheumatic joints.[50]

ACTIVE CONSTITUENTS: The bark is rich in tannins.[3]

Acacia monticola

FAMILY: Mimosaceae

DESCRIPTION: A shrub to about 4 m tall with a dry reddish bark curling off in thin strips. Branchlets are ribbed, sticky and hairy. Leaf-like phyllodes are also sticky with some short hairs on their margins; they are oblong to egg-shaped and broadened near the tip, 13–25 mm long and 7–10 mm wide, and blunt-tipped, sometimes with a slight depression or with a very small terminal point. Phyllodes have three to five translucent longitudinal veins with a rather coarse network of veins between them. Single about 18-flowered heads occur on stalks 13–16 mm long in upper leaf forks. The pod is flat, raised over the seeds, sticky, hairy containing flattened seeds 5–6 mm long, 3.5–4.5 mm wide and about 2 mm thick. Flowers in May.

HABITAT AND DISTRIBUTION: Stony arid regions of Queensland, Northern Territory and Western Australia.

MEDICINAL USES: The Aborigines of Western Australia used it for coughs and colds: mashed roots were soaked in water or branchlets were boiled in water and the resulting solutions drunk or used for bathing.[18]

ACTIVE CONSTITUENTS: Not known.

Adiantum aethiopicum (See colour plate facing page 49)

FAMILY: Adiantaceae

VERNACULAR NAMES: 'Common maidenhair fern', 'small maidenhair fern'.

DESCRIPTION: A terrestrial fern with a creeping rhizome. The overall height of the plant varies from 10 to 60 cm. The main stems are dark brown. Its leaves (fronds) are 10–45 cm high, sometimes very broad, compound (2- to 4-pinnate) with their slender, wiry and shining main stalk attached to the middle of the base. The short-stalked leaf segments are almost circular to somewhat triangular (with the pointed end attached to the stalk) with lobed margins; they are bright green in colour.

HABITAT AND DISTRIBUTION: Along the banks of creeks, in gullies and generally in damp open situations. Occurs in all states.

MEDICINAL USES: It is reputed to be slightly astringent and emetic. A soothing drink prepared from *Adiantum capillus-veneris* (that name means 'Venus-hair'; this is the original maidenhair fern, although Venus was no maiden; moreover the real resemblance of the fine dark stalks is to pubic hair, not that of the head) and from *Adiantum peltatum* has been used in Europe and elsewhere under the name of 'sirop de capillaire' in diseases of the chest;[3,36] our common maidenhair fern has been used for the same purpose as an infusion of one to five parts of plant in 100 parts of water.[3]

ACTIVE CONSTITUENTS: Possibly tannins;[36] the plant has not yet been properly investigated.

Alphitonia petriei

FAMILY: Rhamnaceae

DESCRIPTION: A tall tree up to 45 m high and 60 cm in diameter, with a dark brown to grey and almost black bark which is usually deeply fissured in old trees. Young shoots, young branchlets and the underside of leaves are hairy. Leaves are alternate, tapered at both ends, fairly narrow to quite broadly elliptical, sometimes more rounded near the base. The upper leaf surface is smooth and glossy, the underside much paler and hairy, with conspicuous veins. Length of leaves varies from 7.5 cm to 15 cm. Its small, cream-coloured, fragrant flowers occur in clusters in leaf forks or at the end of branchlets. The fruit is round and black, about 12 mm in diameter and contains three (sometimes two) hard cells. Each cell contains a rusty-brown and glossy oval seed. Flowers in October.

HABITAT AND DISTRIBUTION: In coastal tropical and subtropical rainforest of the Northern Territory, northern Queensland and adjacent islands.

MEDICINAL USES: A decoction of the bark has been used by the Aborigines of northern Queensland externally for the relief of body pains.[13]

ACTIVE CONSTITUENTS: The decoction smells of methyl salicylate,[13] a substance commonly used by external application for the relief of muscular pain. The wood contains several triterpenoid acids (alphitolic acid, ceanothic acid and betulic acid) as well as alphitonin, a flavonoid-like substance.[16]

Alyxia spicata *(See colour plate facing page 49)*

FAMILY: Apocynaceae

DESCRIPTION: A shrub with angular branchlets. Its oval-shaped leaves are round-tipped and are arranged in groups of three to four around the stem. Single stalkless flowers occur along the axis of short-stalked spikes growing from leaf forks. The fruit is an orange berry.

HABITAT AND DISTRIBUTION: Coastal tropical Queensland.

MEDICINAL USES: The Aborigines used it for breathlessness and 'short wind'. A decoction of the roots drunk daily was reputed to achieve the desired cure after two applications.[20]

ACTIVE CONSTITUENTS: Not known.

Ammannia baccifera

FAMILY: Lythraceae

SYNONYMS: *Ammannia indica, Ammannia vesicatoria.*

DESCRIPTION: An erect and strongly aromatic plant that may reach 60 cm in height. Its oblong leaves are tapered at both ends and vary from 12 to 25 mm in length; leaves on side branches are usually smaller. Petal-less flowers occur on slender stalks in small clusters in leaf forks. The fruit is a flattened globular capsule. The leaf juice is acrid.

HABITAT AND DISTRIBUTION: In swampy land; northern Queensland, Northern Territory and Central Australia.

MEDICINAL USES: Freshly bruised leaves are used in India to raise blisters in rheumatic pains and fevers; about thirty minutes are sufficient to achieve this.[3]

ACTIVE CONSTITUENTS: Not known.

Amyema quandang *(See colour plate facing page 49)*

FAMILY: Loranthaceae

SYNONYMS: *Loranthus quandang*

VERNACULAR NAMES: 'Grey mistletoe'

DESCRIPTION: A parasitic shrub on tree branches with pendulous branches, 0.6–1.8 m long. Its leaves are thick and flat, greyish and almost always densely hairy. Leaves are opposite, alternate, or scattered, 3–12 cm long, tapered at both ends to elliptical, often sickle-shaped and less than 2 cm wide (var. *quandang*) or oblong to ovate, not sickle-shaped, more than 2 cm wide and contracted at the base (var. *bancroftii*). Veins are not prominent. Its very short-stalked brown to yellow flowers are red inside and occur in groups of two or three in leaf forks. Individual petals are about 2.5 cm long. The fruit is egg-shaped to globular, greyish and hairy, 6–10 mm long. Flowers from late autumn to early spring.

HABITAT AND DISTRIBUTION: Exclusively parasitic on species of *Acacia;* distributed somewhat discontinuously in temperate dry inland areas. All states except Tasmania.

MEDICINAL USES: The Aborigines bruise the leaves in water and drink the water for fever.[2]

ACTIVE CONSTITUENTS: Not known.

Antidesma dallachyanum

FAMILY: Euphorbiaceae

VERNACULAR NAMES: 'Herbert River cherry', 'top-kie', 'je-jo'.

DESCRIPTION: A small tree with brittle branches and hairy young shoots. Its alternate leaves are egg-shaped, 5–10 cm long, with a blunt or very shortly tipped apex. Flowers are very small and inconspicuous. The fruit is a white or more frequently rosy pink berry, 1–2 cm in diameter and containing one or two flat seeds. Dense fruit clusters are borne by female trees along the flowering stalks. The fruit has a sharp acid flavour.

HABITAT AND DISTRIBUTION: Along the tropical coasts of the Northern Territory and Queensland.

MEDICINAL USES: The fruit juice has been used as a cooling drink for people suffering from fever.[19]

ACTIVE CONSTITUENTS: Not known.

Basilicum polystachyon

FAMILY: Lamiaceae

SYNONYMS: *Moschosma polystachyum*

DESCRIPTION: An erect annual about 30–60 cm tall. Its leaves are opposite, 2–5 cm long on long petioles. Its white or blue flowers are very small in slender, loose, spike-like clusters and are all turned to one side. The calyx, when in fruit, is either sharply turned backwards or very bell-shaped. The corolla tube is straight, the upper four lobes are united in a broad upper lip with the fifth lower lobe left undivided. The fruit is a small dry and smooth nut.

HABITAT AND DISTRIBUTION: Tropical coastal Queensland.

MEDICINAL USES: North Queensland Aborigines mixed the plant with water and drank it for fever.[2]

ACTIVE CONSTITUENTS: Not known.

Beyeria leschenaultii

FAMILY: Euphorbiaceae

VERNACULAR NAMES: 'Pale turpentine bush'

DESCRIPTION: A small shrub up to 1.5 m high. Its leaves are white and hairy on the underside; they are narrow with their margins turned under. Small, stalked flowers occur in leaf forks. The stems of the plant are often covered with a hard resin.

HABITAT AND DISTRIBUTION: On sandy soils in the more arid regions of Western Australia.

MEDICINAL USES: The Aborigines took a leaf decoction against tuberculosis; this leaf decoction was also reputed to be efficaceous against fevers as well as being a universal remedy.[20]

ACTIVE CONSTITUENTS: The resin coating on the stems contains triterpenoid alcohols;[51] it is not known whether they are responsible for the plant's medicinal usefulness.

Boerhavia diffusa

FAMILY: Nyctaginaceae

SYNONYMS: *Boerhavia pubescens, Boerhavia procumbens.*

VERNACULAR NAMES: 'Tarvine', 'tah vine', 'goitcho' (Cloncurry).

DESCRIPTION: A slender prostrate, rarely ascending perennial herb, up to several metres long, usually hairy and sometimes sticky. The leaves of each opposite pair are unequal, almost circular to egg-shaped, heart-shaped or oblong, 1–4 cm long, often with wavy margins and paler green on the underside. Its small flowers occur either singly or in clusters of two to four in the forks of leaves on wiry stalks. The tubular calyx is about 5 mm long, pale pink or lilac; petals are absent. Flowers in summer.

HABITAT AND DISTRIBUTION: A pioneer species on bare areas of warm regions. Sometimes invades land disturbed by man and thus often, slanderously, referred to as a weed. All states except Tasmania.

MEDICINAL USES: As an expectorant in asthma; in India, the root is used for its diuretic and emetic action.[19] The dried herb is also used as a diuretic.[16]

ACTIVE CONSTITUENTS: The plant contains the water soluble alkaloid punarnavine.[16,19]

Calamus caryotoides

FAMILY: Palmae

VERNACULAR NAMES: A 'lawyer vine'; sometimes spelt 'loya' in Queensland (a corruption of 'lawyer', not an Aboriginal name). The reference is of course to the difficulty of escaping from its clutches.

DESCRIPTION: A climbing palm with prickles on its stems and leaves. Leaf segments are hooked or jagged at the end; their edges are rough to the touch. Its small flowers are in loose bunches growing out of a prickly sheath.

HABITAT AND DISTRIBUTION: Near rainforest; north-eastern Queensland.

MEDICINAL USES: Young shoots when eaten were reputed to cure headaches.[2]

ACTIVE CONSTITUENTS: Not known.

Cassytha glabella

FAMILY: Cassythaceae

VERNACULAR NAMES: 'Dodder laurel', 'devil's twine'.

DESCRIPTION: A twiner, parasitic on other shrubs and trees. Its thread-like stems are quite hairless with leaves reduced to minute scales. Small white flowers occur in globular heads on a short stalk; the whole flower is about 2 mm long. The floral tube at the fruiting stage is egg-shaped, reddish or yellowish, 4–6 mm long. The fruit is a berry enveloped in the enlarged floral tube but free from it. Flowers in the summer.

Once the plant has made contact with a host, it generally loses its connection with the ground, putting modified roots (known as haustoria) into the host.

HABITAT AND DISTRIBUTION: Heath and mountainous areas of coastal Victoria, New South Wales and Queensland.

MEDICINAL USES: The Aborigines used to drink an infusion of the whole plant in water in cases of high temperature.[2] A decoction in water has been used in northern Queensland for bathing of the body to combat pains.[13]

A *Cassytha* species known locally as 'natcha' has been used by the Aborigines at Hopevale Mission near Cooktown to make an infusion for the alleviation of chest pains.[13]

ACTIVE CONSTITUENTS: Possibly some of the alkaloids such as cassythicine present in the plant.[52]

Chenopodium rhadinostachyum

FAMILY: Chenopodiaceae

VERNACULAR NAMES: 'Green crumbweed', 'yambal'.

DESCRIPTION: An erect annual herb with alternate leaves. The floral structure consists of a 5-lobed perianth, but there are no petals. The fruit is almost black.

HABITAT AND DISTRIBUTION: On stony soils of northern inland Western Australia and Central Australia.

MEDICINAL USES: The fragrant leaves, crushed and soaked in water are used by the Aborigines to bathe the head for the relief of colds and headaches.[18]

ACTIVE CONSTITUENTS: Possibly an essential oil; the plant also gives positive tests for alkaloids.[18]

Cissus hypoglauca

FAMILY: Vitaceae

SYNONYMS: *Vitis hypoglauca, Cissus australasica.*

VERNACULAR NAMES: 'Native grape', 'Gippsland grape'.

DESCRIPTION: A tall evergreen climber, often forming massive 'monkey-ropes', with rusty-hairy young shoots and tendrils opposite to the point of attachment of the leaves. Leaves are compound with five leaflets branching from the stem like fingers on a hand. The leaflets are blunt at the base, elliptical to almost lanceolate (tapered at both ends), 5–8 cm long, sometimes slightly toothed near the tip, pale and bluish on the underside. The leaflet stalks are often more than 25 mm long. Flowers are yellowish. The edible fruits are bluish black globular berries, 1–2 cm in diameter.

HABITAT AND DISTRIBUTION: In rainforest and sheltered places along the coast and nearby ranges of New South Wales, Queensland and Victoria.

MEDICINAL USES: A gargle made from the fruit has been used to relieve sore throat.[56]

ACTIVE CONSTITUENTS: Not known.

Clematis glycinoides

FAMILY: Ranunculaceae

VERNACULAR NAMES: 'Traveller's joy', 'headache vine'.

DESCRIPTION: A woody climber with long wiry stems and opposite leaves. Each leaf is composed of three rather broad leaflets, up to 7 cm long, with undivided margins or having a single tooth near the base. The absence of irregular tooth-like serrations of leaf margins and thinner leaf texture distinguish it from the other common clematis, *Clematis aristata*. Masses of white flowers in loose clusters in leaf forks or at the end of branchlets and stems. Flowers in early spring.

HABITAT AND DISTRIBUTION: Mainly in areas of high rainfall, moist gullies, edges of rainforests and roadsides along the coast and adjacent tablelands of the eastern coast of Australia and of the Northern Territory.

MEDICINAL USES: Both Aborigines and bushmen, used the crushed foliage to cure headaches and colds by inhaling the strong and sharp aroma.[13,19]

ACTIVE CONSTITUENTS: Not known.

Clematis microphylla (See colour plate facing page 64)

FAMILY: Ranunculaceae

VERNACULAR NAMES: 'Small leaf clematis', 'small clematis', 'oldman's beard'.

DESCRIPTION: A woody climber with wiry stems, up to 5 m long. Its long-stalked leaves are divided once or twice into three leaflets; these are narrow and tapered at both ends and very variable in length (between 1 and 5 cm). Flowers occur in short open clusters. The fruit is a compressed elliptical achene, that is, a dry fruit which does not burst open on maturity.

DISTRIBUTION AND HABITAT: Coast and tablelands of New South Wales, Victoria, South Australia and Western Australia. It occurs generally in drier regions than *Clematis glycinoides*.

MEDICINAL USES: A poultice made from leaves was used by early white settlers as a counter-irritant. However, if the poultice was applied for more than three minutes the exact opposite was achieved, in other words it caused irritation and blistering.[55]

ACTIVE CONSTITUENTS: Not known.

Cleome viscosa (See colour plate facing page 64)

FAMILY: Capparidaceae

SYNONYMS: *Polanisia viscosa*

VERNACULAR NAMES: 'Tickweed', 'tjinduwadhu'.

DESCRIPTION: A branched, upright annual herb covered with sticky hair. Its compound leaves are composed of three to seven wedge- or spear-shaped leaflets. Its 4-petalled yellow flowers occur in clusters at the end of branchlets. The fruit is a wrinkled, narrow and oblong capsule. The whole plant is strongly scented.

HABITAT AND DISTRIBUTION: Widespread in the northern tropical half of Australia; in places a troublesome weed.

MEDICINAL USES: The whole mashed plant has been used externally by the Aborigines to relieve rheumatism, swellings, headaches and colds as well as to heal ulcers and open sores.[2,18,41]

The seeds were given to relieve fever and diarrhoea.[3] In India, its leaves boiled in ghee were applied to recent wounds and the leaf juice to ulcers.[3] The plant was also used for the treatment of ear disease.[23]

In the United States the roots were used as a vermifuge, whilst in Cochin-China (southern Vietnam) the plant was used as a counter-irritant (in the same way as mustard plasters in Europe) and to raise blisters.[41]

ACTIVE CONSTITUENTS: The herb contains triterpenes.[43] Various flavonoids are present in the herb as well as in the root and seed.[57] It is not known whether any of these compounds are responsible for the plant's medicinal activity.

Cymbopogon procerus

FAMILY: Poaceae

SYNONYMS: *Cymbopogon exaltatus, Andropogon exaltatus, Andropogon procerus.*

VERNACULAR NAMES: 'Scentgrass', 'scented grass', 'marrankangu'.

DESCRIPTION: A grass with narrow, up to 1 cm wide leaves, often tapering into an awl-like point; leaves are up to 20 cm long. Flower spikes are bristly and erect. The grass is usually lemon or citronella-like scented.

HABITAT AND DISTRIBUTION: Tropical parts of Western Australia and Northern Territory.

MEDICINAL USES: Used by the Aborigines for the treatment of colds: leaves were chewed or eaten slowly. Sometimes, a decoction was drunk.[18,20,26]

ACTIVE CONSTITUENTS: Possibly the lemon-scented oil.[18]

Cynanchum floribundum

FAMILY: Asclepiadaceae

VERNACULAR NAMES: 'Thooromia' (Cloncurry), 'tjipa', 'dthumara', 'djumbu', 'wadura' (Western Australia).

DESCRIPTION: A herb with erect branches, twining or bent in opposite directions, up to 1 m high. Its opposite, rather long-petioled leaves are heart-shaped to rather broad, tapered at both ends and 2.5–5 cm long. The wheel-like corolla is deeply 5-lobed, and the corona, a ring of tissue seated upon the corolla, has twenty lobes. The white flowers are spike-like on separate petioles. The dry, cigar- or spindle-shaped fruit is more or less winged, about 2.5–5 cm long. Flowers in late spring.

HABITAT AND DISTRIBUTION: Tropical regions of northern Australia.

MEDICINAL USES: The latex (milky sap) has been rubbed on the body by the Aborigines to raise the body temperature during cold weather.[18]

ACTIVE CONSTITUENTS: Not known.

Dodonaea attenuata (See colour plate facing page 64)

FAMILY: Sapindaceae

SYNONYMS: *Dodonaea preissiana*

VERNACULAR NAMES: 'Narrowleaf hopbush', 'slender hopbush', or just 'hopbush'.

DESCRIPTION: A slender shrub up to 3 m tall. Its alternate leaves are very narrow, usually 3–7 cm long and about 2 mm wide (rarely up to 4 mm wide), more or less toothed (main distinguishing feature from *Dodonaea viscosa*) and sometimes with wavy edges. The whole shrub may be sticky. The fruit is a winged capsule up to 1 cm long and 1.4 cm wide, sometimes tinged with reddish purple. Flowers in spring and fruits in summer.

HABITAT AND DISTRIBUTION: Widespread throughout Australia; in valleys as well as in mountainous areas; often inland.

MEDICINAL USES: The Aborigines used the cooled infusion of the foliage for sponging of the forehead and body to relieve fever.[15]

ACTIVE CONSTITUENTS: The narrow-leaved form, *D. attentuata* var. *linearis*, yielded the lactone of hautriwaic acid; the leaves are also cyanogenic.[14] However, the active substances are not really known.

Eremophila cuneifolia

FAMILY: Myoporaceae

VERNACULAR NAMES: 'Wedge-leaved eremophila', 't'iranju'.

DESCRIPTION: A bushy, resinous, hairy and somewhat warty shrub up to 1.5 m high with wedge-shaped, notched leaves up to 2 cm long. Flowers are violet-purple. Flowers in spring.

HABITAT AND DISTRIBUTION: On stony, clayey soils of the arid regions of Western Australia.

MEDICINAL USES: The Aborigines boiled the leaves and drank the decoction for colds.[18]

ACTIVE CONSTITUENTS: Not known.

Eremophila freelingii

FAMILY: Myoporaceae

VERNACULAR NAMES: 'Limestone fuchsia', 'rutta'.

DESCRIPTION: A small shrub up to 2 m high. It is much branched with alternate, dull greyish green and quite sticky leaves, 2-6 cm long and 0.6-1.2 cm broad, tapered at both ends and sharp-tipped, crowded towards the extremities of otherwise bare and twisted branches. Flowers are bright blue or lilac with a funnel-shaped tube and five spreading lobes, the lower of which is quite distinct from the other four. They are about 2.5-3 cm long. The crushed plant is quite aromatic.

HABITAT AND DISTRIBUTION: Mainly inland on stony limestone hills; far western Queensland, Central Australia and parts of the Northern Territory.

MEDICINAL USES: Used as a pillow by the Aborigines for a 'sick head'. Sometimes placed into the perforation of the nasal septum.[29]

ACTIVE CONSTITUENTS: Possibly the essential oil present in the leaves. The oil contains various sesquiterpenoid lactones such as eremolactone and freelingyine,[16] but whether any of these is medicinally active is not known.

Eremophila longifolia

FAMILY: Myoporaceae

SYNONYMS: *Stenochilus longifolius*

VERNACULAR NAMES: 'Berrigan'; sometimes 'emu bush' and 'dogwood'.

DESCRIPTION: A tall and erect shrub, up to 6 m high, with drooping branches. Very finely hairy young shoots give it a greyish appearance. Its leaves are alternate, 5-17 cm long, narrow and tapered at both ends. Its purplish, about 2.5 cm long, flowers are hairy on the outside; the flower lobe is longer than broad; flowers occur in groups of up to three. The fruit is egg-shaped or globular, fleshy, dark coloured, with a single hard 4-celled stone. Flowers nearly all year round.

HABITAT AND DISTRIBUTION: Often on limestone soils, usually inland; continental Australia except extreme north.

MEDICINAL USES: The Aborigines applied a decoction to sores and also drank it for colds.[20]

ACTIVE CONSTITUENTS: Leaves and bark contain tannins; leaves also contain an essential oil rich in safrole and methyleugenol.[16] Since safrole has been shown to be quite toxic, the drinking of a tea made from the plant may be hazardous and ought to be discouraged.

Eremophila maculata
(See colour plate facing page 65)

FAMILY: Myoporaceae

SYNONYMS: *Stenochilus maculatus*

VERNACULAR NAMES: 'Fuchsia bush, 'spotted emu bush', 'native fuchsia', 'wild fuchsia', 'spotted fuchsia', 'wedgerra' (Hungerford district, beyond the Darling River), 'tchuldani' (Cooper's Creek near Lake Eyre), 'pitula'.

DESCRIPTION: A much branched shrub, usually 50 cm to 1 m and sometimes up to 2 m high. Branches and young leaves are hoary. Leaves are dark green, shiny and tapered at both ends, 2–4 cm long and 5 mm wide. Solitary flowers on slender, rather S-shaped stalks in leaf forks. The flowers are about 2.5 cm long, red or yellow on the outside and spotted inside. The lower lobe ('petal') of the 4-lobed corolla is characteristically recurved and separated from the rest. The fruit is nearly globular, about 1.5–2.5 cm in diameter, firm and smooth with a tough, brownish grey skin.

Eremophila maculata

HABITAT AND DISTRIBUTION: On clayey soils in the more arid regions of all mainland states of Australia.

MEDICINAL USES: The Aborigines of the Hungerford district used the leaves as a blister when suffering from a cold.[10]

ACTIVE CONSTITUENTS: The activity is probably associated with the resin-secreting glands present in the leaves.[10] The whole plant, and particularly the leaves, contains the cyanogenic glycoside prunasin[21] (which undoubtedly is not associated with the medicinal properties of the plant).

Eriostemon brucei

FAMILY: Rutaceae

VERNACULAR NAMES: 'Noolburra'

DESCRIPTION: A small shrub up to 2 m high; branchlets have a warty apearance (as many other Eriostemons); its stalkless leaves are up to 18 mm long and fairly variable in shape, from oblong to almost round, turned back near the tip, hairless or densely hairy and always with visible oil glands. Its more or less stalkless pink or white flowers are 5-petalled and occur along stems. The seed is thick, about 4.5 mm long. Flowers from winter to late spring.

HABITAT AND DISTRIBUTION: On stony soil in the arid regions of southern Western Australia.

MEDICINAL USES: The Aborigines used to hold twigs above the fire to warm them and to make them sweat. They then inhaled the vapours or rubbed the moisture on their skin for colds.[18]

ACTIVE CONSTITUENTS: The leaves and twigs contain an essential oil rich in 1,8-cineole, which is likely to be the active principle. The plant also contains coumarins, such as bruceol, and the alkaloid maculosidine.[14]

Ervatamia angustisepala

FAMILY: Apocynaceae

SYNONYMS: *Tabernaemontana orientalis* var. *angustisepala*

VERNACULAR NAMES: 'Bitterbark', 'pallabara'.

DESCRIPTION: A shrub or small tree up to 4 m high. Its opposite, elliptical or oblong leaves are usually 5-10 cm long and end in a blunt point. Leaf margins are undivided. Flowers occur in groups of two at the end or in the forks of branchlets; they are white and deliciously scented. The large-valved orange fruit contains a mass of crimson seeds. The bark is intensely bitter. It may be distinguished from *Ervatamia orientalis* by its very narrow and pointed sepals.

HABITAT AND DISTRIBUTION: Northern coastal New South Wales as well as coastal southern Queensland.

MEDICINAL USES: Queensland Aborigines used to rub the fruit on sores to heal them.[46] The root bark has been used for tropical fever.[13] According to Dr T. Bancroft the bark, even though bitter, has no pharmacological activity.[46]

ACTIVE CONSTITUENTS: Root bark, stem bark, leaves, and stems give strong positive tests for alkaloids. Leaves and fruit contain triterpenes. The fruit latex is probably proteolytic (by analogy with *E. orientalis*).[13,31,42,43]

NOTE: Some confusion exists in the older literature about the identities of *Ervatamia orientalis* and *E. angustisepala* with respect to their reported uses. Since the two species are botanically very similar, they may also have similar medicinal properties. It is also possible that they have occasionally been confused with one another.

Eucalyptus papuana   (See colour plate facing page 80)

FAMILY: Myrtaceae

VERNACULAR NAMES: 'Ghost gum', 'desert gum', 'drooping white gum', 'goonooru', 'coolbidgi'.

DESCRIPTION: A large handsome tree with a smooth, white and deciduous bark. Juvenile leaves are opposite; mature leaves are alternate, narrow, tapered at both ends, sometimes quite sharply pointed, 12–20 cm long, thin and wavy. Flowers in small bunches in upper leaf forks or at the end of branchlets. Flowers in summer.

HABITAT AND DISTRIBUTION: A tropical species most common on alluvial flats; northern Australia.

MEDICINAL USES: The Aborigines soak the broken up bark in water until it is red and drink the infusion for colds; also used for bathing sore eyes.[18]

ACTIVE CONSTITUENTS: Not known; bark contains the triterpenoid morolic acid; leaves contain stilbenes.[16]

Eucalyptus pruinosa

FAMILY: Myrtaceae

VERNACULAR NAMES: 'Silverleaf box' or 'silver-leaved box', 'silver box', 'kullingal'.

DESCRIPTION: A small tree, up to 10 m high, with a rough persistent bark and opposite juvenile as well as mature leaves. Both types of leaf are stalkless, egg-shaped to circular, about 5 cm long and mealy white. Flowers occur in small clusters in upper leaf forks or at the end of branchlets. The fruit is egg-shaped with a cut off top, to almost cylindrical, nearly white and about 10 mm long. Flowers in late spring.

HABITAT AND DISTRIBUTION: Prefers level country with calcareous soils; northern tropical Australia.

MEDICINAL USES: The Aborigines used to strip the inner bark and wind it around body and limbs for pains and rheumatism.[23]

ACTIVE CONSTITUENTS: Not known.

Eucalyptus tetrodonta

FAMILY: Myrtaceae

VERNACULAR NAMES: 'Darwin stringybark', 'emenungkwa'.

DESCRIPTION: A tree up to 25 m high with a rough, fibrous and persistent bark. Juvenile leaves are opposite for an indefinite number of pairs. Mature leaves are either opposite or alternate, broadly oblong, sickle-shaped and tapered at both ends, 10–23 cm long and 3–5 cm broad. Three-flowered umbels in upper leaf forks with flattened stalks. Fruits are bell-shaped to cylindrical with prominent triangular teeth. Flowers in winter (dry season), rarely in summer.

HABITAT AND DISTRIBUTION: Poor sandy soils in wetter regions of northern Australia.

MEDICINAL USES: The Aborigines drank an infusion of the inner bark and sapwood for diarrhoea. An infusion from young leaves, prepared by bruising and rubbing the leaves in water until it turns green and thick, was drunk for fevers and headache. A leaf decoction was drunk for influenza.[2,20,25]

ACTIVE CONSTITUENTS: Not known.

Euphorbia alsiniflora

FAMILY: Euphorbiaceae

SYNONYMS: Has been spelt alsinaeflora.

DESCRIPTION: A hairless perennial herb with a dull, bluish appearance. The lower portion of its much-branched stem tends to lie on the ground, whilst its tips grow upwards to a height of about 15 cm. The rootstock is hard and knotted. Its very short-petioled leaves are opposite, egg-shaped to oblong and slightly heart-shaped near the base. Leaf margins are minutely toothed with the tips pointing forward; the leaves vary from 8–12 mm in length. Flowers occur in solitary groups in upper leaf forks.

HABITAT AND DISTRIBUTION: Northern New South Wales, Queensland and Northern Territory.

MEDICINAL USES: An infusion of the whole herb has been used by bushmen in cases of chronic dysentery and low fever.[3]

ACTIVE CONSTITUENTS: Not known.

Euphorbia hirta

FAMILY: Euphorbiaceae

SYNONYMS: *Euphorbia pilulifera, Chamaesyce hirta.*

VERNACULAR NAMES: 'Queensland asthma plant', 'asthma plant', asthma herb', 'snake weed'.

DESCRIPTION: An annual or perennial herb, spreading to semi-prostrate. Its stems are dull or reddish to reddish green and densely hairy. Its opposite leaves are 1–5 cm long and about half as wide, also reddish green and hairy (sometimes hairless on the upper side), broadly elliptical to rhomboid-oblong and rounded at the tip; margins are finely toothed. Flowers are very small and occur in clusters in leaf forks. Fruit capsules are very small and hairy; seeds are tiny, oblong, 4-angled and reddish in colour.

HABITAT AND DISTRIBUTION: Disturbed areas, often as a weed along roadsides, in gardens and waste ground; warmer districts of northern subtropical and tropical Australia.

MEDICINAL USES: As a decoction for asthma and bronchitis and generally as a sedative in conditions of the respiratory apparatus.[18,19] The decoction is prepared by gently boiling about 25 g of carefully dried herb in 1 L of water, until the volume has reduced to about one half. A glassful is taken three times a day.[3] It may also be smoked in a pipe or the smoke inhaled if burnt on a slab.[3] There are reports, though, that it is not always effective in the treatment of asthma.[3]

Cures emphysema;[53] it also has been used for the treatment of worms; in bowel complaints, dysentery, colic, and against warts.[54] It also possesses hypoglycaemic and anti-cancer activity on laboratory animals.[54]

ACTIVE CONSTITUENTS: Not known with certainty; contains various triterpenoids, flavonoids and sugars as well as substances said to have antispasmodic and antihistamine-like properties.[43,54,55]

Exocarpos aphyllus

FAMILY: Santalaceae

DESCRIPTION: An erect shrub, up to 3 m high, with finely furrowed branches sometimes terminating in a sharp point. Leaves are reduced to minute elliptical scales, flattened against the branches. Flowers are minute. The fruit is a very small nut resting on the succulent enlarged flower stalk.

HABITAT AND DISTRIBUTION: Inland of Queensland and New South Wales.

MEDICINAL USES: The Aborigines used a decoction internally for colds and sores; also used as a poultice on the chest for 'wasting diseases'.[20]

ACTIVE CONSTITUENTS: Not known.

Goodenia scaevolina

FAMILY: Goodeniaceae

VERNACULAR NAMES: 'Ngurbi' or 'ngurubi'.

DESCRIPTION: A dense green plant with blue flowers in leaf forks.

HABITAT AND DISTRIBUTION: On rocky soil in northern coastal Western Australia and Northern Territory.

MEDICINAL USES: The Aborigines chewed the roots of the variety growing near the sea, discarded the vegetable matter and swallowed the juice for coughs.[18]

ACTIVE CONSTITUENTS: Not known.

Heteropogon contortus

FAMILY: Poaceae

VERNACULAR NAMES: 'Black speargrass', 'bunch speargrass'.

DESCRIPTION: A tufted perennial grass with up to 1 m high stems and narrow leaves with flattened sheaths. Flower spikes are 2–5 cm long.

HABITAT AND DISTRIBUTION: From northern Western Australia through northern parts of the Northern Territory into coastal tropical Queensland.

MEDICINAL USES: A cold or hot infusion of the mashed leaves in water has been drunk by the Aborigines for coughs. The Aborigines also chew it like tobacco (appears to be therefore an intoxicant).[20]

ACTIVE CONSTITUENTS: Not known.

Indigofera linnaei

FAMILY: Fabaceae

SYNONYMS: *Indigofera dominii, Indigofera enneaphylla.*

VERNACULAR NAMES: 'Birdsville indigo', 'nine-leaved indigo'.

DESCRIPTION: A prostrate, much branched, hairy herb with a taproot and thin woody stems forming flat thickets up to 1.5 m across; sometimes erect and then up to 50 cm high. The plant has a greyish green appearance owing to the presence of the grey hairy coating. Its alternate, compound (somewhat fern-like) leaves consist of five to eleven alternate leaflets, each 3–6 mm long, wedge-shaped to oblong, and folded upwards along the midrib. Flowers are bright vermilion inside; they are very small and occur in short crowded spikes in leaf forks. The fruit is a grey pod with somewhat cube-shaped seeds.

HABITAT AND DISTRIBUTION: Widespread in tropical regions, preferable in sandy, silty soils; coastal Queensland, Central Australia, Northern Territory, northern South Australia, Western Australia and northern coastal New South Wales.

MEDICINAL USES: An infusion of the whole plant is diuretic and has been given in India for coughs and fevers.[41]

ACTIVE CONSTITUENTS: Not known; contains beta-nitropropionic acid.[21]

Melaleuca hypericifolia *(See colour plate facing page 80)*

FAMILY: Myrtaceae

DESCRIPTION: A hairless shrub, rarely up to 6 m high but usually much smaller, with spreading and often rambling branches and corky bark. Its very short-stalked, opposite leaves are elliptical to oblong, tapered at both ends with a sharp, sometimes blunt tip, 15–40 mm long and 4–10 mm wide and a prominent midrib. Young leaves have a velvety, dull appearance. Its striking red 'bottlebrush'-like flowers occur in dense 3–5 cm long spikes. Fruits, woody capsules up to 10 mm in diameter and crowned with conspicuous teeth, surround stems in dense spike-like clusters. Flowering time is in summer. The crushed foliage is quite aromatic.

HABITAT AND DISTRIBUTION: Prefers wet places on coastal headlands; also on moist ledges and clefts along the Great Dividing Range. Widespread in the coastal districts in New South Wales and southern Queensland.

MEDICINAL USES: Crushed foliage sniffed for the relief of headache.[58]

ACTIVE CONSTITUENTS: The essential oil present in the foliage; its 1,8-cineole content is about 80 per cent.[39]

Melaleuca quinquenervia

FAMILY: Myrtaceae

SYNONYMS: *Metrosideros quinquenervia, Melaleuca smithii, Melaleuca maidenii* and several others; *Melaleuca leucadendron* var. *viridiflora* and *Melaleuca viridiflora* have been misapplied to this species, the last particularly in publications dealing with the chemistry of the volatile leaf oils (before 1968).

VERNACULAR NAMES: 'Broad-leaved tea-tree', 'broad-leaved paperbark', 'paperbark'; 'numbah' (southern New South Wales), 'belbowrie' (originary of the county of Gloucester as far as Kempsey); many other common (including Aboriginal) names used in Queensland may have applied also to other paperbark Melaleucas.

DESCRIPTION: Shrub or tree up to 25 m high with a dull green or slightly yellowish green crown and spreading twigs. The bark is papery, creamy white to light brown, sometimes grey on the surface. Its leaves are alternate, stiff, tapered at both ends, mostly 5–9 cm long and 0.6–2.5 cm wide and often showing 5 prominent longitudinal veins. Young shoots are silky grey owing to a dense coat of fine hair. The dense-flowered spikes are up to 8 cm long, the flowers being nearly always white to creamy white and only exceptionally greenish, red or partly red. Fruit capsules are broadly cylindrical and about 5 mm in diameter. The tree flowers from late summer to winter.

HABITAT AND DISTRIBUTION: It relishes swampy ground; also on hillsides where ground water is close to the surface. Common along the coastal strip of New South Wales north of Kurnell near Sydney, all the way to Cape York Peninsula at the northern tip of Queensland. Often in extensive and pure stands. Also in New Caledonia, where it is known as 'niaouli', and in Papua.

MEDICINAL USES: Young leaves are bruised in water and the liquid drunk for the relief of headaches, colds and during general sickness.[59]

The volatile leaf oil, obtained by steam distillation has been used for coughs and colds and externally for neuralgia and rheumatism;[11] also as an expectorant during colds.[49] Oil of niaouli formerly used as a vermifuge.[49]

It should be noted that there are two chemical forms of *M. quinquenervia*. One is rich in cineole and the other in nerolidol and linalool. Only the cineole form has the properties mentioned. The two forms may readily be distinguished by rubbing a leaf or two between one's fingers and smelling the crushed leaf: the nerolidol-linalool form has a sweetish, floral odour; the cineole form reminds of medicinal eucalyptus oil.

Also compare with the uses of *Melaleuca cajuputi*, the oil of which is very similar and has been used in the same way. It is probable that the oil of *M. quinquenervia*

Cleome viscosa (see page 56)

Clematis microphylla (see page 56)

Dodonaea attenuata (see page 57)

Eremophila maculata (see page 59)

has occasionally been substituted for cajuput oil.

ACTIVE CONSTITUENTS: Undoubtedly 1,8-cineole (eucalyptol, cajeputol), the major component of the steam-distilled oil.[16] The oil also contains some alpha-terpineol which possesses bactericidal properties and has been used as an antiseptic.[49]

Melaleuca symphyocarpa

FAMILY: Myrtaceae

VERNACULAR NAMES: 'Liniment tree', 'mawilyaburna' (Groote Eylandt).

DESCRIPTION: An almost hairless shrub, sometimes with a bluish frosted appearance. Its leaves are alternate, oblong, blunt at the tip, many-nerved and 3.5–6.5 cm long. Flowers occur in dense, globular and stalkless clusters at the end of the former year's branches. Fruiting heads are about 1.2 cm in diameter and consist of a number of closely pressed together (or even fused) woody capsules. Crushed leaves are quite aromatic.

HABITAT AND DISTRIBUTION: Mainly in swampy woodland and open forest around the coast of the Gulf of Carpentaria, including islands.

MEDICINAL USES: The Aborigines of Groote Eylandt use it as a liniment; crushed leaves were inhaled to relieve headache. Also, leaves were boiled in water and the steam inhaled to ease colds. The decoction was used as an embrocation for aches and pains, swollen limbs and the like. Crushed leaves were rubbed on chest to ease difficult breathing.[25]

ACTIVE CONSTITUENTS: Undoubtedly the 1,8-cineole-rich volatile leaf oil.[58]

Melaleuca uncinata

FAMILY: Myrtaceae

VERNACULAR NAMES: 'Broombush', 'broom honey myrtle'.

DESCRIPTION: A spindly shrub, 1–2 m high with alternate, very narrow and cylindrical leaves, usually with a recurved point. Flowers are very small in nearly globular heads through which the stem grows, often before flowering is over. Fruits are about 4 mm in diameter crowded in nearly spherical clusters. Flowers in early summer and late spring.

HABITAT AND DISTRIBUTION: Usually on sandy, gravelly soils of the fairly arid inland areas of Victoria, South Australia and western New South Wales.

MEDICINAL USES: Leaves have been chewed to alleviate catarrh.[60]

ACTIVE CONSTITUENTS: Most probably the 1,8-cineole-rich essential oil present in the foliage.[58]

Mentha australis

FAMILY: Lamiaceae

VERNACLUAR NAMES: 'River mint', 'Australian mint', 'native mint', 'native peppermint'; 'panaryle' of the Aborigines of Coranderrk Station in Victoria is almost certainly a mispronunciation of 'pennyroyal'.

DESCRIPTION: A small hairless to hairy herb, strongly aromatic when crushed. Its opposite leaves are 1.2–2.5 cm long, tapered at both ends, bright green on pale green stems and sometimes have sparsely toothed margins. Numerous flowers are situated in leaf forks; the 5-lobed calyx is longitudinally striated, individual lobes are narrow and hairy inside; the corolla is white, 4-lobed and less than 8 mm long.

HABITAT AND DISTRIBUTION: Widespread along streams, usually in semi-shade; inland areas of all states.

MEDICINAL USES: A decoction of the plant has been used by the Aborigines for coughs and colds. Also as abortifacient. The crushed plant may be sniffed for the relief of headache.[19]

ACTIVE CONSTITUENTS: Undoubtedly the essential oil present in all parts of the plant;[19] its constitution is not yet fully known.

Mucuna gigantea

FAMILY: Fabaceae

VERNACULAR NAMES: 'Velvet bean', 'cow-itch'.

DESCRIPTION: A tall climber with compound, alternate leaves, each being composed of three, 7–10 cm long elliptical leaflets which are tapered at both ends. Flowers are pale greenish, 2–5 cm long and hang in loose clusters on about 30 cm long stalks. The calyx is covered with long hair; the large upper petal is concave and bent back at a sharp angle. The thick pod is about 15 cm long and 2.5 cm broad and usually contains 4 black seeds; it is covered with irritating hairs.

HABITAT AND DISTRIBUTION: From northern coastal New South Wales into Queensland and the Northern Territory, including islands.

MEDICINAL USES: In India, the powdered bark is mixed with dry ginger and used in rheumatic complaints by rubbing it over the parts affected.[19,41]

ACTIVE CONSTITUENTS: Not known.

NOTE: The Australian plants belong to the subspecies *gigantea*. There is no record of their ever having been used locally for medicinal purposes.

Ochrosia elliptica

FAMILY: Apocynaceae

VERNACULAR NAMES: 'Ochrosia plum'

DESCRIPTION: A tree with pale yellow wood and a bark which, unlike all other *Ochrosia* species, does not exude a milky sap when cut. Leaves are mostly in groups of three or four, rarely here and there opposite, broadly elliptical in shape, sometimes broader near the rounded apex, 7–15 cm long. Its pale yellow flowers are stalkless and occur in small, dense clusters. The fruit is a scarlet, plum-like berry, 2–5 cm long, exuding a milky juice when cut.

HABITAT AND DISTRIBUTION: Coastal Queensland, mainly in the tropical north.

MEDICINAL USES: The bark has been apparently used with success in the treatment of malaria.[19]

ACTIVE CONSTITUENTS: Fruit and bark contain alkaloids[42] but no quinine.[19]

Owenia acidula

FAMILY: Meliaceae

VERNACULAR NAMES: 'Emu apple', 'gruie'; less comonly 'sour plum', 'native peach', 'native nectarine', 'mooley apple', 'rancooran', 'warrongan'.

DESCRIPTION: A small tree with sticky young shoots and a rounded crown. Its alternate, compound leaves are crowded at the end of pendulous branches; each leaf is composed of nine to thirty smaller, dark green and glossy leaflets. The fruit is a reddish, fleshy, globular berry, about 3 cm in diameter. The red and hard flesh surrounding the stone is intensely sour. The tree tends to sucker from roots, hence occurs in small groups.

HABITAT AND DISTRIBUTION: Inland areas of southern Queensland, northern South Australia, northern New South Wales and Central Australia.

MEDICINAL USES: The Aborigines used a wood decoction to bathe sore eyes.[20] Apparently used in the treatment of malaria (but no mention is made of which part of the tree was used).[19]

ACTIVE CONSTITUENTS: Not known; leaves and bark contain saponins.[19]

Pimelea microcephala

FAMILY: Thymeleaceae

SYNONYMS: *Pimelea distinctissima, Calyptrostegia microcephala.*

VERNACULAR NAMES: 'Mallee riceflower', 'small-head rice-flower', 'scrub kurrajong', 'yackahber' (St George), 'willparee' (Mt Lyndhurst), 'wondari' and 'wondai' (Musgrave Ranges S.A.), 'wirri-pirri' (Flinders Ranges).

DESCRIPTION: A small, much branched shrub with spreading branches, hairless except for the flowers and up to 5 m high. Its bark is tough and fibrous. Leaves are opposite, narrow and tapered at both ends, pointed, sometimes blunt, and up to 2.5 cm long. Flower heads are small and occur at the end of branchlets together with two to four leaf-like bracts. The fruit is a fleshy yellowish green or red berry. Seeds are black and wrinkled. Flowers in summer or after rain in dry districts.

HABITAT AND DISTRIBUTION: Usually on sandy soils in inland Australia (never near the coast).

MEDICINAL USES: The Aborigines drink the decoction of the root bark for throat and chest complaints. The tough root bark is twisted around the head and other parts of the body to remove pain.[61] Bark put around the neck is reputed to cure colds.[38]

ACTIVE CONSTITUENTS: Not known.

Planchonella laurifolia

FAMILY: Sapotaceae

SYNONYMS: *Achras laurifolia, Sideroxylon richardii, Sideroxylon laurifolium.*

VERNACULAR NAMES: 'Sweet bark, 'sycamore', 'coondoo'.

DESCRIPTION: A large tree up to 50 m high and 1 m in diameter. Its rough and scaly brown bark is shed in large irregular pieces and exudes a milky juice when cut. Young shoots are finely hairy. Its alternate leaves are broadly oval-shaped, tapered at both ends, 7-13 cm long and crowded towards the end of branchlets. Flowers are in clusters of two to seven in leaf forks. Their calyx may be hairy. The fruit is fleshy and narrow oval, up to 2 cm long, black when ripe and enclosing one or two brown, smooth and shiny seeds (up to 12 mm long).

HABITAT AND DISTRIBUTION: Coastal district of central and northern New South Wales, Queensland and Northern Territory.

MEDICINAL USES: The extract of the sweet and astringent bark may be useful for throat lozenges.[3]

ACTIVE CONSTITUENTS: Bark contains glycyrrhizin;[3] otherwise not yet investigated.

Prostanthera cineolifera

FAMILY: Lamiaceae

VERNACULAR NAMES: A 'mintbush'

DESCRIPTION: In the open, it is a bushy shrub about 1–2 m high; in the deep sandstone gorges near Cox's Gap it may grow up to 5 m in height. Its stems and branchlets are covered with short white hair. Leaves are tapered at both ends, pale green and dotted on the underside, darker green on the upper side, 2–5 cm long and 1–1.5 cm wide with straight margins. Spike-like groups of stalked white, mauve, or violet flowers occur at the end of branchlets.

This species differs from the very similar *P. ovalifolia* by the shape of its leaves and a somewhat hairy calyx. In *P. ovalifolia* leaves are more oval-shaped and rarely exceed 1.5 cm in length; also, the calyx is hairless or nearly so.

HABITAT AND DISTRIBUTION: This is a very restricted species. It is confined to the sandstones in and around Singleton in New South Wales, in the vicinity of Broke, Siberia, Cox's Gap, Cedar Creek and Millfield.

MEDICINAL USES: The vapour from the crushed leaves has been inhaled by local people against influenza and similar complaints.[62]

The crushed leaves are also said to be fly repellent.[62]

ACTIVE CONSTITUENTS: Undoubtedly the essential oil present in the foliage. The oil is rich in 1,8-cineole; it also contains small amounts of the bactericidal and fungicidal phenolic compounds thymol and carvacrol.[62]

Pterigeron odorus

FAMILY: Asteraceae

VERNACULAR NAMES: 'Smelly bush'

DESCRIPTION: A stiff, erect herb up to 30 cm tall with alternate, stalkless and fragrant leaves. Leaves are oblong and tapered at both ends, about 2.5 cm long with irregularly toothed margins. Flower heads are egg-shaped. Seed capsules are silky hairy. Flowers from late autumn to early winter.

HABITAT AND DISTRIBUTION: In spinifex country; inland tropical northern Australia.

MEDICINAL USES: The Aborigines used an infusion of the crushed leaves for the relief of colds and headaches: the head was bathed in it.[18]

ACTIVE CONSTITUENTS: Possibly the essential oil. The plant also gives a positive test for alkaloids.[18]

Pterocaulon serrulatum

FAMILY: Asteraceae

SYNONYMS: *Pterocaulon glandulosum*

VERNACULAR NAMES: 'Tjungarai', 'alworm-angka-ina', 'penja-penja'.

DESCRIPTION: A tall, strongly scented, hairy perennial herb with alternate, broad-bladed leaves tapering at both ends, 2–5 cm long, with toothed margins and a wrinkled, blister-like surface. Flower heads occur in oval clusters at the end of stems. Edges of leaf stalks continue downwards along the stem forming a ridge.

HABITAT AND DISTRIBUTION: Tropical Australia.

MEDICINAL USES: The Aborigines used to insert the aromatic leaves in the nose for headcolds.[29,37] Leaves were chewed to relieve congestion of the lungs.[19] Wounds were treated by rubbing the plant over them and stuffing them with the herb.[2]

A leaf decoction was drunk for headache and fever.[2] The leaves are supposedly potent only when green. An overdose stimulates the heart.[19]

ACTIVE CONSTITUENTS: The plant may contain alkaloids.[31]

Raphidophora australasica

FAMILY: Araceae

SYNONYMS: Sometimes spelt *Rhaphidophora.*

DESCRIPTION: A climbing plant with large undivided leaves; these are egg-shaped and tapered at both ends. Flower spikes are cylindrical.

HABITAT AND DISTRIBUTION: Coastal Northern Territory and northern Queensland.

MEDICINAL USES: The Aborigines have used a decoction of leaves and roots for rubbing on their body to cure rheumatic pains. It causes an itchy sensation.[13]

ACTIVE CONSTITUENTS: Not known.

Remirea maritima

FAMILY: Cyperaceae

DESCRIPTION: A low, branching, grass-like perennial herb with stems 7–20 cm high growing from a creeping rhizome. Its leaves are narrow and rigid, about 2–8 cm long. Its flowers occur in small egg-shaped spikes surrounded by leaf-like bracts at the end of stems. The fruit is a 3-angled nut.

HABITAT AND DISTRIBUTION: In sand on the seashore of northern and north-eastern Queensland.

MEDICINAL USES: Said to be a powerful diuretic and diaphoretic.[40]

ACTIVE CONSTITUENTS: Not known.

Santalum spicatum

FAMILY: Santalaceae

SYNONYMS: *Santalum cygnorum, Fusanus spicatus, Eucarya spicata.*

VERNACULAR NAMES: 'Sandalwood', 'fragrant sandalwood', 'darjen', 'munyun', 'wideerba'.

DESCRIPTION: A crooked, rough-barked tree up to 8 m high; its wood is very fragrant. Its opposite leaves are tapered at both ends and are stalkless. Its tiny but fragrant flowers are green outside and reddish inside; they occur in bunches in leaf forks. Flowers in early winter.

HABITAT AND DISTRIBUTION: On sandy loamy soils in the arid regions of northern South Australia and Western Australia.

MEDICINAL USES: The Aborigines made a cough medicine by soaking or boiling the inner bark in water. The inside of the nuts was used as a 'rubbing medicine' for colds and stiffness.[18,20]

ACTIVE CONSTITUENTS: The volatile wood oil is rich in alpha- and beta-santalols and should thus have antibacterial activity.[36]

Sida rhombifolia

FAMILY: Malvaceae

SYNONYMS: *Sida retusa*

VERNACULAR NAMES: 'Common sida', 'sidratusa', 'Paddy's lucerne', 'Queensland hemp', 'native lucerne', 'jelly leaf'.

DESCRIPTION: A shrubby but short-lived plant varying from 0.3–2 m in height with narrow oval to rhomboid, alternate leaves, 2.5–7 cm long, with toothed margins, whitish on the underside only (var. *rhombifolia*) or on both sides (var. *incana*) owing to the presence of soft short hairs. Its flowers are yellow, small on long stalks in leaf forks. Petals vary from 6 to 8 mm in length.

HABITAT AND DISTRIBUTION: A common and widespread weed in vacant land, sometimes described as one of our greatest pests. Tropical and subtropical Queensland, Northern Territory, New South Wales and South Australia. Almost certainly not native in the non-tropical parts of its range in Australia.

MEDICINAL USES: In India an infusion (of leaves?) is used against pulmonary consumption (phthisis);[19] a root infusion is used in the treatment of rheumatism.[40] A decoction of leaf tips is reported to be useful for diarrhoea.[19] Australian Aborigines have used a root decoction for diarrhoea and eaten the whole plant for indigestion.[20]

In Europe it has apparently been used in pulmonary tuberculosis, rheumatism and in the treatment of snakebite.[19]

ACTIVE CONSTITUENTS: The mucilage content accounts for its usefulness in chest diseases.[19] The root bark contains alkaloids.[16]

Spartothamnella juncea

FAMILY: Verbenaceae

SYNONYMS: *Spartothamnus junceus*

DESCRIPTION: A mostly hairless shrub, rigid or scrambling, up to 3 m tall with green, broom-like, 4-angled branches. Leaves are opposite, often reduced to tiny scales. Its very small white flowers occur in leaf forks; the fruit is an orange or red globular berry with a smooth surface, about 3 mm in diameter, attached to a wire-like recurved stalk.

HABITAT AND DISTRIBUTION: Mostly in swampy ground in coastal areas of New South Wales and Queensland.

MEDICINAL USES: The Aborigines have used a decoction of the plant internally for the treatment of lung complaints and coughs; also for post-partum fever.[20]

ACTIVE CONSTITUENTS: Not known.

Stemodia grossa

FAMILY: Scrophulariaceae

VERNACULAR NAMES: 'Mindharri', 'mindjaarra'.

DESCRIPTION: An erect herb, up to 2.5 m high. Its rich blue flowers are strongly scented; the corolla is twice as long as the calyx. Flowers from mid-autumn through winter until late spring.

HABITAT AND DISTRIBUTION: Prefers loamy soils in the tropical areas of Western Australia and coastal Northern Territory.

MEDICINAL USES: Leaves crushed and soaked in water or boiled in water were used by the Aborigines to rub on for rheumatism or to bathe the head for the relief of colds and headaches. A sweetened leaf decoction was also drunk for the relief of colds.[18]

ACTIVE CONSTITUENTS: Not known.

Stemodia lythrifolia

FAMILY: Scrophulariaceae

VERNACULAR NAMES: 'Bunu-bunu'

DESCRIPTION: A tall aromatic herb. Its flowers are blue; the corolla exceeds the calyx only shortly. Flowers in autumn and early winter.

HABITAT AND DISTRIBUTION: Northern parts of Western Australia and rocky islands off the north-western coast of the Northern Territory.

MEDICINAL USES: The Aborigines applied the fragrant infusion of the whole plant in water externally for the relief of headaches (by pouring it over the head).[18]

ACTIVE CONSTITUENTS: Not known.

Stemodia viscosa

FAMILY: Scrophulariaceae

VERNACULAR NAMES: 'Kwatjinga-unbunamba', 'penja-penja', 'minjakara'.

DESCRIPTION: A sticky, hairy perennial herb, up to 50 cm high with roughly elliptical opposite leaves and irregularly toothed margins. The herb is strongly scented. Its blue flowers occur in leaf forks. Flowers from autumn to winter.

HABITAT AND DISTRIBUTION: Grows on moist ground and river banks in northern parts of Western Australia.

MEDICINAL USES: The Aborigines used the bruised plant as a remedy for colds;[29] rubbed on the body it was reputed to prevent sickness. During outbreaks of contagious diseases the plant was covered with paperbark and used to make beds for babies to keep them healthy.[18]

ACTIVE CONSTITUENTS: Not known; probably the aromatic oil.

Tephrosia varians

FAMILY: Fabaceae

SYNONYMS: *Galactia varians*

DESCRIPTION: A hairless herb with more or less angular trailing stems and a cigar-shaped root. Its compound leaves are very variable in shape and size; near the base often reduced to a single oblong leaflet less than 2.5 cm long; larger leaves bear up to twelve almost stalkless leaflets, alternate or opposite along the leaf axis. Leaflets are 2.5-5 cm long and up to 2 cm broad, very rounded at both ends, displaying a prominent network of veins, paler on the underside. Flower stalks are almost 30 cm long and bearing several widely spaced, pale and purplish stained, softly hairy flowers upon the upper half. The calyx is also slightly hairy. The pod, about 5 cm long, is straight and not flattened, and contains about seven smooth, grey and handsomely veined seeds.

HABITAT AND DISTRIBUTION: In open eucalypt forest; northern Queensland near the coast and adjacent ranges.

MEDICINAL USES: Roots, eaten as such, or boiled in water and the decoction drunk, are reported to have cured rheumatism.[45]

ACTIVE CONSTITUENTS: Not known.

Trachymene hemicarpa

FAMILY: Apiaceae

VERNACULAR NAMES: 'Wilawanggan'

DESCRIPTION: A herbaceous perennial up to 1.5 m high. Leaves on lower portions of the stems are small, wedge-shaped or 3-lobed, coarsely and sharply toothed, whereas the upper leaves are small and narrow to linear. Its very small white flowers occur in dense umbels. Flowers in winter.

HABITAT AND DISTRIBUTION: On barren plains and in semi-desert; Northern Territory and northern parts of Western Australia.

MEDICINAL USES: The Aborigines rubbed the green leaves and roots all over the body for cramps and tiredness.[18]

ACTIVE CONSTITUENTS: Not known.

Zieria smithii

FAMILY: Rutaceae

VERNACULAR NAMES: 'Sandfly zieria', 'sandfly bush', 'lanoline bush'.

DESCRIPTION: A small to tallish shrub with opposite leaves. Each leaf consists of three nearly hairless leaflets which vary from narrow to broadly egg-shaped and are tapered at both ends, 2.5–5 cm long. When crushed they exhibit a strong odour. Small 4-petalled white flowers occur in loose clusters in the forks of leaves. Flowers in spring.

HABITAT AND DISTRIBUTION: Common in sandy forest or cleared areas along the eastern Australian coast from Victoria to northern Queensland.

MEDICINAL USES: The Aborigines reputedly used it for the relief of headache by sniffing the crushed plant.[19] This appears rather strange since the plant is also capable of giving a severe headache if one is exposed to a concentrated vapour of the oil.[58]

ACTIVE COMPONENTS: Probably the essential oil present in the foliage. The oil may vary widely in composition and this may possibly explain the contradictory effects mentioned above. Safrole, methyleugenol and elemicin may be present in major amounts in the steam-distilled leaf oil.[21]

NOTE: It is possible that in some instances *Zieria arborescens* may have been used instead of *Z. smithii*. The two species are fairly similar and sometimes difficult to differentiate.

CHAPTER FOUR
Tonics

Atriplex nummularia

THE TERM 'TONIC' is one of those words gradually disappearing from our everyday vocabulary. Accordingly, it may be appropriate to remind the reader that a tonic is any agent that will give, on continued administration, strength and renewed vigour to the body without any adverse side or after effects, such as sudden excitement or depression. It need not necessarily be a drug or chemical compound. Fresh air, sunlight, or perhaps a cold shower also refresh and invigorate and thus qualify as tonics.

Tonics can be subdivided into different classes according to the organs they tone up: there are nerve tonics, blood tonics, digestive tonics, muscle tonics, and several others. In any case the term tonic is a vague one since it refers only to the treatment of certain symptoms without taking into account their underlying causes. In days past, when the knowledge of disease processes and of their causes was less than it is today, when expert medical attention was at times not readily available, a real need undoubtedly existed for remedies that would help to combat loss of appetite, weakness, and lassitude that accompanied most illnesses. As medical knowledge increased it became apparent that in many cases treatment of the symptoms alone may have been more harmful than useful. It is one thing to prescribe a bitter digestive tonic for someone suffering from a lack of appetite whilst convalescing after some serious illness, and another, and a totally inappropriate one at that, to prescribe it in the case of lack of appetite due to stomach cancer. And so, as more discrimination was exercised in the usage of tonics, their naming became more precise, reflecting more closely their chemical nature (e.g. vitamins) and the term 'tonic' started to become obsolete. Fashion has undoubtedly also had a hand in its gradual extinction. It is so much trendier to pop a vitamin pill into one's mouth than to swallow an oldfashioned spoonful of tonic elixir or syrup.

A quick glance at the list of native plants shows that only about a quarter of the fifty or so species in this category has been used by the Australian Aborigines. A good example is their use of the roasted stalks of young leaves of the 'rough tree fern' *(Cyathea australis)* after any kind of disease.

To the early settlers tonics were very important. It is likely that after arriving here, weakened by a long and exhausting sea voyage, suffering from the effects of inadequate nutrition, and confronted by a hostile and harsh environment, they were prone to all kinds of fevers, digestive disorders and so on. Since bitters and certain other bitter-tasting remedies were held in high repute at that time as nerve tonics and digestives, any local bitter tasting plants were eagerly sought and investigated for medicinal use. An indication of this interest in bitterness may be gathered from some of the entries in the chapter on medicinal plants in Maiden's book on *The Useful Native Plants of Australia*. For example:

> *Codonocarpus cotinifolius* . . . This bark contains a peculiar bitter, and no doubt possesses medicinal properties.
>
> *Croton phebalioides* . . . The bark contains an agreeable bitter.
>
> *Geijera salicifolia* . . . 'Balsam of Copaiba tree' . . . The bark contains a powerful bitter and has the odour of the drug from which it obtains one of its vernacular names.

> *Daphnandra micrantha* ... The bark of this tree is intensely bitter, and is in much repute as a tonic amongst sawyers. Dr. Bancroft has quite recently drawn attention to the properties of this bark, which are similar to those of *D. repandula*.[3]

Bitterness in plants is often, even though by no means always, caused by alkaloids. Some of these nitrogenous substances may possess medicinal properties in very small dosages, but almost invariably act as violent poisons in larger amounts. Strychnine is a case in point: it is a valuable ingredient in Easton's syrup, a well known tonic containing iron phosphate and quinine in addition to small amounts of strychnine; in large doses it is a violent poison formerly used for the extermination of vermin.

Consequently, the greatest care and caution should be exercised in the use of bitter and, therefore, possibly alkaloid-containing plants. For instance, the previously mentioned *Daphnandra micrantha* exhibits a certain degree of variation in its bark alkaloids. South of Brisbane and in New South Wales it contains three alkaloids: micranthine, daphnandrine, and daphnoline, whereas north of Brisbane micranthine is the only alkaloid so far identified.[16] Furthermore, Dr. Bancroft's remark that its bark has similar properties to those of *Daphnandra repandula* should be carefully noted; particularly in view of the toxicity of the latter: 'The extract is very poisonous, one grain being a fatal dose for a frog, and ten for warm-blooded animals ... Its poisonous action is chiefly due to its action on the heart.'[10]

Some of the most popular tonics were prepared from the two small, pleasantly bitter gentianaceous herbs *Centaurium spicatum* and *Sebaea ovata* as well as from the bark of the apocynaceous tree *Alstonia constricta*, the 'bitter bark' of northern New South Wales and southern to central Queensland.

George Althofer remembers his mother giving the children early each spring a decoction of *Centaurium* to help them get over the effects of winter colds:

> It was the custom in those days to either get a tonic from the chemist or to make one up. They used various things. Horehound, nettles and the native *Erythraea* [a species of *Centaurium*]. It is a little, tiny pink flower that grows in wet places ... My mother used to use the *Erythraea* [*Centaurium*] by just boiling the whole plant, making a little toddy of it and giving it to us about once a week.[47]

The bitter principles in *Centaurium spicatum* and probably in *Sebaea ovata* as well are not alkaloids. It has been reported that they may be used indiscriminately.

Unlike the 'pleasantly bitter' *Centaurium*, even the tiniest nibble of the fibrous *Alstonia constricta* bark will leave a long-lasting and very bitter after-taste in the mouth. A powerful bitter tonic is prepared from it by steeping the broken up bark in ethanol. One recipe is to take about 75 grams of bark to 600 mL of proof spirit and, after leaving it to stand for a day or so to complete the extraction process, to use between five to ten drops of the alcoholic extract either diluted in a glass of water or on a lump of sugar.

It seems that not only humans derive some benefit from this tree. George Althofer witnessed bees in the Warrumbungles getting intoxicated by the nectar of *Alstonia constricta* flowers:

> sure enough the bees would get on to the flowers which were exuding nectar. Then they would drop onto the ground in a comatose state and stay there for quite a long time. Then... they would waddle up to the plant and climb laboriously up and get stuck into these flowers again ... and down they would come ... absolute drunkards they became.[47]

Whilst on the subject of flower nectar it may be interesting to quote briefly from a report by a Mr Shallard to J.H. Maiden in which he commented on the startling behavioural changes which took place in bees collecting honey from the 'tea tree' *(Melaleuca quinquenervia)*:

> There is one peculiarity about Ti-tree [Tea tree] honey and that is the fiendish bad temper it always creates in (at other times) peaceful bees. As soon as the flow stops, every hive will mount three or four hundred guards, and they are all looking for a fight. If a hive is opened they are at it to rob it out at once, and extracting at this time is a work of art, and not likely to be tackled by anyone who does not know the Alpha and Omega of robbing preventives.[10]

Insects other than bees were also important in the therapeutic history of *Alstonia constricta*, so important that J.H. Maiden felt it necessary to quote extensively from a fascinating paper on the properties of the bark published in 1901 by J. Gordon Sharp, M.D., in the *Pharmaceutical Journal*. In his description of the action of *Alstonia* extract on 'the Small Life of Pond Water and Hay Infusion' he noted:

> Movements of inhabitants much slowed in fifteen minutes, and all evidently dead in two hours. The animalcules appear to ingest the alstonine, and gradually die, due to coagulation of their protoplasm. When the alstonine is first added, it acts as a stimulant, and the inhabitants rush across the field [of the microscope] with increased activity, and even the lazy *Amoeba* raises himself up; but in a few seconds all is changed, and instead of bounding over the field [of the microscope] the *Paramaecium* moves within a narrower circle, and more slowly, and finally dies. In Rotifera the alstonine seems first to paralyse the fine cilia.[59]

After these and other labours, Dr Sharp declared *Alstonia constricta* a useful tonic, particularly in the case of influenza: 'It acts on the skin and kidneys, and so aids in the elimination of the influenzal poisonous products, and thus it can be employed as soon as the acute symptoms have passed off.'

Smilax glyciphylla, commonly known as 'native sarsaparilla' has been once extensively used as a tonic and antiscorbutic. The naturalist T.W. Shepherd pointed out in one of his 'Stray Notes on Indigenous and Acclimatized Medicinal Plants of N.S.W.' in the N.S.W. Medical Gazette (1871/2) that true South American sarsaparilla was not only in short supply, but that most of that imported into Australia was adulterated. He further expressed astonishment at the neglect of our own native sarsaparilla:

> it is, to say the least, singular that, although New South Wales possesses an indigenous sarsaparilla growing in abundance over a wide area, and of a quality thought to be far superior to the South American plant, yet so little attention

has been paid to it. But perhaps we should not say singular, for it only affords another example of the characteristic apathy of the people of the oldest Australian colony, in all such matters.[63]

After pointing out that this intensely sweet plant, also known as 'sweet tea', probably because of its use as a substitute for both tea and sugar, was quite common in and around Sydney, he went on to say that

> For many years past poor people have been accustomed to use infusions of the leaves as draughts to relieve colds, and to counteract debility, and amongst them there is a general belief that its effects are beneficial. Their mode of preparation is to boil the leaves in water until a kind of thin syrup is formed, which is then bottled and put away for use as wanted.[63]

The usefulness of this decoction as an effective antiscorbutic seems highly doubtful. No significant amount of vitamin C could possibly survive unchanged such a lengthy boiling process.

In another 'stray note' Shepherd mentions the use of 'native pennyroyal' as a medicinal aid:

> In our rural or 'bush' pharmacy, the 'Native Penny Royal' is administered to old and young in the shape of 'tea', as it is familiarly termed. Strong infusions of the fresh or dried leaves and stems are prepared by boiling in water fifteen minutes, more or less: after straining, the 'tea' is sweetened with sugar, and taken warm at bed time q.a.l. [*sic*] It is supposed to be a specific for colds, catarrhs, coughs, and a host of other aches and ills peculiar to both our first and second childhood. It is also esteemed by domestic physicians as a useful alterative, a blood purifier, and an invigorator of the whole system.[64]

He then goes on to comment on the preference of the settlers for the native plant, seemingly more powerful in both taste and odour, over the widely cultivated English species. In fact the native Australian pennyroyal, *Mentha satureioides*, contains more menthol than the English pennyroyal, thus giving the impression of greater strength. In its essential oil composition the Australian plant lies midway between English peppermint and English pennyroyal.

Finally, brief mention should be made of the 'native pepper vine', *Piper novae-hollandiae*, an excellent mucous membrane tonic according to Dr Bancroft. The plant is related to *Piper methysticum* used in the making of 'kava' by Fijian natives.

Ailanthus triphysa

FAMILY: Simaroubaceae

SYNONYMS: *Ailanthus imberbiflora, Ailanthus malabarica.*

VERNACULAR NAMES: 'White bean', 'white siris'.

DESCRIPTION: A tree up to 30 m high with a grey or brown, sometimes minutely scaly bark. Young shoots and the underside of leaves may be covered with fine hairs. Its alternate, compound leaves consist of fifteen to sixty leaflets each. These are tapered at both ends, usually sickle-shaped, 5–12 cm long, with a long blunt point at the apex. The upper side is glossy, the underside is dull. Flowers are small and occur in slender spike-like groups in the forks of upper leaves. Fruits consist of one to five dry, flattened bodies, each about 5 cm long and 2 cm wide and enclosing a single seed near the middle in a circular thickened area. Flowering time is December.

HABITAT AND DISTRIBUTION: In coastal districts of northern New South Wales and southern and central coastal Queensland.

MEDICINAL USES: The resin exuded from the wounded trunk is mixed with lard or wax and is applied to inveterate chronic ulcers;[19] it should not be used for fresh cuts and sores because of the acrid oil present in the resin. In India, the bitter bark is used as a tonic and febrifuge and is administered in cases of dyspepsia. The powdered resin, mixed with milk, is given in small amounts for dysentery and bronchitis.[23] The bark is used for asthma.[14]

ACTIVE CONSTITUENTS: The resin contains the triterpenoids malabaricol, malabaricandiol, epoxymalabaricol, etc.[14] The bark contains the bitter principle not malanthin,[14] as well as a number of beta-carboline alkaloids.[65] Branchlets and wood give positive tests for triterpenes.[43] It is not known whether any of these substances are responsible for the medicinal activity.

NOTE: The bark of a tree growing in the Royal Botanic Gardens in Sydney did have a bitter taste. It is possible that the species exists in different chemical varieties.

Alstonia constricta (See colour plate facing page 80)

FAMILY: Apocynaceae

VERNACULAR NAMES: 'Bitterbark', 'quinine bark', 'quinine tree', 'fever bark', 'Peruvian bark', 'whitewood' on the Herbert River and 'lacambie' or 'lecambil' by the Aborigines of the Clarence River.

DESCRIPTION: A shrub or tree up to 12 m high, sometimes in dense thickets growing from root suckers. Its yellowish grey outer bark is thick, corky, and deeply fissured. The inner bark is yellow, somewhat fibrous, and intensely bitter to the taste. Its leaves are opposite, soft, bright green, slightly glossy on the upper side and usually duller and paler on the underside owing to a dense coating of short hair. They are narrow and taper at both ends, about 7.5–12.5 cm long and 1.5–2.5 cm wide. The leaf stalk exudes a milky sap when cut or bruised. Flowers are creamy white, star-shaped and about 4 mm across. They occur in open bunches either at the end of branches or in the forks of the upper leaves. The fruits consist of pairs of long narrow pods.

HABITAT AND DISTRIBUTION: Prefers sandy and loamy soils; sometimes on rocky outcrops. Also in rainforest clearings, in open scrub and on alluvial sand ridges along watercourses. In central and southern Queensland; also on the far North Coast, northwest slopes and northwest plains in New South Wales, for example, Baradine–Warrumbungle Range distict, near Moree, Brewarrina.

MEDICINAL USES: The stem bark has been used as a febrifuge and tonic. It has been said to be a better antiperiodic than quinine or cinchonidine, and a cerebro-spinal stimulant, particularly useful during influenza and early stages of typhoid fever. It has little antimalarial activity.

It has been used in the form of a tincture prepared by extraction of 100 g of bark with 750 mL of proof spirit; five to ten drops is the usual dose. It has also been used by making pills from powdered bark and liquorice.[3,19,56]

The root bark is not being used as such, even though it could be used as a source of the hypotensive alkaloid reserpine.

The latex or milky sap has been used for infectious sores. Care should be exercised, however, since it is very severe to the skin.[20]

ACTIVE CONSTITUENTS: The stem bark contains several alkaloids such as alstonine, alstonidine etc. The root bark contains reserpine, alstonilidine, 0-3,4,5-trimethoxycinnamoylamajine, vincamajine, alstonidine etc.[33]

WAYS OF DISTINGUISHING *Alstonia constricta* stem bark from *Alstonia scholaris* stem bark: Some reference books (quite wrongly) lump these two barks under the same heading of 'dita bark' (see *A. scholaris*). Apart from the somewhat less pronounced bitterness of *A. scholaris* bark, the following tests may help in differentiating the two. The reagents are applied to the inner bark.[59]

Reagent	*A. constricta*	*A. scholaris*
strong sulphuric acid	no change	beautiful red
strong nitric acid	almost blood red	yellowish green
alcoholic iodine solution	brown	almost black

Alstonia scholaris

FAMILY: Apocynaceae

SYNONYMS: *Alstonia cuneata, Echites scholaris.*

VERNACULAR NAMES: 'Milky pine', 'white cheesewood', 'white pine', 'whitewood', 'dita bark'; Aboriginal names include 'birrba' (Forest Hill) and 'koorool' (Barron River). It is also the 'devil tree' of India.

DESCRIPTION: A tall tree up to 30 m high and 75 cm in diameter. The trunk bark is brownish grey on the outside, yellowish brown on the inside, somewhat spongy and exuding a milky sap when cut; longitudinally furrowed on large trees. Its leaves are in clusters of five to seven, with elliptical blades tapering towards the base and rounded to bluntly pointed tips, 10–15 cm long, paler on the underside. Its small cream-coloured flowers are about 12 mm long with a bell-shaped 5-lobed calyx; the corolla is egg-shaped and also 5-lobed. The whole flower is highly fragrant. Fruits are dry capsules up to 30 cm long, containing numerous hairy seeds.

HABITAT AND DISTRIBUTION: Lowland rainforests of northern coastal Queensland.

MEDICINAL USES: The bark is used in India against various bowel complaints, such as chronic diarrhoea; also as an antiperiodic, anthelmintic and general tonic after fever and general illness.[3]

The Aborigines of northern Queensland have used it for abdominal pains and dysentery;[13] also in fevers[13] (but not malaria).[19]

The bark is used in the form of a tincture prepared by extraction of 1 part of bark with 10 parts of 60 per cent ethanol (ethyl alcohol). The dose is 3 to 7 g of tincture in the treatment of dysentery.[36]

The milky sap is also reputed to be useful in neuralgia and toothache.[19]

ACTIVE CONSTITUENTS: Undoubtedly the alkaloids present in the bark and latex. They include ditamine, echitamine, echitenine and echitamidine. The bark also contains several non-alkaloidal components (echiretine, echiteine, echitine, echicerine).[19,49]

NOTE: See under *Alstonia constricta* for chemical differentiation of the two barks.

Atherosperma moschatum

FAMILY: Atherospermataceae (included by some in the Monimiaceae).

VERNACULAR NAMES: 'Sassafras', 'native sassafras', 'black sassafras', 'Victorian sassafras', 'southern sassafras'.

DESCRIPTION: A small- to medium-sized tree, aromatic in all its parts. Young branches, flowers and the underside of leaves are brownish or greyish hairy. Its opposite leaves are rigid and tapered at both ends, sometimes with toothed margins. The leaves are often arranged in one plane. Their length varies from 3 to 10 cm. Solitary flowers occur in leaf forks. Flowers in summer.

HABITAT AND DISTRIBUTION: In rainforest and in moist gullies of Tasmania, Victoria and New South Wales as far north as the Barrington Tops district.

MEDICINAL USES: A tea made from the bark (fresh or dried) is reputed to have slightly laxative as well as tonic properties and has been used by both Aborigines and early settlers.[3,15] It has also been used as a diuretic and diaphoretic, in asthma, in some forms of heart disease (as a sedative for the heart), and in lung disease (bronchitis). In all these cases a tincture prepared from about 100 g of bark to 550 mL of rectified spirit has been used; thirty to sixty drops were taken on a lump of sugar.[3]

The bark has also been apparently used for the treatment of rheumatism and syphilis,[66] but doubts have been expressed as to its medicinal value.[27]

ACTIVE CONSTITUENTS: The bark oil probably contains safrole. A number of alkaloids are also present in the bark: berbamine (major alkaloid), isotetrandrine, isocorydine, atherospermidine, atherosperminine, spermatheridine, atheroline, moschatoline, and methoxyatherosperminine.[16]

NOTE: Since safrole has in recent years been found to be a potential carcinogen and its use, in consequence, has been restricted, it may be advisable not to make use of the bark for medicinal purposes involving oral ingestion.

Atriplex nummularia

FAMILY: Chenopodiaceae

VERNACULAR NAMES: 'Oldman saltbush', 'cabbage saltbush'.

DESCRIPTION: A greenish grey, scaly, hairy shrub up to 2 m tall. Its alternate, long-petioled leaves are round to oval-shaped and broadened near the base, with straight or toothed margins, and 12–30 mm long. Flowers occur in spikes either in leaf forks or at the end of branchlets. Its 2-valved fruit is semi-circular and toothed, with the valves free nearly to the base. Flowers from summer to autumn.

HABITAT AND DISTRIBUTION: On heavy soils in the dry inland regions of Victoria, Western Australia, South Australia, central and western New South Wales and south-western Queensland.

MEDICINAL USES: Early settlers used it in the treatment of scurvy and blood diseases.[47]

ACTIVE CONSTITUENTS: Not known; like other saltbushes, the plant accumulates common salt.[3]

Eucalyptus papuana (see page 60)

Melaleuca hypericifolia (see page 63)

Spartothamnella junea (see page 70)

yathea australis (see page 84)

Alstonia constricta (Bark) (see page 78)

Exocarpos cupressiformis (see page 86)

Abrus precatorius (see page 100)

Smilax glyciphylla (see page 91)

Cycas media (see page 106)

Ajuga australis (see page 102)

Bacopa monniera

FAMILY: Scrophulariaceae

SYNONYMS: *Bramia indica*

DESCRIPTION: A hairless perennial creeper. Its opposite leaves are small, thick and oblong to somewhat broadened near the tip. Its white to pale blue flowers occur in leaf forks; the corolla is tubular at the base with the upper lip erect, notched or lobed and the lower lip spreading, 3- or 5-lobed. The fruit is a capsule.

HABITAT AND DISTRIBUTION: Usually found on very wet, swampy ground in coastal areas of Queensland and New South Wales to south of Sydney.

MEDICINAL USES: In India, leaves were mixed with petroleum and rubbed on parts of the body affected by rheumatism.[41] The efficacy of this remedy is doubtful, the only benefit is probably due to the petroleum.[3] Also in India, the plant has been used as a powerful diuretic and laxative,[3] as well as a nerve tonic and cardiac tonic.[14] In Ceylon it has been used as a mild laxative in fevers.[23]

ACTIVE CONSTITUENTS: Contains nicotine as well as other alkaloids in addition to 3-formyl-4-hydroxy-alpha-pyrone[14] and the triterpenoid saponins bacoside A and bacoside B.[67]

Caesalpinia bonduc

FAMILY: Caesalpiniaceae

SYNONYMS: *Guilandina bonduc, Guilandina bonducella, Caesalpinia bonducella.*

VERNACULAR NAMES: Seeds are called 'Molucca beans', 'bonduc nuts', and 'nicker nuts'.

DESCRIPTION: A large rambling shrub with numerous hooked prickles. Its large alternate leaves are compound, twice divided into leaflet-covered sub-units. The fruit is a short, broad and prickly pod containing two or three polished blue-grey seeds. The seeds are very bitter.

HABITAT AND DISTRIBUTION: Coastal areas of far northern New South Wales, Queensland, Northern Territory and also Lord Howe Island.

MEDICINAL USES: The seeds are used in India as a tonic and febrifuge (for intermittent fevers) and externally, pounded and mixed with castor oil, for hydrocele. In Amboina seeds are considered to be anthelmintic and the root tonic in dyspepsia. In Cochin-China (southern Vietnam) the leaves are reputed to be emmenagogue and deobstruent and the roots astringent. The leaf oil is used in convulsions and palsy.[3]

ACTIVE CONSTITUENTS: A bitter principle, bonducin (= guilandinin) is present in the seeds and in the bark; it has been considered for malaria treatment.[19] Seeds also give a positive test for triterpenes.[43]

Carissa lanceolata

FAMILY: Apocynaceae

VERNACULAR NAMES: 'Conkerberry', 'concle berry', 'bush plum', 'kungsberry bush', 'marnuwiji', 'gung gara', 'biwil'.

DESCRIPTION: An erect, bright green shrub up to 2 m high with narrow opposite leaves, tapered at both ends, 2.5–5 cm long. The bush is clothed in 1–2.5 cm long thorns. Its pure white, 5-petalled flowers occur in almost stalkless groups, giving rise to purple egg-shaped berries. roughly 1–2.5 cm in diameter. Flowering time is in autumn.

HABITAT AND DISTRIBUTION: It tends to grow on ridges near rivers, from northern Western Australia, through the Northern Territory into north-western Queensland.

MEDICINAL USES: The Aborigines used the oily sap obtained from the whole plant by chipping into small pieces as a liniment for rheumatism. They also were reported to boil the wood pulp in water for some one to two hours and to drink the decoction for colds.[18] They also used to smoke themselves in burning leaves to 'get strength' for long trips.[20]

ACTIVE CONSTITUENTS: Triterpenes have been reported from the leaves[43] and carissone from the roots.[33] Whether these compounds are responsible for the medicinal properties is not known.

Cassytha filiformis

FAMILY: Lauraceae (sometimes separated as Cassythaceae).

VERNACULAR NAMES: 'Dodder laurel', 'devil's guts', 'devil's twine'.

DESCRIPTION: A sprawling parasitic vine, often binding together shrubs and trees by its wiry, thread-like stems. Hairless, except for young shoots which may be hairy. Leaves are reduced to minute scales. Flowers spikes are 1–5 cm long. Fruits are globular and smooth without prominent ribs.

HABITAT AND DISTRIBUTION: Mainly along the coast of Queensland; also throughout the Northern Territory.

MEDICINAL USES: In India, the whole pulverized plant is mixed with dry ginger and butter and used in the cleaning of inveterate ulcers; the juice of the plant mixed with sugar is occasionally applied to inflamed eyes. It is also used as an alterative (tonic) in bilious affections and for piles.[3] The macerated plant has been applied externally to sick people.[20]

ACTIVE CONSTITUENTS: Originally reported to contain the alkaloid laurotetanine;[19] however, our Queensland plants contain two different alkaloids, cassyfiline and cassythidine.[68,69] According to Dr Bancroft our *Cassytha* species are medicinally inert.

Centaurium spicatum

FAMILY: Gentianaceae

SYNONYMS: *Erythraea australis, Centaurium australe.*

VERNACULAR NAMES: 'Australian centaury', 'native centaury', 'centaury'.

DESCRIPTION: An erect annual herb, up to 40 cm high with slender quadrangular stems. Its opposite leaves are stalkless, broad- to narrow-oblong, tapered at both ends and 1–3 cm long. Its small flowers are pink. Flowers in spring. The whole plant is pleasantly bitter to the taste.

HABITAT AND DISTRIBUTION: In pastures, grasslands and waste ground. All states. It may not be truly native, as it is also a Mediterranean species.

MEDICINAL USES: A decoction of the whole plant (collected in summer and stored in small bundles) is useful as a stomach-strengthening tonic,[36] particularly in dysentery and diarrhoea;[70] it has also been used to relieve 'bilious headaches'.[50]

A decoction has been applied externally by the Aborigines to piles and inflammations of external genitals. Also used for the treatment of eczema.[20]

ACTIVE CONSTITUENTS: A bitter glycoside 'erythrocentaurin'.[19]

Cinnamomum laubatii

FAMILY: Lauraceae

SYNONYMS: [Sometimes referred to as *Cinnamomum tamala*.]

VERNACULAR NAMES: 'Camphorwood', 'pepperberry', 'pepperwood', 'brown beech'.

DESCRIPTION: A tree up to 35 m high with a straight, somewhat buttressed trunk and a smooth, light brown bark, sometimes scaly on large trees. The freshly cut bark has a pleasant aroma. Young shoots and branchlets may be finely hairy. Leaves are mostly opposite, oblong and tapered at both ends, 7.5-15 cm long showing three prominent ribs. Bunches of white flowers occur in upper leaf forks.

HABITAT AND DISTRIBUTION: Coastal rainforests of northern Queensland.

MEDICINAL USES: In India, both bark and leaves have been used as a carminative, diuretic, stimulant, diaphoretic, lactagogue and deobstruent.[3]

ACTIVE CONSTITUENTS: Leaves contain a volatile oil rich in eugenol and sesquiterpenoid compounds. The bark oil contains safrole.[71] Since safrole is toxic it may be advisable not to use the bark medicinally.

The species appears to exhibit chemical variation in its oil composition;[71] only the eugenol variety has been used in India.[3]

The bark also contains the alkaloid reticuline.[72]

Croton insularis

FAMILY: Euphorbiaceae

SYNONYMS: Has been confused with *Croton phebalioides*, a different species.

VERNACULAR NAMES: 'Queensland cascarilla', 'warrel'.

DESCRIPTION: A small and rather compact tree or tall shrub. Branchlets, undersides of leaves and flowers are covered with a thick coat of silvery, scaly hair. Leaves are egg-shaped, tapered at both ends, 5-8 cm long with slightly wavy margins; they are spirally arranged along branchlets. Small flowers occur in clusters, 6-10 cm long. Fruits are globular, about 6 mm in diameter.

HABITAT AND DISTRIBUTION: Widespread in or near rainforest; coastal Queensland and New South Wales.

MEDICINAL USES: Tonic and appetite inducing remedy, particularly in cases of stomach and intestinal catarrh; it is used as a bark infusion or powder and is a good substitute for cascarilla bark. Cascarilla is used in doses of 1 to 2 g several times a day.[19,36]

ACTIVE CONSTITUENTS: Not known.

Croton phebalioides

FAMILY: Euphorbiaceae

VERNACULAR NAMES: 'Native cascarilla'

DESCRIPTION: A small tree with slender pendulous branches. A hairy coating gives the branchlets and foliage a silvery appearance. Leaves are tapered at both ends, sometimes slightly elliptical, 5-8 cm long with straight margins (sometimes with a few teeth); they are green on the upper side and alternately arranged around branches. Flowers are small and occur in clusters. The fruit is globular and hairy, 6–8 mm in diameter.

HABITAT AND DISTRIBUTION: In or near rainforest; Queensland.

MEDICINAL USES: The bark contains an agreeable bitter tonic.[3]

ACTIVE CONSTITUENTS: Not known.

NOTE: The similar *Croton stigmatosus* ('warrel' of the Aborigines of northern New South Wales, wrongly quoted as a synonym of *C. phebalioides* in some older literature is a separate species growing in northern New South Wales.

It is not known whether its bark has bitter tonic properties similar to those of *C. phebalioides*.

Cyathea australis (See colour plate facing page 80)

FAMILY: Cyatheaceae

SYNONYMS: *Alsophila australis*

VERNACULAR NAMES: 'Rough tree fern', 'tree fern'.

DESCRIPTION: A tree fern 2.5–20 m high. Old bases of leaf stalks are persistent on the main stem. The scales of these bases are bright brown, glossy and leathery. Leaves (fronds) are compound (bi-pinnate). The mid-veins of secondary leaflets are covered with bubble-like (never star-shaped) scales. Scale margins are fringed with long, fawn or white hairs. Secondary leaf axes are yellow-brown or brown on the underside.

HABITAT AND DISTRIBUTION: In rainforest gullies or on mountain slopes of Queensland, New South Wales, Victoria and, rarely, Tasmania.

MEDICINAL USES: The Aborigines ate the roasted stalks of young leaves as a tonic after any kind of disease.

ACTIVE CONSTITUENTS: Not known.

Daphnandra micrantha

FAMILY: Atherospermataceae (which is sometimes included in the family Monimiaceae).

SYNONYMS: *Atherosperma micranthum*

VERNACULAR NAMES: 'Light yellow wood', 'socketwood', 'yellow wood', 'satinwood', 'sassafras', 'tdun-dambie' (Clarence River).

DESCRIPTION: A small to medium tree up to 30 m high and 60 cm in diameter. 'Socketwood' refers to the rounded knobs, up to 5 cm in diameter, present at the junction of branches and stem. Leaves are tapered at both ends, sometimes elliptical in shape with more or less toothed margins, 7–10 cm long and green on both sides. Flowers, occurring in axillary panicles, are not numerous. Fruits are hairy. Flowers in summer. Wood is yellow and the bark bitter to the taste.

HABITAT AND DISTRIBUTION: A common rainforest species. It extends from Minnamurra Falls near Kiama in New South Wales to Gympie in Queensland.

MEDICINAL USES: The bitter bark has been used by sawyers as a tonic. Dr T.L. Bancroft has used a tincture prepared from the bark in the treatment of heart disease. It appeared to act in a way similar to digitalis.[10]

ACTIVE CONSTITUENTS: The bark of trees growing south of Brisbane and in New South Wales contains the alkaloids daphnandrine, daphnoline and micranthine, whereas north of Brisbane only micranthine appears to be present.[16] It is possible that more than one species is involved (the group is under revision by scientists of the CSIRO).

Doryphora aromatica

FAMILY: Atherospermataceae (included by some in the Monimiaceae).

SYNONYMS: *Daphnandra aromatica*

VERNACULAR NAMES: 'Grey sassafras', 'northern grey sassafras', 'net sassafras', 'cheedingnan' (Barron River).

DESCRIPTION: A tree up to 35 m high with a grey bark exhibiting large pustules, up to 6 mm across. Both the yellow wood and the bark are very aromatic. Young branchlets are sometimes 4-angled. Young shoots and flower stalks are hairy. Leaves are opposite, elliptical, tapered at both ends, 6–15 cm long and have toothed margins. Flowers are borne in upper leaf forks and at the end of branchlets; fruits are club-shaped or tubular, 1.5–2.5 cm long; they split lengthwise when mature and release several tufted seeds. Differs from *Daphnandra micrantha* by being more aromatic and having less-toothed leaves as well as by a larger plume of hairs on the seed.

HABITAT AND DISTRIBUTION: In the rainforests of northern Queensland.

MEDICINAL USES: Bark decoction drunk as a tonic.[13]

ACTIVE CONSTITUENTS: The bark contains the alkaloids isocorydine, daphnoline, aromoline, homoaromoline, daphnandrine, isotetrandrine and 1,2-dehydroapateline.[16,84]

The bark also contains a volatile oil rich in safrole.[16] **Since safrole is toxic, it may be advisable to avoid the use of the bark as a tonic.**

Doryphora sassafras

FAMILY: Atherospermataceae (which is sometimes included in the Monimiaceae).

VERNACULAR NAMES: 'Sassafras', 'New South Wales sassafras', 'caalang' (Illawarra), 'boobin' (northern New South Wales), 'tdjeundegong' (Brisbane Water).

DESCRIPTION: A large tree 20–30 m and exceptionally up to 40 m high. Its opposite leaves are dark green and glossy, with coarsely toothed edges and showing prominent veins on their underside. They are elliptical, tapered at both ends, narrowed at the base and 4–10 cm long. Young shoots are silky hairy. Its short-stalked, star-like flowers (usually three together) are pure white and occur in leaf forks, forming a striking contrast to the dark shining foliage. Flowers in early spring.

The crushed leaves, the bark, and, in fact, all parts of the tree are highly aromatic.

HABITAT AND DISTRIBUTION: In rainforest in the eastern districts of New South Wales and south Queensland. It occurs, for instance, in the Blue Mountains west of Sydney and extends as far west as Jenolan Caves.

MEDICINAL USES: The fragrant tea made from the bark is supposed to have tonic properties.[3,59]

ACTIVE CONSTITUENTS: The bark contains about 0.5 per cent of a mixture of alkaloids named 'doryphorine' by Petrie, who first investigated the bark of this species.[73] 'Doryphorine' consists of a mixture of liriodenine, doryafranine, doryanine, as well as other bases.[16] Because of the poisonous properties of these alkaloids **caution should be exercised in the use of the bark.**

The leaves contain the same alkaloids, as well as an essential oil rich in the very toxic safrole[16] and should, therefore, **not be used for tea making.**

Eclipta prostrata

FAMILY: Asteraceae

SYNONYMS: *Eclipta alba*

VERNACULAR NAMES: 'White eclipta', 'white twin heads'.

DESCRIPTION: An upright herb, about 1–1.2 m tall with opposite leaves tapered at both ends, sometimes broadened near the base and 2.5–8 cm long. Small stalked heads of white flowers occur at the end of stems as well as in the forks of leaves.

HABITAT AND DISTRIBUTION: Coastal areas of northern New South Wales and Queensland.

MEDICINAL USES: In India the roots are used in dropsy and in liver complaints; they are also purgative and emetic.[41] In Ceylon, it is used as a tonic, capable of changing a morbid state to one of health, without causing distress.[23,55]

ACTIVE CONSTITUENTS: The plant contains nicotine; the leaves contain the complex coumarin wedelolactone.[33] It is not known whether these compounds are responsible for the plant's reputation.

Eucalyptus dichromophloia

FAMILY: Myrtaceae

VERNACULAR NAMES: 'Variable barked bloodwood', 'gum topped bloodwood', 'red barked bloodwood', 'gardgu', 'palgarri', 'walgalu', 'mardaudhu', 'punaangu'.

DESCRIPTION: A medium-sized tree with a smooth ash-grey bark, peeling to reveal the inner reddish bark. Mature leaves are alternate, narrow and sometimes sickle-shaped, tapered at both ends, 8–22 cm long. Leaf venation is inconspicuous except for the midrib. Blossoms are in 3- to 6-flowered bunches at the end of branchlets. Fruits are spherical to slightly urn-shaped, 10–13 mm in diameter, thick and firm. Flowers in late autumn.

HABITAT AND DISTRIBUTION: Restricted to northern parts of the Northern Territory and Western Australia.

MEDICINAL USES: The Aborigines drank the flower nectar for coughs and colds. The red kino exuding from the trunk was used as a tonic: either a small grain was sucked or a weak solution was drunk. The solution was also used as a mouth rinse for toothache and the kino itself was used to plug holes in teeth and to stop the pain. Kino solutions, sometimes sweetened with sugar, were drunk for colds and bronchial diseases, and lung and heart diseases (it is possible that some 'heart disease' was merely indigestion). The usual strength of these kino solutions was two spoons of kino to one tin of water.[18,20]

ACTIVE CONSTITUENTS: Probably tannins.[26]

Exocarpos cupressiformis *(See colour plate facing page 81)*

FAMILY: Santalaceae

VERNACULAR NAMES: 'Native cherry', 'cherry ballart'.

DESCRIPTION: A tall shrub or small tree parasitic upon the roots of other species. Young specimens are erect and not unlike a common cypress; the branches of older trees tend to droop. Leaves alternate, reduced to minute scales. Branchlets are green. As the fruit matures its stalk increases in size until, at maturity, it becomes a fleshy, bright red somewhat egg-shaped structure, 5–6 mm in diameter, with the true fruit, a dull green nut situated at its apex.

HABITAT AND DISTRIBUTION: It is common in eucalyptus forests in coastal as well as inland areas.

MEDICINAL USES: Twigs have proved a good bitter tonic and astringent (like the South American rhatany, *Krameria triandra*).[19]

ACTIVE CONSTITUENTS: Stems and old branches contain a triglyceride of exocarpic acid. Leaves and twigs contain various flavonoid glycosides, the triterpenoid oleanolic acid, a saponin of oleanolic acid as well as mannitol. The stem bark contains about 22 per cent tannin.[14] The last named substance is probably responsible for the plant's astringent properties. No work has been carried out on the identification of the actual tonic principle present.

Gnaphalium luteoalbum

FAMILY: Asteraceae

VERNACULAR NAMES: 'Jersey cudweed', 'karkar' (Mitchell River).

DESCRIPTION: An annual or biennial herb with erect stems, 30–50 cm high (rarely taller), wholly covered with woolly hair. Leaves are alternate with straight margins; lower leaves are stalked and spoon-shaped, that is, enlarged and rounded at the apex, up to 7 cm long, whereas upper leaves are quite narrow and stalkless. Greenish or whitish yellow flowers in dense clusters at the end of stems. Flowers all year round.

HABITAT AND DISTRIBUTION: In grassland and often along roadsides, etc. Widespread throughout Australia.

MEDICINAL USES: A drink prepared from the plant by the Aborigines of the Mitchell River area was used for general sickness.[2]

ACTIVE CONSTITUENTS: The plant contains acetylenic pigments in the roots,[33] but otherwise it has not been investigated.

Heliotropium ovalifolium

FAMILY: Boraginaceae

VERNACULAR NAMES: 'Kai-kai'

DESCRIPTION: A diffuse annual herb covered with woolly greyish hair. Its leaves are oval-shaped and rounded at the apex, about 2.5 cm long. Flowers occur in slender spikes. The corolla has a hairy cylindrical tube with a bearded throat. It is composed of five spreading, longitudinally folded lobes. The fruit separates into small sticky nuts.

HABITAT AND DISTRIBUTION: Tropical coastal Queensland, northern South Australia and Northern Territory.

MEDICINAL USES: The plant was bruised in water and used as a drink or wash in cases of general sickness.[2]

ACTIVE CONSTITUENTS: Not known.

Isopogon ceratophyllus

FAMILY: Proteaceae

VERNACULAR NAMES: 'Horny conebush'

DESCRIPTION: A semi-shrubby woody plant, 15 cm to about 1 m tall. Its leaves are twice or three times pinnately divided with oblong, not too narrow leaf segments, altogether 5–10 cm long, stiff and fairly leathery. Flower heads are yellow and occur at the end of stems. Fruit cones are almost stalkless.

HABITAT AND DISTRIBUTION: Widely spread on sandy soils in Victoria, temperate South Australia and in the far south-east of New South Wales.

MEDICINAL USES: The bark has been used to prepare a bitter tonic.[27]

ACTIVE CONSTITUENTS: Not known.

Mentha satureioides

FAMILY: Lamiaceae

VERNACULAR NAMES: 'Native pennyroyal', 'wild pennyroyal', 'Brisbane pennyroyal'.

DESCRIPTION: A small perennial herb, green and almost free from hairs and usually under 30 cm high. Its opposite leaves are oblong to tapered at both ends, stalkless and 5–30 mm long. In contrast to *Mentha diemenica* they are not broader towards the base. The 5-toothed calyx is longitudinally striated, the individual teeth being triangular and sometimes tapering to a point; it is covered with dense white hair inside. The 4-lobed flowers are white and occur in groups of four to eight. Like most other *Mentha* species, the whole herb is strongly scented. Flowers in spring.

HABITAT AND DISTRIBUTION: Near banks of creeks and rivers; also in open forest and in pastures, usually on shale. Usually near the coast and adjacent ranges and tablelands. All states except Tasmania.

MEDICINAL USES: A strong decoction (tea) prepared from fresh or dry herb by boiling in water for some fifteen minutes is sweetened and taken warm at bedtime to relieve colds, catarrhs, coughs, and various aches and pains; also for stomach cramps, intestinal cramps and similar complaints. Used for the treatment of dysmenorrhoea. The tea has also been used as a tonic, alterative, blood purifier, and an invigorator of the whole system in general.[3,19,36,56]

Apparently used illegally as an abortifacient.[19]

As with *Mentha diemenica* it should be used carefully owing to its 'greater pungency'. This probably refers to its more powerful aroma subconsciously linked to the more powerful effect of the drug as compared with *Mentha piperita* (common 'peppermint').

ACTIVE CONSTITUENTS: The essential oil rich in pulegone (40 per cent of oil), l-menthone (20 to 30 per cent), l-menthol (12 per cent), menthyl acetate (8 per cent) as well as other minor components. Pulegone is somewhat toxic and is probably responsible for the increased 'pungency' of the oil.[74]

Oil yield and composition vary with plant development.[74]

Morinda citrifolia

FAMILY: Rubiaceae

SYNONYMS: *Morinda quadrangularis*

VERNACULAR NAMES: 'Morinda', 'great morinda', 'Indian mulberry', 'ko-on-je-rung' (Moorehead River).

DESCRIPTION: A tall shrub to small tree with 4-angled branches. It has large shining egg-shaped leaves occurring in opposite pairs; leaves are 15–30 cm long and short-stalked. There are large leafy stipules at the base of leaves. Flower heads occur in leaf forks, with the leaf subtending the flower head much smaller than the opposite leaf. The mature fruit is greenish white and resembles a bumpy football; it is up to 5–6 cm in diameter and has a rancid, cheese-like aroma.

HABITAT AND DISTRIBUTION: Along the shores of northern Queensland and of the Northern Territory.

MEDICINAL USES: The Aborigines used a rootbark infusion as an antiseptic.[13] In India leaves were applied to wounds and ulcers. They were also administered orally as a tonic and febrifuge. In Cochin-China (southern Vietnam) the fruits were believed to have deobstruent and emmenagogue properties.[3,19] A drug made from roots and trunk has been marketed for its hypotensive properties.[14]

ACTIVE CONSTITUENTS: Roots and bark as well as wood contain the glycoside morindin, alizarin and a number of anthraquinones. Leaves give a positive test for alkaloids.[14,19,42]

Nauclea orientalis

FAMILY: Rubiaceae

SYNONYMS: *Sarcocephalus coadunatus, Sarcocephalus cordatus.*

VERNACULAR NAMES: Leichhardt tree', 'canary cheesewood', 'oolpanje', 'coobiaby', 'toka', 'koo-badg-aroo', 'bul-bocra'.

DESCRIPTION: A large tree, sometimes covered with fine hairs. Its opposite leaves are oval-shaped, blunt at the apex and tapered at the base, 15 cm or longer. Leafy stipules at the base of leaf stalks are large, broad and deciduous. Flowers occur in globular heads; corolla tube is slender with four or five spreading lobes. Fruits are fused together in a globular mass. The bark and wood are very bitter.

HABITAT AND DISTRIBUTION: Coastal northern Queensland and Northern Territory.

MEDICINAL USES: An alcoholic bark infusion has been used as a bitter tonic.[19] The Aborigines used an infusion of the bark in water to induce vomiting and to cure 'sore belly'; also to treat certain snakebites.[2,19] They also used a bark decoction externally for rheumatic pains[13] and bushmen used it for the ague (i.e. malarial fever) and fever in general. A wood decoction was also reputed to cure fevers.[2,19]

ACTIVE CONSTITUENTS: Not known; the heartwood contains triterpenoid compounds and noreugenin.[14]

Ocimum sanctum var. *angustifolium*

FAMILY: Lamiaceae

SYNONYMS: *Ocimum anisodorum, Ocimum caryophyllinum.*

VERNACULAR NAMES: 'Sacred balm', 'mooda', 'bulla-bulla'.

DESCRIPTION: A branching perennial shrub, about 30 cm tall. It is hairy with opposite leaves, about 2.5 cm long, on long stalks. Its white or purple flowers occur in groups of six. The two upper stamens have tufts of hair at the base. The crushed herb smells of either anis or oil of cloves.

HABITAT AND DISTRIBUTION: Tropical inland of Queensland and of the Northern Territory.

MEDICINAL USES: North Queensland Aborigines drank an infusion of the leaves for fever and general sickness and ascribed to it tonic properties.[19] In India, it was used as snuff for infections of the nasal cavity and to kill larvae in wounds.[40] A leaf infusion has also been used in the treatment of skin diseases and of malaria.[19]

ACTIVE CONSTITUENTS: May be the essential oil rich in phenolic compounds such as eugenol (oil of cloves).[19]

Polygonum hydropiper

FAMILY: Polygonaceae

VERNACULAR NAMES: 'Water pepper', 'smartweed', 'water smartweed', 'tang-gul'.

DESCRIPTION: A slender, weak, erect or trailing, hairless annual herb, up to 1 m high. Its alternate leaves are almost stalkless, narow and tapered at both ends with a pointed tip. They are 3–10 cm long with a membranous sheath at the base of each petiole encircling the stem. Flowers are pink or greenish white, small, in elongated arching clusters up to 10 cm long. Flowers are densely dotted. Flowers in summer.

HABITAT AND DISTRIBUTION: Wet places, river and creek banks and swampy ground. Eastern coast of Australia.

MEDICINAL USES: Stimulant, diuretic, and emmenagogue; the juice is haemostatic (if somewhat irritant) and has been used to treat sores on horses.[19]

ACTIVE CONSTITUENTS: A blood-coagulating glycoside and a water-soluble alkaloid are present. Also much tannin and some essential oil. Two flavonoids, persicarin and its 7-methyl ether, have been isolated from the whole plant.[16,19,31]

Portulaca oleracea

FAMILY: Portulacaceae

VERNACULAR NAMES: 'Pigweed', 'purslane', 'munyeroo', 'thukouro' (Cloncurry).

DESCRIPTION: A prostrate, succulent annual with reddish or brownish stems and mostly alternate leaves. Leaves are wedge-shaped or oblong wedge-shaped, sometimes becoming more rounded near the apex, 1–2 cm long. Its stalkless flowers are yellow, solitary or in clusters in leaf forks. The flower's four to six petals are as long as its sepals. Seeds are rough and black. Flowers in summer.

HABITAT AND DISTRIBUTION: Mostly on sandy and loamy soils, especially in inland areas and northern areas. It is an introduced weed in many southern settled areas. Not in Tasmania.

MEDICINAL USES: It is a cooling diuretic and possesses antiscorbutic properties.[3,19] It has been used by Aborigines and early settlers alike as a blood cleanser.[47] In India, it has been used internally when spitting blood.[41]

The anthelmintic properties of the seed have been disproved.[19]

ACTIVE CONSTITUENTS: The plant contains small amounts of alkaloids (such as noradrenaline, dopamine); also calcium oxalate and potassium nitrate, both in potentially toxic amounts.[16]

Rorippa islandica

FAMILY: Cruciferae

SYNONYMS: *Nasturtium palustre, Nasturtium terrestre, Nasturtium semipinnatifidum.*

VERNACULAR NAMES: 'Marsh watercress', 'yellow cress', 'native cabbage', 'yellow swampcress', 'yellow marshcress'.

DESCRIPTION: An erect or ascending leafy biennial herb. Leaves are alternate, pinnately lobed with individual leaf segments toothed. Flowers are yellow and small in clusters at the end of branchlets. Sepals as well as petals are about 1–2 mm long. The fruit is oblong, less than 10 mm long and about 2 mm wide with numerous seeds arranged in two rows in each of the two valves.

HABITAT AND DISTRIBUTION: In damp ground near swamps, along creeks, ditches and the like. Quite widespread; occurs in all states except Western Australia and Northern Territory.

MEDICINAL USES: Early settlers used it to prevent and alleviate scurvy.[47]

ACTIVE CONSTITUENTS: Not known.

Sebaea ovata

FAMILY: Gentianaceae

SYNONYMS: *Exacum ovatum*

VERNACULAR NAMES: 'Yellow centaury'

DESCRIPTION: An erect annual herb, up to 50 cm high. Its stalkless opposite leaves occur in distinct pairs; they are egg-shaped to almost circular with blunt tips and measure 6–15 mm in length and 5–10 mm in width. Small yellow flowers occur in spike-like groups; corolla is 5-lobed. The fruit is an egg-shaped capsule, about 5 mm long. Flowers in spring.

HABITAT AND DISTRIBUTION: In coastal lowlands, pastures etc. Widespread through Australia, in all states, but now uncommon.

MEDICINAL USES: As a tonic in dysentery; has been used by early settlers indiscriminately.[56]

ACTIVE CONSTITUENTS: Said to contain a bitter principle; however, this plant has not yet been fully investigated.

Smilax australis

FAMILY: Smilacaceae, sometimes placed under Liliaceae

DESCRIPTION: A branched shrubby climber. Leaves are alternate, oblong to almost circular, 5–15 cm long with five longitudinal veins, green on both sides and quite leathery. Stems have prickles. Fruits are black globular berries, 10–15 mm in diameter, with one to three hard shining seeds. Flowers are greenish white and arranged in umbels in leaf forks. Flowers in summer.

HABITAT AND DISTRIBUTION: In or near rainforest, or moist eucalypt forests, also on sand dunes; near the coast and coastal ranges of New South Wales and Queensland.

MEDICINAL USES: As alterative and tonic.[19]

ACTIVE CONSTITUENTS: Not known.

Smilax glyciphylla *(See colour plate facing page 81)*

FAMILY: Smilacaceae, sometimes placed under Liliaceae.

VERNACULAR NAMES: 'Native sarsaparilla', 'sarsaparilla', 'sweet tea', 'wild liquorice'.

DESCRIPTION: A branched shrubby climber with wiry stems, free from prickles but with numerous tendrils. Its alternate leaves are more or less broadly egg-shaped, tapered at both ends, 4–14 cm long and 1–5 cm broad, exhibiting three prominent longitudinal veins. They are shiny above, paler and duller on the underside and leathery in texture. After flowering in summer, the plant produces clusters of small black berries, each containing one to three hard and shining seeds. When chewed, the leaves are peculiarly sweet and astringent. The plant should not be confused with the similar-looking *Hardenbergia violacea* or certain species of *Kennedia*.

HABITAT AND DISTRIBUTION: Quite common in valleys and in humid positions along the coast of New South Wales and Queensland.

MEDICINAL USES: It was once a common article of trade amongst Sydney herbalists. It was used as an alterative and tonic, and a decoction of the leaves was used as an effective antiscorbutic and medicine for coughs and chest complaints.[3,20] This decoction was prepared by prolonged boiling of the leaves until a thin syrup was obtained, then being bottled for later use.[63] This procedure undoubtedly destroyed any vitamin C that may have originally been present.

It has been claimed that a decoction of its leaves was more pleasant in taste but similar in properties to *Smilax officinalis* (Jamaica sarsaparilla).[3] The root of the latter, as well as of a number of South and Central American species of *Smilax*, has been used as a blood purifier in the form of teas,[36] as a diuretic, and during mercuric salt treatment of syphilis. Salts of mercury cause uraemia as a result of their kidney-damaging action but this may be prevented by the antiuraemic action of true sarsaparilla.[22] The claims that *S. glyciphylla* has similar activity have never been checked or in any way substantiated.

ACTIVE CONSTITUENTS: The leaves, stems, and flowers contain the glycoside glyciphyllin, which imparts to them their bitter-sweet taste and may be responsible for the plant's medicinal properties.[22]

Tasmannia lanceolata

FAMILY: Winteraceae

SYNONYMS: *Drimys lanceolata, Drimys aromatica, Tasmannia aromatica.*

VERNACULAR NAMES: 'Mountain pepper', 'pepper tree'.

DESCRIPTION: A shrub or small tree usually up to 3 m high. Leaves are alternate, narrow, tapered at both ends, distinctly paler on the underside, with undivided margins, 4–7 cm long, gland-dotted and aromatic when crushed. Bunches of white or brownish flowers occur at the end of branchlets. The fruit is a purple pea-sized berry. Flowers from spring to summer.

HABITAT AND DISTRIBUTION: In woodland and mountain gullies of Tasmania, Victoria and southern to central New South Wales.

MEDICINAL USES: The bark has been used as a remedy for scurvy[60] and as a substitute for Winter's bark.[3] The latter is used as a stomachic.

ACTIVE CONSTITUENTS: Not known; probably contains an essential oil.

Wedelia calendulacea

FAMILY: Asteraceae

DESCRIPTION: A prostrate herb, up to 90 cm high. Its opposite leaves are oblong and tapered at both ends, 2–8 cm long with coarsely tooth margins. Stalked, yellow 'marigold'-like flower heads, about 2 cm in diameter, occur in leaf forks or at the end of stems. Outer leaf-like bracts surrounding the flowers are 8–10 mm long. Fruits are dry, flattened capsules which do not open at maturity.

HABITAT AND DESCRIPTION: Coastal Queensland

MEDICINAL USES: Tonic; in Ceylon said to change a morbid state to health without distress.[19,23]

ACTIVE CONSTITUENTS: Contains wedelolactone,[33] but it is not known whether this compound has any medicinal properties.

CHAPTER FIVE
Antiseptics and bactericides
Treatment of wounds and inflammations

Abrus precatorius

As WE HAVE SEEN in the previous chapter, the Aborigines appeared to know little about tonics; perhaps they did not have much use for them. Quite the reverse applies to germicides and antiseptics. In 1903, in one of the earliest compilations of Australian medicinal plants, Roth lists a total of forty-two species, ten of which have been used by the Aborigines of northern Queensland for the treatment of wounds and inflammations.

There appears to be little doubt that the hot, and often humid, climate had a lot to do with the Aborigines' search for means of curbing infection and speeding the healing process. Bacterial growth is much faster in tropical climates, as anyone who has left a scratched mosquito bite or a minor cut untreated will know. And so the impressive number of different plant species used for this purpose, about 150 in all and belonging to some 57 widely separated botanical families, may not come altogether as a surprise.

The Aborigines seemed to have been aware of the fact that often the bactericidal components could be extracted from the plant into water. Dulcie Levitt has reported cases of wounds being first disinfected by bathing with a warm infusion of one plant and being dressed with the bark of another germicidal plant afterwards. For instance, the Aborigines of Groote Eylandt would use an infusion of the bulb of the 'crinum lily' *(Crinum asiaticum)* for an initial disinfection and follow it by wrapping the wound with the bark of 'cocky apple' *(Planchonia careya)*.

Another example, this time from northern Queensland, is the use of the milky juice or latex of one of the native figs, *Ficus coronata,* as disinfectant, followed by tying the scraped root of *Grewia* around the wound. Even though little is known about the medicinally active constituents of these plants, it has been suggested that proteolytic enzymes and possibly even antibiotics present in the latex of many species of *Ficus* (Moraceae) as well as *Excoecaria* and *Euphorbia* (Euphorbiaceae), *Sarcostemma* (Asclepiadaceae), and *Ervatamia* (Apocynaceae) may be responsible for any of the observed healing properties. Proteolytic enzymes cause the breaking down of proteins into simpler fragments and finally into their component amino acids, allowing their gradual elimination.

The preparation of the plant material also could be varied depending on the way in which it was to be used. Again on Groote Eylandt, when 'cocky apple' was used alone, the bark was cut and the inner part removed. This was then pounded on a stone and shredded in the fingers before extracting it with water. As a result of this breaking-up process, the medicinal substances present in the inner bark were more readily released. At its simplest this may be likened to the grinding of coffee beans before percolating.

Sore and infected eyes were another of the major worries of the Australian Aborigines. Major, since impaired eye-sight or even blindness prevented them from hunting and gathering food. Consequently eyewashes were fairly popular and several species are known to have been used for this purpose. For instance, a carefully strained infusion of 'wild plum' *(Buchanania obovata)* was used and, according to a report by Dulcie Levitt, has even cured a case of blindness:

An old Aborginal man said that he once had very sore eyes. He became blind and his wife had to lead him by the hand, so when they camped he told her to get some 'mangkarrba' *(Buchanania obovata)* and prepare it. She selected a young plant, prepared it in the usual way, and soaked it overnight in a bailer shell. In the morning the man poured the liquid into his eyes. He then lay down and went to sleep. He slept until the afternoon 'began to cool' (about four) then woke, to find that he could see. There was no need to repeat the treatment—he was cured, and able to hunt.[25]

Sandy blight, a kind of eye inflammation (often of the conjunctiva) in which the eye feels as if it was full of sand, purulent ophthalmia, as well as other eye infections, have been reportedly treated by Aborigines and whites alike by bathing the eyes in infusions or decoctions of three of our native 'sneezeweeds', *Centipeda cunninghamii, C. minima* and *C. thespidioides.* It may be opportune to add at this point a few words of warning. Eye infections may be caused by a variety of pathogenic microorganisms and it is, therefore, unlikely that, whatever the active constituent is in *Centipeda,* it would be active against all of them. Also, according to Woolls, the application of too strong a decoction of *Centipeda minima* to the inflamed eye will cause considerable pain. Finally, all latex-producing plants should be handled with particular care. For instance, the milky sap of several species of *Excoecaria,* even though possessing certain medicinal uses, will cause BLINDNESS, sometimes PERMANENT, if allowed to come in contact with the eyes.

Apart from using 'sneezeweed' decoctions for the treatment of eye inflammations (and even that may have been learned from the native population) the early white settlers contributed little in this area. Whether this was due to a somewhat higher standard of hygiene, such as the common use of soap or to the widespread use of methylated spirit and carbolic acid for the purpose of wound disinfection, or possibly to other factors as well is uncertain. Potassium permanganate, popularly known as Condy's crystals, was used in later years as a fairly universal and easily available cleansing agent. One of the authors remembers the use of its faintly pink and very diluted solutions as a mouth wash and, many years later during a prolonged sojourn in eastern Africa, under rather unhygienic conditions, for the washing of fruit before eating it.

Oddly enough, the settlers did use eucalyptus oil as a reputed antiseptic. Odd, since most cineole-rich oils exhibit relatively little bactericidal activity. Perhaps the clean, crisp smell encouraged them. And, should one be permitted to speculate a little, one could possibly explain this belief in terms of the known clearing effect of cineole vapour on the nasal passages resulting in easier and deeper breathing. Plenty of good clean air has always been associated in folk medicine with good health. Whatever the real benefits may have been, the widespread acceptance of the essential oil of eucalyptus may have spurred twentieth century research into other volatile oils of our Australian indigenous flora, particularly those of reputed medicinal value.

In the 1920s A.R. Penfold and his co-workers at the Technological Museum in Sydney (now the Museum of Applied Arts and Sciences) discovered the high germicidal activity of the essential oil obtained by steam-distillation of *Melaleuca alternifolia* foliage. They also established that most of the activity was associated with terpinen-4-ol, a major component of the oil.[75]

To extract the essential oil, the leaves and terminal branchlets of *Melaleuca alternifolia* have to be boiled with water and the oil separated from the condensed aqueous steam distillate. One kilogram (about 2.2 pounds) of foliage will yield only between 12 and 25 grams (about ½ to 1 ounce) of oil. The small oil yield as well as the relatively complicated procedure for its extraction may well explain why this shrub's medicinal properties were not discovered earlier.

'Tea-tree oil', as the volatile oil of *Melaleuca alternifolia* is often referred to, is still being produced and sold in pharmacies and health food shops throughout Australia, although one could hardly call it popular. The oil can penetrate unbroken skin and is particularly useful for the treatment of infected fingernail beds, coral cuts, tinea, some types of boils, mouth ulcers, as well as all kinds of cuts and abrasions. One manufacturer used it a few years ago as an additive in a dog shampoo composition.

A report[76] on the medical and dental uses of Ti-trol (the commercial name for the oil) published in 1936 by Australian Essential Oil Ltd in Sydney included the treatment of pyorrhoea and of diabetic gangrene in addition to the uses mentioned earlier. Its use in the alleviation of unpleasant symptoms of gonorrhoea will be dealt with in chapter 9. The numerous commendations all stressed the non-toxic and non-irritant properties of the oil. Its non-toxic character is perhaps best highlighted by its use as a flavouring agent, particularly as an additive to nutmeg oil.

Its remarkable bactericidal properties have even contributed to our Second World War effort! A bulletin published in 1946 by the Sydney Technological Museum states:

> An interesting application of the oil is its incorporation in machine cutting oils, the germicidal and healing properties having reduced to a minimum infection of skin injuries, especially abrasions to the hands by metal filings and turnings.
>
> Large quantities of *Melaleuca alternifolia* oil were used for this purpose in the various ammunition annexes during World War II.[75]

Even though the oil was popular at that time, its fame was fleeting. According to Mrs Tod Berry who, with her husband took over Australian Essential Oils Ltd, the eventual decline of tea tree oil was due to several factors, such as unreliable supply, inconsistent quality, and, most importantly, lack of promotion. When Mrs Berry retired in 1975, her company, renamed Pacific Manufacturing, was sold, and all records dealing with tea tree oil, its history, and medical applications apparently destroyed.

Some aspects of the commercial failure of tea-tree oil lie in the very nature of the species itself. *Melaleuca alternifolia* favours swampy ground. This makes access for harvesting purposes, particularly during wet years, difficult and sometimes impossible. Consequently, oil supplies fluctuate depending on whether the area is experiencing periods of prolonged wet or drought conditions. Furthermore, the oil composition is not constant throughout the species' natural habitat. Only in the Casino district of north-

Cymbonotus lawsonianus (see page 107)

Eucryphia lucida (see page 110)

Ervatamia orientalis (see page 109)

Lavatera plebeia (see page 114)

Melaleuca alternifolia (see page 115)

Persoonia falcata (see page 116)

Planchonia careya (see page 117)

Solanum lasiophyllum (see page 118)

ern coastal New South Wales does it have the desired composition, namely a high terpinen-4-ol content and a low cineole content. As one progresses south along the coast the cineole content of the oil tends to increase until, around Port Macquarie it starts to resemble a cineole-rich eucalyptus oil. This does not mean that all *M. alternifolia* south of Casino is unsuitable for medicinal use. It means that oils of variable quality will be produced owing to random proportions of good and not-so-good foliage in the distillation charge. Unlike in *Melaleuca quinquenervia* ('paperbark' or 'broad-leaved tea tree') where the nerolidol and cineole forms are readily distinguished by the vastly different odour of their crushed foliage, variations in cineole content in *M. alternifolia* are not easy to estimate in this crude but simple manner.

Cineole, even though useful for the relief of colds, is a mucous membrane and skin irritant and thus quite undesirable for use in healing wounds and inflammations. Penfold warned against the use of tea tree oil containing more than 10 per cent of cineole.

It is interesting to note that a significant proportion of our indigenous plants reputed to have bactericidal or disinfectant properties belong to plant families well known for their essential oils: Myrtaceae (including all eucalypts and tea trees), Asteraceae (previously known as Compositae), Lauraceae, and several others.

The obvious question, as to whether essential oils are in fact responsible for the bactericidal activity, has been answered, at least in part, by Penfold and Grant. Possibly encouraged by the observation that the high boiling residues of eucalyptus oil refining exhibited greater germicidal power than the oils themselves, they determined the phenol coefficients of a number of essential oils and essential oil components by the Rideal–Walker method using *Salmonella typhi* (in their original papers referred to as *Bacillus typhosus*) as the test micro-organism.[77] This so-called Rideal–Walker or R–W test compares the germicidal power of the substance tested with that of the well-known germicide phenol (carbolic acid). Their findings suggested that many of the oils were indeed quite powerful disinfectants. Even though the R–W test has been superseded in recent years by the Sykes–Kelsey test, at least in part owing to the introduction on the market of new types of germicidal compounds, such as the quaternary ammonium salts, it still remains a valid test, albeit of more restricted application. Some of Penfold and Grant's results are shown in Tables 5.1 and 5.2.

Table 5.1	Essential oils	
Species	R–W Coefficient	Major oil components
Melaleuca alternifolia	11	terpinen-4-ol
Melaleuca linariifolia	10	terpinen-4-ol, cineole
Eucalyptus dives 'Type'	8	piperitone, piperitol
Eucalyptus elata	11	piperitone, piperitol
Eucalyptus citriodora	8	citronellal, citronellol

Table 5.1	Essential oils	(continued)
Species	R-W Coefficient	Major oil components
Eucalyptus polybractea	5	cineole, some australol
Leptospermum petersonii	15	citral, citronellal
Backhousia citriodora	16	citral
Doryphora sassafras	13	safrole

Table 5.2	Essential oil components	
Compound	R-W Coefficient	Chemical type
Cineole	3.5	monoterpenoid ether
Geraniol	21	monoterpenoid alcohol
Piperitol (*cis* + *trans*)	13	monoterpenoid alcohol
Citronellol	14	monoterpenoid alcohol
Linalool	13	monoterpenoid alcohol
Terpinen-4-ol	13	monoterpenoid alcohol
alpha-Terpineol	16	monoterpenoid alcohol
Menthol	19	monoterpenoid alcohol
Piperitone	8	monoterpenoid ketone
Thujone	12	monoterpenoid ketone
Citral	19.5	monoterpenoid aldehyde
Citronellal	13.5	monoterpenoid aldehyde
Safrole	11	phenolic ether
Methyleugenol	13.5	phenolic ether
Anethole	11	phenolic ether
Thymol	25	phenol
Eugenol	15	phenol
Australol	22.5	phenol

Pine oil (from *Pinus palustris*), a mixture of alpha-terpineol and other monoterpenoid alcohols, has long been used as a good general disinfectant, often in the form of a soap solution, for the disinfection of railway carriages, hospital floors and classrooms. Menthol-rich mouth washes and gargles are equally popular, and many people use lavender oil (rich in linalool) as a local bactericide. Eugenol, with the characteristic odour of clove oil, is used to this day as a dental antiseptic.

Work done outside Australia on several perfumery and flavouring oils such as citronella, clove, lemongrass, gingergrass and many others has also shown considerable antibacterial activity in all of them.

Screening of well over a thousand native Australian plant species by Dr Nancy Atkinson's group at the University of Adelaide, some twenty to twenty five years after Penfold's pioneering investigations, has revealed almost a hundred species showing antibacterial properties with respect to one or more of the three micro-organisms used: *Staphylococcus aureus, Salmonella typhi,* and *Mycobacterium phlei.*[78] Once again, in the majority of cases, the essential oils present in these plants appeared to be responsible for the activity.

In most cases, the essential oils studied were obtained from the leaves of the plants investigated. The finding that certain flower oils, such as those of *Darwinia citriodora, Agonis linearis* and *Chamaelaucium uncinatum* (more popularly known as 'Geraldton wax'), have equally germicidal properties appears of special interest. Perfumes have, in the past, been compounded largely from flower oils and flower extracts. Could it be that their popularity and widespread use, since antiquity, has had something to do with their hidden disinfectant properties? According to Rovesti the germicidal properties of Eau de Cologne are due to its essential oil components rather than to its alcohol content.[79]

Furthermore, it has been reported that the bactericidal power of essential oils is enhanced by aerial oxidation[79.] This spontaneous reaction with the oxygen present in air is accelerated by sunlight; hence, essential oils or perfumes kept for prolonged periods of time in only partly filled bottles of white glass tend to darken in colour and thicken at the same time. One of the authors (E.V.L.) has personal experience of oxidized, slightly yellowed terpinen-4-ol (obtained from *Melaleuca alternifolia* oil) having cleared up an ugly and persistent tinea infection, where fresh, unoxidized terpinen-4-ol acted slowly, and certain proprietary preparations not at all. From all accounts it seems, therefore, that there is more to a perfume than just perfume.

More recently, Beylier[80] obtained good results with Australian sandalwood oil *(Santalum spicatum)* against the 'golden staph' *(Staphylococcus aureus)* whereas the chemically almost identical Indian sandalwood oil *(Santalum album)* has been reported to have negligible activity. Penfold and Grant rated both oils very low on the R–W scale, giving each a coefficient of 1.5 only. Indian sandalwood oil has been used in the past as a good urinary antiseptic. Its use as a perfume ingredient has become widespread only in the last hundred years or so.

Antibacterial activity is not confined to essential oils only. A bladder inflammation has reportedly been cured by drinking a solution of *Eucalyptus maculata* kino in water.[81] An antibiotic substance, citriodorol, has been isolated from the yellow-brown kino of the botanically close *Eucalyptus citriodora,*[16] and it may not be unreasonable to assume that citriodorol, or a very similar substance, may be present in *E. maculata* kino as well.

Quite recently a group of Japanese workers, intrigued by the almost total absence of micro-organisms inside or outside the leaves of *Eucalyptus gunnii,* not only isolated three fungistatic substances from its leaves but also found indications of antifungal compounds in another eleven out of twenty seven species of *Eucalyptus* screened.[82] One of these fungistatic substances was gallic acid, a common enough natural product. The other two appear to be phenolic in nature but have not yet been fully identified. Whether any of these compounds will prove of use to man is a question as yet without answer.

Abrus precatorius *(See colour plate facing page 81)*

FAMILY: Fabaceae

SYNONYMS: *Abrus pauciflorus, Abrus squamulosus.*

VERNACULAR NAMES: 'Crab's eye', 'prayer bean', 'rosary pea', 'precatory bean', 'jequirity bean', 'Indian liquorice', 'gidgee-gidgee', 'do-anjin-jin', 'pundir-pundir', 'boan'.

DESCRIPTION: A perennial woody climbing shrub that often twines around other plants. It has tough branches and alternate compound leaves consisting of seven to fifteen pairs of oblong leaflets, about 12 mm long. Leaflets are thin and bright green. Pink, white or purple 'peaflower'-like blossoms occur in groups either at the end of branchlets or along branches. Flower petioles are about 2.5 cm long. The fruit is a pod, 4–5 cm long and 12 mm wide, dark grey or brown in colour and when ripe containing several 'crab's eyes', that is, scarlet seeds with a large black spot at their base. They are rounded, hard, shiny and about 6 mm in diameter. On rare occasions the seeds may be white without any spotting.

HABITAT AND DISTRIBUTION: Mainly on sandy soils, often just behind the beaches of tropical Queensland, Northern Territory, and northern Western Australia.

Abrus precatorius

MEDICINAL USES: The roots have been used in India as a substitute for liquorice, for example as a soothing medicine when suffering from catarrh and coughs, and as a blood diluent.[3] It has been put to similar uses in Java.[3] Leaf decoctions have also been used for the same purposes.[41] Leaves mixed with honey may be applied to swellings.[3] The **exceedingly toxic seeds** have been used in cases of ophthalmia (in India and in Brazil);[3] a sterile solution obtained from the seeds has been used in Western medicine for the treatment of trachoma.[49]

ACTIVE CONSTITUENTS: The ophthalmically active component of the seeds is the protein abrin which is **extremely toxic**; the seeds also contain several alkaloids such as abrine (N-methyl-L-tryptophan), hypaphorine, precatorine, choline, trigonelline etc.[21,83,85] The seeds also contain the flavonoids abrectorin, desmethoxycentaureidin-7-0-rutinoside, luteolin, orientin and isoorientin.[86] In addition, the seeds of the scarlet variety have been shown to contain the steroids abricin and abridin as well as cycloartenol, beta-amyrin, campesterol, cholesterol, stigmasterol, beta-sitosterol and squalene.[87]

Acacia leptocarpa

FAMILY: Mimosaceae

VERNACULAR NAMES: 'Manggar manggal', 'i-wa-wal' (Palmer River).

DESCRIPTION: A small erect tree up to 7 m high with angular branches that later become rounded. Leaf-like phyllodes are narrow and sickle-shaped and tapered at both ends, 10–15 cm long and 8–15 mm broad with three prominent nerves. Its yellow flowers occur in 5 cm long spike-like clusters. The legume is very narrow, nearly straight, about 10 cm long with longitudinally arranged seeds. Flowers in winter.

HABITAT AND DISTRIBUTION: Mainly near creeks in the north of Western Australia, tropical coastal Northern Territory and Queensland.

MEDICINAL USES: The Aborigines used to soak the mashed green phyllodes in water and apply the infusion to sore eyes.[18]

ACTIVE CONSTITUENTS: Not known.

Acacia translucens

FAMILY: Mimosaceae

VERNACULAR NAMES: 'Banmung', 'nilura'(?).

DESCRIPTION: A small, semi-prostrate spreading shrub. Its yellow flowers last from mid-summer through winter to early spring.

HABITAT AND DISTRIBUTION: Northern parts of Western Australia and Northern Territory; often on sandstone ridges.

MEDICINAL USES: The Aborigines mash leaves and twigs in water and use the liquid to bathe skin sores and the head for headache.[18]

ACTIVE CONSTITUENTS: Not known; probably tannins.

NOTE: Several other *Acacia* species occurring in the deserts of Western Australia and of Central Australia have been used for similar purposes by the Aborigines. *Acacia trachycarpa*, a small tree with a peeling bark, and *A. ancistrocarpa*, also a small shrub, have been used for the treatment of headaches in exactly the same way as *A. translucens*; furthermore, twigs and young leaves of both species were heated in a fire until they started sweating, and they were then rubbed on the body for swellings and internal pains. The infusions used for headache treatment were also used externally for bathing skin sores.[18,26] Skin sores were also treated with bark decoctions of *Acacia inaequilatera,* a straggly shrub, and *Acacia pyrifolia,* a prickly shrub with a greyish blue appearance. The decoction of the last-named species was applied around the wound, not on it.[18]

Acalypha wilkesiana

FAMILY: Euphorbiaceae

DESCRIPTION: A shrub with hairy branchlets. Leaves are alternate, long-stalked, up to 25 cm long, egg-shaped and tapered at the apex, green or bronzy red. Flowers occur in long spike-like groups in the upper leaf-forks.

HABITAT AND DISTRIBUTION: Tropical areas of northern Australia.

MEDICINAL USES: The shoots were pulped (only when the leaves were red) by the Aborigines and applied to lacerations and open sores.[20] In New Guinea leaves were taken as a sedative.[88]

ACTIVE CONSTITUENTS: Not known.

Ageratum conyzoides

FAMILY: Asteraceae

VERNACULAR NAMES: 'Billygoat weed', 'billygoat plant'.

DESCRIPTION: An erect branched and hairy annual herb, 30–60 cm tall. Its hairy opposite leaves are tapered at both ends; their margins are edged with rounded teeth. Flowers occur in small disc-like heads in bunches at the end of stems and branchlets. The fruit is a dry, black and hairy capsule which does not split open on maturity.

HABITAT AND DISTRIBUTION: Coastal Queensland and Northern Territory.

MEDICINAL USES: The Aborigines of northern Queensland applied the mashed plant to wounds to promote their healing.[13] The herb is used for the same purpose of wound healing in Nigeria.[89] In India, the juice is freely applied in cases of prolapsus ani before replacing the part.[23] In South America it has been used as a remedy for metrorrhagia.[23]

ACTIVE CONSTITUENTS: The activity may be associated with the flavone 5'-methoxynobiletin.[89] The herb also contains the flavone conyzorigin, sitosterol, stigmasterol, 7-methoxy-2,2-dimethylchromen and coumarins, as well as an essential oil containing ageratochromen.[33,89]

Ajuga australis *(See colour plate facing page 81)*

FAMILY: Lamiaceae

VERNACULAR NAMES: 'Australian bugle', 'bugle'.

DESCRIPTION: An erect ascending perennial herb, up to 45 cm high and more or less covered with long weak hair. Its leaves form a rosette at the base of the stem; lower leaves are broad and rounded at the apex to oblong, contracting at the base into a long petiole and with distinctly round-toothed margins. Higher up the plant, the leaves become oblong and stalkless with straight margins. Flowers are blue or purple and occur all the way from the base up; the corolla may be up to 2 cm long; it is 3-lobed with a spreading and long lower lip. The middle lobe is large and notched at the tip.

HABITAT AND DISTRIBUTION: Widespread in open forest in all eastern Australian states.

MEDICINAL USES: The Aborigines used to bathe sores and boils with an infusion of the bruised plant in hot water.[15]

ACTIVE CONSTITUENTS: Not known.

Amyema maidenii subspecies *maidenii*
FAMILY: Loranthaceae
SYNONYMS: *Loranthus maidenii*
VERNACULAR NAMES: 'Mulka wertibi'

DESCRIPTION: A parasitic plant (mistletoe) on the aerial parts of other shrubs and trees. Its leaves are flat, broadly elliptical with parallel veins. Stalkless flower heads containing more than three flowers occur in leaf forks. Leafy bracts at the base of each flower head are conspicuous.

HABITAT AND DISTRIBUTION: Chiefly on *Acacia aneura* and others of the mulga group in the arid interior (Central Australia, northern South Australia, inland New South Wales and Queensland).

MEDICINAL USES: The Aborigines treated inflammations of the genital regions, in both men and women, by drinking a decoction of the mucilaginous fruits in water; an amount that would go into a hollowed hand was drunk three times a day (note the European origin of this cure which mentions precisely how many doses each day are required).[38]

ACTIVE CONSTITUENTS: Not known.

Asparagus racemosus
FAMILY: Liliaceae
SYNONYMS: *Asparagus fasciculatus, Asparagopsis floribunda, Asparagopsis brownei, Asparagopsis decaisnei.*

DESCRIPTION: A slender, much-branched climber with recurved prickles and underground rhizomes. Its 2 to 4 cm long leaf-like branchlets usually occur in groups of three to six; they are only rarely solitary. They are very slender, curved, sometimes straight, flat or with a triangular cross-section and often tapering into a fine point. Its flowers are very small; the fruit is a globular berry containing a single shining, black seed.

HABITAT AND DISTRIBUTION: Cape York Peninsula in northern Queensland, as well as coastal Northern Territory.

MEDICINAL USES: After removal of the poisonous bark, the root is boiled in milk and used in Indian medicine in bilious affections.[41] However, Maiden considers this cure to be ineffective.[3] Also in India, the boiled leaf-like branchlets are mixed with ghee (rendered butter) and applied externally to hasten suppuration of boils and to prevent the confluence of vesicles due to smallpox.[41]

ACTIVE CONSTITUENTS: The root contains essential oil, saponin, and fatty substances.[22] Its aerial parts have not yet been examined chemically.

Breynia stipitata
FAMILY: Euphorbiaceae
DESCRIPTION: A tall shrub with alternate, oval-shaped to almost circular leaves. Its

small top-shaped, flat-tipped flowers have the orifice at the centre almost closed by six short lobes. The fruit is a stalked red, globular berry with triangular seeds. The plant turns black on drying.

HABITAT AND DISTRIBUTION: Coastal tropical Queensland and Northern Territory.

MEDICINAL USES: Aborigines in the Bloomfield River area of northern Queensland have used a decoction of the leaves for the bathing of sore eyes.[13]

ACTIVE CONSTITUENTS: Not known. The decoction exhibits the disagreeable odour of methyl mercaptan.

Canarium muelleri

FAMILY: Burseraceae

VERNACULAR NAMES: 'Queensland elemi tree', 'elemi tree', 'scrub turpentine'.

DESCRIPTION: A tree up to 30 m high with large and prominent buttresses. Its bark is brown with small pustules and depressions and exudes, when cut, a whitish resin with a strong turpentine-like odour. Young shoots are hairy. Its alternate leaves are compound, consisting of five to seven leaflets; these are elliptical or egg-shaped, sometimes asymmetrical, 6–12 cm long, with a short, blunt apex. Flowers occur in 7–10 cm long bunches in the forks of upper leaves. The calyx is 3-lobed and the corolla 3-petalled.

HABITAT AND DISTRIBUTION: Mainly in rainforests of northern Queensland.

MEDICINAL USES: According to Dr Lauterer, the resin is a very good healing agent for cuts, sores, and chronic ulcers and is thus a good substitute for true elemi resin.[23]

ACTIVE CONSTITUENTS: The resin is rich in an essential oil containing alpha-pinene, alpha-terpineol, etc. The alpha-terpineol may be partly responsible for the resin's antiseptic properties.[90] The resin also contains triterpenoids such as canaric acid (of unknown pharmacological properties).[91]

Capparis uberiflora

FAMILY: Capparidaceae

DESCRIPTION: A shrub with spiny stems and large spear-shaped leaves tapered at both ends, about 20 cm long and 8 cm broad. Flowers are small and occur in dense clusters on long stalks in leaf forks. The ovaries are borne on long stalks and protrude from the flowers. The fruit is an almost globular berry, about 8 mm in diameter, and contains numerous seeds immersed in a soft pulp.

HABITAT AND DISTRIBUTION: Tropical coastal Queensland.

MEDICINAL USES: The Aborigines reputedly scraped the reddish outer bark of the roots and after soaking the shavings in water applied the mixture to sores and scratches on legs.[2]

ACTIVE CONSTITUENTS: Not known.

Cassia absus

FAMILY: Caesalpiniaceae

VERNACULAR NAMES: 'Hairy cassia'

DESCRIPTION: A small, quite hairy and somewhat sticky plant, up to 50 cm high. Its alternate leaves are composed of two pairs of leaflets broadened near the tip and narrowed near the petiole; each leaflet is 1–2.5 cm long. Glands between leaflets are very small. Flowers occur in clusters at the end of branchlets. Seed pods are 2.5–4 cm long, about 6 mm broad, flat and pointed. Seeds are extremely bitter.

HABITAT AND DISTRIBUTION: Near the coast of tropical Queensland and Northern Territory.

MEDICINAL USES: The seed has been used in Egypt for the treatment of purulent ophthalmia. The seed, reduced to a fine powder is introduced under the eyelid, one grain or more being used.[19,40] **Should be used with the greatest caution.**

ACTIVE CONSTITUENTS: The plant contains alkaloids,[19] but the actual medicinally active principles are not known.

Centipeda minima

FAMILY: Asteraceae

SYNONYMS: *Centipeda orbicularis, Myriogyne minuta,* and many others; used to include *C. cunninghamii.*

VERNACULAR NAMES: 'Spreading sneezeweed', 'sneezeweed', 'gukwonderuk', 'kandjirkalara', 'kanjirralaa'.

DESCRIPTION: A small, aromatic annual herb with stems up to 20 cm long, spreading along the ground but with ascending tips. It may be hairless or quite woolly. Leaves are alternate, tapered at both ends with toothed margins, broadened near the tip rather than near the base and up to 3 cm long. Small, almost stalkless, flower heads in the forks of leaves. Flowers in the summer.

HABITAT AND DISTRIBUTION: Usually in wet places such as near dams, creeks, swamps. Often in coastal areas; all states.

MEDICINAL USES: A decoction of the plant has been used in cases of purulent ophthalmia and sandy blight. If the decoction used for the bathing of the affected eyes is too strong it may cause considerable pain.[70] The crushed herb is inhaled and rubbed on the nose for colds.[18] Reputed to be anthelmintic.[55]

ACTIVE CONSTITUENTS: Not known; contains a small amount of a volatile oil[58] as well as a bitter principle.[19]

Centipeda thespidioides

FAMILY: Asteraceae

VERNACULAR NAMES: 'Desert sneezeweed'

DESCRIPTION: A slightly fragrant, small perennial herb with alternate toothed leaves, dilated at the base and pointed at the tip. Flower heads are relatively large and stalkless. The fruit is cylindrical, streaked at the top. Flowers in early summer.

HABITAT AND DISTRIBUTION: Mainly in creek beds and near wet places away from the coast, preferably in arid inland areas; Central Australia, western New South Wales and north-western Victoria.

MEDICINAL USES: The Aborigines drank a decoction for colds, sore throat and sore eyes;[20] a poultice was applied externally to sprained and jarred limbs.[20]

ACTIVE CONSTITUENTS: Not known, but leaves, stems and flowers may contain alkaloids.[31]

Chenopodium cristatum

FAMILY: Chenopodiaceae

VERNACULAR NAMES: 'Crested goosefoot', 'crested crumbweed'.

DESCRIPTION: An aromatic annual with branched stems, generally prostrate, pale green and covered with rough hair. Leaves are alternate, oblong or egg-shaped with toothed margins. Flowers are small; ridges on the backs of the flower segments are divided into separate crests.

HABITAT AND DISTRIBUTION: Most inland regions of continental Australia.

MEDICINAL USES: A poultice prepared from the plant was used by the Aborigines for septic inflammations and breast abscesses.[20]

ACTIVE CONSTITUENTS: Not known; contains hydrocyanic acid.[21]

Clerodendrum inerme

FAMILY: Verbenaceae

VERNACULAR NAMES: 'Ta-anji' (Batavia River)

DESCRIPTION: An up to 3.5 m high, somewhat hairy shrub. Leaves are egg-shaped, 5-8 cm long on very long stalks. Flowers occur in groups of three to seven in leaf forks. The corolla tube is 2.5 cm long or longer, with five 8 mm long lobes; four stamens protrude about 2.5 cm beyond the throat. The fruit is a succulent berry, about 12 mm long.

HABITAT AND DISTRIBUTION: Coastal northern New South Wales, Queensland and Northern Territory.

MEDICINAL USES: Queensland Aborigines rubbed the crushed leaves and bark on sores;[13] it has been used to heal spear wounds in New Guinea. On Guam, the crushed leaves were reputedly used against intermittent fever.[19]

ACTIVE CONSTITUENTS: Possibly a bitter principle of the clerodin type.[14]

Crinum uniflorum

FAMILY: Amaryllidaceae

VERNACULAR NAMES: Exactly as *Crinum asiaticum*.

DESCRIPTION: A herbaceous plant with an oval to globular bulb. Its leaves are linear, hang limply and are 5-8 mm wide. As with other Crinums, leaves grow in a rosette-like fashion from the base. The flower-bearing stem is 15-30 cm high, bearing one or rarely two almost stalkless flowers. Flowers tubes are white, tinged with red and are 10-13 cm long.

HABITAT AND DISTRIBUTION: Tropical coastal areas of Queensland and of the Northern Territory.

MEDICINAL USES: The Aborigines of Groote Eylandt used it as an antiseptic exactly as in the case of *Crinum asiaticum*.[25]

ACTIVE CONSTITUENTS: Probably alkaloids, but otherwise not known.

Cycas media *(See colour plate facing page 81)*

FAMILY: Cycadaceae

VERNACULAR NAMES: 'Cycas', 'tree zamia'.

DESCRIPTION: A palm-like plant with a dark brown, thick, woody trunk, up to 3 m high; sometimes branched. Its leaves, at the apex of the trunk are compound, 60–120 cm long; each leaf consists of a stiff central axis and numerous narrow segments which spread out at right angles from it. These segments (leaflets) are about 7–20 cm long and have a prominent rib. Fruit stalks bear four or more 2.5–4 cm long, egg-shaped, yellowish and hairless fruits. Ripe seeds are brown and smooth.

The palm-like appearance is superficial; the cycads are in no way related to true palms.

HABITAT AND DISTRIBUTION: Usually in depressions in open forest; also on stony hills in *Eucalyptus* forest. Coastal tropical northern Australia.

MEDICINAL USES: Seeds have a powerful antibiotic activity.[92]

ACTIVE CONSTITUENTS: Seeds contain about 0.5 per cent of the nitrogenous glycoside macrozamin.[92] It is not known whether this compound is responsible for the activity of the seeds.

NOTE: A species of *Cycas* was used in Papua to treat wounds.[13] In the original reference it was identified as '*Cycas media*?'; however, this identification is almost certainly wrong.

Cymbonotus lawsonianus *(See colour plate facing page 96)*

FAMILY: Asteraceae

VERNACULAR NAMES: 'Bear's ear'

DESCRIPTION: A perennial herb with long-petioled leaves arising from the very base of the plant. Leaves are elliptical, broader at the base, coarsely toothed, sometimes deeply lobed, 5–8 cm long, green above and cottony white underneath. Flowers are yellow. The fruit is a dry dark brown capsule, oblong and kidney-shaped, ribbed without any hair whatsoever, 2–3 mm long. It flowers through most of the year.

HABITAT AND DISTRIBUTION: On loamy or sandy soils, widespread in non-tropical Australia.

MEDICINAL PROPERTIES: Early settlers used to prepare a salve for wounds by extracting leaves with melted lard. Alternate layers of lard and leaves were allowed to cool. After some standing the lard was reheated and run out and was ready for use.[3]

ACTIVE CONSTITUENTS: Not known.

Cymbopogon bombycinus

FAMILY: Poaceae

SYNONYMS: *Andropogon bombycinus*

VERNACULAR NAMES: 'Silky oilgrass'

DESCRIPTION: An erect grass up to 1 m tall. Its narrow leaves are rigid and flat with prominent membranous outgrowths at the junction of the leaf sheath and blade. The flowering tops resemble masses of silk. The bases of stems are highly aromatic.

HABITAT AND DISTRIBUTION: Widespread, particularly in the more tropical regions of Australia.

MEDICINAL USES: The Aborigines used to soak the whole plant in water and use the liquid to treat sore eyes.[2]

Maiden mentions that all *Cymbopogon* species have aromatic roots and that, therefore, they are thought by uneducated people to possess medicinal properties.[2]

Furthermore, the name *C. bombycinus* has been misapplied for a long time and it is quite possible that the plant actually used by the Aborigines of the Palmer River district of northern Queensland was an altogether different species of *Cymbopogon*.

ACTIVE CONSTITUENTS: Not known, possibly an essential oil.

Dianella ensifolia

FAMILY: Liliaceae

DESCRIPTION: A hairless perennial herb with branching stems. The sharply keeled leaves are sword-shaped, 12–25 mm broad and arranged in two opposite rows. The floral stems are erect and often tall with dense bunches of blue flowers. Flower segments are about 8 mm long. The fruit is a blue berry.

HABITAT AND DISTRIBUTION: Usually in wet swampy ground; tropical Queensland and Northern Territory.

MEDICINAL USES: Roots are used in cases of painful urination (dysuria).[19]

ACTIVE CONSTITUENTS: Not known.

Eleocharis dulcis

FAMILY: Cyperaceae

SYNONYMS: In older literature often spelt *Heleocharis*.

VERNACULAR NAMES: 'Chinese water chestnut', 'water chestnut', 'spike rush', 'migirra'.

DESCRIPTION: A leafless, perennial rush-like plant, often with tubers. Its tufted stems are up to 1 m high, cylindrical and finely longitudinally striate. Spikelets are cylindrical, 2.5–5 cm long; numerous dense glumes subtend the spikelets; they are 5–6.5 mm long, rounded at their tips, flattened when dry; dull. Nuts are greyish brown, shining, 1.5–2 mm long and 1.2–1.8 mm wide.

HABITAT AND DISTRIBUTION: In wet places, near stagnant water, near billabongs and swamps; coastal Northern Territory.

MEDICINAL USES: The Aborigines used it for the treatment of wounds; an infusion of the plant in saltwater was poured into the wound and bound up with the soft hollow stems of the same plant. Only the variety growing in or near saltwater was used; the freshwater variety was not utilized.[25]

ACTIVE CONSTITUENTS: The roots contain a heat-unstable, strongly antibiotic substance, puchiin.[22]

Elephantopus scaber

FAMILY: Asteraceae

DESCRIPTION: A stiff-stemmed erect plant, up to 30 cm tall, with its leaves arranged in a rosette-like manner around the base of the stem. Its leaves are 5–10 cm long, oblong but wider near the apex and edged with rounded teeth. Stem leaves are nearly stalkless. Flowers occur in groups of two to five in compound heads.

MEDICINAL USES: In Travancore (India) leaves are boiled and mixed with rice for stomach pains and swellings of the body.[3] Also in India, on the Malabar coast, a decoction of the leaves and roots is used in cases of painful urination (dysuria).[41]

ACTIVE CONSTITUENTS: Not known; the flowers, stalks and leaves contain luteolin-7-glucoside (a flavonoid).[33]

Ervatamia orientalis

(See colour plate facing page 96)

FAMILY: Apocynaceae

SYNONYMS: *Tabernaemontana orientalis*

VERNACULAR NAMES: 'Bitterbark', 'iodine plant', 'pallabara' (north Queensland).

DESCRIPTION: A shrub 3–5 m high very similar in appearance to *Ervatamia angustisepala*, except for the sepals, which are not nearly as narrow.

HABITAT AND DISTRIBUTION: In regions of high rainfall such as northern Queensland, northern Western Australia and tropical Northern Territory.

MEDICINAL USES: The sap has been used like tincture of iodine to disinfect ulcers and sores by the Queensland Aborigines.[13] The fruit, which contains a milky latex, may be rubbed on sores to heal them.[2]

ACTIVE CONSTITUTENTS: Leaves, branchlets, stems, bark as well as mature fruits contain alkaloids.[31,42] Triterpenes are present in roots, leaves, bark and fruits.[43] The milky latex is proteolytic.[13]

Erythrophleum chlorostachyum

FAMILY: Caesalpiniaceae

SYNONYMS: *Erythrophleum laboucheri, Erythrophleum chlorostachys, Laboucheria chlorostachys.*

VERNACULAR NAMES: 'Cooktown ironwood', 'ironwood', 'poison tree', 'camel poison' and 'black bean' in Western Australia, 'ah-pill' (Mitchell River), 'arriga' (Palmer River), 'nanmuta' (Batavia River).

DESCRIPTION: A medium-sized, hard-wooded tree, 12–15 m high, with few branches and a leafy crown. Its bark is rough or coarsely flaky, dark grey to almost black. Its leaves are compound (bipinnate) consisting of four to nine widely spread leaflets alternately arranged on two to three pairs of opposite pinnae. Each leaflet is rounded to oval, prominently veined, blunt or slightly notched at the tip. The bases of the leaflets are often asymmetrical. Leaflets are pink on young shoots turning to dark green and leathery when mature; they are 4–5 cm long. Its very small pale yellow flowers occur in narrow and crowded spikes, 2–7 cm long, forming clusters at the end of branchlets. The fruit is a brown, 10–15 cm long and 2.5 cm broad pod.

HABITAT AND DISTRIBUTION: On sandy soil, from northern Western Australia through the Northern Territory to northern Queensland.

MEDICINAL USES: The Aborigines use a bark infusion to treat spear wounds and to rub all over for general malaise; a root infusion is also used for cuts and open sores.[18,19]

ACTIVE CONSTITUENTS: Contains the alkaloid erythrophlein and the flavonoid pigment luteolin.[19] Erythrophlein has been shown to be a mixture of alkaloidal esters of diterpenoid acids. In some populations, erythrophlein is replaced by toxic esters and amides of cinnamic acid.[21] Recently, the cardiac-slowing alkaloid cassaine has been identified.[18]

Eucalyptus drepanophylla

FAMILY: Myrtaceae

VERNACULAR NAMES: 'Bowen ironbark', 'Queensland grey ironbark'.

DESCRIPTION: A graceful tree up to 30 m high, with a rough and persistent bark on the trunk as well as on the branches. Juvenile leaves are opposite, oblong to egg-shaped, stalked and dull green; mature leaves are alternate, narrow and tapered at both ends, sometimes sickle-shaped and with wavy margins, 8–14 cm long. Flowers occur in umbels in leaf forks as well as at the end of branchlets. Fruit is globular with a cut-off top, slightly narrowed at the orifice and with protruding valves; about 5 mm in diameter. Flowers in early spring.

HABITAT AND DISTRIBUTION: Eastern Queensland, north of Bundaberg.

MEDICINAL USES: The Aborigines used a bark decoction for the bathing of sores.[20]

ACTIVE CONSTITUENTS: Not known; possibly tannins.

Eucalyptus maculata

FAMILY: Myrtaceae

VERNACULAR NAMES: 'Spotted gum'

DESCRIPTION: A tall straight tree, up to 40 m high, with a smooth whitish-to-grey bark, peeling in irregular patches giving the tree its spotted appearance. Juvenile leaves are opposite and variable in shape; mature leaves are alternate, relatively narrow and tapered at both ends, 10–25 cm long and 2–6 cm broad. Flowers occur in clusters at the end of branchlets, The tree resembles *E. citriodora,* but differs from it by having almost odourless leaves. Flowers in winter.

HABITAT AND DISTRIBUTION: On clayey and somewhat sandy soils; far eastern Victoria to central coastal Queensland.

MEDICINAL USES: A water solution of the kino (resinous exudate found on the trunk), taken internally, has been reported to have cured a bladder inflammation.[81]

ACTIVE CONSTITUENTS: The yellow-brown kino contains ellagic acid, various flavonoids and tannins;[16] it is not known which, if any, of these is responsible for the medicinal properties.

Eucryphia lucida *(See colour plate facing page 96)*

FAMILY: Eucryphiaceae

SYNONYMS: *Eucryphia billardieri*

VERNACULAR NAMES: 'Leatherwood'

DESCRIPTION: A tree up to 30 m high, but sometimes shrubby. Its short-stalked leaves are opposite, elliptical to tapered at both ends with a rounded tip, 2.5–4.5 cm long, leathery, dark green and shining on the upper surface, almost white on the underside. Young leaves are sticky. Its white flowers are large, 3–4 cm in diameter, consist of four petals, and occur singly in upper leaf forks. The fruit is a leathery, woody capsule opening into two boat-shaped halves.

MEDICINAL USES: The aromatic resin exuded by certain parts of the plant, sometimes dripping down along branchlets and stems, is reputed to be antiseptic and to stop bleeding; it is thus applied to wounds.[68]

ACTIVE CONSTITUENTS: Not known.

Euphorbia atoto

FAMILY: Euphorbiaceae

VERNACULAR NAMES: 'Miri-miri'

DESCRIPTION: A hairless, diffuse and much-branched perennial, up to 60 cm high with opposite, broadly oblong and rather thick, 2.5–4 cm long leaves. When bruised, the plant exudes a milky sap. The fruit capsule contains smooth seeds. Flowers from autumn to early spring.

HABITAT AND DISTRIBUTION: Loamy and sandy soils along the sea-coasts of Queensland, Northern Territory and Western Australia.

MEDICINAL USES: The nectar from the flowers diluted with water has been used by the Aborigines to cleanse the throat (burns as it goes down, like a cough mixture).[18] The milky sap has been used in the Sandwich Islands (Hawaiian Islands) as an application for ulcers.[41]

ACTIVE CONSTITUENTS: The plant contains alkaloids;[18] otherwise not yet investigated.

Euphorbia australis

FAMILY: Euphorbiaceae

VERNACULAR NAMES: 'Namana' and 'piwi' in Western Australia.

DESCRIPTION: A perennial herb with woody rhizomes and prostrate, branching stems, about 15–30 cm long. Its nearly circular leaves are opposite and about 7 mm in diameter. Flower heads are solitary in upper leaf forks. The fruit is a hairy capsule. When bruised, the plant exudes a milky sap.

HABITAT AND DISTRIBUTION: In spinifex country; widespread in all of Queensland, Central Australia, northern parts of Western Australia and Victoria River district of Northern Territory.

MEDICINAL USES: The milky sap from the crushed plant has been used for the treatment of skin sores and skin cancer.[18,26] It has also been claimed to stimulate milk production when rubbed on the breasts of women.[18] A decoction of the plant has allegedly cured a bad case of sciatica.[23]

ACTIVE CONSTITUENTS: Not known.

Euphorbia coghlanii

FAMILY: Euphorbiaceae

VERNACULAR NAMES: 'Namana'

DESCRIPTION: A small annual, prostrate plant. Exudes a milky sap when broken or bruised. Flowers are white and small. Flowers in winter.

HABITAT AND DISTRIBUTION: Arid northern and central Western Australia.

MEDICINAL USES: The milky sap is rubbed on breasts of women to induce lactation; it is also used to treat skin sores and skin cancer.[18]

ACTIVE CONSTITUENTS: Not known.

Ficus coronata

FAMILY: Moraceae

SYNONYMS: *Ficus stephanocarpa* (and has been included under the non-Australian *Ficus aspera* and *Ficus scabra*).

VERNACULAR NAMES: 'Sandpaper fig', 'rough fig', 'purple fig', 'creek fig', 'noomaie', 'balemo'.

DESCRIPTION: A shrub or small tree without aerial roots. Its oblong-elliptical leaves are very rough on the upper surface; 7–15 cm long and 1.5–6 cm broad, sometimes lobed. The fruit, a fig, is usually densely hairy, egg-shaped to urn-shaped, 8–20 mm in diameter, purple-black when fully ripe and pleasantly flavoured. All parts exude a milky latex when cut.

HABITAT AND DISTRIBUTION: In or near rainforests, usually near the coast; Queensland, New South Wales, far eastern Victoria and Northern Territory.

MEDICINAL USES: The milky latex of young shoots is used in the healing of wounds. Afterwards the scraped root bark of *Grewia* is applied as a poultice by north Queensland Aborigines.[2]

ACTIVE CONSTITUENTS: The latex of many *Ficus* species is proteolytic;[13] however, the latex of this species has not yet been investigated.

Flagellaria indica

FAMILY: Flagellariaceae

VERNACULAR NAMES: 'Lawyer vine', 'supplejack', 'pain-ki' (Tully River), 'yurol' or 'yerroll' (Stradbroke Island).

DESCRIPTION: A tall hairless climbing perennial, up to 10 m tall with woody stems 1-3 cm thick. Its bright green leaves are narrow and tapered at both ends, 10-30 cm long. Each leaf is terminated by a spirally twisted tendril resembling a watchspring; at the base each leaf has a sheath completely surrounding the stem. Small white flowers occur in open, much-branched bunches at the end of stems. The fruit is a small and fleshy globular berry.

HABITAT AND DISTRIBUTION: In rainforests or along their margins and along streams; northern New South Wales, Queensland, Northern Territory and north of Western Australia.

MEDICINAL USES: Its astringent leaves are used in the healing of wounds.[3] Tips applied to sore eyes.[20] Also used as a contraceptive.[13]

ACTIVE CONSTITUENTS: Not known; contains cyanogenic compounds.[22]

Grevillea pyramidalis

FAMILY: Proteaceae

VERNACULAR NAMES: 'Caustic tree', 'blister bush', 'turpentine bush', 'tjungu', 'tjiinngu', 'kura', 'mangarr'.

DESCRIPTION: A shrub to small tree, up to 10 m high, with bluish green divided leaves, each leaf with a few narrow thick segments, 7-12 cm long and veined lengthwise. Its very small white flowers occur in groups at the ends of branchlets. Seedpods are 2-2.5 cm long and sticky.

HABITAT AND DISTRIBUTION: Northern parts of Western Australia along the slopes of tablelands.

MEDICINAL USES: The Aborigines used to mash the greenish inner bark with some water until it was white; the infusion was then rubbed around breasts of women to induce lactation. It was also painted on sores.[18]

ACTIVE CONSTITUENTS: Not known; the exudate from the fruits contains the vesicatory 5-(10-pentadecenyl)-resorcinol.[16]

Gyrocarpus americanus

FAMILY: Hernandiaceae (sometimes separated as Gyrocarpaceae).

SYNONYMS: *Gyrocarpus jacquinii*

VERNACULAR NAMES: 'Shitwood' (in the Kimberleys); 'mida', 'dyiwididiny'; also 'propeller tree'.

Spinifex longifolius (see page 119)

Sterculia quadrifida (see page 119)

Acacia implexa (see page 126)

Acacia tetragonophylla (see page 127)

Barringtonia acutangula (see page 127)

DESCRIPTION: A small to medium tree with a stout smooth trunk and deciduous leaves crowded at the end of branchlets; leaves are egg-shaped to circular, often 25–30 cm in diameter and deeply 3-lobed on young trees, undivided and heart-shaped in older trees. Leaves may be hairy on both sides. Flowers occur in upper leaf forks. Flowers in autumn.

HABITAT AND DISTRIBUTION: Northern districts of Western Australia and Northern Territory; often in rocky places.

MEDICINAL USES: The Aborigines rubbed an infusion of roots and young shoots on cuts (but not fresh cuts) and on parts of the body suffering from rheumatism. Charcoal prepared from the wood was powdered and used to heal fresh cuts and open sores.[18]

ACTIVE CONSTITUENTS: The compounds responsible for the medicinal properties mentioned are not known. However, the bark contains alkaloids and one of them, magnocurarine, is a ganglionic blocking agent and may prove useful in cardiology.[18]

Hakea macrocarpa

FAMILY: Proteaceae

VERNACULAR NAMES: 'Dyaridany'

DESCRIPTION: A small tree, from 3 to 8 m high, robust in appearance and with a rugged bark. Its leaves are alternate, narrow, and tapered at both ends, 15–20 cm long, thick, and hairy on both sides. Its greenish and yellow flowers occur in 7 to 15 cm long clusters; the fruit is egg-shaped and tapered, 3.5–4 cm long.

HABITAT AND DISTRIBUTION: Northern arid regions of Western Australia and of the Northern Territory, usually near the coast.

MEDICINAL USES: The Aborigines applied the charcoal from the wood to open sores and cuts.[18]

ACTIVE CONSTITUENTS: The activity is probably entirely physical, that is, the porous charcoal dries the wound.

Hibiscus tiliaceus subspecies *tiliaceus*

FAMILY: Malvaceae

VERNACULAR NAMES: 'Yellow hibiscus', 'cotton tree', 'talwalpin', 'maband'.

DESCRIPTION: A small tree with large circular alternate leaves. Pairs of leafy appendages at the base of stalks are large and oblong. Its large pale yellow flowers have crimson centres. The fruit is a globular capsule.

HABITAT AND DISTRIBUTION: Usually grows near beaches or along estuaries; coastal regions of northern New South Wales, Queensland and Northern Territory.

MEDICINAL USES: The inner bark and sapwood are heated in seawater or freshwater and the infusion used as an antiseptic for pouring into wounds. The wound is then strapped with the bark of the same plant.[25]

ACTIVE CONSTITUENTS: Not known.

Hibiscus vitifolius

FAMILY: Malvaceae

DESCRIPTION: A shrub with alternate leaves. The 2- to 5-lobed leaves resemble grape-vine foliage. Its flowers are large and pale yellow. The fruit is a depressed globular capsule beaked in the centre.

HABITAT AND DISTRIBUTION: Coastal tropical Queensland.

MEDICINAL USES: The Aborigines of the Daintree Mission area of northern coastal Queensland have found the tuber useful for the treatment of boils. However, there is some doubt on the identity of the species used.[13]

ACTIVE CONSTITUENTS: Not known.

Hydrolea zeylanica

FAMILY: Hydrophyllaceae

DESCRIPTION: A creeping annual herb ascending to about 30 cm. Its alternate leaves are very short-stalked, tapered at both ends, 3–7 cm long with straight margins. Its flowers are blue and occur either at the end of branchlets or in leaf forks; all flowering parts are hairy. The fruit is a small egg-shaped capsule.

HABITAT AND DISTRIBUTION: Coastal areas of the Gulf of Carpentaria.

MEDICINAL USES: In India the pulped leaves have been applied as a poultice to cleanse and heal ulcers (particularly those in which maggots are breeding).[40]

ACTIVE CONSTITUENTS: Not known.

Lavatera plebeia *(See colour plate facing page 97)*

FAMILY: Malvaceae

VERNACULAR NAMES: 'Australian hollyhock'

DESCRIPTION: A somewhat hairy herbaceous annual or perennial plant, between 0.3 and 1.5 m high. Its alternate leaves are 5- to 7-lobed and have long petioles. Its large flowers are lilac, pink and white, about 2.5 cm long with notched petals. The fruit is a capsule which, when dry, splits into ten to fifteen kidney-shaped segments. Flowering time is late spring to summer.

HABITAT AND DISTRIBUTION: Widely spread, especially on clayey soils, chiefly inland. Throughout temperate Australia, also in Central Australia.

MEDICINAL USES: Victorian Aborigines have used a poultice made by boiling leaves in water for application to boils.[50]

ACTIVE CONSTITUENTS: Not known.

Lysiphyllum carronii

FAMILY: Caesalpiniaceae

SYNONYMS: *Bauhinia carronii*

VERNACULAR NAMES: 'Northern beantree', 'red bauhinia', 'Queensland ebony', 'pergunny', 'thalmera' (Cloncurry).

DESCRIPTION: A small tree, up to 8 m high, with compound leaves; leaflets are egg-shaped to sickle-shaped, about 2.5 cm long, rather narrow and 5- to 7-nerved. The calyx is hairy and about 12 mm long. Petals are oval, but broader near the apex, cream coloured and silky outside. The seedpod is 2-valved, flattened, about 4 cm long and contains flattened seeds. Flowers in early spring.

HABITAT AND DISTRIBUTION: Northern districts of Western Australia to inland Queensland.

MEDICINAL USES: The Aborigines used to soak the finely cut bark in water and apply the infusion to sores.[18]

ACTIVE CONSTITUENTS: Not known.

Melaleuca alternifolia (See colour plate facing page 97)

FAMILY: Myrtaceae

SYNONYMS: *Melaleuca linariifolia* var. *alternifolia*

VERNACULAR NAMES: 'Medicinal tea tree'

DESCRIPTION: A shrub or small tree up to 5 m high with a papery bark. Its leaves are mostly alternate, very narrow (up to 1.5 mm), tapered at both ends and rarely exceeding 20 mm in length. Flowers occur in loose cream-coloured spikes. Fruits are woody capsules, about 3 mm in diameter and occur in elongated clusters around branchlets. Flowers in summer. It may be distinguished from the very similar *M. linariifolia* by its more compact habit, smaller overall size, narrower and shorter leaves as well as alternate leaf arrangement. Crushed foliage is aromatic.

HABITAT AND DISTRIBUTION: Usually in swampy or wet ground on the northern coastal strip of New South Wales (from Port Macquarie northwards) and southern Queensland.

MEDICINAL USES: The terpinen-4-ol rich variety yields a bacteriostatic and germicidal oil. The oil, obtained by steam-distillation of the foliage, is used in the treatment of boils, abscesses, sores, cuts and abrasions, as well as in conditions resulting in a pussy discharge such as gonorrhoea. Reputed to cure skin conditions such as ringworm. The oil is applied externally.[76]

ACTIVE CONSTITUENTS: The bactericidal components of the essential oil are terpinen-4-ol and possibly gamma-terpinene. The cineole-rich oils of one of the chemical forms of this species, originating from plants growing near the southern limits of the species' habitat, do not exhibit any of the bactericidal activity of the terpinen-4-ol-rich form and may in fact act as an irritant if applied too often to the skin.[75]

Merremia tridentata

FAMILY: Convolvulaceae

SYNONYMS: *Ipomoea angustifolia*

VERNACULAR NAMES: 'Kal-boo-roon-ga' (Cooktown)

DESCRIPTION: A hairless annual herb with trailing stems, turning black on drying. Its alternate short-petioled leaves are either very narrow, heart-shaped or triangular with spreading lobes, often with a tooth at the base and are 2.5–8 cm long. Flower stalks bear one or two pale yellow flowers. Sepals are elliptical, pointed and fairly broad; the corolla is 12–18 mm long. The fruit is a dry capsule with smooth seeds.

HABITAT AND DISTRIBUTION: Tropical coastal Queensland.

MEDICINAL USES: The Aborigines chewed the whole plant or soaked it in water before placing it on sores.[2]

ACTIVE CONSTITUENTS: Not known.

Mimulus gracilis

FAMILY: Scrophulariaceae

DESCRIPTION: An erect herb, about 15 cm high with opposite, narrow oblong leaves, about 12 mm long, almost stalkless and without hairs. Its solitary violet flowers occur on stalks up to 5 cm long in leaf forks. The corolla lobes are fringed with fine hair.

HABITAT AND DISTRIBUTION: Widespread throughout Queensland and the Northern Territory.

MEDICINAL USES: Used as a remedy in menstrual disorders; also made into a soothing lotion.[19]

ACTIVE CONSTITUENTS: Not known.

Omalanthus populifolius

FAMILY: Euphorbiaceae

SYNONYMS: Sometimes wrongly spelt *Homalanthus.*

VERNACULAR NAMES: 'Native bleeding heart', 'Queensland poplar'.

DESCRIPTION: A tall shrub or small tree up to 10 m high. Its leaves are broadly elliptical to rhomboidal, dull green with a bluish lustre, often reddish on the underside, 5–15 cm long on long petioles; they resemble poplar leaves and turn bright coppery red in autumn. There are small leafy appendages, 1–2 cm long and tapered at both ends, at the base of leaf stalks. Flowers are in clusters 2–10 cm long. Pairs of fruits, capsules about 9 mm long with a bluish frosted appearance, contain seeds half enveloped in a fleshy pulp.

HABITAT AND DISTRIBUTION: Often growing in rocky ravines, or in and around rainforest, especially in second-growth; coastal areas and ranges of New South Wales; also in Queensland.

MEDICINAL USES: The Chinese living in Ingham have used the freshly crushed leaves to stop bleeding.[19]

ACTIVE CONSTITUENTS: Not known.

Persoonia falcata *(See colour plate facing page 97)*

FAMILY: Proteaceae

VERNACULAR NAMES: 'Tarpoon' (Annan River), 'nanchee' and 'booral' (Mitchell River).

DESCRIPTION: A small almost hairless tree, with a dark flaky bark, up to 7 m high. Its alternate leaves are very narrow and sickle-shaped, 10–20 cm long and with a prominent midrib. Its flowers are cylindrical and occur in loose spikes along branchlets. The fruit is a succulent drupe.

HABITAT AND DISTRIBUTION: Across tropical Australia.

MEDICINAL USES: An infusion of the leaves and bark has been drunk by the Aborigines for sore throat and colds;[13] an infusion of the wood has been applied externally to sore eyes.[20]

ACTIVE CONSTITUENTS: Not known.

NOTE: The genus *Persoonia* has been recently subdivided; this species will be transferred to *Pycnonia* at a later date.

Planchonella pohlmanniana

FAMILY: Sapotaceae

SYNONYMS: *Sideroxylon pohlmannianum, Pouteria pohlmanniana, Achras pohlmanniana.*

VERNACULAR NAMES: 'Yellow boxwood', 'engraver's wood', 'Pohlmann's jungle plum', 'Queensland yellow box', 'beleam', 'arlian'.

DESCRIPTION: A tree up to 25 m high, the stem of which is never buttressed. Its bark is grey and scaly, exuding a milky juice when cut. Young shoots are silky, hairy as are branchlets and petioles. Its alternate leaves are oblong, sometimes broadened towards the blunt apex, green on both sides and 8–15 cm long. Clusters of flowers occur in leaf forks. The fruit is globular, about 2.5 cm in diameter and containing usually 5 hard, brown, glossy, slightly flattened seeds about 12 mm long. Fruit develops in October.

HABITAT AND DISTRIBUTION: Coast of northern New South Wales and eastern Queensland.

MEDICINAL USES: An infusion of twigs and leaves has been used by north Queensland Aborigines as a poultice on boils.[13]

ACTIVE CONSTITUENTS: Not known with certainty; the bark contains a triterpenoid saponin (yielding bayogenin on hydrolysis);[93] leaves, bark and branchlets give strongly positive tests for alkaloids.[31]

Planchonia careya (See colour plate facing page 97)

FAMILY: Lecythidaceae, sometimes separated as Barringtoniaceae

SYNONYMS: *Careya australis, Careya arborescens, Planchonia crenata, Barringtonia careya.*

VERNACULAR NAMES: 'Cocky apple', 'cockatoo apple', 'mugwara' (Groote Eylandt), 'go-onje' (Cloncurry), 'gunthamarrah' (Mitchell River), 'barror' (Rockhampton), 'kuiperi' (Batavia River), 'karoo' (Dunk Island), 'ootcho' as well as 'gwiyarbi', 'gulay' and 'jundal' in Western Australia.

DESCRIPTION: A shrub or small deciduous tree of spreading habit, up to 20 m high. Its alternate leaves are tapered at both ends, rounded or even notched at the tip and broadened near the base, sometimes with round-toothed margins, 5–15 cm long and almost as broad. They are bright green but turn orange-red on ageing. Flowers are white, large and stalked, 5–10 cm across and occur in small clusters. They open at night and are usually very short-lived. Fruits are fleshy but hard-rinded, egg-shaped, 4–5 cm long, sour tasting and aromatic.

HABITAT AND DISTRIBUTION: Mainly in open woodland, in flat areas as well as in gullies of north-western Western Australia, Northern Territory and northern Queensland.

MEDICINAL USES: The Aborigines have used the pulped leaves and stems as a sure and safe cure for ulcers and sores.[23,26] In northern Australia it has been used as an antiseptic in the following manner: the red inside bark and sapwood are shredded and soaked in water, and the red liquid is poured into wounds. The wound is then strapped with the root bark of the same tree. Pulped roots have been used to treat burns and sores by rubbing the juice over them.[25] An infusion prepared from the mashed small roots by soaking in water has been applied externally to relieve itching of prickly heat, chicken pox, and various sores.[18] Finally, a bark decoction may be rubbed on the body when feeling sick or out of sorts.[2]

ACTIVE CONSTITUENTS: Leaves contain triterpenes;[43] triterpenes and triterpenoid saponins are present in the bark and include moradiol, erythrodiol etc.[94] It is not known which of these compounds are medicinally active.

Prunella vulgaris

FAMILY: Lamiaceae

SYNONYMS: Sometimes wrongly given as *Brunella*.

VERNACULAR NAMES: 'Self heal'

DESCRIPTION: A creeping perennial herb with ascending angular branches, up to 30 cm tall. Its leaves are opposite, broadly elliptical with tapered ends, stalked and 2–8 cm long with sometimes slightly toothed margins. Its purplish blue (rarely white) flowers occur in dense cylindrical spikes, 2.5–5 cm long at the end of branchlets. The corolla is about 12 mm long. The crushed plant is quite aromatic. Flowers in summer to early autumn.

HABITAT AND DISTRIBUTION: Widespread in wet places, usually near the coast; Victoria, New South Wales, Queensland, South Australia and Tasmania.

MEDICINAL USES: Its astringent leaves are applied to wounds and cuts.[60] Its volatile essential oil has been used as an expectorant, antispasmodic, and for fever and rheumatism.[90]

ACTIVE CONSTITUENTS: The plant contains an essential oil rich in camphor, fenchone and fenchol.[90] The plant also contains free ursolic acid and oleanolic acid, a glycoside of oleanolic acid as well as rutin and hyperoside.[68] It is not known which of these substances are responsible for the healing properties of the plant.

Sesbania sesban

FAMILY: Fabaceae

SYNONYMS: *Sesbania aegyptiaca, Aeschynomene sesban*.

VERNACULAR NAMES: 'Ngean-jerry' (Cloncurry)

DESCRIPTION: A small shrub, 1.5–2 m high with alternate, compound leaves each of which carries a number of pairs of leaflets (less than twenty); each leaflet is blunt and about 6–12 mm long. Flowers are yellow except for the large upper petal which is purple, and occur in pendulous spike-like bunches. The fruit is a pod, roughly 25 cm long and about 4 mm broad.

HABITAT AND DISTRIBUTION: Coastal tropical Queensland.

MEDICINAL USES: In India, the warmed leaves are moistened with castor oil and applied as a poultice to hasten the suppuration of boils.[41]

ACTIVE CONSTITUENTS: Not known.

Solanum lasiophyllum *(See colour plate facing page 97)*

FAMILY: Solanaceae

VERNACULAR NAMES: 'Flannel bush', 'pulgatura', 'taura', 'mindjulu'.

DESCRIPTION: A prickly bushy shrub, 1–2 m high, with alternate, round or broadly egg-shaped, up to 5 cm long leaves, hairy on both sides and with wavy margins. Its flowers are violet with orange-yellow stamens in the centre. Flowering time is from late autumn to spring.

HABITAT AND DISTRIBUTION: Widespread on red sandy soils of Western Australia, particularly of the south-western coastal regions.

MEDICINAL USES: The Aborigines were reputed to boil the roots and apply them as a poultice to leg swellings.[18]

ACTIVE CONSTITUENTS: Not known.

Spinifex longifolius *(See colour plate facing page 112)*

FAMILY: Poaceae

VERNACULAR NAMES: 'Wurruwarduwarda'

DESCRIPTION: A coarse grass with leaves over 30 cm long. It is quite hairless except for a few long hairs at the inner junction of the leaf sheath and blade. Flower spikes are barely 10 mm long and are quite loose.

HABITAT AND DISTRIBUTION: Mainly on beaches; Northern Territory.

MEDICINAL USES: The juice from young growing tips or juicy young shoots, obtained by squeezing between the fingers, is allowed to drip into the eye to relieve soreness. If not enough juice is obtained in this manner, the shoots are hammered and soaked in water and the infusion used. Fresh or seawater was used for this purpose by the Aborigines, usually slightly warmed.[25]

ACTIVE CONSTITUENTS: Not known.

NOTE: This grass is a true *Spinifex*, in the botanical sense. It should not be confused with the so-called 'spinifex' or 'porcupine-grasses' which belong to the genera *Triodia* and *Plectrachne*.

Sterculia quadrifida *(See colour plate facing page 112)*

FAMILY: Sterculiaceae

VERNACULAR NAMES: 'Redfruit kurrajong', 'peanut tree', 'kurrajong', 'calool;', 'gorar-bar' (Cape Bedford), 'ko-ral-ba' (Cooktown), 'ku-man' (Atherton).

DESCRIPTION: A tree up to 20 m high with long-stalked, alternate, somewhat elongated, heart-shaped to oval leaves drawn into a short, blunt point; 5.5–9 cm long and about half as wide. Flowers are in clusters at the end of branchlets; their calyx is bell-shaped and hairy. Fruits are bright red woody capsules, occurring in groups of one to five, splitting laterally to reveal a strikingly orange-red inside with several black oval seeds. The capsules are 5–8 cm long and the seeds about 12–18 mm in size.

HABITAT AND DISTRIBUTION: Mainly in rainforest; northern New South Wales, Queensland and Northern Territory, along the coast.

MEDICINAL USES: The Aborigines of northern Queensland applied the crushed leaves to wounds.[13] An infusion of the bark in water was applied to sore eyes, and the juice from the inner bark was wrung straight into the eyes (like eye-drops).[20]

ACTIVE CONSTITUENTS: Not known.

Swainsona galegifolia

FAMILY: Fabaceae

SYNONYMS: Formerly wrongly spelt *Swainsonia*.

VERNACULAR NAMES: 'Smooth Darling pea', 'Darling pea', 'indigo plant'.

DESCRIPTION: A perennial undershrub with weak undulating branches, up to 50 cm high, with a light grey bark. Its leaves consist of eleven to twenty-five oblong, short-stalked and blunt-tipped leaflets in alternating pairs and one terminal leaflet; leaflets are 1–2.5 cm long, soft, often notched. Red, purplish or even white flowers occur in long bunches. The pod is inflated, 2.5–5 cm long. Flowers in spring.

HABITAT AND DISTRIBUTION: On heavy clayey to light loamy soils; subtropical coastal and inland areas of New South Wales and Queensland.

MEDICINAL USES: The Aborigines prepared a warm poultice from the crushed leaves, stems and roots and applied it to bruises and swellings.[15]

ACTIVE CONSTITUENTS: Not known; leaves and stems give occasionally weak positive tests for alkaloids.[42]

Swainsona pterostylis

FAMILY: Fabaceae

SYNONYMS: *Swainsona occidentalis*

VERNACULAR NAMES: 'Tjarin'

DESCRIPTION: A semi-prostrate shrub with compound leaves. Its sweetly scented flowers are violet; flowering time is from winter into early spring.

HABITAT AND DISTRIBUTION: Sandhills and sterile places in arid regions of northern Western Australia and north-western Northern Territory.

MEDICINAL USES: The Aborigines boiled the mashed plant in water and applied it as a poultice to swellings and bruises.[18]

ACTIVE CONSTITUENTS: Not known.

Syncarpia hillii

FAMILY: Myrtaceae

VERNACULAR NAMES: 'Turpentine', 'peebeen'

DESCRIPTION: A tall tree, 30–70 m high with a thick and stringy bark. Its opposite leaves are elliptical and tapered at both ends, dark green, up to 12 cm long and densely hairy on the underside. Flowers are creamy white in dense globular heads. Fruits are 3-celled capsules united into small heads. It differs from *Syncarpia glomulifera* (= *Syncarpia laurifolia*) by its larger leaves and fruits.

HABITAT AND DISTRIBUTION: Chiefly on Fraser Island off the Queensland coast.

MEDICINAL USES: Resin used as a healing agent on sores and chronic ulcers.[47]

ACTIVE CONSTITUENTS: Not known; myrtaceous exudates frequently contain polyphenolic compounds which may account for the bactericidal properties.

Timonius timon

FAMILY: Rubiaceae

DESCRIPTION: A small tree; its young shoots, leaves, and flowers are quite hairy; its leaves are thin with lateral veins visible on the underside.

HABITAT AND DISTRIBUTION: In open forest in the coastal districts of the Northern Territory and the north of Western Australia.

MEDICINAL USES: The Aborigines applied a wood decoction to sore eyes; an inner bark decoction was drunk at two to three day intervals for colds, influenza and fevers.[20]

ACTIVE CONSTITUENTS: Not known.

Trichosanthes palmata

FAMILY: Cucurbitaceae

VERNACULAR NAMES: 'Thowan'

DESCRIPTION: A large vigorous climber with tendrils. Its large, alternate leaves are palmately divided into three to seven lobes; their petioles are reddish and stout. Its large white flowers have beautifully hair-like fringed petals. The fruit is a succulent, nearly globular gourd with a hard rind; its diameter is about 5–8 cm.

HABITAT AND DISTRIBUTION: Coastal regions of New South Wales and Queensland; in moist open forest or rainforest.

MEDICINAL USES: Leaves have been smoked for asthma.[19] In India, the fruit is pounded and intimately mixed with warm coconut oil and used for the cleansing and healing of sores inside ears; also poured into nostrils for ozaena.[40]

ACTIVE CONSTITUENTS: Not known.

Tricoryne platyptera

FAMILY: Liliaceae

DESCRIPTION: A herb with up to 60 cm high stems ascending from a shortly creeping base. Branches are flattened with winged margins. Star-like, 6-petalled flowers are arranged in umbels at the end of branches, each umbel containing six flowers or more. Fruits are very small nuts; they are strongly ribbed when dry.

HABITAT AND DISTRIBUTION: Tropical coastal Queensland.

MEDICINAL USES: The Aborigines applied the crushed leaves to wounds, cuts and sores and bound them up with fresh leaves for two to three days.[20]

ACTIVE CONSTITUENTS: Not known.

Wikstroemia indica

FAMILY: Thymeleaceae

VERNACULAR NAMES: 'Tiebush'

DESCRIPTION: A tall, much branched woody shrub to small tree, sometimes with silky hairy branches. Its opposite leaves are thin, tapered at both ends, 3–5 cm long and paler on the underside. Greenish yellow flowers occur in small clusters at the end of branchlets. The fruit is a red berry, 5–8 mm long.

HABITAT AND DISTRIBUTION: In open forest, usually near the sea and adjacent mountains; New South Wales, Queensland and Northern Territory.

MEDICINAL USES: In Fiji, the root bark has been applied externally to sores; leaves and stem bark were given for coughs.[27]

ACTIVE CONSTITUENTS: Not known.

Ziziphus oenoplia

FAMILY: Rhamnaceae

SYNONYMS: *Ziziphus celtidifolia*

VERNACULAR NAMES: 'Wine jujube'

DESCRIPTION: A rambling spiny shrub with hairy young parts. Its alternate leaves are elliptical, tapered at both ends, 2.5–5 cm long, with three veins. Its flowers are 5-lobed and occur in clusters of a few individuals. The fruit is black, sour tasting and edible, less than 1 cm in diameter.

HABITAT AND DISTRIBUTION: Tropical coastal Queensland and Northern Territory, including islands of Gulf of Carpentaria.

MEDICINAL USES: In India, a decoction of the bark and of the fresh fruit is used to promote the healing of fresh wounds.[41]

ACTIVE CONSTITUENTS: Not known; the root bark contains the peptide alkaloids ziziphine and ziziphinine; also betulic acid.[14]

CHAPTER SIX
Skin disorders

Entada phaseoloides

MOST OF US have tried to remove, at one time or another, an unsightly wart by resorting to one of the popular folk methods such as the application of crystallized honey or of the milky sap of one of the so-called 'milkweeds', by tightly tying a cotton or silk thread around it, or, by those amongst us with a bent for chemistry, by the carefully repeated application of a drop of the highly corrosive concentrated nitric acid taking great care to protect the surrounding skin by a thin smear of petroleum jelly.

Of all these, the application of the 'milk' (latex) of various plants is probably the most widespread and popular wart removing method. In Europe the alkaloid-rich milky juice of *Chelidonium majus* has been widely used. Likewise, the 'milk' of various figs and particularly that of 'petty spurge' *(Euphorbia peplus)*, a small herbaceous plant introduced into Australia from Europe and Asia and now a common weed in gardens and waste ground, has been used for this purpose. **Care has to be taken to keep the juice of Euphorbias away from the eyes as it may cause extreme irritation and even blindness.**

A more drastic and undoubtedly very painful procedure used by the Western Australian Aborigines consisted of inserting several of the sharp and spiny phyllodes of *Acacia tetragonophylla* under the wart.[18] It has been claimed that the wart would then wither in the incredibly short span of an hour or so allowing it to be pulled out. The method bears some similarities to the earlier-mentioned tying of a thread around the wart since in both cases the drying up of the wart is probably due to its blood supply being restricted or even cut off. Thus, apart from its reputed speed of action, the Aborigines' method is probably quite effective.

Reports that the milky juices of *Euphorbia australis* and of *Euphorbia coghlanii* have been used by the Aborigines of Western Australia for the treatment of skin cancer ought to be investigated in more detail in order to establish whether these two plants really possess anti-skin-cancer activity or whether they merely have wart-removing properties. Warts may sometimes resemble skin cancer in its early stages, for example, small lumps on the surface of the skin, or enlarged moles, and may thus have been wrongly diagnosed by the medically untrained. Also, skin cancer is not very common amongst dark-skinned people. At the same time the 'milk' of the north Brazilian *Euphorbia heterodoxa* has been reported to be extremely useful in the treatment of certain cancers of the epithelium of the lips, nose, and eyelids.

A difficulty often confronting us when it comes to Aboriginal uses of plants is the vagueness of the terms employed. We read of 'skin infections', 'skin diseases', 'rashes' or vague 'itches' without any detailed and precise description of the visible lesions or any mention of possible underlying causes. The great number of skin diseases recognized by medical science is related not only to the varied changes that skin texture may undergo but also to which skin structure is affected. For instance, *Ventilago viminalis*, a small tree growing in the more arid parts of the northern half of Australia, is reputed to be a hair restoring agent.[18] But baldness may have different causes and it is unlikely that this particular species would be effective in all cases. It is known that *Ventilago viminalis* contains a number of anthraquinones,[14] and since certain anthraquinone derivatives, such as chrysophanic acid, anthrarobine and several others, have pronounced bactericidal properties and have been widely used for the treatment of numerous skin diseases (e.g. psoriasis, herpes tonsurans, pityriasis versicolor, eczema marginatum, erythrasma),[36] it is quite likely that the *Ventilago* anthraquinones also have bactericidal activity and thus may be capable of clearing up diseases of the scalp that cause the baldness or impairing hair growth.

Fungal diseases, such as ringworm, have been treated by the Aborigines with some success by the external application of the milky sap of *Ficus opposita,* the resin of *Myristica insipida,* as well as the red exudation ('kino') of *Eucalyptus gummifera,* the 'red bloodwood' of eastern coastal Australia. The active components of all these plants are not known with any certainty. Apart from the polyphenolic compounds present in the 'red bloodwood' kino, and which almost certainly possess some fungistatic and bactericidal properties, all these plant agents appear to be astringent, a property common to many skin cures.

Scabies, sometimes referred to simply as 'the itch', is a highly contagious skin disease caused by a tiny parasite, the Acarus, which burrows into the skin and causes intense irritation, especially at night. It has been treated by the Aborigines by the external application of a decoction of the alkaloid-rich bark of *Litsea glutinosa.* The bruised fresh herb of *Phyllanthus simplex,* usually mixed with buttermilk, as well as a lotion prepared from the leaves of *Cynometra ramiflora* var. *bijuga* by boiling them in cow's milk have been used in India for the same purpose. Both these plants are also indigenous to Australia.

Many of the plant species mentioned in this book have a very wide range of natural distribution: they are often found in India and the Indonesian Archipelago and reach as far as South Africa, Arabia, and even the Americas. In the particular case of skin diseases, almost one-third of all treatments mentioned here have been exclusively practised elsewhere, mainly in India. This prompts us once again to stress the importance of the great care required in their use. Firstly, the plants growing in Australia and those growing elsewhere may be different chemical forms of the same botanical species and thus have different medicinal properties. This may explain why certain plants are put to different uses in different parts of the world. And, secondly, certain minor morphological differences between plants growing in widely separated countries may not have been given adequate taxonomic recognition by the early workers whose reports of medicinal usage we are quoting. This means that in some such cases we may in fact be dealing with either different subspecies (or varieties) of the same species, or even with different, albeit closely related, species. For example, there appears to be evidence that the toxicity of *Melia azedarach* var. *australasica* berries varies considerably from one continent to another; and *Centella asiatica* may really include two closely related species or subspecies. The plants of temperate Australia differ from the typical *Centella asiatica* of the north, a form with many medicinal uses.

Centella asiatica has been widely used in India, and apparently with good success, for the treatment of leprosy.[3] The active constituent of this plant, a triterpenoid saponin asiaticoside, has also been used for the treatment of this dreaded disease.[14] Leprosy is a chronic infectious disease that usually affects the skin and peripheral nerves. In its early stages it manifests itself on the skin as nodules and scaly patches. Most of the remaining nine or so plants used for its treatment are not well known chemically and their efficacy may be doubtful. On the other hand, some of these plants may be quite effective in clearing up certain other similar looking skin afflictions wrongly diagnosed as leprosy. For instance, it is now accepted by many Biblical scholars that much of what was designated as leprosy in the Old Testament included a variety of skin blemishes and was not leprosy at all.

Acacia falcata

FAMILY: Mimosaceae

VERNACULAR NAMES: 'Hickory', 'lignum vitae', 'sally', 'weetjellan'.

DESCRIPTION: A shrub up to 3 m high with angular branches. Its phyllodes (i.e. flat petioles of leaf-like appearance) are sickle-shaped and tapered at both ends, 7–18 cm long, with a bluish, frosted surface. Flower heads are pale yellow, 2–4 mm in diameter with about twenty flowers in each head. The fruit is a bluish hued legume, 7–10 cm long and about 5–6 mm broad, containing egg-shaped seeds. Flowers in late autumn.

HABITAT AND DISTRIBUTION: Widespread on shales, preferably on cleared ground. Coastal New South Wales and southern Queensland.

MEDICINAL USES: The Aborigines used to make an embrocation from the bark for the cure of skin diseases.[3]

ACTIVE CONSTITUENTS: Tannins.[3]

Acacia implexa *(See colour plate facing page 112)*

FAMILY: Mimosaceae

VERNACULAR NAMES: 'Lightwood', 'hickory', 'fish wattle', 'weetjellan', 'millewah'.

DESCRIPTION: A hairless smooth tree or tall shrub. Its phyllodes are thin, sickle-shaped, tapered at both ends, 7–15 cm long or longer and up to 2 cm wide, with sharp, pointed tips. Its globular flower heads contain thirty to fifty individual flowers. The legume is bulging, about 8 cm long and 6 mm wide, much curved and twisted and constricted between the seeds. The seed stalk is folded under the seed. Flowers mostly in late summer to early autumn, but also at other times of the year.

It differs from *Acacia melanoxylon* by its seed stalk which encircles the seed twice in the latter. Also, the pod of *A. melanoxylon* is less twisted and the phyllodes less pointed.

HABITAT AND DISTRIBUTION: Widespread on all kinds of soils; suckers easily and so often occurs in clumps. Reported from Victoria, New South Wales and southern Queensland.

MEDICINAL USES: The Aborigines used to make an embrocation from the bark for the cure of skin diseases.[95]

ACTIVE CONSTITUENTS: Tannins.[95]

Acacia tetragonophylla *(See colour plate facing page 112)*

FAMILY: Mimosaceae

VERNACULAR NAMES: 'Dead finish', 'curara', 'tjilkaru', 'wakalpuka'.

DESCRIPTION: A spreading shrub up to 3 m high. Its leaf-like phyllodes are 4-angled, spiky and less than 3 cm long. They occur in small bunches radiating from a central point along branchlets. Single globular, yellow flowers occur from late spring to early summer.

HABITAT AND DISTRIBUTION: Arid regions of all mainland states.

MEDICINAL USES: The Aborigines soaked the cleaned inner bark in water and drank the infusion as a cough medicine.[18,20] Leaves were chewed in cases of dysentery. Ashes from bark-free wood were used an an antiseptic: applied to wounds following circumcision; acute pain followed, but this apparently subsided after about half an hour and healing of the wound occurred rapidly. Points of the pungent phyllodes are inserted under warts; about an hour later the wart has withered and may be pulled out.[18]

ACTIVE CONSTITUENTS: Not known.

Barringtonia acutangula *(See colour plate facing page 113)*

FAMILY: Lecythidaceae, sometimes separated as Barringtoniaceae.

SYNONYMS: *Barringtonia gracilis*

VERNACULAR NAMES: 'Freshwater mangrove'

DESCRIPTION: A large tree with alternate, oblong to wedge-shaped leaves, about 10 cm long. Leaf margins may be either straight or minutely toothed. Its small pinky red flowers occur in pendulous clusters. The fruit is egg-shaped or oblong, 4-angled, hard and fibrous and about 2.5–6 cm long and 2–4 cm broad.

HABITAT AND DISTRIBUTION: In wet gullies, near streams and along creek banks of tropical coastal northern Queensland, Northern Territory and north-western Western Australia.

MEDICINAL USES: In India the leaf juice was mixed with oil and used for skin eruptions. Kernels, powdered and mixed with sago, were used for the treatment of diarrhoea, whereas mixed with milk they produced vomiting. The bitter root has been used as a laxative.[3]

ACTIVE CONSTITUENTS: Fruits, seeds and leaves contain triterpenoid saponins and triterpenes. Hydrolysis of the saponins yields barringtogenols B, C and D as well as barringtogenic acid and acutagenic acid.[68] It is not known whether these compounds are pharmacologically active.

Barringtonia racemosa

FAMILY: Lecythidaceae, sometimes separated as Barringtoniaceae.

VERNACULAR NAMES: 'Yakooro' (Mitchell River)

DESCRIPTION: A large shrub or small tree with large, short-petioled, alternate leaves. Leaves are elliptical, broadened near the base and tapered at both ends with a blunt tip, and edged with rounded teeth. White, pale pink or cream coloured flowers occur in very long, drooping spike-like clusters. Flowers are smaller than in *Barringtonia asiatica*. The 4-angled, egg-shaped fruits are 5–8 cm long and 2.5–4 cm wide.

HABITAT AND DISTRIBUTION: Mainly in floodplain rainforest, around swamps and in wet situations, and on tidal flats behind the mangrove line of coastal northern Queensland.

MEDICINAL USES: The bitter-tasting root has been used in India as a laxative. Bark and seeds are also used medicinally in India. The former is said to have cinchona-like properties (bitter tonic, astringent and antiseptic taken internally; for external treatment of ulcers, bleeding gums and the like);[3] the latter are reputed to be anthelmintic.[19] The whole pulverised root is applied externally in diseases of the skin.[3]

The Bloomfield Aborigines hammer the bark, dip it into boiling water and dab it over the body of a sick person. Also used in non-venereal stricture.[2]

ACTIVE CONSTITUENTS: Both fruits and bark contain tannin; fruits also contain triterpenoid saponins which yield barringtogenol and barringtogenic acid on hydrolysis.[68]

Calophyllum inophyllum (See colour plate facing page)

FAMILY: Clusiaceae

VERNACULAR NAMES: 'Alexandrian laurel', 'tacamahac tree', 'ulee-ree' (Dunk Island), 'wurri' (Cardwell); 'ndilo tree' and 'doomba oil tree' of India.

DESCRIPTION: A smooth-barked tree with rather beautiful oblong leaves, rounded at the tip, 15 cm long or more, and oppositely arranged along branches. When wounded, the trunk bark exudes a greenish resin. Flower-bearing spikes are longer than the leaves. The fruit is a succulent globular berry containing a hard seed.

HABITAT AND DISTRIBUTION: Coastal tropical Queensland and Northern Territory.

MEDICINAL USES: The green, strongly scented seed oil is used in India externally for rheumatism and for the treatment of leprosy.[2,3] The Aborigines of Queensland use the nut kernels, ground with red pigment and then mixed with water, for rubbing all over the body to relieve pain.[2] The 'resin' from the fruits (the nut oil is probably meant) is used by the Aborigines as an emetic and laxative.[19] It appears that true bark resin is used medicinally in India as well as the seed oil.[2]

ACTIVE CONSTITUENTS: The seed contains an essential oil of unknown composition. The seed also contains a fixed fatty oil (60 per cent by weight) composed of the esters of oleic, linoleic and other fatty acids. The resinous fraction of the seed oil contains several phenylcoumarins: calophyllolide, inophyllolide and the derived calophyllic acid and inophyllic acid. The last named occurs in the bark as well.[23,68] It is not certain whether these compounds are responsible for all of the medicinal properties listed.

Canavalia rosea

FAMILY: Fabaceae

SYNONYMS: *Canavalia obtusifolia, Canavalia maritima.*

VERNACULAR NAMES: 'Wild Jack bean', 'McKenzie bean', 'windi', 'yugam'.

DESCRIPTION: A coarse thick vine or prostrate herb with a twining stem. Except for its young shoots it is hairless. Each leaf is composed of three almost round

Calophyllum inophyllum (see page 128)

Canavalia rosea (see page 128)

Eucalyptus gummifera (Kino) (see page 132)

Dendrocnide excelsa (see page 130)

Melia azedarach var. *australasica* (see page 134)

Ficus opposita (see page 133)

Santalum lanceolatum (see page 136)

leaflets, mostly 4–8 cm in diameter. Its pink flowers occur in clusters in leaf forks on stalks 15–30 cm long. The pod is about 2.5 cm broad with longitudinal wings and contains two to eight seeds.

HABITAT AND DISTRIBUTION: Along the coast of central and northern New South Wales, Queensland, Northern Territory and northern Western Australia.

MEDICINAL USES: The Aborigines used to rub an infusion of the mashed roots on the body for rheumatism, aches and pains, broken bones, colds and even leprosy.[18,26]

ACTIVE CONSTITUENTS: Not known; both mature as well as immature seeds give positive tests for alkaloids.[31]

Cassia barclayana

FAMILY: Caesalpiniaceae

SYNONYMS: This species has sometimes been referred to in the Australian literature as *Cassia sophera* var. *schinifolia*.

VERNACULAR NAMES: 'Pepperleaf senna', 'ant bush'.

DESCRIPTION: An undershrub up to 2 m high with compound leaves, each leaf being composed of four to ten pairs of 2.5 cm long leaflets, tapered at both ends. Near the base of each pair a gland, thickened near the top, is found. Flowers are few and are found on short stalks in clusters at the end of branchlets. The hard, cylindrical pods are 5–10 cm long.

HABITAT AND DISTRIBUTION: Prefers the warmer parts of New South Wales, coast or inland; also in the drier regions of Queensland; New Guinea and Malaysia.

MEDICINAL USES: The species called *Cassia sophera*, which grows in India, has been used as a laxative (like senna) and for the treatment of skin disease.[19,55]

Our *Cassia barclayana* has been suspected of being poisonous to stock, causing purging and a kind of blindness.[19] Since the Australian and Indian species are quite different (and not merely varieties) it is **advisable not to use** the Australian species medicinally.

ACTIVE CONSTITUENTS: Not known.

Centipeda cunninghamii

FAMILY: Asteraceae

SYNONYMS: *Myriogyne cunninghamii*, it was once included in *Centipeda minima*.

VERNACULAR NAMES: 'Common sneezeweed', 'scentwood', 'old man weed', 'gukwonderuk', 'koona puturku'.

DESCRIPTION: An aromatic perennial herb, hairless except for young shoots, which are quite woolly. Its is semi-erect, up to 30 cm high, with stalkless, toothed leaves, tapered at both ends, often broader at the base and 1–3 cm long. Flower heads are stalkless. Growth and flowering occur during the warmer months; semi-dormant during winter.

HABITAT AND DISTRIBUTION: Usually near wet places such as dams, dips along roads, creek beds; widespread in New South Wales, Victoria, and the temperate regions of South Australia and Queensland.

MEDICINAL USES: A decoction of the plant is used in the treatment of purulent ophthalmia and sandy blight; the eyes are bathed in the cooled decoction. It also alleviates eye inflammation.[19] At Cummeragunga a decoction of the plant has been used internally as a cure for ill health, including tuberculosis, and externally as a lotion for skin infections.[50] Plants have been put around head for the relief of bad colds.[32]

ACTIVE CONSTITUENTS: A bitter principle, myriogenin is present.[19] A volatile essential oil, rich in *cis*-chrysanthenyl acetate, may be obtained by steam-distillation of the whole plant.[96] It is not known whether any of these compounds have the medicinal properties mentioned.

Cynometra ramiflora var. *bijuga*

FAMILY: Caesalpiniaceae

SYNONYMS: *Cynometra bijuga*

DESCRIPTION: A small tree with crooked and twisted branches. Its compound leaves are alternate, each consisting of two pairs (rarely one pair) of oblong, and broadened near the rounded apex, leaflets. The 5-petalled flowers occur in short clusters in leaf forks; petals are oblong and tapered at both ends. The fruit is a wrinkled pod, thick, broad and rounded, and containing one seed. The length of the pod is about 12–35 mm.

HABITAT AND DISTRIBUTION: It occurs together with mangroves along the tropical coast of north-eastern Queensland.

MEDICINAL USES: The root is purgative. A lotion prepared by boiling the leaves in cow's milk, and to which honey has been added, is applied externally in India for the treatment of skin diseases such as scabies and leprosy.[3,19]

ACTIVE CONSTITUENTS: Not known.

Dendrocnide excelsa (See colour plate facing page 128)

FAMILY: Urticaceae

SYNONYMS: *Laportea gigas*

VERNACULAR NAMES: 'Giant stinging tree', 'stinging tree', 'giant nettle tree', 'fibrewood', 'gympie', 'braggain', 'irtaie', 'goo-mao-mah'.

DESCRIPTION: A large soft-wooded tree up to 40 m high with a fluted or channelled trunk and a grey, scaly, rough bark. Young shoots, branchlets and leaves are covered with large, stiff stinging hairs capable of inflicting **exceedingly painful stings**. Its very large alternate leaves are heart-shaped or broadly egg-shaped, up to 30 cm long, and hairy on the underside. Differs from *Dendrocnide moroides* by a deeply divided leaf base forming two lobes with the leaf stalk attached in the notch between them and by its much taller growth. Leaf margins are regularly toothed on young trees. Flowers in short bunches in leaf forks. The fruits are small nuts surrounded by light purple fleshy masses.

HABITAT AND DISTRIBUTION: In rainforest, from just north of the Victorian border to about Gympie in southern coastal Queensland. Often occurs as regrowth in rainforest clearings.

MEDICINAL USES: Aborigines used the bark to cure rheumatism; also as a cure for a skin complaint called 'giggle-giggle' and for mange in dogs.

The leaves have reportedly been used to cure rheumatism by stinging the part affected (although this seems rather too drastic a cure). A more gentle cure for rheumatism consisted of the application of the pounded and boiled (to a treacle-like consistency) leaves.[46]

Cure for stings: it has been suggested to rub the juice of the cunjevoi *(Alocasia macrorrhizos*) on the part affected, or even the bark of the stinging tree itself.[3,46] Antihistamines are used now (but are of little use if one is not carrying them when stung).

ACTIVE CONSTITUENTS: The stinging hairs contain acetylcholine, histamine and 5-hydroxytryptamine;[14] the constituents of the bark are not known.

Entada phaseoloides

FAMILY: Mimosaceae

SYNONYMS: *Entada scandens, Mimosa scandens.*

VERNACULAR NAMES: 'Matchbox bean', 'Queensland bean', 'Leichhardt bean', 'gogo vine', 'barbaddah' (Cleveland Bay), 'na-gobar' (Cardwell), 'parpangata' (Batavia River).

Entada phaseoloides

DESCRIPTION: A tall woody climber with compound leaves on 5–15 cm long stalks; the leaflets of the upper pairs of leaves are often converted into tendrils; otherwise each leaf if composed of two or three (rarely four or five) pairs of oblong leaflets, broadened towards the apex or slightly notched and 5–12 cm long. Flower spikes vary from 3 cm to almost 30 cm in length with white 'peaflower'-like blossoms 3.5 cm long. Petals are tapered at their apex. The fruit is a woody pod, 30–120 cm long and 5–10 cm broad, containing 10–30 large (about 5 cm across) round and flat seeds. The seeds are dark red to almost black with a hard, woody and shining coat.

HABITAT AND DISTRIBUTION: In rainforest or dense scrub just above high-water mark of coastal tropical Queensland.

MEDICINAL USES: The seeds are used in India as a febrifuge, for pains in the loins, for general debility, and as an emetic. In the Philippines an infusion of the spongy fibres of the trunk is used for diseases of the skin.[3,41]

ACTIVE CONSTITUENTS: Not known.

Eucalyptus gummifera (See colour plate facing page 128)

FAMILY: Myrtaceae

SYNONYMS: *Eucalyptus corymbosa*, *Metrosideros gummifera*.

VERNACULAR NAMES: 'Red bloodwood', 'bloodwood'.

DESCRIPTION: A medium to large tree, up to 30 m high, which may be stunted near the coast. Its branches, often gnarled, form a dense crown. Rough, flaky bark showing numerous transverse as well as longitudinal cracks covers the whole tree with the exception of the smallest branches and twigs, which are smooth. Leaves are tapered at both ends, 10–16 cm long and 2–5 cm wide with lateral veins parallel and close together, forming an angle of 60–70° with the mid-rib. The underside of the leaves is usually paler than the upper side. Very young leaves and shoots are often covered with a shiny film of rubber which can be stripped off if some care is exercised. Flowering time is summer; the flowers occur in large terminal clusters. The very distinctive fruits are more or less urn-shaped (size: 12–20 mm by 10–18 mm) with large reflected broad rims which distinguish it from *Eucalyptus eximia* (which has a yellowish grey flaky bark) and *Eucalyptus intermedia* in which the bark is rough to the smallest branches. A bright red gum (kino) often exudes from splits and cracks in the bark and has given the species its name.

HABITAT AND DISTRIBUTION: It is a widely distributed coastal species extending from sea level to about 1000 m. It prefers sandy gravelly to loamy sandy soils. It extends from the north-eastern corner of Victoria through New South Wales to north Queensland.

MEDICINAL USES: The gum (kino) is a good astringent and has been used by the Aborigines for the treatment of venereal sores, by both local external as well as internal application. It also is said to cure ring-worm.[19] Charcoal from tree bark has been used for antiseptic purposes, but Dr J. Bancroft suggests that this may be due to the scaly nature of the bark, which facilitates charcoal making.[97]

ACTIVE CONSTITUENTS: The kino contains the phenolic compounds ellagic acid, kaempferol and aromadendrin,[98] which may have some antiseptic and bactericidal qualities.

Excoecaria agallocha

FAMILY: Euphorbiaceae

SYNONYMS: Sometimes spelt *Excaecaria*.

VERNACULAR NAMES: 'Milky mangrove', 'river poison tree', 'blind-your-eyes', 'balavola karping'.

DESCRIPTION: A small tree containing an acrid milky juice exuding from the cut bark. Its acrid fumes affect the eyes and throat (burning sensation). **One drop in the eye will blind,** fortunately only temporarily. Its alternate, fig-like leaves are bright green, fleshy and shining, broader towards the tip, 4–6 cm long and 2–4 cm wide, with somewhat toothed margins. Flowers are very small in slender spikes in leaf forks. Fruits are somewhat fleshy capsules, 6 mm in diameter.

HABITAT AND DISTRIBUTION: Northern New South Wales, Queensland and Northern Territory as well as Western Australia, usually along tidal streams and rivers, and margins of tidal salt meadows.

MEDICINAL USES: The Aborigines used the poisonous juice to cure chronic ulcerous diseases such as leprosy;[3] they also used it to treat marine stings (particularly the painful punctures caused by the spines of certain fish, particularly flathead).[21] In India, a decoction of the foliage is used (in addition to the latex itself) to treat ulcers that won't heal.[3] The Aborigines also used a heated infusion of the mashed bark for rubbing on the body for pains and sickness.[27] The latex is violently purgative.[40]

ACTIVE CONSTITUENTS: The latex is proteolytic;[13] bark contains tannin.[19] Otherwise it is not fully investigated.

Ficus opposita *(See colour plate facing page 129)*

FAMILY: Moraceae

SYNONYMS: There are three varieties of this species: var. *opposita,* var. *indecora* and var. *micracantha;* it is not clear which of these was used medicinally.

VERNACULAR NAMES: 'Sandpaper fig', 'murn-tyul' (Moorhead River), 'moinjal' (Palmer River).

DESCRIPTION: A small tree with softly hairy young branches and undersides of leaves. Leaves are opposite, heart- to oval-shaped and about 5 cm long or somewhat elongated and tapered at both ends and then 15–20 cm long, with wavy and slightly round-toothed margins; rough on the upper side. Leaves may also be 3-lobed with spreading bases. A milky juice is exuded on breaking leaves or branches. Figs are pear-shaped at first, globular later on, 15 mm or slightly more in diameter, solitary or in pairs.

HABITAT AND DISTRIBUTION: Coastal Queensland and Northern Territory.

MEDICINAL USES: Latex applied to ringworm.[13] Leaves rubbed on hands by Aborigines for diarrhoea[20] (perhaps the latex acted as a disinfectant).

ACTIVE CONSTITUENTS: Not known.

Litsea glutinosa

FAMILY: Lauraceae

SYNONYMS: *Litsea chinensis, Tetranthera laurifolia.*

DESCRIPTION: A small tree with greyish-hairy branches and leaves. Older leaves may be hairless. Leaves are egg-shaped to broadly spoon-shaped or even fairly narrow and elongated, blunt or sharp-tipped, 10–20 cm long, either green on both sides or bluish frosted on the underside; primary veins are prominent on the underside. The fruit is globular, 6–8 mm in diameter.

HABITAT AND DISTRIBUTION: Tropical rainforest of northern Queensland and of the Northern Territory.

MEDICINAL USES: A decoction of the bark has been applied by north Queensland Aborigines to sores and scabies;[13] a leaf and bark decoction has been applied externally for aches and pains.[20] Sometimes, chewed leaves were applied directly to sores, cuts and skin infections. The juice from crushed leaves has been applied by the Aborigines to infected eyes.[20]

ACTIVE CONSTITUENTS: The bark gives strongly positive tests for alkaloids.[31]

Mallotus philippensis

FAMILY: Euphorbiaceae

VERNACULAR NAMES: 'Poodgee-poodgera' and 'poodgee-poodgee' of the Aborigines of Queensland; 'kamala tree' of India.

DESCRIPTION: A tree up to 17 m high, but often small and bushy. Its bark is deep red when cut. Branchlets and leaf stalks are rusty hairy. Its long-stalked (up to 5 cm), alternate leaves are oblong to broadly elliptical, tapered at both ends, 5–15 cm long and terminated by a pointed apex. The leaf's under-side is paler than the upper-side and is dotted with numerous minute red glands; sometimes it is downy. Flowers occur either in bunches at the end of branchlets or in spikes in leaf forks. The fruit is a 3-lobed and 3-celled capsule, 6–9 mm broad with one seed to each cell. The capsule is covered with a coat of red hair.

HABITAT AND DISTRIBUTION: Coastal areas of Queensland and northern New South Wales.

MEDICINAL USES: The red mealy powder coating the capsules ('kamala') is used in India in skin complaints, particularly parasitic skin diseases. It is also used for the treatment of worms, particularly taenia, 3 drachms being the usual dose for a robust individual and half that amount for one of weaker constitution. It has been official in the B.P. Codex (1934).[19,41]

It has been recommended by the Arabs for internal use in leprosy and in solution for the removal of freckles and pustules.[41]

ACTIVE CONSTITUENTS: The red 'kamala' contains the complex chalcone rottlerin as its active ingredient. In addition it contains *iso*rottlerin, 4-hydroxyrottlerin, 3,4-dihydroxyrottlerin, resins and waxes.

The seed contains the cardenolides corotoxigenin, coroglaucigenin, and their respective rhamnosides.

The bark contains the *iso*coumarin bergenin.[68]

Melia azedarach var. *australasica* (See colour plate facing page 129)

FAMILY: Meliaceae

SYNONYMS: *Melia composita*, *Melia dubia* (this name has been applied to the Australian plant by some authors who regard it as a separate species), *Melia australasica*.

VERNACULAR NAMES: 'White cedar', 'Cape lilac', 'chinaberry', 'bastard cedar', 'bead tree', 'dygal', 'dtheerah', 'kilvain'.

DESCRIPTION: A large deciduous tree, up to 45 m high (in rain forest), but much smaller in open situations. Bark is dark grey, slightly furrowed and reddish brown when cut. Its branches are widely spread giving the tree a handsome appearance. Leaves are compound with numerous bright green leaflets, 2–7 cm long and 1–4 cm wide, egg-shaped to narrow egg-shaped tapering to a point. Leaf margins are either straight or coarsely toothed. Flowers occur in loose open bunches in leaf forks; they are lilac in colour and very fragrant; petals are up to 10 mm long. Fruits are fleshy, yellow berries, egg-shaped and 12–20 mm long containing a hard stone in a fleshy pulp. Flowers in late spring.

HABITAT AND DISTRIBUTION: Rainforest and moist but sunny places near rivers; central New South Wales to northern Queensland and Northern Territory. Often planted as an ornamental tree.

MEDICINAL USES: The poisonous pulp of the fruit has been used in India for the treatment of leprosy and scrofula (a condition with glandular swellings). In the United States the dried berries were soaked in whisky and used as an anthelmintic (no mention was ever made of their poisonous nature; they may come from a different chemical strain). The root bark was also used for the same purpose in the United States. In fact, all parts of the plant are bitter and have purgative and anthelmintic properties. Before the advent of quinine the bark was used for the treatment of malaria in India.[19,99]

ACTIVE CONSTITUTENTS: There is no general agreement on this. However, vanillic acid present in the bark is probably the anthelmintic principle. Alkaloids are present in the bark, leaves and roots; triterpenes are present in fruits. Leaves contain polyphenols and traces of saponins.[16]

Myristica insipida

FAMILY: Myristicaceae

SYNONYMS: *Myristica muelleri, Myristica cimicifera, Myristica cimicifera* var. *muelleri.*

VERNACULAR NAMES: 'Queensland nutmeg', 'kurroonbah', 'gooroombah' (Tully River).

DESCRIPTION: A medium to tall tree, up to 30 m high. Its trunk is at best only slightly buttressed and is covered with a brown, sometimes scaly, bark. When cut, the bark exudes a red sap. Young shoots and branchlets are rusty-hairy. Its leaves are tapered at both ends and vary from being quite narrow to elliptical in shape. They are green above and much paler, almost white underneath, with brown veins and vary from 10 to 20 cm in length. Three-lobed cylindrical flowers occur in clusters of nine or so in leaf forks. Fruits are brown hairy, egg-shaped, and about 3 cm long; their single seeds are aromatic when cut.

HABITAT AND DISTRIBUTION: Coastal tropical northern Queensland and Northern Territory.

MEDICINAL USES: Resin exuded from bark has been used by the Aborigines to cure ringworm.[13]

ACTIVE CONSTITUENTS: Not known.

Pittosporum phillyraeoides

FAMILY: Pittosporaceae

VERNACULAR NAMES: 'Butterbush', 'weeping pittosporum', 'native willow', 'poison berry tree', 'cattle bush', 'meemeei'.

DESCRIPTION: A slender shrub or small tree with attractive pendulous branchlets, up to 10 m high. Its deep green, alternate leaves are oblong, quite narrow and tapered at both ends, often with a hooked point, 5–10 cm long. Its yellow flowers are small, either solitary or in small short-stalked clusters in leaf forks. The fruit is a yellow-skinned, compressed egg-shaped capsule, 6–20 mm long, opening into two valves with several sticky orange to dark red seeds inside. The seeds are very bitter. Flowers in winter to early summer.

HABITAT AND DISTRIBUTION: In the more arid regions of all states of mainland Australia.

MEDICINAL USES: The Aborigines used an infusion of the seeds, fruit pulp, leaves or wood internally for the relief of pain and cramps.[70,99] Decoction of the fruits was drunk and applied for eczema and pruritus.[19] Used for colds and as a lactagogue.[18,20] Should not be used too frequently, since the haemolytic saponin present may prove injurious.[60,99]

ACTIVE CONSTITUENTS: Fruits and leaves contain a haemolytic saponin hydrolysing to the triterpenoid compounds pittosapogenin (R_1-barrigenol) and phillyrigenin.[16]

Plumbago zeylanica

FAMILY: Plumbaginaceae

DESCRIPTION: A shrub more than a metre high with alternate leaves and leafy branches. Leaves are tapered at the lower end, whereas the tip may be blunt and rounded to pointed; 5–8 cm long. The inflorescence is coated with a sticky substance. White, pink, or blue flowers occur in simple, stalkless spikes. The corolla is a cylindrical tube with spreading lobes.

HABITAT AND DISTRIBUTION: Subtropical and tropical Australia: northern New South Wales, Queensland and Northern Territory.

MEDICINAL USES: The fresh bruised bark is vesicatory. The root bark is used in India as an antiperiodic, for dyspepsia, as a poultice for abscesses, and as a powerful sudorific; also reputed to be an abortifacient. In South Africa the root is used for the treatment of leprosy.[19]

ACTIVE CONSTITUENTS: The drug prepared from the roots contains 1 to 2 per cent of the naphthoquinone plumbagin.[19]

Pongamia pinnata

FAMILY: Fabaceae

SYNONYMS: *Pongamia glabra*

VERNACULAR NAMES: 'Indian beech', 'napum-napum', 'karum'.

DESCRIPTION: A small tree with leaves consisting of five to seven broad egg-shaped leaflets, about 7.5 cm long and with bluntly pointed tips. Pairs of flowers occur in loose up to 13 cm long bunches; their large upper petal is about 12 mm in diameter. The one-seeded pod is broadly oblong, asymmetrical, thick and flat; the seed is kidney-shaped.

HABITAT AND DISTRIBUTION: Coastal regions of Northern Territory and of northern Queensland.

MEDICINAL USES: The seed oil has been used in India for certain skin diseases, such as scabies and herpes; it has also been used as an embrocation in rheumatism. A poultice of leaves has been used for foul ulcers.[3] All parts of the plant are toxic and emetic.[23]

ACTIVE CONSTITUENTS: The seed oil contains pongamol and several flavonoids.[100] It is not known whether any of these are pharmacologically active.

Santalum lanceolatum (See colour plate facing page 129)

FAMILY: Santalaceae

SYNONYMS: *Santalum oblongatum*

Skin disorders

VERNACULAR NAMES: 'Plumbush', 'plumwood', 'bush plum', 'sandalwood', 'northern sandalwood', 'black currant tree', 'bolan', 'tharragibberah', 'gumamu', 'yarnguli', 'birmingal'.

DESCRIPTION: A small tree or erect shrub. Its leathery, opposite leaves are oblong and tapered at both ends, 2.5–5 cm long. The leaves are more noticeably grey and the branches more pendulous than in the similar *Santalum acuminatum*. Small clusters of flowers occur in leaf forks. Fruits are succulent, 6–15 mm in diameter, with a distinctive scar encircling the top; they are reddish, turning deep blue or almost black at full maturity. They are edible, sweetish to the taste.

HABITAT AND DISTRIBUTION: Mainly on rocky ground over much of continental Australia; sometimes near the coast in drier districts, as well as inland.

MEDICINAL USES: The berries may have slightly narcotic properties.[92] A decoction of the leaves and bark has been drunk as a purgative by Queensland Aborigines. A decoction of the scraped outer wood was drunk for sickness of the chest.[18] The leaves were also used by the Aborigines for boils, sores, and gonorrhoea.[99] An infusion from mashed roots was strained and the liquid applied for rheumatism and to relieve itching;[18] it was also applied to the body for refreshment when hot and tired.[20] People used to smoke themselves in burning leaves to gather strength for long trips.[20]

ACTIVE CONSTITUENTS: Not known; however, the tree contains an essential oil rich in the sesquiterpenoid alcohol lanceol[39] which may be responsible for some of the activity (lanceol has bactericidal properties).

NOTE: It is probable that both varieties *lanceolatum* and *angustifolium* were used in these ways.

Sarcostemma australe (See colour plate facing page 144)

FAMILY: Asclepiadaceae

VERNACULAR NAMES: 'Caustic vine', 'caustic bush', 'caustic plant', 'pencil caustic', 'milkbush', 'milk vine', 'ngamul-ngamul', 'gaoloowurrah', 'ipi-ipi', 'meeninya', 'parde-bardettee'.

DESCRIPTION: A small straggling shrub or sometimes twiner growing to the top of trees, with smooth, jointed, rather cylindrical and somewhat succulent branches covered with a greyish green bloom. Foliage is reduced to minute scales, which gives the impression of a leafless shrub. When wounded, the twigs exude a corrosive milky sap. Flowers are creamy white, waxy, star-shaped, in clusters in leaf forks. The fruit is pointed, pod-like, 5–8 cm long, splitting lengthwise; it contains many silky flat seeds. Flowers from late winter to late spring.

HABITAT AND DISTRIBUTION: Scattered over dry districts of mainland Australia; on stony soils inland and also a form near the coast, sometimes in rainforest in the north.

MEDICINAL USES: The Aborigines have been reported to use the milky sap to cure smallpox.[3] White settlers and Aborigines used the sap to stop bleeding of wounds, to cure sores,[3,61] skin rashes,[18,20] and to remove warts and corns quickly. The Aborigines also used an embrocation for sprains and sores.[18] The whole vine and sap were warmed and put on women's breasts to induce lactation.[18]

There is a report that on Mornington Island the sap was used to cure eye troubles;[18] **owing to the corrosive nature of the sap this should be treated with caution.**

ACTIVE CONSTITUENTS: Possibly proteolytic enzymes and antibiotics.[35] The plant gives positive tests for alkaloids.[18] It also contains steroidal saponins and triterpenes.[19] However, so far no compounds responsible for any of the abovementioned activities have been isolated from the plant.

Scaevola spinescens (See colour plate facing page 144)

FAMILY: Goodeniaceae

VERNACULAR NAMES: 'Prickly fanflower', 'currant bush'.

DESCRIPTION: A rigid, scrubby bush, 1–2 m tall and covered with fine hairs; its short branchlets are often converted into short, sharp spines. Its alternate leaves are clustered, narrow or broadened near the rounded apex and 10–25 mm long. Each bush carries a few solitary white to yellowish flowers (sometimes bronze coloured) on short slender stalks in leaf forks. The corolla is hairy inside.

HABITAT AND DISTRIBUTION: On sandy loams and on hills in inland regions of Central and Western Australia as well as western New South Wales.

MEDICINAL USES: The Aborigines used to drink root decoctions for stomach ache and urinary troubles; an infusion of the roots in water was drunk for pains of the alimentary tract.[18,38] A decoction of broken up stems was reputed to cure boils, sores and rashes when drunk for three or four days.[18] The whole plant was burned and the fumes inhaled for colds.[18] Sores were also treated by burning leaves and twigs in a hole in the ground, then pouring water into the embers and steaming the parts affected.[38]

An infusion of leaves and twigs together with *Codonocarpus cotinifolius* was reputed to cure cancer. Later work on this cure was inconclusive.[18,26]

ACTIVE CONSTITUENTS: Furocoumarins are present,[26] but it is not known whether they are responsible for any of the medicinal activities mentioned.

Scaevola taccada

FAMILY: Goodeniaceae

SYNONYMS: *Scaevola sericea, Scaevola koenigii, Scaevola frutescens.*

VERNACULAR NAMES: 'Sea lettuce tree', 'native cabbage', 'ko-po' (Cardwell).

DESCRIPTION: A thick-stemmed shrub or small tree, sometimes covered with silky hair. Its large, rich green, alternate leaves are oblong and rather broad near the very rounded tip; 7–15 cm long and up to 7 cm wide. Small flowers occur in leaf forks. The corolla is about 18 mm long and more or less hairy. The fruit is very succulent.

HABITAT AND DISTRIBUTION: Often along sandy beaches of the coasts of northern Queensland and of the Northern Territory (including islands).

MEDICINAL USES: Crushed fruits were rubbed on the skin to cure tinea.[1] A leaf decoction was used by the Aborigines externally to treat sores.[13]

ACTIVE CONSTITUENTS: Not known; leaves give a positive test for saponins.[43] A bitter principle, scaevolin, and two glycosidic compounds of unspecified nature have been found in the plant.[21]

Securinega melanthesoides

FAMILY: Euphorbiaceae

SYNONYMS: *Securinega obovata, Securinega virosa, Phyllanthus baccatus, Phyllanthus reticulatus, Flueggia microcarpa, Flueggia virosa.*

VERNACULAR NAMES: 'White raisin', 'guwal', 'anbamar'.

DESCRIPTION: A large shrub, 1.5–2.5 m high. Its leaves are arranged in two ranks on opposite sides of the stems in the same plane; usually they are stalked. The fruit is a fleshy, succulent capsule.

HABITAT AND DISTRIBUTION: Always near rivers; northern districts of Western Australia and Northern Territory, including Gulf of Carpentaria islands.

MEDICINAL USES: The Aborigines drank an infusion of young leaves in water for internal pains or severe sickness; the liquid was applied externally for itches, heat rash, chicken pox, open sores and leprosy.[18]

ACTIVE CONSTITUENTS: Aerial parts of the plant contain several alkaloids.[101]

Semecarpus australiensis

FAMILY: Anacardiaceae

VERNACULAR NAMES: 'Tar tree', 'marking nut', 'marking tree', ''jaln-ba', 'eger'.

DESCRIPTION: A spreading tree up to 20 m high with thick branches and a rough, dark grey bark. Leaves are alternate, broad and rounded tapering gradually into a short stalk; 7–20 cm long, whitish on the underside owing to fine hair, conspicuously veined with prominent nerve-like margins. Flowers are very small, white, in bunches. Fruits are large, 3.5–4 cm broad, flattened, attached to a large fleshy stalk.

HABITAT AND DISTRIBUTION: North-eastern coastal Queensland, Torres Strait Islands and coastal Northern Territory.

MEDICINAL USES: In India, the shell juice is used externally for the treatment of sprains and rheumatic conditions, in scrofulous eruptions, and for the removal of warts. The nut is used in the fumigation of piles, causing them to slough. It is also used internally, after steeping in buttermilk, for the treatment of asthma. Also used as a vermifuge.[3]

ACTIVE CONSTITUENTS: Oily fruit exudate contains a mixture of unsaturated phenolic compounds (urushenols).[33]

Striga curviflora

FAMILY: Scrophulariaceae

SYNONYMS: In Roth's paper (1903) misspelt *S. curvifolia*.

DESCRIPTION: A rough (to the touch), erect annual with linear leaves. Lower leaves are opposite whilst upper leaves are alternate. The corolla is nearly 2 cm long; the upper lip is less than half as long as the lower lip. The calyx is tubular and bell-shaped with prominent nerves. The whole flower is without a stalk. The fruit is a 2-valved capsule. The plant turns black on drying.

HABITAT AND DISTRIBUTION: Tropical coastal Northern Territory and Queensland.

MEDICINAL USES: The Aborigines use this plant in the treatment of certain skin diseases. The plant is first chewed or soaked in water and then rubbed into the sores on the skin.[2]

ACTIVE CONSTITUENTS: Not known.

Thespesia populnea

FAMILY: Malvaceae

SYNONYMS: *Hibiscus populneus*

VERNACULAR NAMES: 'Tulip tree'

DESCRIPTION: A moderately large evergreen tree with broadly heart-shaped leaves tapering to a point and 10–15 cm long. Its large flowers are reddish yellow. Its fruit is a hard capsule, 2.5–5 cm in diameter, which opens lengthwise only when very dry. The flower buds and unripe fruit yield a yellow viscous juice.

HABITAT AND DISTRIBUTION: Tropical coastal areas of the Northern Territory and of Queensland.

MEDICINAL USES: Scabies and other skin diseases have been treated in India with the yellow juice of the unripe fruit; the affected skin is also washed daily with a decoction of the tree bark.[3]

ACTIVE CONSTITUENTS: Fruits, flowers and roots contain thespesin; the flowers also contain a variety of flavonoids; epoxyoleic acid is present in the seed oil.[16] It is not known whether any of these compounds is responsible for the alleged medicinal properties.

CHAPTER SEVEN
Digestion and elimination

Rubus hilbii

THE GENERALLY HOT Australian climate, a lack of hygiene as well as poor nutrition undoubtedly contributed in varying degrees to all kinds of digestive complaints common amongst Aborigines and settlers alike. However, by a fortunate accident of Nature, the Australian flora was also very rich in plant species that could be used to alleviate some of the unpleasant manifestations of these conditions.

So, for instance, astringents capable of stemming the secretion of body fluids, and thus able to check diarrhoea, be they various plant exudates or plant extracts, were in regular use almost from the inception of the Colony. Some of these were the red or, less commonly, orange-brown exudations of eucalypts and angophoras, often referred to as 'kino'. Dr Lauterer writing in 1894 discussed this most widely used plant remedy:

> Of an immense value for the bushman are the gums (erroneously styled 'kinos') of the Eucalypts. They were introduced into Europe as early as 1810, when the gum of our common ironbark *(E. siderophloia)* was collected by the convicts under the name of 'Botany Bay Kino' ... When I left Europe, twelve years ago, there was great demand for Eucalypti gum, and its superiority over other vegetable astringents was pointed out by German investigation as due to their power to adhere firmly and kindly to the mucilaginous membranes of the body.[81]

According to Lauterer, the true kinos (the dried juice of certain Indian and African species of *Pterocarpus*) are very inferior drugs. He pointed out that the astringent contained in them adhered only slightly to the mucous membranes and were not tolerated by weak stomachs.

In spite of their alleged superiority, the arrival of 'Botany Bay Kino' in Europe was hardly greeted with joy. It seems the market had already been flooded with kinos and Lauterer described the reaction thus: '"Have we not too many kinos already! Must we have another one from Botany Bay?" This was the outcry of the European pharmacists; and still how little did our Myrtaceous gums deserve such a slander!'

Terms such as 'gum', 'kino', 'resin', extensively used in older literature, and to a lesser extent even to this day, are at best vague and should, therefore, be commented upon.

Originally the term 'gum' was applied to sticky, viscous exudations of shrubs and trees which, after drying to hard, sometimes even brittle, transparent or translucent masses, would once again redissolve in water to clear solutions. Gum arabic, a clear water-soluble exudate of certain African species of *Acacia* (used as adhesive and food thickener) is possibly one of the best known examples of a gum. Since it is also a polymer composed of a large number of simple (D-galactopyranose, D-arabofuranose, L-rhamnopyranose) as well as oxidised (D-glucuronic acid) sugar units the term 'gum' has often been reserved for mainly polysaccharidic plant exudates, regardless of their solubility in water, for example, the gums of *Acacia decurrens, Acacia deanii* subspecies *paucijuga,* gum tragacanth (exudate of the genus *Astragalus*) and many others which mostly only swell in water without dissolving to any great extent.

'Resins' (in the original sense) are generally water-insoluble but alcohol-soluble plant exudates. They too are largely polymeric in nature and thus, though not playing an important role in the context of this chapter, they serve to illustrate the extent and diversity of naturally occurring polymeric materials. Often their building blocks are terpenoid hydrocarbons or terpenoid acids. In the latter case, the resins, even though water-insoluble, will dissolve in dilute aqueous solutions of alkalis (for example the so-called Australian sandarac obtained from *Callitris columellaris* and *C. endlicheri*). If devoid of essential oil, they are usually hard and brittle. On the other hand if substantial quantities of essential oil are present, acting as a plasticizer, the resins will be soft and sticky and are now called 'oleoresins' (for example pine resins from various species of *Pinus*). If resinous material exists in mixture with a gum we speak of 'gum resins' (e.g. myrrh).

In fact, the apparent solubility of a polymer in water (or any other solvent for that matter) is related to its chemical structure, that is, the type and relative number of functional groups present, as well as to the arrangement of its atoms in space. Whilst greatly oversimplifying the problem, one may nevertheless say that the more hydroxyl groups that are present in a molecule of polymer, the more likely it is to be colloidally soluble in water, a hydroxylic solvent itself (e.g. polysaccharidic polymers such as certain wattle gums). As the relative number of hydroxyls decreases and that of other, less water-attracting groups (acid groups, hydrocarbon units) increases, the polymer will gradually lose it solubility in water and become more soluble in organic solvents such as alcohol, acetone (e.g. *Callitris columellaris* and *C. endlicheri* resins) or even in hydrocarbon solvents (certain natural rubbers). The other parameters affecting solubility are molecular weight and molecular shape of the polymer. In general, solubility decreases as the molecular weight increases. Likewise, linear polymers, with their component units strung together like beads on a necklace, will tend to be soluble (within the limits imposed by their molecular weight), whereas three-dimensional polymers, having their component units cross-linked in all directions throughout space, are almost invariably quite insoluble.

From the foregoing it should be clear how difficult, or indeed how futile, it would be to attempt to draw a line between gum, resin and so on. They are nothing but special, almost extreme, cases within the very large family of naturally occurring polymeric substances. Thus it is only reasonable to expect that many natural polymers will not fit into the rigid and arbitrary categories established a long time ago and based only on visually observable, and, therefore, often subjective, physical characteristics (e.g. colour, consistency, transparency, solubility) since chemistry was at the time still in its infancy. The structural complexity of polymers, the fact that they are almost invariably complex mixtures, makes their study difficult even to this day.

Tannins, that is the water-soluble astringent principles of many barks and woods (once extensively used in medicine) belong also to the class of natural polymers. Even though little is known about their detailed chemical structure they may conveniently be subdivided into two major subdivisions: hydrolysable tannins and condensed tannins. Hydrolysable tannins break down on acid hydrolysis to either gallic acid and glucose (gallotannins) or ellagic acid and glucose (ellagitannins); it has been suggested that they are polyesters formed by self-condensation of gallic acid (and of its oxidative coupling products) with occasional glucose units attached to the main polymer chain by way of ether or ester linkages. Under the same acidic conditions of hydrolysis, condensed tannins precipitate insoluble substances known collectively as 'phlobaphene' or 'tanner's red'. Owing to their resistance to chemical degradation even less is known about them except that they may be polymeric flavans, that is, substances related to flavonoids. Hydrolysable and condensed tannins often occur together, albeit in varying proportions. Acacia (wattle) and myrtaceous, e.g. eucalypt and angophora tannins belong primarily to the condensed type. Although natural tannins may differ greatly in chemical constitution, all will precipitate proteins from solution or react with them. It is this property that is responsible for their astringent qualities.

Little research has been conducted in recent years into the chemistry of angophora and eucalypt kinos. Consequently the old classification, dating from last century, into ruby, gummy, and turbid kinos is still the only one available. All myrtaceous kinos appear to be composed of a polysaccharidic gum ('metarabin'), a tannin component (often referred to as 'kinotannic acid') and a host of simple benzenoid compounds such as eudesmin, aromadendrin, and ellagic acid. Ruby kinos are so called because their solutions in water are a rich, deep red. On acid hydrolysis they precipitate 'phlobaphene' and contain thus mainly tannins of the condensed type. They have been used medicinally as astringents. Gummy kinos, medicinally of most value, contain a larger proportion of the polysaccharidic component and thus are more stable and more active in the acid environment of the stomach. Finally, turbid kinos dissolve to more or less clear solutions only in boiling water, but they become turbid on cooling owing to the precipitation of sparingly soluble compounds, such as eudesmin. For that reason they are not popular as astringent remedies.

The preparation of kinos for commercial use (it should be remembered that kinos were once very popular in pharmacy the world over) involved dissolving them in water followed by straining in order to remove bits of adhering bark. The cleared solution was then poured on glass or porcelain plates, the water allowed to evaporate, and the purified kino scraped off and packed for sale. Evaporation on metal plates or, for that matter, any contact at all of the kino solution with metals, should be carefully avoided. Phenolic hydroxyls present in the kino's tannin component, as well as in some of its flavonoid and other aromatic constituents, are capable of dissolving certain metals, often resulting in quite poisonous metal complexes.

According to the literature, the so-called true kino from species of *Pterocarpus* has a very similar chemical composition to our myrtaceous kinos. It contains 70 to 80 per cent of 'kinotannic acid', some gum as well as small amounts of simple phenolic compounds such as catechol.[49] However, the incomplete solubility of *Pterocarpus* in water appears to make it, in agreement with Dr Lauterer, a second rate product indeed.

The question whether a kino is a gum, or a resin, or something else is unimportant from the scientific point of view. Chemically it is too complex to be categorized, physically it is an exudate. To the layman it will remain

Sarcostemma australe (see page 137)

Scaevola spinescens (see page 138)

Angophora costata (Kino) (see page 147)

Araucaria cunninghamii (Bark) (see page 148)

Cassia odorata (see page 149)

Convolvulus erubescens (see page 151)

Cymbidium canaliculatum (see page 151)

Cymbidium madidum (see page 152)

a matter of individual taste or of compliance with local custom.

A note of warning should be included at this point. A preliminary study recently conducted by Dr J.F. Morton on the geographic distribution of oesophageal cancer throughout the world strongly suggests that condensed tannins may be the cause.[102] Areas where tannin-rich beverages, be they herbal teas, ordinary tea without milk, tannin-rich wines, or whatever, are regularly consumed, also show greatly increased incidence of this type of cancer. However, Dr Morton adds that the risk from consuming tannin-containing plant products is in proportion to quantity, frequency, and length of time. This means that occasional intake is not likely to be harmful.

Another point worth mentioning is the occurrence of toxic alkaloids in the stem barks of certain species of *Acacia*, such as *A. holosericea*,[48] *A. polystacha*[103] and *A. maidenii*.[104] Even though only the roots (not the tree bark) of *A. holosericea* have been used medicinally it should be nevertheless quite clear that careless experimentation with previously untested *Acacia* barks may kill rather than cure.

The Reverend William Woolls in his *Flora of Australia* written in 1867 mentions the usefulness of *Centaurium spicatum (Erythraea australis)* and *Sebaea ovata* in the treatment of diarrhoea and in certain stages of dysentery.[56] Even though the first named species may not be truly native the reader may nevertheless be interested in Woolls's comments on these, two of Australia's earliest plant remedies:

> The two little plants of the Gentian Family ... are great favourites with those persons who know the value of them, and they have proved highly efficaceous in certain stages of dysentery. The pink one is generally called Centaury and is the more powerful, and like the allied European species 'possesses all the essential properties of the gentian of the shops and although not used professionally, is a very valuable medicine;' A learned physician ... was so impressed with the efficacy of this little herb, from noticing the use of it amongst certain old women in his neighbourhood, that he was not too proud to adopt their remedy and recommended it to his patients. This was an instance of candour in a great mind which deserves to be recorded, for medical men generally are so wedded to what is popularly called 'Doctor's Stuff' that nature with all her endearments appeals to them in vain.[56]

According to T.W. Shepherd, a contemporary of Woolls, the plant is gathered when in bloom and dried. A more or less strong decoction of the plant is then drunk.

On the other side of the coin, several native plants have been used as laxatives. For instance north Queensland Aborigines have used the resin of *Calophyllum inophyllum*. The leaves of *Cassia odorata* and the leaves and pods of *Cassia pleurocarpa* are also purgative, but have to be used with some care lest they cause pain or even injury.

One of the more unusual, but most certainly more pleasant, treatments came from eating the so-called manna, a sweet exudation of certain eucalypts, particularly *Eucalyptus viminalis*. It is produced by insects puncturing leaves and twigs whilst feeding on the tree. Chemically it consists largely of the sugar-like substance mannitol, which is also the laxative principle. The laxative manna from *Fraxinus ornus* (manna ash tree) growing in southern Europe and Asia Minor, official in several pharmacopoeias, also contains mannitol as its main and active ingredient and has been given in the past to children, owing to the mildness of its action.

Maiden also commented on its mildness:

The Manna, as it is called by our ultramontane settlers ... is frequently taken by persons at Bathurst as a pleasant purgative, so gentle in its operation that it may be administered to the tenderest infant—the dose for a healthy adult being from two and a half to three tablespoonsful ...

... It sounds strange to English ears—a party of ladies and gentlemen strolling out in a summer's afternoon to gather manna in the wilderness; yet more than once I was so employed in Australia.[10]

Another manna, this time obtained from *Myoporum platycarpum* was also used as a laxative. J.H. Maiden commented on this as follows:

In spite of its sweetness, Mr. Helms informs me that the natives were not partial to it, preferring the gum of *Acacia leiophylla;* probably because of its laxative property, and not from any objection to its sweetness.[105]

It should be noted that some mannas, like that of *Tamarix mannifera* (the manna of the Bible), which is caused by an insect, *Coccus manniparus,* puncturing its branches, do not contain mannitol and are therefore not laxative and have been used only as a food.

Plants with diuretic and to a lesser extent emetic properties are in most cases also native to India, where alone they have been used medicinally. Whether the Aborigines had no need for them or whether the plants growing here were chemically different is not certain but may be worthy of examination.

Acacia decurrens

FAMILY: Mimosaceae

SYNONYMS: The *Acacia decurrens* mentioned in Woolls's article probably included the superficially similar, and then as yet undescribed, *Acacia parramattensis* and *Acacia parvipinnula* (and possibly other closely related species).

VERNACULAR NAMES: 'Green wattle', 'wat-tah' (Camden and Cumberland).

DESCRIPTION: A small to medium-sized tree up to 14 m high. Its trunk is dark grey, almost black. Leaves are alternate, compound (bipinnate), distinctly feathery in appearance and rich green in colour. The ultimate leaflet segments are hairless, 0.5–1.5 mm broad. Stems and branchlets have broad wing-like ridges, 0.5–2 mm high, imparting to them a distinctly angular appearance. There are usually four to twelve pairs of pinnae in each leaf, each pinna being composed of fifteen to thirty-five pairs of pinnules. Pinnules are 5–14 mm long. Flower heads contain twenty to thirty yellow flowers. The fruit is a brown or dark brown legume, 4–11 cm long and 4–7 mm broad. Flowers from late winter to spring.

The similar *Acacia parramattensis* has insignificant stem ridges; in *Acacia parvipinnula,* pinnules are 3–5 mm long and the legume is blue-brown to blue-black.

HABITAT AND DISTRIBUTION: Mostly on shales and sandstones of eastern Australia, mainly New South Wales.

MEDICINAL USES: A decoction of the bark has been used in cases of extreme dysentery.[70]

ACTIVE CONSTITUENTS: Tannin is present in the bark.[3]

Allophylus serratus

FAMILY: Sapindaceae

SYNONYMS: *Allophylus ternatus*

DESCRIPTION: A straggling shrub with alternate leaves consisting of three egg-shaped leaflets tapered at both ends, 5–10 cm long and with either straight or irregularly toothed margins. Its small flowers occur in slender spikes; the fruit is a small, red egg-shaped berry.

HABITAT AND DISTRIBUTION: In swamps in tropical coastal Queensland and Northern Territory.

MEDICINAL USES: In India, the astringent roots are used for the checking of diarrhoea.[3]

ACTIVE CONSTITUENTS: Not known.

Alyxia buxifolia

FAMILY: Apocynaceae

SYNONYMS: *Alyxia capitellata*

VERNACULAR NAMES: 'Dysentery bush', 'heath box', 'sea box', 'tonga bean wood', 'camel bush'.

DESCRIPTION: A hairless densely branched shrub, 0.6–4 m high with short-stalked elliptical to rounded leaves, 1.2–2.5 cm long, usually in groups of two or three. Its small flowers consist of an about 6 mm long orange corolla tube with five white short and spreading lobes. The fruit is a small orange-red globular berry, 8–10 mm in diameter, containing one or two seeds. The timber has a strong aroma reminiscent of coumarin. Flowers in summer.

HABITAT AND DISTRIBUTION: Sea-coasts of temperate Australia, from southern New South Wales to the south of Western Australia, in the west also extending inland in rocky places.

MEDICINAL USES: Bushmen have used the bark for dysentery.[19]

ACTIVE CONSTITUENTS: The constituents of the bark are not known. Leaves contain the triterpenoid compounds betulic acid, oleanolic acid, and ursolic acid.[33]

Angophora costata *(See colour plate facing page 144)*

FAMILY: Myrtaceae

SYNONYMS: *Angophora lanceolata*

VERNACULAR NAMES: 'Smoothbark apple', 'rusty gum', 'orange gum', 'mountain apple tree', 'toolookar'.

DESCRIPTION: A tall tree with a pinky red trunk and spreading twisted branches. The smooth reddish bark is shed yearly. Its opposite leaves are narrow, tapered at both ends, and up to 16 cm long. Oil glands are not visible. Cream to white coloured flowers occur in clusters at the end of branchlets. The fruit is a ribbed capsule surmounted by persistent teeth. Flowers in early spring or summer.

HABITAT AND DISTRIBUTION: Chiefly on sandstones, usually in open forest near the coast and adjacent tablelands; New South Wales and Queensland.

MEDICINAL USES: The kino, a reddish exudate found on the trunk (often in large amounts), has been used by the early settlers for the treatment of diarrhoea; 150 to 200 g of a 10 per cent solution in water was the usual daily dose taken internally.[106]

Other *Angophora* gums used for the same purpose were obtained from *A. subvelutina, A. woodsiana* and *A. floribunda* (synonym: *A. intermedia*).[106]

ACTIVE CONSTITUENTS: Probably tannins and various phenolic substances.

Araucaria cunninghamii (See colour plate facing page 144)

FAMILY: Araucariaceae

VERNACULAR NAMES: 'Hoop pine', 'colonial pine', 'Queensland pine', 'Moreton Bay pine', 'Richmond River pine'; 'coorong', 'cumburtu' and 'coonam' are Queensland Aboriginal names.

DESCRIPTION: A very tall tree up to 60 m high with an almost cylindrical trunk and a dark brown, almost black, bark marked by circular horizontal wrinkles and fissures. Leaves are crowded around branchlets and are without stalks. They are curved, very narrow or triangular narrowing into a sharp point and are about 6–8 mm long. Male and female flowers usually on separate trees. Male catkins are stalkless, cylindrical, very dense and about 5–8 cm long. The fruit is an egg-shaped cone 8 cm long and 5 cm in diameter. The bark exudes a clear resin when injured.

HABITAT AND DISTRIBUTION: In some rainforest of northern New South Wales and Queensland. It may grow well over 100 km inland.

MEDICINAL USES: The resin has been used in the treatment of kidney complaints and in stricture causing urine retention: a solution of the resin in alcohol is prepared and twenty to thirty drops are given in a single dose in some water. Three to four doses are said to be sufficient for a cure.[8]

ACTIVE CONSTITUENTS: The resin contains some essential oil as well as diterpenoids such as dundathic acid.[92] Whether these compounds are pharmacologically active is not known.

Breynia cernua

FAMILY: Euphorbiaceae

DESCRIPTION: A hairless, drooping bush with alternate, broad to almost circular leaves. The small top-shaped, flat-tipped flowers have the small opening in the centre almost closed by six short lobes. The fruiting perianth (corolla and calyx collectively) spreads flat to a diameter of about 6 mm. The fruit is a round red berry with triangular seeds. The plant turns black on drying.

HABITAT AND DISTRIBUTION: Mainly on Cape York Peninsula in northern Queensland.

MEDICINAL USES: An infusion from the bark of a plant described as being probably this species has been used by the Aborigines in dysentery.[13]

ACTIVE CONSTITUENTS: Not known.

Digestion and elimination

Caesalpinia nuga

FAMILY: Caesalpiniaceae

DESCRIPTION: A woody climber with numerous recurved prickles. Leaves are compound, and each leaflet is further subdivided. Ultimate leaf segments are shining, oval-shaped, broadened towards the lower half and tapered at both ends. Flowers occur in bunches 10–20 cm long at the end of branchlets; each flower consists of five yellow, spreading petals of unequal size. The fruit is a flattened, asymmetrical pod, roughly elliptical in shape and contains a single flat and broad seed.

HABITAT AND DISTRIBUTION: Tropical coastal Queensland.

MEDICINAL USES: A decoction of the roots has been used in Asia for various calculous and nephritic complaints.[41]

ACTIVE CONSTITUENTS: Not known.

Canarium australianum

FAMILY: Burseraceae

VERNACULAR NAMES: 'Kame' (Batavia River), 'tchaln-ji' (Bloomfield River).

DESCRIPTION: A tree up to 12 m high with its branches marked with the scars of fallen leaves. Leaves are compound, alternate, composed of five to nine oblong-oval leaflets, each being 5–10 cm long. Flowers consist of a 3-lobed calyx and a 3-petalled corolla and occur in bunches in leaf forks. The fruit is hard, succulent inside, egg-shaped and about 2.5 cm long. The trunk bark is resinous.

HABITAT AND DISTRIBUTION: Coastal areas of Queensland, coast of the Gulf of Carpentaria (including islands) and northern Western Australia; north coast of New South Wales.

MEDICINAL USES: The resinous bark, broken up and rubbed in water to a milky suspension was strained and the infusion drunk by the Aborigines for diarrhoea and stomach pains.[2]

ACTIVE CONSTITUENTS: Not known.

Cassia odorata *(See colour plate facing page 144)*

FAMILY: Caesalpiniaceae

SYNONYMS: *Cassia australis, Cassia schultesii.*

VERNACULAR NAMES: 'Australian senna'

DESCRIPTION: A tall erect shrub with angular branches. Its alternate leaves are compound, 5–10 cm long; each leaf consists of six to ten pairs of narrow to elliptical leaflets, 1–2.5 cm long with recurved margins, paler green on the underside than above. A stalk-like gland, 1–1.5 mm long is situated between most pairs of leaflets. Loose bunches of two to six yellow flowers with five conspicuously veined petals produce flat pods after flowering in late spring.

HABITAT AND DISTRIBUTION: Widely spread but otherwise uncommon; throughout New South Wales, Queensland and the Northern Territory.

MEDICINAL USES: Leaves have been used as a substitute for senna, that is, as a laxative.[19] Up to 2 g taken in one dose does not cause undesirable side effects. Larger amounts, and up to 10 g, cause abdominal pain.[36,49]

ACTIVE CONSTITUENTS: The leaves contain triterpenes,[43] but the active compounds have not been identified yet.

Cassia pleurocarpa

FAMILY: Caesalpiniaceae

VERNACULAR NAMES: 'Ribfruit senna', 'firebush', 'native senna', 'kabil-kabil'.

DESCRIPTION: A shrub growing to 3 m in height with alternate compound leaves. Individual leaflets are pale green and occur in four or five rather distant pairs; they are rather thick without glands, narrow to oblong, 2–5 cm long and blunt-tipped. Loose, long bunches of pale yellow flowers occur in upper leaf forks; petals are conspicuously veined (veins are dark). Seed pods are flat, oblong with rounded tips, about 5 cm long and 1 cm broad and black when ripe. Seeds are large and rattle in the pod when shaken. Pod valves exhibit a longitudinal furrow along the centre.

HABITAT AND DISTRIBUTION: Mainly in arid and dry areas of Queensland, Northern Territory, Central Australia and Western Australia.

MEDICINAL USES: Leaves and pods have laxative properties, practically as efficient as common senna. **Large doses may be fatal.**[83]

ACTIVE CONSTITUENTS: Not known.

Casuarina equisetifolia

FAMILY: Casuarinaceae

VERNACULAR NAMES: 'Coast sheoak', 'coast oak', 'beachoak', 'whistling tree', 'swamp oak', 'beefwood', 'dalgan', 'wunna-wuuarumpa', 'muwarraga'.

DESCRIPTION: A tree, occasionally attaining 30 m in height, with wide spreading limbs. Smaller branches are often pendulous. Hairless; sometimes, particularly when young, covered with fine hair. Young shoots are very hairy in the southern race known as variety *incana*. Male spikes about 20 mm long; fruit cones are short-stalked, globular and about 12–15 mm in diameter.

HABITAT AND DISTRIBUTION: Prefers exposed coastal areas; northern New South Wales, Queensland and Northern Territory including islands of the Gulf of Carpentaria.

MEDICINAL USES: Bark is an excellent astringent and is useful in chronic diarrhoea and dysentery.[3,95] On Groote Eylandt it is used as a mouthwash prepared from young twigs by soaking in fresh or salt water.[25]

Also said to be used in China (where it is not native) as an astringent.[3]

ACTIVE CONSTITUENTS: Not known.

Cinnamomum oliveri

FAMILY: Lauraceae

VERNACULAR NAMES: 'Sassafras', 'Oliver's sassafras', 'camphorwood'.

DESCRIPTION: A tall tree up to 45 m high with a brown, nodular bark, very fragrant when cut. Its opposite leaves are narrow and tapered at both ends, glossy above and much paler below, 20 cm long and 3.5 cm broad. Velvety, cream-coloured flowers occur in bunches 15–20 cm long in upper leaf forks or at the end of branchlets. Fruits are oval berries, 12 mm long and containing a single seed; sometimes irregular in shape owing to numerous galls. Flowers in late spring or early summer.

The similar *Beilschmiedia obtusifolia* has much broader leaves.

HABITAT AND DISTRIBUTION: Rainforests of northern New South Wales and southern Queensland.

MEDICINAL USES: The bark is astringent and has been used in diarrhoea and dysentery in the form of a tincture prepared from about 75 g of bark to 1 L of rectified spirit.[95,107]

ACTIVE CONSTITUENTS: Tannin in the bark; the bark also contains an essential oil rich in camphor, safrole and methyleugenol or cinnamic aldehyde and eugenol depending on the chemical variety of the species.[107,108]

NOTE: *Beilschmiedia obtusifolia* (synonym: *Nesodaphne obtusifolia*) has been erroneously reported to have been used in the above manner.

Cissampelos pareira

FAMILY: Menispermaceae

VERNACULAR NAMES: 'Velvet leaf'

DESCRIPTION: A climber with kidney-shaped, softly hairy leaves. Male flower clusters are stalked; female flower spikes are elongated with large leafy heart-shaped bracts at their base. The fruit is densely hairy, succulent with a stony centre.

HABITAT AND DISTRIBUTION: Northern coastal Queensland.

MEDICINAL USES: An infusion of the bitter root (known as the drug 'pareira brava') is used as a laxative;[19] also for the treatment of diseases of the bladder and urinary organs.[41]

ACTIVE CONSTITUENTS: Root contains a variable mixture of alkaloids, depending on where the drug originated; also contains some essential oil and quercitol.[16]

Convolvulus erubescens (See colour plate facing page 145)

FAMILY: Convolvulaceae

VERNACULAR NAMES: 'Australian bindweed', 'blushing bindweed'.

DESCRIPTION: A prostrate perennial creeper or twiner with a thick rootstock and extremely variable leaves. They vary from linear to heart-shaped and slightly toothed to deeply lobed, 1-5 cm long and are usually hairy. Pink or white flowers, 6-20 mm in diameter, are bell-shaped, and occur in stalked groups of one to four in leaf forks. The fruit is a globular capsule up to 6 mm in diameter.

HABITAT AND DISTRIBUTION: In grassland and open forest on loamy soils throughout Australia except the extreme north.

MEDICINAL USES: A decoction of the whole plant was drunk by the Aborigines for diarrhoea, indigestion, and stomach pains.[20]

ACTIVE CONSTITUENTS: Not known.

Cymbidium canaliculatum (See colour plate facing page 145)

FAMILY: Orchidaceae

SYNONYMS: *Cymbidium sparkesii, Cymbidium leai.*

DESCRIPTION: An epiphytic herb with stem-like pseudobulbs, 5-10 cm long, covered with the sheathing bases of leaves. Leaves are rigid, dull green and keeled (ridged like the keel of a boat), 15-35 cm long and 2-4 cm broad, deeply channeled above. Flowers are numerous in spikes up to 30 cm long; green, purple, and brown, spotted with red or reddish brown and 3-4 cm in diameter. The labellum (the unique petal) is 3-lobed with two longitudinal raised, hairy or fringed plates on the disc near its base. Flowers in spring and early summer.

HABITAT AND DISTRIBUTION: Grows on trees in open forest. Coastal New South Wales, Victoria, South Australia, Queensland and Northern Territory.

MEDICINAL USES: The 'stems' (pseudobulbs) used in dysentery by the Aborigines of northern Queensland.[13]

ACTIVE CONSTITUENTS: Not known with certainty; the pseudobulb is rich in starch.[13]

Cymbidium madidum *(See colour plate facing page 145)*

FAMILY: Orchidaceae

SYNONYMS: *Cymbidium albuciflorum*

VERNACULAR NAMES: 'Arrowroot orchid', 'curry orchid', 'dampy-dampy', 'bungkiam'.

DESCRIPTION: An epiphytic herb with stem-like pseudobulbs, 15–30 cm long and covered with the sheathing bases of leaves. Leaves are limp, 60 cm long (sometimes longer) and about 2.5 cm broad, keeled (ridged like the keel of a boat). Flowers occur in elongated clusters on stems 30–60 cm long. Sepals and petals are nearly free and spreading, without any conical or cylindrical projections arising from the base or side of individual groups of flowers. The unequal petal is 3-lobed and red at the base. The fruit is a capsule with a multitude of tiny seeds.

HABITAT AND DISTRIBUTION: Coastal Queensland.

MEDICINAL USES: The stem-like pseudobulbs are chewed by the Aborigines of northern Queensland when suffering from dysentery.[2]

ACTIVE CONSTITUENTS: Not known; pseudobulb contains starch.

Diplocyclos palmatus

FAMILY: Cucurbitaceae

SYNONYMS: *Bryonopsis laciniosa, Bryonia laciniosa.*

VERNACULAR NAMES: 'Native bryony'

DESCRIPTION: A slender climbing herb with 2-branched tendrils and broad, deeply 5-lobed alternate leaves with wavy margins. Its small greenish yellow flowers occur in clusters in leaf forks; their corolla is also deeply 5-lobed. The fruit is a red to yellow globular berry resembling a gooseberry and is about 2 cm in diameter.

HABITAT AND DISTRIBUTION: Northern coastal districts of New South Wales, coastal Queensland and Northern Territory, chiefly in rainforest.

MEDICINAL USES: The whole bitter plant, albeit toxic, has been used in India as a laxative.[19] It should be mentioned that the plant has been a fairly common stock poisoner.

ACTIVE CONSTITUENTS: Not known.

Eremophila bignoniiflora

FAMILY: Myoporaceae

VERNACULAR NAMES: 'River angee', 'creek wilga', 'emu bush', 'gooramurra'.

DESCRIPTION: A small erect tree with drooping branches and a rough grey bark. Its alternate leaves are pale green, pendulous, fairly thick and tapered at both ends, 5–15 cm long. Young shoots are often sticky. Its large bell-shaped flowers are white with green spots inside. The fruit is a succulent oval-shaped berry, about 12 mm long with a pointed apex.

HABITAT AND DISTRIBUTION: Usually along creeks or flooded flats in inland areas of Queensland, New South Wales, South Australia and of the Northern Territory.

MEDICINAL USES: A decoction of the fruit was used by the Barcoo Aborigines as a laxative.[19]

ACTIVE CONSTITUENTS: Not known.

Eucalyptus camaldulensis

FAMILY: Myrtaceae

SYNONYMS: *Eucalyptus rostrata, Eucalyptus longirostris.*

VERNACULAR NAMES: 'River red gum', 'Murray red gum', 'biall', 'yarrah', 'moolerr', 'polak' are some of the numerous Aboriginal names.

DESCRIPTION: A medium-sized tree with a deciduous, smooth, grey-white bark; its timber is red. Juvenile leaves are opposite with a slightly bluish appearance, narrow to broad and tapered at both ends, 6–9 cm long and 2.5–4 cm broad; mature leaves are alternate, narrow, tapered at both ends and usually slightly sickle-shaped, 12–22 cm long and 0.8–1.5 cm wide; they are relatively thin and green on both sides, except in some arid-country forms. The fruit is hemispherical to almost globular with a broad rim and entirely protruding valves, about 6–7 mm in diameter. Flowers nearly all year round.

HABITAT AND DISTRIBUTION: One of the most widespread species; confined to river banks, alluvial flats and damp, low-lying areas subject to flooding. Inland of all states except Tasmania.

MEDICINAL USES: Kino is astringent and has been used in cases of diarrhoea,[10,50] the dose is 0.3–1.3 g of kino mixed with water and drunk.[49] An infusion of leaves and twigs has been used to bathe the head for colds and fevers.[18]

ACTIVE CONSTITUENTS: Not recently investigated; kino said to contain kinotannic acid, catechol, pyrocatechol, etc.[49]

NOTE: Kinos of the following species are also useful as astringents for the treatment of diarrhoea (in addition to those species already mentioned separately):[106] *E. crebra, E. saligna* (both belonging to the gummy group and used as a 10 per cent solution in water; dose is about 150 g of solution every twenty-four hours), *E. acmenioides, E. tereticornis* (belonging to the ruby group; a 5 per cent solution in water is used internally) and *E. microcorys* (turbid group of kinos). Stronger solutions are used if they are applied externally to sores and the like.

Eucalyptus haemastoma

FAMILY: Myrtaceae

VERNACULAR NAMES: 'Scribbly gum', 'white gum'.

DESCRIPTION: A medium tree up to 15 m high, often of a deformed appearance and of mallee-like habit (with several stems). Its bark is smooth, white-grey and mottled with green, and usually riddled with insect 'scribbles'; it falls off in brittle flakes. Adult leaves are alternate, thick and leathery, sickle-shaped and tapered at both ends, 8–12 cm long and 2–3 cm wide. Flowers occur in small bunches either at the end of branchlets or in leaf forks. Fruits are somewhat pear-shaped with a broad, flat, reddish disc, 9–10 mm in diameter. Flowers in autumn and spring.

HABITAT AND DISTRIBUTION: Mainly on sandstone and poor soils in general. Common near the coast in central New South Wales.

MEDICINAL USES: The bright red kino is used externally in the treatment of cuts, wounds and ulcers. Also used internally for the treatment of dysentery.[47]

The kinos of the botanically close *E. sclerophylla*, *E. signata* and *E. racemosa* may also have been used in the abovementioned manner, particularly since some of them were falsely identified with *E. haemastoma*.

ACTIVE CONSTITUENTS: Possibly tannins.

Eucalyptus pilularis

FAMILY: Myrtaceae

VERNACULAR NAMES: 'Blackbutt', 'great blackbutt'; 'yarr-warrah' (Illawarra) and 'benaroon' in New South Wales; 'toi' and 'tcheergun' in southern Queensland.

DESCRIPTION: A tall and usually straight tree, up to 50 m high. Its outer bark is shortly fibrous and thickly matted resembling the bark of the so-called 'peppermint' gums; it is dark brown to black and confined to the lower part of the trunk. The upper portion of the tree trunk and branches are greenish white and smooth. Juvenile leaves are opposite and stem-clasping. Adult leaves are tapered at both ends, thick, smooth and paler on the underside, 10–12 cm long and 2–4 cm wide. Intramarginal veins are distinct; lateral veins are parallel and at 30 to 45° to the midrib. Blossoms occur in 7- to 15-flowered clusters along twigs. Fruits are more or less globular, with enclosed valves, 9–12 mm in diameter and attached to short stalks. Flowering time is in the summer.

HABITAT AND DISTRIBUTION: A very common forest species on a variety of soils in moist climatic regions along the coast from southern New South Wales to southern Queensland.

MEDICINAL USES: Kino is an astringent remedy.[8]

ACTIVE CONSTITUENTS: Probably tannins; also contains ellagic acid, gallic acid and leucodelphinidin.[16,109]

Eucalyptus piperita

FAMILY: Myrtaceae

VERNACULAR NAMES: 'Sydney peppermint'; sometimes 'white stringybark'.

DESCRIPTION: A medium tree up to 20 m high, often with a short bole and widespreading branches. The bark is rough, shortly fibrous on the trunk and larger branches, smooth and ribbon-like on small branches. Juvenile leaves are opposite and somewhat stem-clasping. Mature leaves are alternate, dull green, tapered at both ends, 6–12 cm long and 1–2 cm wide. Flowers occur in clusters in leaf forks. Fruits are either urn-shaped (subspecies *urceolaris*) or ovoid (subspecies *piperita*) with deeply enclosed valves and are about 6–7 mm in diameter. Flowering time is in early summer.

The crushed foliage usually has a strong pepperminty odour.

HABITAT AND DISTRIBUTION: Most commonly on sandstone, preferring the cool sides of valleys and ridges. Coast and tablelands of New South Wales, within 200 km north and south of Sydney.

MEDICINAL USES: The volatile leaf oil has been used in stomach upsets: it is reputed to remove 'cholicky' complaints.[8]

ACTIVE CONSTITUENTS: The leaf oil contains 45 to 55 per cent *l*-piperitone when distilled from foliage collected in the Sydney area.[110] Since the oils used medicinally came originally from around Sydney, low piperitone strains growing near Wingello, Gosford and north of Wyong[111] (piperitone usually below 10 per cent) may not be medicinally useful.

OTHER USES: *l*-piperitone is used as the starting material for the manufacture of *l*-menthol and thymol. Menthol is used for the treatment of migraine; thymol is a powerful fungicide.[49]

Eucalyptus polycarpa

FAMILY: Myrtaceae

SYNONYMS: The name was once misapplied to *E. terminalis.*

VERNACULAR NAMES: 'Longfruit bloodwood'

DESCRIPTION: A small to medium-sized tree with a persistent rough and flaky bark, on the trunk and large branches. Mature leaves are alternate, narrow and tapered at both ends, 7–12 cm long, smooth, thick and leathery. Flowers in profuse bunches at the end of branchlets. Fruits are stalked, urn-shaped and contracted at the orifice, thick, 22 mm by 10 to 15 mm. Seeds are brown and winged. Flowers from late autumn to winter.

HABITAT AND DISTRIBUTION: Mainly on sandy loams; far north-western New South Wales, inland Queensland and drier parts of Northern Territory.

MEDICINAL USES: Kino eaten by the Aborigines for dysentery.[13]

ACTIVE CONSTITUENTS: Possibly tannins; kino has not yet been investigated.

Eucalyptus racemosa

FAMILY: Myrtaceae

SYNONYMS: *Eucalyptus micrantha*

VERNACULAR NAMES: 'Snappy gum', 'scribbly gum'.

DESCRIPTION: A medium-sized tree with spreading branches and drooping branchlets; its deciduous bark is smooth, greyish white with blotches of pale blue and various shades of green. Juvenile leaves are opposite, narrow and oblong, tapered at both ends, 1–3 cm long; mature leaves are alternate, similar in shape but 7–14 cm long, dull grey-green on both sides. Flower clusters occur at the end of branchlets or in leaf forks. Fruits are almost globular with a convex reddish disc. Flowers in spring, sometimes in autumn.

HABITAT AND DISTRIBUTION: Prefers sandy soils near the coast mostly between Sydney and Newcastle in New South Wales.

MEDICINAL USES: The kino has been used against diarrhoea.[19]

ACTIVE CONSTITUENTS: Kino contains about 60 per cent tannin.[19]

NOTE: *Eucalyptus signata* and *Eucalyptus sclerophylla* have been confused with this species.

Eucalyptus tessellaris

FAMILY: Myrtaceae

VERNACULAR NAMES: 'Moreton Bay ash', 'carbeen', 'ori', 'woonara', 'urrgula', 'tchunba', 'wonkara', 'algoori'.

DESCRIPTION: A medium to large tree with a rough bark with square cracks, persistent on lower trunk, white and smooth above and on branches. Juvenile leaves are opposite, narrow and tapered at both ends, 10 cm long; mature leaves are alternate and similarly narrow but 8–18 cm long and sharply pointed. Small flower clusters at the end of branchlets with slightly angular to round stalks. Flowers in summer.

HABITAT AND DISTRIBUTION: Queensland and northern New South Wales.

MEDICINAL USES: Queensland Aborigines soaked the bark in water and drank the infusion for dysentery. Kino used too.[2]

ACTIVE CONSTITUENTS: Possibly tannins.

Eucalyptus viminalis

FAMILY: Myrtaceae

VERNACULAR NAMES: 'Manna gum', 'roughbark ribbon gum', 'ribbon gum'.

DESCRIPTION: A large tree up to 40 m high. Its bark is smooth but may be rough near the base, usually with ribbons hanging on the trunk or caught in branches. Adult leaves are prominently veined, alternate, 11–18 cm long and 1.5–2 cm broad, tapered at both ends. Twigs are green or yellowish. Umbels are 3-flowered; its hemi-spherical fruits are stalkless or short-stalked, reddish and shining with projecting valves, 7–9 mm in diameter. Flowers most of the year round.

HABITAT AND DISTRIBUTION: Usually on better soils; along the Great Dividing Range in New South Wales, also in South Australia, Victoria, Tasmania and Queensland.

MEDICINAL USES: The manna found on its leaves has been used as a mild laxative.[10]

ACTIVE CONSTITUENTS: Mannitol, the main component of the manna.[36]

Euphorbia mitchelliana

FAMILY: Euphorbiaceae

DESCRIPTION: A hairless, branched perennial plant up to 45 cm high with opposite leaves. Lower leaves are egg-shaped, whereas the upper leaves are narrow, almost linear and tapered at both ends. Solitary flower heads, giving the impression of being single flowers, occur in upper leaf forks. The fruit capsule is hairless with transversely wrinkled seeds. When bruised, the plant exudes a milky sap.

HABITAT AND DISTRIBUTION: Tropical Northern Territory and Queensland.

MEDICINAL USES: The Aborigines chewed the flowers for diarrhoea.[20]

ACTIVE CONSTITUENTS: Not known.

Flindersia maculosa

FAMILY: Rutaceae (sometimes separated as Flindersiaceae or wrongly referred to Meliaceae).

SYNONYMS: *Flindersia maculata, Elaeodendron maculosum.*

VERNACULAR NAMES: 'Leopardwood', 'leopard tree'.

DESCRIPTION: A tangled scrubby bush when young, it eventually grows into a medium-sized tree, up to 15 m high, with a characteristically spotted trunk. This spottiness is due to the bark being shed in irregular patches. Its leaves are opposite, fairly narrow, about 2–7 cm long, and may be 3-lobed. Small white flowers occur in open clusters at the end of branchlets. The fruit is a hard capsule, covered with hard protuberances, 2.5–4 cm long and containing flat winged seeds. A pleasant-tasting gum is exuded from the trunk in summer.

HABITAT AND DISTRIBUTION: Usually in lightly timbered areas in the more arid and dry regions of central and western New South Wales and Queensland.

MEDICINAL USES: The resinous exudate has been used by bushmen against diarrhoea.[3]

ACTIVE CONSTITUTENTS: The exudate contains about 80 per cent arabin;[3] it has not been investigated recently.

Grewia latifolia

FAMILY: Tiliaceae

VERNACULAR NAMES: 'Dysentery plant', 'dog's balls'.

DESCRIPTION: A shrub with broadly heart-shaped alternate leaves, 10–13 cm in diameter. Flowers occur in groups of two to three stalks, each stalk bearing two to five individual flowers. Sepals are pointed, about 8 mm long; petals are shorter and there are five of each. The fruit is a succulent 2- to 3-lobed berry.

HABITAT AND DISTRIBUTION: Coastal Queensland and Northern Territory.

MEDICINAL USES: The Aborigines drank a decoction of the roots for diarrhoea.[20]

ACTIVE CONSTITUENTS: Not known; leaves contain free triterpenes.[43]

Haemodorum spicatum

FAMILY: Haemodoraceae

DESCRIPTION: A stout perennial herb 60 cm to 1 m high; flowers are subtended by small leafy bracts alternating along the stems. Flowers are dark purplish black.

HABITAT AND DISTRIBUTION: Western Australia.

MEDICINAL USES: The Aborigines used it to cure dysentery.[19]

ACTIVE CONSTITUENTS: Not known.

Hybanthus enneaspermus

FAMILY: Violaceae

SYNONYMS: *Ionidium suffruticosum, Pigea banksiana.*

VERNACULAR NAMES: 'Spade flower', 'yellow spade'.

DESCRIPTION: There are two varieties: var. *enneaspermus* and var. *banksianus.* Since it is not known which variety was used medicinally, only the general botanical description is given.

It is a shrubby perennial, 30–60 cm high, with very narrow, alternate leaves and a slightly hairy stem. Single small yellow flowers, all the petals of which are minute except the lowest, which may be as long as 12 mm, are borne on wiry stalks in leaf forks. Sepals are tapered with a prominent green midrib. The fruit is a tiny capsule containing seeds beautifully marked with longitudinal furrows.

HABITAT AND DISTRIBUTION: Widely distributed throughout the warmer parts of New South Wales, South Australia, Northern Territory and Queensland.

MEDICINAL USES: In India the roots were used in diseases of the urinary organs.[40]

ACTIVE CONSTITUENTS: Not known.

Ipomoea mauritiana

FAMILY: Convolvulaceae

SYNONYMS: *Ipomoea paniculata*

DESCRIPTION: A large smooth twining or trailing plant with alternate palmately divided leaves, 15–30 cm long as well as broad. The five to nine lobes are tapered at both ends. Its flowers are large, purple or pink; the corolla is about 5 cm long. The fruit capsule is about 12 mm in diameter and contains densely woolly seeds. The roots are thick and fleshy.

HABITAT AND DISTRIBUTION: Along the coast of tropical northern Queensland.

MEDICINAL USES: Roots are said to be purgative.[40]

ACTIVE CONSTITUENTS: Not known.

Jacksonia dilatata

FAMILY: Fabaceae

DESCRIPTION: An erect shrub covered with silky hair, more or less rusty coloured under the flowering parts. Branchlets are leaf-like, flat, spear-shaped and tapered at both ends, 5–10 cm long. Flowers are stalkless in spikes or heads at the end of these branchlets. The pod is egg-shaped.

HABITAT AND DISTRIBUTION: Northern coastal Northern Territory.

MEDICINAL USES: The Aborigines drank a wood infusion for stomach upsets.[20]

ACTIVE CONSTITUENTS: Not known.

Lythrum salicaria

FAMILY: Lythraceae

VERNACULAR NAMES: 'Purple loosestrife', 'willow-like loosestrife'.

DESCRIPTION: An erect, often hairy perennial herb, 50–100 cm high with opposite leaves tapered at one end and slightly stem clasping, 2–8 cm long, with undivided margins. Reddish, pink-purple or bluish flowers in groups at the end of leafy branchlets, 10–12 mm long. There are twelve stamens, six of which are longer than the rest and protrude from the flower tube.

HABITAT AND DISTRIBUTION: Widespread in wet places and swamps in New South Wales and the cooler districts of southern Queensland. May well be introduced from Europe.

MEDICINAL USES: The whole plant is astringent and reputed to be useful in inveterate diarrhoea.[55] The medicinal attributes of this plant have been known since antiquity. It has been recommended for dysentery, as an antihemorrhagic and for the moderation of the menstrual flow. It is also used in folk medicine as a hypoglycaemic agent; flowers and stems and to a lesser extent leaves possess the hypoglycaemic activity.[113]

ACTIVE CONSTITUENTS: The astringent properties may be due to tannin-like substances since gallic acid and ellagic acid have been identified in hydrolyzed leaf extracts.[68] The plant also contains the flavonoids vitexin and orientin.[112]

Leaves contain alkaloids.[68] The hypoglycaemic principles have not yet been identified.[113]

Mallotus mollissimus

FAMILY: Euphorbiaceae

SYNONYMS: *Mallotus ricinoides*

VERNACULAR NAMES: 'Barrinya' (Cairns)

DESCRIPTION: A tall shrub up to 6 m high, more or less hairy and resembling the castor oil plant. Its leaves are mostly alternate, broadly egg-shaped to circular but with a pointed apex, with the stalk attached to the back of the leaves or near their base; leaves are 10–25 cm in diameter. Flowers occur in spikes at the end of branches. The fruit is a 3-lobed capsule, densely mossy hairy, 12 mm in diameter. When bruised, exudes a milky sap from the trunk.

HABITAT AND DISTRIBUTION: In rainforests in northern coastal Queensland.

MEDICINAL USES: The milky sap mixed with coconut juice has been used as a cure for dysentery.[13]

ACTIVE CONSTITUENTS: Not known.

Myoporum platycarpum

FAMILY: Myoporaceae

VERNACULAR NAMES: 'Sugarwood', 'red sandalwood', 'dogwood', 'yumburra' (in South Australia).

DESCRIPTION: A tall hairless shrub or small tree, 2–7 m high, with slender, sometimes drooping branchlets. Its sometimes slightly sticky leaves are comparatively thick, narrow, tapered at both ends, and 4–8 cm long. Clusters of small white flowers, often dotted with purple spots, occur in leaf forks. The corolla is 6–8 mm long, bearded inside and sometimes yellowish at the base. Fruits are egg-shaped, narrow-edged and pointed and about 6 mm long. Insect-caused injuries to the trunk are responsible for the white to pinkish, sweet exudate formed on the bark. Flowering time is in late spring. The wood (including rootwood) is quite aromatic.

HABITAT AND DISTRIBUTION: On loamy and clayey soils of the drier parts of Western Australia, South Australia, Victoria and New South Wales.

MEDICINAL USES: The insect-induced exudate found on the bark (manna) has slightly laxative properties.[105]

ACTIVE CONSTITUENTS: Mannitol in the exudate.[36]

Nelumbo nucifera *(See colour plate facing page 160)*

FAMILY: Nelumbonaceae

SYNONYMS: *Nelumbium speciosum.*

VERNACULAR NAMES: 'Sacred lotus', 'pink water lily', 'aquaie'.

DESCRIPTION: An aquatic herb with large, more or less circular leaves supported above water by erect stalks attached roughly near the centre of their underside. Flowers have four to five sepals and numerous pink petals; these are large and fragrant.

HABITAT AND DISTRIBUTION: In pools, stagnant river arms; coastal areas of Queensland, Northern Territory and Western Australia (Kimberley region).

MEDICINAL USES: In India the viscous milky juice from leaf and flower stalks has been used for diarrhoea and sickness. Flower petals are astringent.[3]

ACTIVE CONSTITUENTS: Leaf- and flower-stalk juice contains alkaloids such as nuciferine, nornuciferine and roemerine. Leaves also contain quercetin, whereas flower petals contain flavonoid glycosides and tannins.[16]

Operculina turpethum

FAMILY: Convolvulaceae

SYNONYMS: *Ipomoea turpethum*

VERNACULAR NAMES: 'Onion vine', 'kar-kor' (Cloncurry).

DESCRIPTION: A vigorous twiner whose young shoots and flowering parts are somewhat hairy. Older stems often bordered by narrow longitudinal wings. Its alternate leaves are broad, heart-shaped and up to 15 cm wide. Its large white bell-shaped flowers are up to 5 cm long. The globular seed capsule contains smooth seeds.

HABITAT AND DISTRIBUTION: Tropical coast of Queensland.

MEDICINAL USES: The roots are used in India as a purgative. A piece of root 15 cm long and as thick as a little finger is rubbed up with milk and taken in a single dose.[19,41]

ACTIVE CONSTITUENTS: Not known.

Plectranthus congestus

FAMILY: Lamiaceae

VERNACULAR NAMES: 'Kai-kai (Mitchell River)

DESCRIPTION: A tall herb, 1–2 m high, whitish-hairy with soft, opposite, wrinkled, elliptical leaves tapered at both ends and 5–8 cm long. Its small blue flowers occur in dense, crowded, spike-like groups of about twenty.

HABITAT AND DISTRIBUTION: Coastal tropical Queensland.

MEDICINAL PROPERTIES: Leaves and branchlets crushed in water and drunk for internal complaints (by north Queensland Aborigines).[2]

ACTIVE CONSTITUENTS: Not known.

Prostanthera rotundifolia *(See colour plate facing page)*

FAMILY: Lamiaceae

SYNONYMS: *Prostanthera retusa, Prostanthera cotinifolia.*

VERNACULAR NAMES: 'Round-leaf mint-bush'.

DESCRIPTION: A tall bushy shrub up to 3 m high, with opposite leaves. The latter are very variable in size, texture and shape, often 6–12 mm long, stalked and rather thick, more or less rounded, sometimes somewhat spoon-shaped and notched at the tip or tapered to a blunt point. Leaf margins are sometimes obscurely toothed. Flowers are pink, lilac, purple but mostly violet and occur in terminal bunches or in leaf forks. The crushed leaves are aromatic. Flowers in late spring and early summer.

HABITAT AND DISTRIBUTION: Usually on sheltered hillsides west of the Great Dividing Range in New South Wales; also in Queensland, Victoria and Tasmania.

MEDICINAL USES: The volatile oil is carminative.[60]

ACTIVE CONSTITUENTS: Probably 1,8-cineole which is the main component of the volatile oil.[58]

Rhizophora mucronata

FAMILY: Rhizophoraceae

SYNONYMS: *Rhizophora candelaria*

VERNACULAR NAMES: 'Black mangrove', 'binaroley'.

DESCRIPTION: A tree with opposite elliptical leaves, tapered at both ends and with a projecting, pointed tip when young, 7–10 cm long and fairly broad. Leafy appendages (stipules) at the base of leaf stalks are fairly large, oblong and deciduous. Flowers occur in loose groups in leaf forks. Fruits are egg-shaped, 2.5–4 cm

Eucalyptus saligna (see page 153)

Nelumbo nucifera (see page 159)

Prostanthera rotundifolia (see page 160)

Rubus hillii (see page 161)

Sophora tomentosa (see page 163)

Digestion and elimination

long with single root-bearing seeds with the root penetrating through the summit of the fruit.

HABITAT AND DISTRIBUTION: Along the sea coast of far northern New South Wales, Queensland, Northern Territory and Western Australia.

MEDICINAL USES: The bark has been used as an astringent.[3]

ACTIVE CONSTITUENTS: The bark contains about 30 per cent tannin and around 35 per cent mucilage. Leaves contain flavonoids.[14]

Rubus hillii *(See colour plate facing page 160)*
FAMILY: Rosaceae

SYNONYMS: Has been classified in the past as *Rubus moluccanus,* which is not an Australian species.

VERNACULAR NAMES: 'Wild raspberry', 'Queensland bramble'; 'native raspberry' has been applied to several other species of *Rubus* as well.

DESCRIPTION: A tall scrambling shrub or climber, covered with prickles. The equally prickly leaves are round to elliptical, broadly 3- to 5-lobed and covered with rusty hair on the underside. The leaf margins are serrate, that is, edged with forward pointing teeth. The flowers are white or red. The pointed sepals are usually silky hairy. The fruit is a red nearly globular berry (about 12 mm in diameter). Fruiting time is in summer.

Rubus hilbii

HABITAT AND DISTRIBUTION: In or near rainforest along the coast of New South Wales and Queensland; also in the Northern Territory.

MEDICINAL USES: Small leaves are soaked in warm water and the infusion drunk for stomach upsets.[15]

ACTIVE CONSTITUENTS: The leaves contain the triterpenoids rubusinic acid and rubitinic acid.[14] It is not known whether these compounds are responsible for the medicinal properties of the plant.

Rubus parvifolius

FAMILY: Rosaceae

SYNONYMS: In some references incorrectly referred to as *Rubus parviflorus*, which is actually the name of a North American species.

VERNACULAR NAMES: 'Small leaf raspberry', 'small leaf bramble', 'native raspberry' (see also under *Rubus hillii*).

DESCRIPTION: A scrambling softly-hairy shrub. Its leaves are composed of three to five leaflets, egg-shaped to almost circular, irregularly and often deeply toothed, 5–30 mm long, wrinkled above and whitish-hairy underneath. Pink or red flowers occur in upper leaf forks or in short bunches at the end of branchlets. Sepals are hairy. The fruit is a globular, red and very succulent berry. Flowers in spring and early summer.

HABITAT AND DISTRIBUTION: In eucalyptus forest and rocky places in grassland; southern and eastern Australia, except dry inland.

MEDICINAL USES: It is astringent and has been used by country people in cases of diarrhoea.[70]

ACTIVE CONSTITUENTS: Not known.

Scirpus validus

FAMILY: Cyperaceae

SYNONYMS: *Schoenoplectus validus*

VERNACULAR NAMES: 'River clubrush'.

DESCRIPTION: A perennial rush-like sedge with stout, almost cylindrical stems, 0.6–1.5 m high. It is leafless but has long sheaths, never more than half as long as the stems. Numerous flower spikelets with recurved hairs (not feather-like) occur at the end of stems. Flowers from late spring to early autumn.

HABITAT AND DISTRIBUTION: In swampy places and near river banks; widespread along the eastern Australian coast.

MEDICINAL USES: The roots are astringent and diuretic.[40]

ACTIVE CONSTITUENTS: Roots contain anthocyanins;[22] otherwise not yet investigated.

NOTE: From Bailey's original reference[23] it appears that some confusion may have existed about the identity of the plant. Thus it is not clear whether the uses mentioned refer to *Scirpus validus* or to the non-Australian *Scirpus lacustris*. Our native *S. validus* was in the past wrongly included under *S. lacustris*. Also, it is not clear whether the plant was used locally or whether the uses reported by Bailey refer to overseas usage.

Scleria lithosperma

FAMILY: Cyperaceae

DESCRIPTION: A slender perennial sedge, 30 cm to 1 m tall, with triangular stems. Leaves are very narrow and long, with 3-angled sheaths, hairy on the sides and fringed at the orifice. Flower stalks are either in leaf forks or at the end of stems, each bearing one to four clusters of two to three spikelets. The fruit is a hard, smooth and shining white nut.

HABITAT AND DISTRIBUTION: Tropical coastal Queensland and Northern Territory.

MEDICINAL USES: Reputed to be antinephritic (e.g. cure kidney inflammations) in India.[40]

ACTIVE CONSTITUENTS: Not known.

Sophora tomentosa *(See colour plate facing page 161)*

FAMILY: Fabaceae

VERNACULAR NAMES: 'Sea coast laburnum', 'golden chain'.

DESCRIPTION: A tall shrub covered with silky hairs. Its leaves are compound and consist of eleven to seventeen leaflets broadened towards the base and very rounded at the apex, about 25 mm long. Large golden yellow flowers occur in loose grape-like clusters at the end of branchlets. Bead-like pods contain five to ten globular seeds.

HABITAT AND DISTRIBUTION: Coasts of Queensland and northern New South Wales.

MEDICINAL USES: Roots and seeds have been used in bilious sickness.[41]

ACTIVE CONSTITUENTS: The plant, particularly the seeds, is supposed to contain the **very toxic alkaloid cytisine**.[19]

Syzygium suborbiculare

FAMILY: Myrtaceae

SYNONYMS: *Eugenia suborbicularis*

VERNACULAR NAMES: 'Wild apple', 'red wild apple', 'oloorgo', 'pudginjacker', 'yinumaninga', 'e-sie', 'murl-kue-kee'.

DESCRIPTION: A hairless medium-sized tree with almost circular opposite leaves, 10–15 cm long. Its large flowers are 4-lobed and occur in short bunches at the end of branchlets. Petals are up to 2 cm in diameter. The fruit is a red berry.

HABITAT AND DISTRIBUTION: Coastal northern Queensland and Northern Territory, including Gulf of Carpentaria islands.

MEDICINAL USES: The Aborigines use an infusion of bark and roots for stomach pains.[13] The juice squeezed out of baked or boiled fruits is used to ease congestion in the chest.[25]

ACTIVE CONSTITUENTS: Not known.

Vigna vexillata

FAMILY: Fabaceae

VERNACULAR NAMES: The variety *youngiana* is called 'wild cowpea'.

DESCRIPTION: A thick-rooted, prostrate plant with weak stems, covered with recurved hairs. Leaves are compound; the leaflets are 5–10 cm long and linear.

Its purplish flowers are often large and very fragrant. The pod is round, straight, 7–10 cm long and only about 4 mm broad.

HABITAT AND DISTRIBUTION: Tropical coastal regions of the Northern Territory (variety *youngiana*); also coastal Queensland.

MEDICINAL USES: The Aborigines used to chew and eat the roots for constipation.[20]

ACTIVE CONSTITUENTS: Not known.

Ximenia americana

FAMILY: Olacaceae, sometimes separated as Ximeniaceae.

SYNONYMS: *Ximenia elliptica, Ximenia laurina, Ximenia exarmata.*

VERNACULAR NAMES: 'Yellow plum', 'gotoobah', 'bed-yew-rie'.

DESCRIPTION: A shrub or small tree with spreading branches, sometimes with thorns in the forks of leaves. Its pale green leaves are egg-shaped to oblong and shining, about 5 cm long. Its fragrant yellowish flowers are small and occur in groups of three to seven blossoms on each stalk in leaf forks. Each individual flower has four recurved petals. The fruit is a yellow succulent plum-like berry, 2.5 cm across containing a single seed. Flowers in December.

HABITAT AND DISTRIBUTION: Along the sea shore of northern Queensland as well as in softwood scrub of the central eastern highlands of Queensland.

MEDICINAL USES: A decoction of the roots has been used by South African natives to cure diarrhoea in calves.[19]

ACTIVE CONSTITUENTS: Contains glycerides of acetylenic acids;[19] whether these are pharmacologically active is not known.

CHAPTER EIGHT
Miscellaneous cures

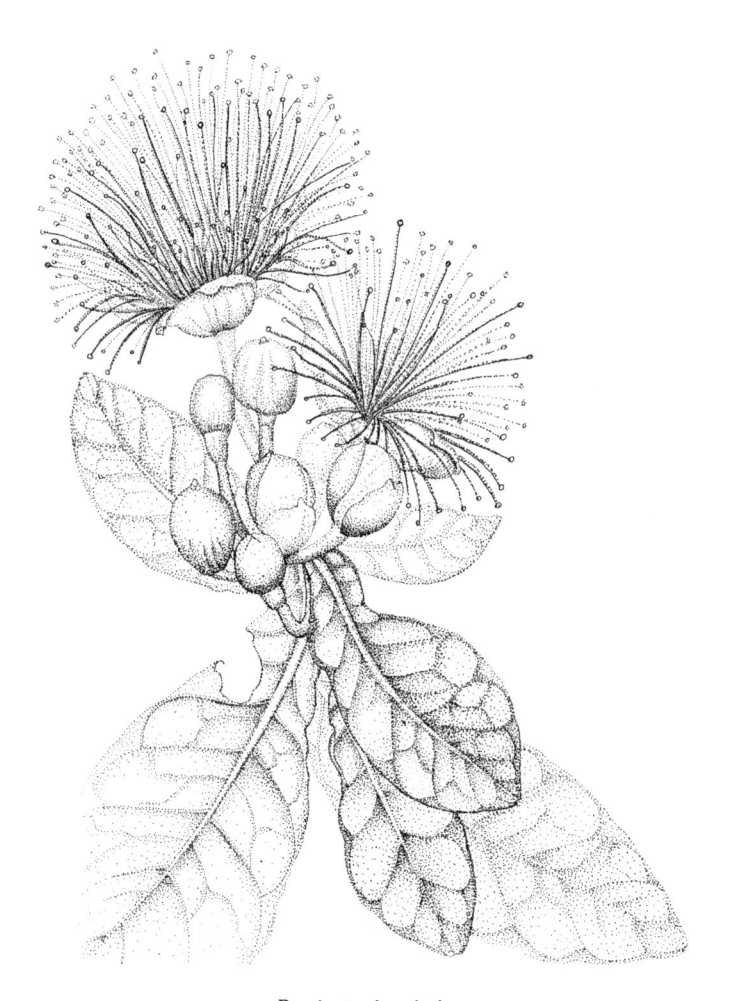

Barringtonia asjatica

IT APPEARS THAT the Australian Aborigines did not know of any methods for the treatment of intestinal parasite infestations (e.g. worms), and all plants mentioned here as having anthelmintic properties have been either used overseas, or, if locally, by the early European settlers. Since it is most unlikely that intestinal worms were unknown before the arrival of the white man, one may assume that the Aborigines were either unaware of the problem, or much more likely, learned to live with it and possibly didn't even ascribe to it any great importance.

The relatively short time interval between the Europeans' arrival in Australia and the introduction of modern twentieth century medication probably cut short any experimentation with native plants by those in need of treatment, and may explain why, for instance, the anthelmintic properties of *Aegiceras corniculatum* ('river mangrove'), due to its content of 'rapanone' (a complex mixture of related quinones),[17] had not been recognized and put to some practical use.

The anthelmintic properties of cajuput oil *(Melaleuca cajuputi)* and niaouli oil (*Melaleuca quinquenervia*, 1,8-cineole form) are usually attributed to their high cineole contents, particularly since 1,8-cineole, either by itself or in conjunction with santonin, has been used as a vermifuge.[36,49] More recent screening tests by McKern and Parnell[114] have shown that several other common essential oil components, such as limonene, alpha-phellandrene, alpha-terpineol, linalool, and piperitone, also have appreciable larvicidal activity; since some of these are present in the two *Melaleuca* oils just mentioned, they undoubtedly contribute to their anthelmintic activity. Furthermore, aged essential oils, which have had time to partly oxidise by long exposure to air, tend to have greater activity than freshly distilled oils. Its should be remembered that one of the best-known plant anthelmintics, ascaridole (the main component of oil of American wormseed, *Chenopodium ambrosioides*), is a terpene peroxide.

The use of the leguminous plant, *Daviesia latifolia* for the expelling of hydatid cysts has been reported by Joseph Bosisto in 1890, who also mentions that it was a favourite remedy amongst the settlers in Victoria.[117] R. Mendham, a farmer living in Barry, a small village near Blayney in eastern New South Wales, remembers an elderly friend of his, living near Trunkey Creek, who some forty years ago used it, reputedly with great success for the same complaint. After several months of drinking a decoction of the leaves in water he apparently coughed up the sac containing the cyst. Mr. Mendham added that he knew of several other cases where this treatment had been tried, stressing that in those days few doctors lived in the country and that their treatments for this complaint were considered to be mostly ineffective anyway.[115] Little recent chemical work exists on the constituents of *Daviesia latifolia* leaves. Those compounds that are known to be present, for example, rutin, salicylic acid, benzoic acid, and *p*-coumaric acid, are hardly likely to account for the alleged medicinal properties.

In a continent as rich in poisonous snakes as Australia, and surrounded by a huge expanse of ocean teeming with unfriendly creatures, apparently only waiting to inflict their painful stings upon the careless bather, it is not in the least surprising that its native inhabitants should have searched, if not for a cure, then a least for some kind of palliative.

Snake venom, a secretion primarily used in killing and digesting prey, is by and large a complex mixture of various proteins. It contains haemolysins, which destroy red blood cells; heamorrhagins, which destroy the lining of blood vessels, allowing blood to escape into surrounding tissues; proteolysins, which break down proteins; cytolysins, which cause disintegration of cells, be they those of blood or of any other tissue with which they come into contact; neurotoxins, which act on the nervous system, often causing death by asphyxiation by paralysing the nerves controlling the heart and the lungs; anticoagulins, which retard the clotting of blood; and thrombase, which causes blood to clot inside the blood vessels. The relative proportions of these substances vary not only from one family to another, but also in different species of the same genus. It appears, therefore, somewhat illusory to expect a given single plant species to contain all the necessary antidotes to counteract such a diversity of harmful agents. Indeed, it is now fairly universally accepted that plants have little remedial value in cases of snake poisoning, even though they may alleviate some of the side effects of snakebite. For instance, the analgesic properties of *Tinospora smilacina* and of *Nauclea orientalis* may be the reason for their use, since snakebite, particularly that of vipers, may be extremely painful. Likewise, the swelling-reducing properties of *Capparis lasiantha* may explain its use, as in some cases the bitten area may become very swollen. The external application of the astringent bark of *Eucalyptus microtheca* probably achieves a similar effect. Roth reported another example where treatment was aimed at relief rather than at a cure:

> In the case of accidents with black snakes on the Palmer River, the limb is held tightly with the hand, just above the injury, and the patient made to eat some raw bark of the Leichhardt-tree *(Sarcocephalus cordatus)* [now called *Nauclea orientalis*] which soon makes him vomit, and so gives him relief.[2]

As with snakebite, the use of *Tinospora smilacina* for marine stings was undoubtedly related to its painkilling properties. The plant contain alkaloids, but it is not known whether they are the active constituents. Another alkaloid-rich plant, *Crinum pedunculatum,* has also been used for the stings of marine organisms (probably cubomedusae). Its main alkaloid, lycorine, is probably the active principle.

Native plants have also been used, mostly by the Aborigines, for such diverse purposes as the treatment of diabetes, piles, various female complaints related to the menstrual cycle, as well as agents to stimulate milk flow in nursing mothers, abortifacients, and even contraceptives.

Alstonia actinophylla
FAMILY: Apocynaceae
SYNONYMS: *Alstonia verticillosa*

DESCRIPTION: A tree similar in appearance to *Alstonia scholaris,* but differing from it in having stalked flowers in loose clusters; the tree is hairless.

HABITAT AND DISTRIBUTION: North-western coastal Northern Territory.

MEDICINAL USES: The Aborigines believed that the latex, which exudes from cut bark, when painted on the breasts of nursing mothers will improve their milk supply.[20]

ACTIVE CONSTITUENTS: Leaves and bark give strongly positive tests for alkaloids.[13,31] The bark also contains esters of various triterpenoid alcohols.[33] However, there is no evidence to suggest that these compounds possess any of the properties mentioned. It could well be that the Aborigines' beliefs were based only on the milky look of the sap.

Ampelocissus acetosa

FAMILY: Vitaceae

SYNONYMS: *Vitis acetosa*

VERNACULAR NAMES: 'Native grape', 'mbau-nu' (Batavia River).

DESCRIPTION: A woody climber with leaf-opposed tendrils. It is mostly hairless, but young shoots may be finely hairy. Each leaf is composed of five to seven leaflets, with the lateral leaflets further subdivided, the whole resembling a foot or a claw. Each leaflet is 5–7 cm long. Flowers are purple and the fruit is a sharp, sour-tasting globular berry.

HABITAT AND DISTRIBUTION: Coastal northern Queensland and Northern Territory.

MEDICINAL USES: The Aborigines of Cape York Peninsula have used the juice as a supposed antidote for snakebite, even that of the death adder.[23]

ACTIVE CONSTITUENTS: Not known.

Barringtonia asiatica *(See colour plate facing page 176)*

FAMILY: Lecythidaceae, sometimes separated as Barringtoniaceae.

DESCRIPTION: A large tree with very large, stalkless, alternate leaves, 20–40 cm long and 10–15 cm wide. The leaves are rounded at the tip and have undivided margins. Its beautiful large white or cream-coloured flowers occur in spikes at the end of branchlets; their stamens are red. The fruit is about 9–12 cm long and almost as broad, 4-angled or exhibiting four distinct ridges.

HABITAT AND DISTRIBUTION: Mainly along beaches in northern Queensland.

MEDICINAL USES: Apparently, all parts of the tree are used medicinally in India (even though the reference consulted did not state any specific uses); the plant is **toxic and quite dangerous.**[19]

ACTIVE CONSTITUENTS: Seeds contain the deadly hydrocyanic acid; triterpenoid saponins and gallic acid are also present.[19]

Brasenia schreberi

FAMILY: Cabombaceae

SYNONYMS: *Brasenia peltata, Brasenia purpurea, Hydropeltis purpurea, Cabomba peltata.*

VERNACULAR NAMES: 'Water-shield', 'water target', sometimes referred to as one of the water lilies.

DESCRIPTION: An aquatic plant with a submerged rhizome and up to 1 cm thick, forked and completely submerged stems. Young parts are coated with a transparent jelly-like substance. Its floating leaves are usually reddish, alternate, elliptic in

Miscellaneous cures

shape, 4–11 cm long and slightly more than half as wide, with long stalks attached to the centre of their underside. Young leaves are often longitudinally inrolled. Its small, solitary flowers are dull purple and attached to completely submerged long stalks, with only the flower floating above the surface. Its fruits are beaked, 6–8 mm long; each contains one or two tiny globular seeds (about 2.5 mm in diameter). Flowers in summer.

HABITAT AND DISTRIBUTION: A fresh water plant growing in shallow ponds, lagoons and rivers of north-eastern Victoria, New South Wales and Queensland, but very scattered in its occurrence.

MEDICINAL USES: Its astringent leaves have been employed in dysentery and phthisis (a wasting disease, usually pulmonary tuberculosis).[3]

ACTIVE CONSTITUENTS: The jelly-like slimy coating is of a polysaccharidic nature and is composed of various simple sugars as well as glucuronic acid. Leaves contain some gallic acid.[33]

Capparis lasiantha

FAMILY: Capparidaceae

VERNACULAR NAMES: 'Split Jack(s)', 'nipan', 'balgarda'.

DESCRIPTION: A softly hairy shrub with egg-shaped, 2–5 cm long leaves. Its 4-petalled flowers are white or yellow. The fruit is a berry containing numerous seeds immersed in a soft pulp. Flowering time extends from autumn to early spring.

HABITAT AND DISTRIBUTION: Throughout northern tropical Australia, except along the coast.

MEDICINAL USES: The Aborigines used the flower nectar as a cough remedy; an infusion in water of the whole, mashed plants (leaves, stems and roots) was applied externally for swellings, snakebite, insect bites and stings.[18]

ACTIVE CONSTITUENTS: The whole plant gives fairly strong positive tests for alkaloids;[18] the bark appears to contain saponins.[43] However, none of the constituents have been as yet specifically identified.

Cayratia trifolia

FAMILY: Vitaceae

SYNONYMS: *Vitis trifolia*

VERNACULAR NAMES: 'native grape', 'corwora' (Palmer River), 'takking' (Staaten River), 'tampara' and 'lenn' (Charlotte Bay), 'pulkun' (Butcher's Hill).

DESCRIPTION: A woody climber, the whole plant being softly hairy. Its leaves are rhomboid, 2.5–8 cm long with toothed margins, the teeth being either pointed or rounded. Opposite each leaf there is a tendril. The fruit is a flattened globular berry.

HABITAT AND DISTRIBUTION: Coastal northern Queensland and Northern Territory.

MEDICINAL USES: The juice is reputed to be an antidote for snakebite (in India).[23]

ACTIVE CONSTITUENTS: Not known.

Coelospermum decipiens   (See colour plate facing page 192)

FAMILY: Rubiaceae

SYNONYMS: *Morinda reticulata*

VERNACULAR NAMES: 'Mapoon', 'ada-a' of the Mapoon natives.

DESCRIPTION: A low shrub with round to egg-shaped, opposite leaves, prominently netted. The stipules at the base of leaves are triangular and pointed. Flowers occur at the end of branchlets, with four stalks together to each head with a large, white, round leafy bract fused to one of the flowers. The compound fruit is a succulent berry.

HABITAT AND DISTRIBUTION: Coastal tropical Queensland (Cape York Peninsula) including islands.

MEDICINAL USES: The Aborigines have been reported to drink a decoction of the roots as an oral contraceptive.[13]

ACTIVE CONSTITUENTS: Contains at times large concentrations of selenium; it is not known with any certainty whether this is the pharmacologically active principle.[13,35]

Crinum pedunculatum (See colour plate facing page 176)

FAMILY: Amaryllidaceae

VERNACULAR NAMES: 'Swamp lily'

DESCRIPTION: A tall erect herbaceous plant with an underground bulb, growing to 1.2 m in height. Its large, strap-like and succulent leaves may vary from 10 to 20 cm in width and reach 80 cm in length. They grow rosette-like from the base of the stem. Flowers grow in groups of eight to twenty at the apex of a fleshy upright stalk which rises from the centre of the leaf cluster. Flowers are white and fragrant. The large succulent fruit contains a hard seed. Flowers in early summer.

HABITAT AND DISTRIBUTION: In swampy ground, along banks of upper reaches of tidal creeks and streams; coast of northern New South Wales and southern Queensland.

MEDICINAL USES: Crushed and rubbed on body for marine stings.[13]

ACTIVE CONSTITUENTS: Contains the alkaloid lycorine.[13]

Curcuma australasica (See colour plate facing page 176)

FAMILY: Zingiberaceae

VERNACULAR NAMES: 'Kumbiji' (Cooktown), 'andan' (Starcke River).

DESCRIPTION: A stemless shrub with a perennial rhizome and 30–45 cm long, narrow-bladed, pointed leaves, tapering into a long sheathing base. Its pale yellow flowers are in 12–17 cm long, dense spikes at the end of up to 15 cm long petioles. Its leaf-like upper bracts are 2.5–4 cm long, spreading and have pink ends. The fruit is a 3-celled capsule.

HABITAT AND DISTRIBUTION: Occurs on the Cape York Peninsula in northern Queensland and along the coast of the Gulf of Carpentaria.

MEDICINAL USES: It has apparently been used by the Aborigines in the Cooktown area for contraceptive purposes. However, the method of use has not been specified.[13]

ACTIVE CONSTITUENTS: Not known.

Cyanotis axillaris

FAMILY: Commelinaceae

DESCRIPTION: A creeping herb with linear (i.e. very narrow) leaves, 5–10 cm long. Its blue flowers occur in clusters of two or three within the short loose leaf sheaths.

The calyx is 3-lobed. The flower tube is also 3-lobed and contains six stamens with their stalks thickened above a dense tuft of hairs.

HABITAT AND DISTRIBUTION: Tropical coast of northern Queensland and of the Gulf of Carpentaria.

MEDICINAL USES: In India, a decoction of the whole plant has been given in cases of tympanitis, that is, swellings of the abdomen due to air in the intestines.[41]

ACTIVE CONSTITUENTS: Not known.

Cyperus rotundus
FAMILY: Cyperaceae

VERNACULAR NAMES: 'Nutgrass'

DESCRIPTION: A perennial with creeping wiry rhizomes forming numerous tubers. Its triangular (particularly towards the top) stems are up to 60 cm high and bear narrow, short, loosely sheathed leaves. The flowering tops consist of clusters of three to ten flattened spikelets united in an umbel. The glumes subtending these spikelets are dark brown and 3–3.5 mm long. Flowers in summer, but does not seed in Australia.

HABITAT AND DISTRIBUTION: Very common in waste ground, gardens etc. of warm regions. Throughout Australia except Tasmania. It is certainly introduced in the non-tropical parts, and may even be introduced there too.

MEDICINAL USES: In India, the tubers are used as emmenagogue[22] and in cholera.[40] The latter use is probably ineffective. Also used by the ancient Romans and Greeks medicinally.[19]

ACTIVE CONSTITUENTS: Probably the essential oil present to the extent of 0.5 to 1 per cent in the dried tubers. The chief component is alpha-cyperone. The oil has a weak but definite oestrogenic activity.[22]

Daviesia latifolia (See colour plate facing page 177)
FAMILY: Fabaceae

VERNACULAR NAMES: 'Hop bitter-pea'

DESCRIPTION: A hairless shrub, 1–3 m high. Its alternate leaves are rigid, strongly veined, 3–10 cm long and 2–5 cm wide on roughly 1 cm long petioles. They are elliptical to ovate and tapered at both ends. Leaf margins are not rolled backwards, nor are the leaves much reduced on the upper part of the stem. Flowers are bright yellow with a dark purplish centre inside, 4–7 mm long in spike-like groups up to 5 cm in length. The fruit is a triangular pod. Flowering time is in spring. Leaves as well as the whole plant are bitter to the taste.

HABITAT AND DISTRIBUTION: In open forest, particularly in hilly and mountainous areas of Tasmania, Victoria and New South Wales.

MEDICINAL USES: Leaves are used as a tonic; the expressed juice or an infusion made at a temperature below 80°C should be used since the active principle is said to decompose above that value.[116] Also used for the treatment of fever and as a remedy for hydatids.[19]

ACTIVE CONSTITUENTS: Contains an oleoresin and a bitter substance daviesine;[116] otherwise not fully investigated yet.

Deeringia amaranthoides

FAMILY: Amaranthaceae

SYNONYMS: *Deeringia celosioides*

DESCRIPTION: A tall woody and hairless climber. Its alternate leaves are egg-shaped, tapered at both ends and 5–8 cm long. The flowers are composed of five equal segments and occur in bunches at the end of branchlets or in leaf forks. The fruit is succulent with several seeds. Its leaves are bitter and acrid to the taste.

The similar *Deeringia altissima* has rusty-hairy young shoots.

HABITAT AND DISTRIBUTION: Coastal areas of Queensland.

MEDICINAL USES: In Java the leaves are used against measles.[19]

ACTIVE CONSTITUENTS: Leaves may contain alkaloids.[31,42]

Eucalyptus microtheca

FAMILY: Myrtaceae

VERNACULAR NAMES: 'Coolibah', 'flooded box', 'white gum', 'jimbul', 'kurleah', 'moolar'.

DESCRIPTION: A small tree up to 12 m high, with the bark varying in different regions; sometimes it is entirely smooth and white but more often brownish, rough and fibrous on the trunk or on the branches as well. Mature leaves are alternate, narrow, tapered at both ends, sometimes quite pointed, 6–20 cm long; dull green to slightly bluish, paler on the underside. Small bunches of flowers on angular stalks in leaf forks or at the end of branchlets. Fruits are egg-shaped to top-shaped, 3–4 mm in diameter. The fruits are very frail and fall off as soon as they are ripe. Flowers in winter.

HABITAT AND DISTRIBUTION: All of northern Australia.

MEDICINAL USES: The beaten up inner bark has been used by the Aborigines as a poultice for snakebite.[23]

ACTIVE CONSTITUENTS: The activity may be due to the astringent principle contained in the bark. Since many eucalypts have astringent barks the activity should not be restricted to this species alone.

NOTE: There are a number of geographic races of this species, differing in bark and fruit.

Goodenia ovata *(See colour plate facing page 177)*

FAMILY: Goodeniaceae

VERNACULAR NAMES: 'Hop goodenia'

DESCRIPTION: A hairless and often sticky erect shrub, up to 2 m high. Its stalked leaves are rather thin, closely and finely toothed, tapered at both ends, egg-shaped or sometimes somewhat heart-shaped, 2–5 cm long. Its yellow flowers occur in leaf forks. The corolla is 10–15 mm long with a deep cleft between the posterior lobes. The fruit is a narrow cylindrical capsule. Flowers in spring to summer.

HABITAT AND DISTRIBUTION: Widespread in forests, near cliffs, river banks, streams etc. It occurs throughout Australia except the far north.

MEDICINAL USES: An infusion of the leaves and twigs has been reported to have antidiabetic virtues.[19]

ACTIVE CONSTITUENTS: Leaves contain ursolic acid,[68] a compound not likely to be responsible for the alleged medicinal properties.

Miscellaneous cures

Gratiola pedunculata

FAMILY: Scrophulariaceae

VERNACULAR NAMES: 'Stalked brooklime', 'heartsease', 'tangran' (Corranderrk Station, Victoria).

DESCRIPTION: A perennial herb with stems up to 30 cm high ascending from a common rootstock. Its opposite leaves are more or less stem-clasping, narrow to broad and tapering towards the apex, 10–25 mm long with margins that may be bordered by a few teeth. Flowers have long stalks and occur in leaf forks. The corolla is white and yellowish inside, sometimes with pink lips. The fruit is a globular capsule. The whole plant may be hairy and sticky. Flowers in early summer.

HABITAT AND DISTRIBUTION: Very common in wet or damp, sandy-clayey soils. Occurs in New South Wales, Victoria, South Australia, Western Australia and Queensland.

MEDICINAL USES: A decoction of the plant has been used for liver complaints in the Braidwood district of New South Wales.[3] Since the related *Gratiola officinalis* slows the heart and is generally poisonous, it may be advisable to **exercise great care** in the use of *G. pedunculata*.

ACTIVE CONSTITUENTS: Not known.

Grevillea striata

FAMILY: Proteaceae

SYNONYMS: *Grevillea lineata*

VERNACULAR NAMES: 'Beefwood', 'silvery honeysuckle', 'turraie', 'willer', 'aroo-in'.

DESCRIPTION: A medium to large tree, up to 30 m high and covered with fine silky hair. Its leaves are alternate, undivided, narrow but long (4–10 mm by 15–45 cm), prominently striated on the underside with nine to thirteen parallel, raised veins. Small flowers occur on 5–7 cm long, erect spikes. The fruit is a broad, 2 cm long capsule.

HABITAT AND DISTRIBUTION: Mainly inland areas of the northern half of Australia; also near the coast in Queensland and the north-west of Western Australia.

MEDICINAL USES: The dark reddish brown resin exuded by the tree melts with body heat and may be used as a substitute for pitch in the preparations of ointments and plasters.[3] Charcoal from this tree has been used to stop bleeding from certain spear wounds.[2]

ACTIVE CONSTITUENTS: Not known.

Haemodorum corymbosum *(See colour plate facing page 177)*

FAMILY: Haemodoraceae

SYNONYMS: *Haemodorum coccineum*

VERNACULAR NAMES: 'On-tho', 'tandi', 'anto' are all northern Queensland Aboriginal names.

DESCRIPTION: A red-flowered erect shrub with up to 1.2 m high stems and almost equally long, 4–6 mm wide leaves with sheathing bases. Fruits are 8–10 mm broad capsules, often occurring in pairs. The freshly broken bulbous roots are bright red; the colour darkens on exposure to air and on drying.

HABITAT AND DISTRIBUTION: On wet land throughout Queensland and the coastal districts of the Northern Territory.

MEDICINAL USES: Aborigines were reported to use it against snakebite.[20]

ACTIVE CONSTITUENTS: Not known; contains the red pigments haemocorin and its aglycone.[22]

Helichrysum apiculatum (See colour plate facing page 177)

FAMILY: Asteraceae

VERNACULAR NAMES: 'Yellow buttons', 'common everlasting'.

DESCRIPTION: A perennial herb, branching near the base, herbaceous and not woody except at the base and about 30–50 cm tall. Its broadly oblong leaves are tapered at both ends terminating in a little point, alternate and 2–5 cm long, the whole plant being covered with silky hair. Flower heads are semi-globular clusters at the end of stems, bright yellow, sometimes (particularly in Western Australia) passing into red, brown or white and about 10–12 mm in diameter. Flowers in spring and summer.

The very similar *Helichrysum semipapposum* has narrower, almost linear leaves without a silvery hairy cover; it is sometimes not regarded as a distinct species.

HABITAT AND DISTRIBUTION: It grows on better soils in grasslands, on sandy loams and on decomposed basalt. It is found in all states.

MEDICINAL USES: Reputed to be anthelmintic.[19]

ACTIVE CONSTITUENTS: Not known.

Hernandia peltata

FAMILY: Hernandiaceae

DESCRIPTION: A tree with a large spreading crown. Its long-stalked, alternate leaves are pointed at the tip, broad and rounded near the base, with the stalk attached to the underside of the leaf near the base, and about 10 cm long. Flowers and fruit are enclosed in a cup-shaped white structure (involucel), transversely cut off at the top. The fruit is about 2.5 cm in diameter marked with eight longitudinal ribs. The seed is globular.

HABITAT AND DISTRIBUTION: Along the coast of tropical Queensland.

MEDICINAL USES: The bark, seeds and young leaves are slightly laxative; the leaf juice is depilatory.[19]

ACTIVE CONSTITUENTS: Not yet identified. Most parts of the plant contain an essential oil.[68] The bark gives a positive test for alkaloids.[42]

Hibiscus diversifolius (See colour plate facing page 177)

FAMILY: Malvaceae

SYNONYMS: Has been misidentified as *Hibiscus ficulneus*.

VERNACULAR NAMES: 'Cooreenyan' (Cloncurry River)

DESCRIPTION: A spreading shrub or small tree with prickly branches. Leaves are alternate, oblong to heart-shaped or nearly circular, irregularly toothed, angular or more or less 5-lobed, 5–7 cm across and covered with some short hair. Flowers are pale yellow, darker on the underside and about 5 cm long; they occur at the end of branchlets with a leafy bract under each flower. The calyx is densely hairy. The fruit is a very hairy pointed capsule, about 2 cm long.

HABITAT AND DISTRIBUTION: Mainly along the coast, often near rainforest, especially where disturbed; New South Wales and Queensland.

MEDICINAL USES: In Fiji the leaf juice has apparently been used to procure abortions.[3] However, according to Maiden, the juice has no activity.[19]

ACTIVE CONSTITUENTS: Not known.

Leichhardtia australis

FAMILY: Asclepiadaceae

SYNONYMS: *Marsdenia australis*

VERNACULAR NAMES: 'Cogola bush', 'kukula', 'wira'.

DESCRIPTION: A twining creeper, long and slender with very narrow opposite leaves; up to 5 cm long. Its greenish yellow flowers occur in leaf forks. Seeds are tufted. Flowers from late spring to summer.

HABITAT AND DISTRIBUTION: Arid regions of Australia but not in Queensland.

MEDICINAL USES: The dried and ground seeds were used by the Aborigines as an oral contraceptive. Its efficacy has been doubted.[18]

ACTIVE CONSTITUENTS: Not known.

Mentha diemenica

FAMILY: Lamiaceae

SYNONYMS: *Mentha gracilis*

VERNACULAR NAMES: 'Slender mint', sometimes also 'native pennyroyal'.

DESCRIPTION: A strongly scented green and almost hairless herb. Its stalkless opposite leaves are narrowly to broadly elliptical, tapered at both ends but broader towards the base and 5–30 mm long. The calyx is 5-toothed and carries longitudinal striations. The calyx teeth are tapered at both ends. Its 4-lobed white or pinkish flowers occur in groups of two to eight. Flowers in spring.

HABITAT AND DISTRIBUTION: Common, in moist and usually sunny situations. In all states except Western Australia and Queensland.

MEDICINAL USES: An infusion or decoction of the whole plant has been used in southern New South Wales to treat menstrual disorders in women (dysmenorrhoea). The herb is used in the same way as ordinary peppermint *(Mentha piperita)* to treat stomach cramps, intestinal cramps, that is, in the form of a tea. It is also used as a diuretic and diaphoretic.[3,36]

The herb strewn on the floor inside houses is reputed to keep away fleas and other insects.[3]

ACTIVE CONSTITUENTS: The essential oil present in the whole plant. Its composition is not yet known.

NOTE: As with *Mentha satureioides* it should be used with care.

Oldenlandia galioides

FAMILY: Rubiaceae

SYNONYMS: *Hedyotis galioides*

DESCRIPTION: A slender, small and rather diffuse annual herb. Its opposite leaves are very narrow, almost linear and 1–3 cm long. Stipules, that is leafy appendages at the base of leaf stalks, are very small with one or two bristle-like lobes on each side. The fruit is a capsule which splits along the carpel walls or along the carpel junction. Flowers occur in leaf forks on rather long stems.

HABITAT AND DISTRIBUTION: In swamps in northern Queensland.

MEDICINAL USES: As an antidote for snakebite (used by the Chinese in Ingham): as much as possible of the dry plant was steeped in spirits, usually rum, and the resulting mixture given internally in repeated doses, as much as the victim could stand.[19]

ACTIVE CONSTITUENTS: Not known.

Ottelia alismoides

FAMILY: Hydrocharitaceae

DESCRIPTION: An aquatic plant with its leaves completely submerged in depths of up to 1.5 m of fresh water or partly emergent in shallower waters. Leaf blades are broadly egg-shaped, 15–20 cm wide, to almost circular or broadly heart-shaped, thin and translucent. Flower clusters enclosed in large leafy bracts with five to ten longitudinal wings. Leaves emerge from a common base.

HABITAT AND DISTRIBUTION: Still water of northern Queensland and of the Northern Territory.

MEDICINAL USES: In India, reputed to remove the effects of the venom of the sea dog.[40]

ACTIVE CONSTITUENTS: Not known.

Owenia reticulata

FAMILY: Meliaceae

VERNACULAR NAMES: 'Desert walnut'

DESCRIPTION: A hairless tree up to 10 m high. Its leaves, which are over 30 cm long, consist of four, six or eight stalkless leaflets with a prominent vein on the underside; leaflets are egg-shaped, blunt, 10–20 cm long, leathery and smooth on the upper side. Their common petiole is angular or broadened, terminating in a short point. The fruit is woody and globular. Flowers from late winter to late spring.

HABITAT AND DISTRIBUTION: On red sandy soils in coastal areas of the Northern Territory and the northern districts of Western Australia.

MEDICINAL USES: The Aborigines roast the oily kernels on a fire and rub them into small sores, infected insect bites, and scratches.[18]

ACTIVE CONSTITUENTS: Not known.

Pagetia medicinalis

FAMILY: Rutaceae

DESCRIPTION: A handsome tree with a smooth and light coloured bark. Its opposite leaves are 7.5–15 cm long and 5–10 cm broad and are dotted with oil glands. Flowers are small, 5-sepalled and 5-petalled.

HABITAT AND DISTRIBUTION: Coastal tropical Queensland.

MEDICINAL USES: The leaf oil is reputed to have medicinal properties, but their nature has not been stated.[41]

ACTIVE CONSTITUENTS: Not known.

Curcuma australasica (see page 170)

Barringtonia asiatica (see page 168)

Crinum pedunculatum (see page 170)

Daviesia latifolia (see page 171)

Haemodorum corymbosum (see page 173)

Goodenia ovata (see page 172)

Hibiscus diversifolius (see page 17)

Helichrysum apiculatum (see page 174)

Pratia purpurascens

FAMILY: Lobeliaceae

SYNONYMS: *Lobelia purpurascens*

VERNACULAR NAMES: 'White root'

DESCRIPTION: A perennial herb with angular stems, up to 30 cm long. Its alternate leaves are almost stalkless, elliptic with irregularly toothed margins, 10–25 mm long; the underside is often purplish. Flowers are pale purple and are borne on single stalks in leaf forks. Flowers from late summer to autumn. Roots are very white.

HABITAT AND DISTRIBUTION: Very widespread in damp places such as in wet sclerophyll forest; occurs in all eastern states as well as in South Australia.

MEDICINAL USES: Reputed to be effective against snakebite.[27]

ACTIVE CONSTITUENTS: Alkaloidal tests are positive;[31,42] said to contain lobeline.[60]

Psilotum nudum

FAMILY: Psilotaceae

SYNONYMS: *Psilotum triquetrum*

DESCRIPTION: A perennial fern-like plant with a branched, wiry, creeping rhizome. The plant is from 15–60 cm long, either hanging down from trees or rocks or erect if growing on the ground. It has flat, forked branches and triangular fruiting branches with minute pointed scale-like leaves in three rows. Spore-producing organs consisting of three fused globular capsules are present in the forks of branchlets.

HABITAT AND DISTRIBUTION: It grows on rockwalls and in crevices in cliffs, and on the trunks of tree ferns and other rainforest species. All states except Tasmania.

MEDICINAL USES: An infusion of the plant has been used in the Pacific islands for visceral complaints.[27]

ACTIVE CONSTITUENTS: Contains flavonoids and sugars,[92] but it is not known whether any of these are pharmacologically active.

Pteridium esculentum

FAMILY: Dennstaedtiaceae

SYNONYMS: Has been included under the related non-Australian species *Pteridium aquilinum*.

VERNACULAR NAMES: 'Common bracken'

DESCRIPTION: A perennial fern with an extensive creeping rhizome, 2–10 mm in diameter and covered with rusty red hair. Stems are up to 1.5 m long, brown and stiff bearing large, deeply divided fronds. Fronds are divided several times into narrow, yellow-green to dark green leathery and tough segments, smooth and glossy on top and paler underneath. Segments have inrolled edges and a line of brown spores inside them. Ultimate segments are often sickle-shaped, linear to broadly oblong. Fronds including stems vary from 0.6–3 m in height.

HABITAT AND DISTRIBUTION: In dry sclerophyll forest, on damp sandy flats, in pastures and the like. Common in moister parts of moister and cooler areas of all states.

MEDICINAL USES: Reputed to be anthelmintic and astringent. Juicy young stems, well rubbed in, have been used by the Aborigines for insect bites. A tea made from leaves and leaf stalks has apparently been used for rheumatism.[19,92]

ACTIVE CONSTITUENTS: Condensed tannins as well as leucocyanidin are present. Leaves contain the taenicidal (tapeworm-killing) saponin pteridin.[92]

Rhyncharrhena linearis

FAMILY: Asclepiadaceae

SYNONYMS: *Pentatropis linearis*

DESCRIPTION: A slender twining creeper, up to 2 m tall, with opposite, narrow and very short-stalked leaves, about 6 cm long and tapered at both ends. Its brown-violet flowers occur in spike-like groups in leaf forks. Seed pods are very long with soft, silky hairs inside them. Flowers from early spring to early autumn.

HABITAT AND DISTRIBUTION: Southern and south-western districts of Western Australia, inland as well as near the coast.

MEDICINAL USES: The Aborigines used the seeds, ground to a paste, as an oral contraceptive.[18]

ACTIVE CONSTITUENTS: Not known.

Rhynchosia minima

FAMILY: Fabaceae

VERNACULAR NAMES: 'Rhynchosia'

DESCRIPTION: A slender trailing herb. Its leaves consist of usually three egg-shaped to rhomboidal leaflets, about 2.5 cm in length. Flower bunches are erect and much longer than leaves; individual flowers are small and pendulous. The pod is pointed, sickle-shaped, flattened and narrowed at the base and about 2.5 cm long. Leaves show resinous dots.

HABITAT AND DISTRIBUTION: Throughout Queensland and the Northern Territory.

MEDICINAL USES: Listed as pharmacologically active without its activity being specifically recorded.[19]

ACTIVE CONSTITUENTS: Not known.

Ripogonum papuanum

FAMILY: Smilacaceae, sometimes included in the family Liliaceae.

SYNONYMS: Sometimes wrongly spelt *Rhipogonum*.

DESCRIPTION: A tall climber, without prickles; its leaves are narrowly elliptical, opposite as well as alternate, tapering into a long point; they are 12–17 cm long and 3–4.5 cm broad. Flowers occur in upper leaf forks.

HABITAT AND DISTRIBUTION: Tropical coast of northern Queensland.

MEDICINAL USES: An infusion of the bark and roots of a species appearing to be this particular plant has been drunk, as well as applied externally, by Queensland Aborigines as a poultice to stingray injuries.[13]

ACTIVE CONSTITUENTS: Not known.

Scoparia dulcis

FAMILY: Scrophulariaceae

VERNACULAR NAMES: 'Scoparia'

DESCRIPTION: A small thickly branched plant, somewhat shrubby (up to 1.2 m tall) and short-lived. Its leaves are grouped in threes around the stem. The petals of its white flowers are fused together with a short tube and a spreading top resembling a wheel. The fruit is a two-valved capsule.

HABITAT AND DISTRIBUTION: A pioneer species in disturbed ground, and therefore often weedy; in coastal areas of Queensland and of the Northern Territory.

MEDICINAL USES: An infusion of the plant has been used to treat malarial fever both in India and North America.[3,41] The Australian Aborigines have been reported to have drunk a decoction for stomach pains and influenza;[20] also, the pulped plant wrapped around sores and cuts would speed healing in a few days.[20] Even though the plant contains an antidiabetic compound, amellin, it has not been used as such for the treatment of diabetes.[19]

ACTIVE CONSTITUENTS: The whole plant contains triterpenes.[43] Amellin, in the purified state, has been given in amounts of 15-20 mg in the treatment of diabetes.[19]

Toona australis

FAMILY: Meliaceae

SYNONYMS: *Cedrela australis, Cedrela toona* var. *australis*. Sometimes confused with *Cedrela toona,* a non-Australian species.

VERNACULAR NAMES: 'Red cedar', 'cedar', 'polai', 'woolia', 'mumin', 'mugurpul', 'woota'.

DESCRIPTION: A large deciduous tree with spreading branches, up to 60 m high, with a grey or brown scaly bark which, after falling off, leaves a smooth reddish brown surface. Its alternate leaves consist of three to eight pairs of 7-12 cm long, pointed leaflets; they are deciduous in winter. White or pinkish flowers occur in large pyramidal bunches on rather long stalks. The fruit is an oblong, 2-3 cm long capsule containing long, winged seeds. Flowers in late spring.

HABITAT AND DISTRIBUTION: Grows on rich soils with abundant moisture available, usually in rainforests; from southern coastal New South Wales to northern Queensland; also in adjacent mountain ranges.

MEDICINAL USES: In India, the astringent bark is used in fevers and dysentery; also used as a reliable antiperiodic. It is used in conjunction with a little powdered *Caesalpinia bonduc* seed for the treatment of fevers. Bark is also used in bilious fevers. Flowers considered to be an emmenagogue.[3,19,40,59]

ACTIVE CONSTITUENTS: Bark contains some tannin. Flowers contain various pigments of flavonoid nature.[16,19] The species has not been very well investigated as yet.

Trichodesma zeylanicum var. *zeylanicum* (See colour plate facing page 192)

FAMILY: Boraginaceae

SYNONYMS: *Pollichia zeylanica*

VERNACULAR NAMES: 'Camel bush', 'pigurga', 'padjapadja', 'kumbalin', 'pardan'.

DESCRIPTION: A coarse, more or less hairy herb, up to 1 m high, with alternate or opposite leaves, 7-10 cm long. Its flowers are blue and have a small leaf-like bract under each flower stalk; all five petals are broad with narrowly pointed tips. The fruit consists of four 1-seeded shining nuts attached by their whole inner face, which when detached, leaves four cavities in the thick, prominently 4-angled axis.

HABITAT AND DISTRIBUTION: Widely distributed over the whole of the warmer, arid regions of Western Australia, Northern Territory, Queensland and New South Wales.

MEDICINAL USES: The Aborigines used to rub the boiled plant on sores.[18] In India considered to be diuretic; also used as a cure for snakebite.[40]

ACTIVE CONSTITUENTS: Leaf constituents are not known; seed contains the alkaloid supinine.[33]

Vitex trifolia

FAMILY: Verbenaceae

DESCRIPTION: A shrub with opposite and rather variable foliage; leaves may be either simple or compound and formed by three or five leaflets. Leaves are often white underneath and sometimes on both sides. White or blue flowers in stalkless, opposite spikes form bunches at the end of branchlets. The corolla is 5-lobed, the lowest lobe, which is the largest, may be notched. The fruit is a succulent, globular berry.

HABITAT AND DISTRIBUTION: Common in coastal areas of Queensland and of the Northern Territory.

MEDICINAL USES: The leaves are used in India as a powerful discutient. A leaf decoction made into a poultice is applied to an enlarged spleen.[40]

ACTIVE CONSTITUENTS: The foliage contains various flavonoids and agnuside. Fruits contain the alkaloid vitricine.[14] However, it is not known which of these compounds, if any, are responsible for the medicinal activity of the plant.

CHAPTER NINE
More myth than medicine?

Ipomoea brasiliensis

IT HAS BEEN ALREADY SUGGESTED that many of the cures and treatments should be viewed with some scepticism. Some may be merely ineffective and the disease or condition will follow its normal course and the patient will recover, or die, regardless of the treatment. For instance, the use of a decoction of *Smilax glyciphylla* as an anti-scorbutic, that is, a remedy aimed at correcting a vitamin C deficiency, is ludicrous; all vitamin C would have been completely destroyed during prolonged boiling involved in the preparation of the plant for use. However, if the patient ate occasionally some green vegetables, whilst continuing with the *Smilax* treatment, all the symptoms would no doubt have gradually subsided and no harm would have come from it. The seeds and flowering spikes of *Achyranthes aspera*, a plant native to both India and Australia, have been used in India in cases of hydrophobia (rabies). There is no simple remedy for this disease and the patient will die, treatment or no treatment (unless he receives, of course, early anti-rabic serum injections). And if he does not, then the dog probably did not have rabies. Fortunately, rabies is absent from Australia and so this particular example is of academic interest only.

On the other hand certain treatments, besides being ineffective, may in fact be dangerous. Not so much because of any toxic hazards involved, but rather because they do not get to the real cause of the disease and thus may lull the patient into believing he has been cured and so does not need further treatment, whereas in actual fact only some minor outward symptoms have been removed and the disease continues to spread unchecked. All so-called cures for syphilis fall into this group. It has been reported that the Aborigines used the astringent kino of the red bloodwood *(Eucalyptus gummifera)* to treat the sores typical of this disease. Their reasons for this particular treatment were probably based on a wrong analogy. Whilst ordinary sores and ulcers are often quite curable in this way, that is, by thorough disinfection followed by the application of an astringent to speed the drying up process, syphilis, as a blood disease, will not respond to such mild local treatment. Since the sores of primary syphilis will disappear after some time, even without treatment, the mistaken impression could have arisen that the cure was successful.

There are other instances of treatments based on false analogies and thus of no medicinal value. The Aborigines' use of a decoction of caustic weed *(Euphorbia drummondii)* for the treatment of gonorrhoea may be attributed to the dictum *similia similibus curantur,* meaning similar cures same. The sticky, milky juice of the *Euphorbia* probably reminded them of the pussy discharge from the sexual organs which is characteristic of this disease. In any case, as venereal diseases are generally thought to have been introduced by European or Asian navigators, the Aborigines' attempts to find cures would not have had the benefit of long established tradition and experimentation. Applying the same principle, western Queensland Aborigines believed that any kind of grass or shrub growing at the water's edge (such as various euphorbias) would relieve difficult or painful urination.

Exallage auricularia, a plant reputed to be a cure for deafness, has been included here mainly because of the lack of precision in the description of the type of deafness. It is unlikely that it would have any effect in the case of a structurally damaged or defective ear. However, the plant contains alkaloids and it may be that one of them may cure deafness due to inflammation or some other type of infection of the ear.

It is well known that some faith in the cure as well as in the practitioner administering it have a significant role to play in the ultimate success of any treatment. An element of mind-over-matter works often as strongly as the most potent drug. This may be particularly so as far as the efficacy of aphrodisiacs is concerned. Medical science does not generally subscribe to the existence of a drug with true aphrodisiac properties, and one may, therefore, be tempted to dismiss reports of the usefulness of *Lycopodium phlegmaria* and *Pittosporum venulosum* as being largely subjective or imaginary. However, the precision of the entry on *P. venulosum* makes one wonder: 'bruised roots have a powerful aromatic odour and are placed near shelters of gins [Aboriginal women] and are alleged to cause sexual excitement'.[13] Could it be that the volatile substances present in the roots are in fact a kind of human sex pheromone? Since, according to a statement in a recent article by B. Kullenberg and G. Bergstrom the 'Study of the biological significance of scents by man has been hampered by his being essentially a sight-and-sound animal.'[117] the species in question may be of some interest to behavioural scientists. The study of sex pheromones, that is, chemical substances by which living organisms communicate, is a relatively new science. It deals with the study of the effect of scents on the behaviour of insects as well as of higher animals, and was pioneered by Adolf Butenandt and his co-workers who, in 1959, discovered and determined the chemical structure of the sex-stimulating signal substance of the female silk moth (*Bombyx mori*). The term pheromone was coined at about the same time.

Achyranthes aspera

FAMILY: Amaranthaceae

VERNACULAR NAMES: 'Chaff flower'

DESCRIPTION: An erect, sometimes spreading annual, up to 90 cm high. The hairy, herbaceous stems have a somewhat woody base. Its opposite short-stalked leaves are broadly elliptical to oblong, tapered at both ends, 2–7 cm long, slightly hairy on the upper side and more woolly on the underside. Numerous shining green flowers occur in long and rigid spikes at the end of branchlets.

HABITAT AND DISTRIBUTION: A plant of disturbed areas; it may be often weedy. It occurs in tropical and subtropical areas of Australia.

MEDICINAL USES: In India, the ashes of the burned herb are used together with an infusion of ginger in the treatment of dropsy.[3,118] The plant is also used for chills.[19] Its seeds are given in cases of ophthalmia, certain skin diseases, snakebite, and hydrophobia (rabies).[3] The flowering spikes, rubbed together with a little sugar, are made into pills and given orally to people bitten by mad dogs. Fresh leaves are ground to a pulp and applied to the bite of scorpions.[3] Seeds and roots are reported to be useful as diuretics and antispasmodics.[33]

Its efficacy in the treatment of rabies is, in the authors' opinion, highly questionable.

ACTIVE CONSTITUENTS: The roots contain the nitrogenous compound achyranthine. Seeds and roots also contain triterpenoid saponins.[33] However, the pharmacologically active compounds are not known.

Aleurites moluccana

FAMILY: Euphorbiaceae

SYNONYMS: *Aleurites triloba, Jatropha moluccana.*

VERNACULAR NAMES: 'Candlenut tree', 'tarkal' (Cooktown), 'nappalla' (Barron River).

DESCRIPTION: A large evergreen tree with spreading branches, up to 20 m high. Its long-stalked leaves are alternate, hairy and often crowded near the ends of branches. They are broadly elliptical and somewhat broadened near the base, tapered at both ends and without lobes, or 3-, 5- or 7-lobed with a heart-shaped base; they will reach up to 20 cm in length. Young leaves and branchlets are covered with a pale rusty, fluffy coating. Flowers are in bunches 10–15 cm long at the end of branchlets; individual petals are about 6 mm long. Fruits are fleshy and rounded, 5–6 cm in diameter, slightly 3- to 4-ridged, hairless and green to olive-green in colour. The fruit contains one or two large seeds, slightly pointed at the apex; seed kernels are very oily. Old seeds that have been lying on the ground are hard and black.

HABITAT AND DISTRIBUTION: In moist gullies along the coast of northern New South Wales and Queensland.

MEDICINAL USES: The kernel oil is used in India as a mild and sure laxative, more pleasant than castor oil. The usual dose is 25–50 g, and it acts within 3–6 hours.[40] **Whole kernels are poisonous** and violently purgative.[13] The oil has also been used in rheumatism.[55] After roasting, the kernels are reputed to have an aphrodisiac effect.[55]

ACTIVE CONSTITUENTS: The kernel oil contains esters of linolenic acid.[68] Mature as well as immature fruits give strongly positive tests for alkaloids.[42] However, the identities of the pharmacologically active constituents are not known.

Centella asiatica

FAMILY: Apiaceae

SYNONYMS: *Hydrocotyle asiatica, Hydrocotyle repanda, Hydrocotyle cordifolia.*

VERNACULAR NAMES: 'Indian pennywort'

DESCRIPTION: A perennial herb creeping along the ground and rooting at leaf nodes. Its leaves are heart-shaped to circular or kidney-shaped with straight or regularly shallow-lobed margins. They may be slightly hairy and vary from 2–3 cm in length. Flowers occur in small heads of three to four with small leaf-like bracts under the flower head. Petals are pink or white and overlap. The fruit is compressed sideways and measures 3 mm or so in diameter.

HABITAT AND DISTRIBUTION: Widespread in damp ground, along roads, near swamps, in gardens. It is found in all states.

MEDICINAL USES: It is used mainly for the treatment of skin diseases. The juice, taken internally or applied locally, has been used for leprosy, skin lesions due to secondary syphilis, and non-specific ulcerations.[3] Powdered and mixed with lime, it has been used for the treatment of sores on babies.[13] Leaf juice stops irritation caused by prickly heat.[55]

If taken internally it has been claimed to have a narcotic effect; it has also been used as a tonic and alternative in diseases of the skin, nervous system, and blood.[55]

Powdered leaves sniffed in cases of ozaena.[55]

The Indian drug 'brahmi' is both *Centella asiatica* and *Herpestis monniera*.[14]

ACTIVE CONSTITUENTS: Asiaticoside, a triterpenoid sugar ester, has been used for the treatment of leprosy. An alkaloid, hydrocotyline, as well as flavonoids, sugars and triterpenoid acids are present.[14] The bitter principle vellarin (probably an impure mixture of all above-mentioned compounds) has been used to treat syphilis and leprosy.[19]

NOTE: There may be two species or subspecies involved here; the plants of temperate Australia differ from the typical *Centella asiatica* of the north.

Codonocarpus cotinifolius

FAMILY: Gyrostemonaceae

SYNONYMS: *Gyrostemon cotinifolius, Gyrostemon pungens, Gyrostemon acaciiformis.*

VERNACULAR NAMES: 'Desert poplar', 'horseradish tree', 'quinine tree', 'medicine tree', 'bell fruit', 'native poplar', 'western poplar', 'mustard tree', 'firebush', 'cucurdie', 'cundilyong', 'kandurangu'.

DESCRIPTION: A tall shrub or narrow-crowned small tree, up to 10 m high, but short-lived. Its pale green, alternate leaves are elliptical, broadened near the tip, oblong and tapered at both ends, usually with a short point. Leaves have a mustardy flavour when chewed. Bark may be marked with dark red, yellow and pale green wavy lines. Flowers in spikes in upper leaf forks, sometimes forming a terminal cluster. Male flowers are circular with stamens radiating around central disc. Fruits are green, bell-shaped, about 1 cm across.

HABITAT AND DISTRIBUTION: Often on red sandy soils in the drier regions of Australia; not near the coast.

MEDICINAL USES: Leaves chewed to relieve toothache; sometimes used for this purpose in conjunction with the bark of *Acacia cuthbertsonii;* also relieves rheumatism. Rheumatic limbs are soaked in an infusion of the root bark together with *Acacia cutherbertsonii* bark. Roots chewed as narcotic. An infusion (together with *Scaevola spinescens*) is reputed to be a cancer cure.[18,26]

ACTIVE CONSTITUENTS: Volatile leaf oil contains benzyl cyanide and a sulphur containing glycoside, cochlearin.[68] May contain alkaloids.[18] The active principles have not yet been positively identified.

Crinum asiaticum (See colour plate facing page 192)

FAMILY: Amaryllidaceae

VERNACULAR NAMES: 'Crinum lily', 'adikalyikba' (Groote Eylandt).

DESCRIPTION: A tall herbaceous plant with its underground bulb produced into an above-ground column. Its long, strap-like, succulent leaves grow rosette-like from the base. Flowers are short-stalked or stalkless and grow in terminal clusters of eight to twenty on 30–60 cm long stems. They are white, 8 cm or so long. The fruit is large and succulent.

There are two varieties: *C. asiaticum* var. *asiaticum* has leaves wider than 2.5 cm; *C. asiaticum* var. *angustifolium* has leaves less than 2.5 cm wide.

HABITAT AND DISTRIBUTION: Confined to tropical coastal areas of northern Queensland and of the Northern Territory.

MEDICINAL USES: The crushed bulb is reputedly antiseptic. The mashed bulb is soaked in water and may be applied to rectal abscesses. The liquid is splashed over it as well. The liquid from soaked bulbs is poured into spear wounds taking care that no solid matter gets into the wound.[1,25] The corm juice is drunk by New Guinean natives regularly for gonorrhoea; a cure allegedly takes about two months.[13]

ACTIVE CONSTITUENTS: Bulbs contain the alkaloid lycorine;[22] whether it is responsible for the plant's medicinal uses is not known.

Cyperus bifax

FAMILY: Cyperaceae

SYNONYMS: *Cyperus retzii*

VERNACULAR NAMES: 'Downs nutgrass'

DESCRIPTION: A perennial grass-like plant with wiry rhizomes carrying narrow egg-shaped tubers. Its 50–75 cm high stems are 3-angled with grass-like leaves which are shorter than the stems. Spikelets are 2.5 mm wide; glumes subtending the spikelets are 3.5–4 mm long, spreading and inrolling. Flowers from late autumn to winter.

HABITAT AND DISTRIBUTION: Widespread; warmer regions of Australia.

MEDICINAL USES: A tuber decoction was used by the Aborigines of northern Queensland for the treatment of gonorrhoea.[19]

ACTIVE CONSTITUENTS: Not known.

Dioscorea transversa

FAMILY: Dioscoreaceae

SYNONYMS: *Dioscorea punctata*

VERNACULAR NAMES: 'Long yam', 'kowar' (in Central Queensland).

DESCRIPTION: A hairless, wiry twiner, several metres long, with tuberous underground rhizomes. Leaves are alternate or almost opposite, triangular with spreading basal lobes, or heart-shaped with spreading lobes, pointed 6–10 cm long with five to seven prominent longitudinal veins. The very fragrant flowers occur in fairly large clusters. The fruit in a 3-angled capsule, 1.5–2 cm long with the protruding lobes about 12 mm long. Flowers in spring to summer.

HABITAT AND DISTRIBUTION: Mainly along the coasts of central and northern New South Wales, Queensland and Northern Territory.

MEDICINAL USES: A decoction has been claimed to be useful for the treatment of skin cancer (applied externally).[13]

ACTIVE CONSTITUENTS: Not known.

Eucalyptus resinifera

FAMILY: Myrtaceae

VERNACULAR NAMES: 'Red mahogany', 'red stringybark', 'Jimmy Low', 'forest mahogany', 'roangga', 'torumba', 'booah'.

DESCRIPTION: A large tree, up to 30 m high, with a reddish fibrous stringy bark, persisting throughout, even on small branches. Juvenile leaves are stalked, opposite, narrow, and tapered at both ends; mature leaves are also stalked, alternate, and tapered at both ends, 10–16 cm long, dark green above and paler underneath. Flowers from late spring to summer.

HABITAT AND DISTRIBUTION: A coastal species that grows in sheltered positions on clayey and sandy soils; central New South Wales to northern Queensland.

MEDICINAL USES: Queensland Aborigines drank a leaf decoction and rubbed the inner bark into syphilitic sores.[2,97]

The older literature refers to the high medicinal value of the kino and to its powerful astringent properties, useful in the treatment of diarrhoea and dysentery.[106] However, this species does not yield much kino; the name was applied because of an initial confusion in the information given to Smith when he described it. The kino referred to may in fact have come from *Eucalyptus siderophloia*.

ACTIVE CONSTITUENTS: Not known.

Euphorbia drummondii

FAMILY: Euphorbiaceae

VERNACULAR NAMES: 'Caustic weed', 'caustic creeper', 'milk plant', 'pox plant', 'creeping caustic', 'mat spurge', 'ngama-ngama', 'widda pooloo', 'piwi', 'munya-munya', 'currawinya clover'.

DESCRIPTION: A small much-branched prostrate herb with a thick tap-root. Its very short-stalked opposite leaves are oblong, smooth, up to 8 mm long, sometimes sparsely toothed. Small flower heads occur in leaf forks. Most parts of the plant are dull to bluish green, sometimes dull dark red. When bruised, the plant exudes a milky sap.

HABITAT AND DISTRIBUTION: Mainly inland areas of all mainland states. It colonizes bare soil after rain; thus it also occurs as a weed in gardens, pastures and disturbed ground, even on the coast in places.

MEDICINAL USES: An infusion of the herb has been claimed to be an almost certain cure for chronic diarrhoea, dysentery, and low fever;[40] also drunk by the Aborigines for rheumatism.[18] A decoction in boiling water has been applied to skin itches, sores, and possible scabies;[50] also drunk for gonorrhoea (undoubtedly ineffective in this case).[32] The milky sap has been applied for venereal disease and sores on the genital organs.[3,18] Also used by the Aborigines against snakebite.[19] A report that the latex has been applied to sore eyes should be treated with the greatest caution.[20]

ACTIVE CONSTITUENTS: Not known.

Exallage auricularia

FAMILY: Rubiaceae

SYNONYMS: *Hedyotis auricularia, Oldenlandia auricularia*.

DESCRIPTION: A herb up to 1 m high. Its opposite leaves are elliptical and tapered at both ends, 2.5–8 cm long, with raised and prominent veins. Flowers are numerous in stalkless clusters in leaf forks. The fruit is a hard capsule which may split into two parts each containing four to six angular seeds.

HABITAT AND DISTRIBUTION: Mainly in Cape York Peninsula in northern Queensland.

MEDICINAL USES: Reputed as a cure for deafness.[19]

ACTIVE CONSTITUENTS: Triterpenoids, triterpenoid saponins, alizarin, alkaloids, such as hedyotine.[14,19,43] It is not known which, if any, of the compounds mentioned have the pharmacological qualities mentioned.

Ficus racemosa

FAMILY: Moraceae

SYNONYMS: *Ficus glomerata, Ficus vesca.*

VERNACULAR NAMES: 'Cluster fig', 'moochai' (Cooktown), 'parpa' (Rockhampton).

DESCRIPTION: A large, almost completely hairless tree. Its leaves are alternate, tapered at both ends, 8–15 cm long and 3–7 cm wide, on stalks 2–5 cm long. The large, fleshy fruits are up to 5 cm in diameter, reddish when ripe, and they occur in dense clusters on short and branched stalks in leaf forks as well as along branches. Wounding of the bark results in the discharge of a white milky sap.

HABITAT AND DISTRIBUTION: Tropical coastal Queensland and Northern Territory.

MEDICINAL USES: Widely used in India for medicinal purposes. In Bombay, for instance, the milky sap was used as a remedy for mumps and other inflammations;[19] also for the treatment of gonorrhoea.[27] The root juice was used as a tonic.[27] The bark and fruit are astringent and have been prescribed in haematuria, menorrhagia, and haemoptysis, usually in 200-grain doses.[3] Galls, common on leaves, are soaked in milk and mixed with honey and given to prevent pitting in smallpox.[27]

It is noteworthy that the Aborigines do not appear to have been aware of the tree's medicinal properties.

ACTIVE CONSTITUENTS: Not known; the latex is probably proteolytic.[35]

Ipomoea brasiliensis (See colour plate facing page 192)

FAMILY: Convolvulaceae

SYNONYMS: Has been included in *Ipomoea pes-caprae*, sometimes as a subspecies; true *I. pes-caprae* (synonym: *Ipomoea biloba*) is not an Australian species.

VERNACULAR NAMES: 'Goatsfoot convolvulus', 'waljno-jo', 'endabari'.

DESCRIPTION: A trailing, branched, woody plant with individual stems 10 m long or longer, rooting at intervals and with a fleshy, up to 4 cm thick taproot. Its prominently veined, long-stalked (about 10 cm), alternate leaves, 5–8 cm long, are elliptical, sometimes broadened towards the apex, notched, or bluntly 2-lobed. Pink flowers, around 4 cm in diameter, are borne on long stalks. The fruit is a globular, 2-celled capsule containing two to four woolly seeds. Flowers in autumn.

HABITAT AND DISTRIBUTION: Along beaches, coastal cliffs; New South Wales, Queensland, Northern Territory and Western Australia.

MEDICINAL USES: The juice has been given as a diuretic in dropsy; the bruised leaves are applied at the same time to the dropsical part.[3] In Brazil, the boiled foliage has been made up into a poultice in cases of scrofulous enlargement of the joints.[40] A decoction was used in rheumatism.[3] Also, boiled leaves were used externally as a painkiller in cases of colic.[3]

The Australian Aborigines applied a leaf decoction to sores and drank it for venereal disease. Heated leaves were applied to boils to make them discharge.[20]

ACTIVE CONSTITUENTS: Not known.

Ipomoea brasiliensis

Lycopodium phlegmaria

FAMILY: Lycopodiaceae

VERNACULAR NAMES: 'Tasselled club-moss'

DESCRIPTION: A terrestrial moss-like plant with elongated pendulous stems. Leaves are tapered at both ends and are about 8–12 mm long. Spikes are several times forked, 15–30 cm or so long. It has leaf-like bracts with closely overlapping edges in four rows. A most graceful epiphyte.

HABITAT AND DISTRIBUTION: On rocks and trees of tropical Queensland.

MEDICINAL USES: Reputed to have aphrodisiac properties.[19]

ACTIVE CONSTITUENTS: Not known.

Myoporum debile   *(See colour plate facing page 193)*

FAMILY: Myoporaceae

SYNONYMS: *Myoporum diffusum*

VERNACULAR NAMES: 'Winter apple', 'amulla'.

DESCRIPTION: A prostrate, trailing shrub with a thick root. Its alternate, short-stalked to almost stalkless leaves are oblong to elliptical, tapered at both ends, often with a few teeth near the base, and 3–10 cm long. Its white or purplish flowers occur singly or in twos on short stalks in leaf forks. The pinkish red fruit is egg-shaped and slightly compressed and somewhat succulent when ripe. It is about 7 mm long and mildly bitter to the taste.

HABITAT AND DISTRIBUTION: In grassland and dry areas along the coast and adjacent tablelands of New South Wales and Queensland.

MEDICINAL USES: It has been used by the Aborigines against venereal diseases.[19]

ACTIVE CONSTITUENTS: Not known.

Phyllanthus virgatus

FAMILY: Euphorbiaceae

SYNONYMS: *Phyllanthus simplex*

DESCRIPTION: A more or less simple-stemmed plant about 30 cm tall, flattened when young, with its leaves arranged in two opposite rows along the stem. Leaves are tapered at both ends and are about 12 mm long. Minute flowers occur in clusters in leaf forks. The fruit is a depressed capsule, smooth and hairless, about 3 mm in diameter.

HABITAT AND DISTRIBUTION: Coastal areas of Queensland and of the Northern Territory.

MEDICINAL USES: Used against gonorrhoea in India: the fresh plant is mixed with equal parts of cumin seed and sugar and a teaspoonful is taken once a day. The fresh plant is bruised, mixed with buttermilk and used as a wash to cure the itch in children.[40]

ACTIVE CONSTITUENTS: Not known.

Piper novae-hollandiae

FAMILY: Piperaceae

VERNACULAR NAMES: 'Native pepper vine', 'climbing pepper', 'native pepper', 'curtain vine', 'Australian pepper vine', 'mao-wararg'.

DESCRIPTION: A tall climber resembling ivy growing over shrubs and trees. Its alternate leaves are broadly ovate (elliptical, broadened near the base and with a pointed apex), 7-10 cm long, with five to seven very noticeable veins. Flower spikes are leaf-opposed, 12-20 mm long. The fruit is a red, stalked, egg-shaped berry.

HABITAT AND DISTRIBUTION: Mainly in coastal rainforest; New South Wales, Queensland and Northern Territory.

MEDICINAL USES: An excellent stimulant and tonic for mucous membranes according to Dr Bancroft, who also used it to treat gonorrhoea and other mucous discharges.[3,19] It has been chewed for sore gums.[13] This may be due to the benumbing effect of one of its components (which may be extracted with ether).[19]

ACTIVE CONSTITUENTS: Not known; may contain alkaloids.[42]

Pittosporum venulosum

FAMILY: Pittosporaceae

DESCRIPTION: A small tree with alternate leaves, 5-10 cm long and 2.5-4 cm broad. Veins are conspicuous and form a dense network. The fruit is a globular capsule, somewhat compressed from the sides and opening into two valves revealing a number of sticky seeds.

HABITAT AND DISTRIBUTION: Tropical coastal Queensland.

MEDICINAL USES: The scent of its bruised oily roots is said by the Aborigines to have aphrodisiac properties.[13]

ACTIVE CONSTITUENTS: The roots contain an essential oil;[13] it is not known whether the oil is responsible for the activity.

Santalum acuminatum *(See colour plate facing page 193)*

FAMILY: Santalaceae

SYNONYMS: *Fusanus acuminatus, Santalum preissianum, Santalum cognatum, Eucarya acuminata.*

VERNACULAR NAMES: 'Sweet quandong', 'native peach', 'kelango', 'gutchu'.

DESCRIPTION: A tall shrub or small tree up to 10 m high. Its leathery, grey-green leaves are opposite, short-stalked, tapered at both ends with a short hooked tip when young; 5–8 cm long but very variable. Flowers occur in bunches at the end of branchlets. The pendulous mature fruit is red, fleshy and about 2.5–3 cm in diameter. Flowers in spring.

HABITAT AND DISTRIBUTION: In sandy soils of the dry interior of Australia.

MEDICINAL USES: Ground seed kernels have been used by the Aborigines as a liniment;[18,25] pounded leaves have been applied to boils, sores, and for gonorrhoea.[59]

ACTIVE CONSTITUENTS: The nuts are rich in a fixed oil.[14] Its leaves have not yet been investigated.

Tylophora erecta

FAMILY: Asclepiadaceae

DESCRIPTION: A perennial plant with simple erect, hairy stems, up to 60 cm high. Its opposite leaves are tapered at both ends, vary between 7 and 15 cm in length and have straight undivided margins. Flowers are wheel-like, deeply divided into five lobes and occur in simple clusters; they are dark purple in colour.

HABITAT AND DISTRIBUTION: Coastal areas of the Gulf of Carpentaria and of northern Queensland.

MEDICINAL USES: Aphrodisiac; the Aborigines have used the sap to prepare a love potion.[20]

ACTIVE CONSTITUENTS: Not known.

Verbena officinalis

FAMILY: Verbenaceae

VERNACULAR NAMES: 'Common verbena', 'common vervain'.

DESCRIPTION: An erect perennial herb with square stems and branchlets; the latter are quite wiry. The plant is between 30 cm and 1.2 m high. Its short-petioled leaves are wedge-shaped to spear-shaped, with undivided leaf margins or deeply lobed. Its small purple, lilac or blue flowers have five spreading, slightly unequal lobes and occur in long and slender spikes on petioles becoming leafy immediately below the spike.

HABITAT AND DISTRIBUTION: Widespread in all states, except Western Australia, and it occurs in a variety of situations. Most likely introduced from Europe but spread very early.

MEDICINAL USES: Used internally for the treatment of fevers and as a healing agent for wounds; externally as a rubefacient in rheumatism and pains in the joints. In Australia, it has been used in the form of a decoction to keep the stomach in good working order and to arrest the early stages of consumption.[56]

The Aborigines of north-western New South Wales have apparently used it to cure venereal diseases.[27]

ACTIVE CONSTITUENTS: The herb contains verbenalin and 5-hydroxyverbenalin,[14] but it is not known whether they exhibit the medicinal activities described.

Coelospermum decipiens (see page 169)

Crinum asiaticum (see page 185)

Trichodesma zeylanicum (see page 179)

Ipomoea brasiliensis (see page 188)

Myoporum debile (see page 189)

Santalum acuminatum (see page 191)

Acacia ixiophylla (see page 197)

Bursaria spinosa (see page 197)

Callitris columellaris (Fruit and leaves) (see page 198)

CHAPTER TEN
The medicinal plant industry

Solanum aviculare

ONE MIGHT HAVE EXPECTED that the wealth of medicinal plants found in Australia would have initiated an active and vigorous extractive and pharmaceutical industry. Unfortunately, this is not so. In all, not more than some thirty plant species have been exploited commercially, and of these about twenty are various species of *Eucalyptus,* yielding very similar medicinal oils rich in 1,8-cineole.

The pharmacist Joseph Bosisto, a Yorkshireman who migrated to Australia in 1848, began the first serious investigation of the volatile oils of Australia's native flora, particularly of the eucalypts, and in 1854 started the first commercial production of eucalyptus oil in Victoria. In this he was greatly assisted by Dr Ferdinand Mueller, a German pharmacist turned botanist who later became Government Botanist of Victoria and received both British and German titles (as well as others) to become no less than Baron Sir Ferdinand von Mueller. It was in fact he who, in 1852, recommended that eucalyptus oil be distilled on a commercial scale.

Bosisto, who had established himself by the sixties of the last century as the first commercial producer of eucalyptus oils in Australia, extracted the oil from the foliage by the process of steam distillation, an ancient art traceable to the alchemists of the Middle Ages. In brief, the leaves are placed in a vessel fitted with a lid and an outlet pipe connected to a water cooled condenser. After the addition of a certain amount of water, the leaves are boiled and the steam, enriched with oil vapour, is passed through the water cooled condenser. There, the steam and essential oil vapours are again reliquefied. Since the oil and water are immiscible, the lighter-than-water oil may be skimmed off the surface of the condensed water. This method at its simplest is still being carried out with considerable success by a number of small distillers in our country areas, particularly around Braidwood, Tumut, Cooma and Casino in New South Wales and around Bendigo in Victoria. A refinement introduced by some of the larger distillers is to pass live steam, generated in a separate boiler, through the charge of leaves.

Bosisto produced mainly medicinal oils, that is, oils rich in a compound called 1,8-cineole (sometimes also called eucalyptol), which gives the oils their characteristic 'eucalypty' odour. There are some twenty or so species of *Eucalyptus* used for the production of this type of oil. The species most commonly used are the 'blue mallee' *(Eucalyptus polybractea),* the cineole variety of the 'broad leaf peppermint' (*E. dives* var. C), *E. leucoxylon, E. sideroxylon, E. oleosa, E. radiata* var. australiana (this last named species yields a particularly fine oil) and several others. Even though Australia is the home of eucalypts, our medicinal oil production is barely 5 per cent of the world production of about two thousand tonnes per annum. Portugal and Spain account for well over 60 per cent of the world production. They derive the oil from the foliage of the 'Tasmanian blue gum' *(E. globulus)* introduced into Europe during the last century and grown mainly for the timber used as mine props and more recently for paper pulp production. Apart from the oil being used as such in various pharmaceutical preparations it serves as the raw material for the manufacture of pure 1,8-cineole, which is used phamaceutically in the preparation of liniments, inhalants, cough syrups, and even flavourings.

It is ironical that the oil of another Australian eucalypt, *E. dives* 'type' (the piperitone-rich form of the 'broad leaf peppermint') is produced in Australia (mainly around Braidwood and Cooma in New South Wales) in such small amounts that the greater part of our requirement has to be imported from Swaziland in South Africa. As mentioned before, the main component of this oil is the monoterpenoid ketone piperitone, a compound with a rather pronounced pepperminty odour. The reader is reminded that Surgeon Considen claimed to have produced the first-ever sample of eucalyptus oil in 1788 from the 'Sydney peppermint' *(E. piperita)*, which is also rich in piperitone.

Piperitone-rich oils are not used these days as such medicinally but serve as a source of *l*-piperitone, which is chemically transformed to *l*-menthol, a white crystalline solid with the clean, fresh odour of true peppermint. Menthol is used in gargles, mouth washes, liniments (often together with 1,8-cineole), as well as in flavourings. The chemical process involved in changing piperitone into menthol is called a hydrogenation and involves the addition of four atoms of hydrogen to each molecule of piperitone. This process was pioneered before the Second World War at the Museum of Applied Arts and Sciences in Sydney, an institution involved since 1897 in essential oil reseach and enjoying a world wide reputation in this field. It is sad that this long-standing tradition came to an end in 1979 when the essential oil research was transferred in a somewhat reduced format to another New South Wales government department.

Another medicinal essential oil produced to this day on a commercial scale is that of the 'medicinal tea-tree' *(Melaleuca alternifolia)*. It is produced by a number of small distillers centred around Casino and Lismore in north-eastern New South Wales by the same process of steam distillation mentioned in connection with eucalyptus oil production. The total quantity of oil produced is of the order of five tonnes a year. Apart from its bactericidal applications, the oil is used in the flavouring industry.

The only other medicinal oil produced once in quantity is the West Australian sandalwood oil *(Santalum spicatum)*. Owing to the slow regrowth of this parasitic plant, oil production has ceased and it is quite unlikely that it will ever restart on any commercial scale.

Non-volatile natural products that were once produced on a reasonably large scale include the phenolic pigment rutin and the coumarin esculin. Both rutin and esculin are soluble in boiling water and may thus be extracted by boiling the finely ground plant material in water, followed by filtration of the boiling decoction in order to remove the extracted plant material and finally cooling of the clear filtrate. Rutin and esculin are almost insoluble in cold water and will thus separate in the form of a powdery solid. Rutin used to be produced particularly around Taree in New South Wales and also in Victoria from the leaves of *Eucalyptus macrorhyncha* and *Eucalyptus youmanii*. At present there is very little, if any production. Esculin occurs in the leaves of the common native but often noxious weed 'blackthorn' *(Bursaria spinosa)*. It is common in all of south-eastern and eastern Australia. It was once produced on a modest scale at Taree.

The leaves of 'corkwood' *(Duboisia myoporoides)* contain a large proportion of the alkaloid hyoscine (also known as scopolamine), which is used in the treatment of stomach ulcers and sea sickness. The production of corkwood foliage on the north coast of New South Wales has been for quite some time a steady if not very large industry. The collected leaves are carefully dried out of direct sunlight and sold overseas to pharmaceutical firms engaged in the extraction of its alkaloidal constituents. The related *Duboisia leichhardtii* growing in Queensland is utilized in a similar way. There is as yet no scopolamine produced on a commercial scale in Australia, even though there are indications that this may change in the near future.

Finally, the pale yellow resinous exudate from the cut trunks of the 'white' and 'black' cypress pines (*Callitris columellaris* and *C. endlicheri* respectively) is sold overseas under the name of Australian sandarac. It appears that this resin has been used for the coating of pills which are to dissolve in the intestine and not in the stomach. The collection of this resin is a real cottage industry. It involves visiting those parts of our cypress pine forests which have been logged say a year and a half beforehand. In that time enough resin has collected on the stumps to allow it to be gathered in worthwhile quantities. The fresh air inhaled by the collector during this activity is undoubtedly a special medicinal bonus.

There are quite a few potentially useful plants which await commercial exploitation some time in the future. Dr Len Webb's article 'Alkaloidal Potentialities of the Australian Flora' published as early as 1953 contains numerous references to plants containing physiologically active alkaloids.[119] For instance, *Cryptocarya pleurosperma,* the so-called 'poison walnut', contains cryptopleurine, an exceedingly toxic substance in its bark and sapwood that causes severe blistering and headaches and makes handling of the plant a very hazardous undertaking indeed. However, in minute concentrations cryptopleurine stimulates nerve regeneration. From the 'propeller tree' *(Gyrocarpus americanus)* comes d-magnocurarine, which is a ganglionic blocking agent that may have uses in the treatment of certain heart diseases. The crude alkaloids of the 'tape vine' *(Stephania hernandiifolia)* inhibit the growth of certain micro-organisms such as *Mycobacterium phlei* and *Staphylococcus aureus.* Several species of *Solanum* contain steroidal alkaloids such as solasodine, which may be chemically converted to the medicinally valuable drug cortisone as well as to other steroidal drugs. *Strychnos lucida* of northern Queensland, rich in the alkaloid brucine, and the so-called 'rough eriostemon' *(Eriostemon trachyphyllus)* rich in the skin-sensitizing coumarin bergapten, which has been used in various skin conditions requiring repigmentation, are further examples of possibly useful plants.

One may well ask whether there are really any prospects for an increased growth of the medicinal plant industry. Difficult as an answer to such a question may be, one can nevertheless put forward at least two reasons for the affirmative case. Firstly, synthetic organic chemicals, including of course medicinal compounds, may be contaminated with toxic by-products of their synthesis and with residues of any catalysts employed. Synthetic anethole, for example, often contains very noticeable amounts of the toxic *cis*-anethole whereas natural *trans*-anethole, from aniseed oil or fennel seed oil, contains none. Secondly, synthetic organic chemicals are almost always dependent on the petroleum industry. Since this natural resource is becoming increasingly scarce it would be only logical to resort to a greater use of plants, a source which is renewable and thus unlimited.

Acacia ixiophylla (See colour plate facing page 193)

FAMILY: Mimosaceae

DESCRIPTION: A sticky, bushy, dark green shrub up to 2.5 m high. The leaf-like phyllodes are oblong, tapered at both ends, often with a recurved point, 2–5 cm long and 4–8 mm wide and striated with veins. Flowers occur in small dark yellow globular heads. The pod is twisted and wavy.

HABITAT AND DISTRIBUTION: It usually occurs as an under-storey in eucalypt woodland or mallee scrub, often on hillsides and rocky ridges. It is often associated with *Callitris columellaris* ('white cypress pine') and *Casuarina luehmannii* ('bull oak'). Occurs in southern Queensland as far north as Jericho and Alpha, central and northern New South Wales, and south-western Western Australia.

MEDICINAL USES: None as such.

ACTIVE CONSTITUENTS: The lower polymeric tannins from the phyllodes and twigs show antitumour activity[120] and should thus be investigated for possible uses.

Bauerella simplicifolia

FAMILY: Rutaceae

SYNONYMS: *Acronychia simplicifolia, Acronychia baueri.*

VERNACULAR NAMES: 'Scrub ash'

DESCRIPTION: A tall shrub or small tree, up to 20 m high with a finely fissured, grey and corky bark. The inner bark is bright yellow. Its glossy opposite leaves are quite hairless, elliptical, and broadened near the tip, 7–13 cm long. Small, finely hairy flowers occur on short petioles in leaf forks, either singly or in narrow groups up to 3 cm long. The fruit is somewhat 4-angled, globular or egg-shaped, hard, and about 1.5 cm long. The inner bark turns red on application of a few drops of concentrated hydrochloric acid.

HABITAT AND DISTRIBUTION: Usually in or near drier rainforests, from central coastal New South Wales to northern Queensland.

MEDICINAL USES: None as such.

ACTIVE CONSTITUENTS: Contains a number of alkaloids, one of which, acronycine, shows activity against certain tumours.[35]

Bursaria spinosa (See colour plate facing page 193)

FAMILY: Pittosporaceae

VERNACULAR NAMES: 'Blackthorn', 'native box', 'box thorn', 'native olive', 'sweet bursaria', 'kurwan', 'geapga'.

DESCRIPTION: A rigid much branched shrub or small tree, often with thorny branches. Leaves are alternate, oblong, tapered at both ends with a rounded tip, or even triangular, often notched, or appear as if cut off at the tip, but always narrowed at the base, 10–25 mm long. Flowers are numerous and occur in pyramidal clusters at the end of branchlets. They are creamy white in colour and pleasantly scented. The fruit is a compressed rusty-brown capsule. Flowers in summer.

HABITAT AND DISTRIBUTION: Widespread, in forests, along roads and in pastures as a weed. All states but not in arid areas.

MEDICINAL USES: None as such.

ACTIVE CONSTITUENTS: Its leaves contain the coumarin aesculin which has been used in the treatment of lupus (an ulcerous condition of the skin) by irradiation (used subcutaneously). Aesculin has also been used as an ultraviolet radiation screen in suntan lotions.[19,36]

Callitris columellaris *(See colour plate facing page 193)*

FAMILY: Cupressaceae

SYNONYMS: *Callitris glauca* and many others. *Callitris hugelii* has been used for it, almost certainly incorrectly.

VERNACULAR NAMES: 'White cypress pine', 'white pine', 'coorung-coorung', 'pooragri', 'coolooli'.

DESCRIPTION: A medium to large tree, 10–30 m high. It is evergreen, with a dark grey, rough and furrowed bark, but less so than in *Callitris endlicheri*. Its foliage often shows a dull bluish white lustre and is responsible for the generally lighter appearance of the tree (compared with *Callitris endlicheri*). Its tiny scale-like leaves grow in groups of three to four along the branchlets. Fruiting cones are dark brown and globular, about 2 cm in diameter, with hard and woody scales.

It may be distinguished from *Callitris endlicheri* by its more spreading branches, imparting to the tree a distinctly less pyramidal appearance (except in very young trees).

HABITAT AND DISTRIBUTION: On light soils sometimes near the coast but more often in the drier inland; all mainland states.

MEDICINAL USES: None as such; the resinous exudate often found on stumps or on cut logs ('Australian sandarac') is used by the pharmaceutical industry for the coating of pills.

ACTIVE CONSTITUENTS: The resinous exudate is composed of a number of diterpenoid acids.

NOTE: The species as treated here includes three geographic races, which might well be regarded as distinct species, but the correct name for the most common of these (the inland 'white pine') has yet to be finally determined.

Callitris endlicheri

FAMILY: Cupressaceae

SYNONYMS: *Callitris calcarata, Frenela calcarata, Frenela endlicheri* and many others.

VERNACULAR NAMES: 'Black cypress pine', 'black pine', 'red pine', 'scrub pine', 'Murray pine'.

DESCRIPTION: A tree of characteristically pyramidal appearance, evergreen and up to 13 m high. Its bark is hard and dark, deeply furrowed. Leaves, 2–4 mm long, occur in groups of three or four around the branchlets. Mature female fruiting cones are almost globular, about 2 cm in diameter, the scales hard and woody, with hard, compressed and winged seeds. The crushed leaves have a faint lemony-rosy odour. The overall impression is that of a much darker tree than *Callitris columellaris*. For distinguishing features see the entry for that species.

HABITAT AND DISTRIBUTION: Prefers rocky ridges and rising stony ground along the Great Dividing Range and its western slopes. Occurs in north-western Victoria and continues through New South Wales into south-eastern Queensland.

MEDICINAL USES: As an anthelmintic for horses: twigs are used with fodder to expel worms.[3] The pale yellow resin that exudes from cut logs and stumps is used by the pharmaceutical industry for the coating of pills. It is known under the name 'Australian sandarac'.

ACTIVE CONSTITUENTS: The resinous exudate is composed of a number of diterpenoid acids. The leaves contain an essential oil rich in geranyl acetate.[58]

Casuarina decaisneana

FAMILY: Casuarinaceae

VERNACULAR NAMES: 'Desert oak'

DESCRIPTION: The juvenile form of this tree is conical and tapering, sparsely foliaged, rather tall and slender. Its mature form is up to 12 m high, altogether denser and much more spreading. It has a characteristic 'weeping willow' habit. The foliage is reduced to mere ribs on stems. These are dull green. Its straight trunk is dark brown to brown-black and deeply furrowed. The cones are the largest of the genus, being 5 cm long and 4 cm broad.

HABITAT AND DISTRIBUTION: Prefers deep sand; arid inland and sandhill country of Western Australia, Northern Territory and the far north of South Australia.

MEDICINAL USES: None as such; exhibits a moderate inhibition in the growth of *Staphylococcus aureus*.[19]

ACTIVE CONSTITUENTS: Not known; may contain bacteriostatic compounds.

Duboisia leichhardtii

FAMILY: Solanaceae

VERNACULAR NAMES: 'Corkwood'

DESCRIPTION: A small tree with a pale brown to grey, fissured bark, similar in appearance to *Duboisia myoporoides*. The bark is bitter to the taste. Leaves are alternate, narrowly elliptical and tapered at both ends, 4–10 cm long and 1–2 cm wide. Flowers are in open bunches at the end of branchlets. They are mostly white but may be tinged with mauve. The corolla is bell-shaped with five petal-like lobes. The fruit is a black oval berry, about 6 mm long, containing a few granular kidney-shaped seeds. It flowers from late winter to early spring.

It may be distinguished from *Duboisia myoporoides* by its narrower leaves tapering from the centre and by its slightly larger flowers.

HABITAT AND DISTRIBUTION: In fertile loamy soils, often in open softwood scrub in southern central Queensland and in the Far Western Plains district of New South Wales, never near the coast.

MEDICINAL USES: None as such; source of pharmaceutically used alkaloids.

ACTIVE CONSTITUENTS: Leaves contain up to 5 per cent of a very variable mixture of alkaloids which includes hyoscyamine (10 to 80 per cent), scopolamine (6 to 46 per cent), norhyoscyamine (3 to 42 per cent), tigloidine, apoatropine, aposcopolamine, isobutyroyl tropine.[14,121] The two first named compounds are used in pharmacy.

NOTE: Unlike in *Duboisia myoporoides*, chemical races do not occur.

Duboisia myoporoides (See colour plate facing page 208)

FAMILY: Solanaceae

VERNACULAR NAMES: 'Corkwood' and sometimes 'cork tree'; the former has also been applied to *Duboisia leichhardtii* and to other species with a corky bark, for example, *Erythrina* and *Hakea*. Aboriginal names include 'ngmoo', 'onungunabie' or 'orungurabie'.

DESCRIPTION: A tall shrub or small tree; its bark is yellowish brown to pale grey, fissured, corky and bitter to the taste. Its leaves are alternate, pale green, smooth and hairless, soft in texture, about 3–10 cm long and 1–2.5 cm wide and tapered towards both ends. Flowers occur in open bunches at the end of branches. After flowering in spring the plant produces small juicy, black, almost globular berries, each containing a few granular, kidney-shaped seeds.

HABITAT AND DISTRIBUTION: It grows mainly in areas of high rainfall, preferring sandy and loamy soils on the edges of rainforests, in rainforest clearings and on stabilized dunes behind shore lines. It extends from Sydney (Illawarra Range, Kurrajong district) along the coast and tablelands of northern New South Wales to the Cape York Peninsula in northern Queensland. It also occurs in New Guinea and in New Caledonia.

MEDICINAL USES: The Reverend Dr W. Woolls has reported its use by the Aborigines as a narcotic. Holes were made in the trunk of the tree and filled with fluid (water) which, when drunk the following day, produced stupor. Some people experience giddiness and nausea when staying in a closed room containing branches of the species.[3,10]

Dr Joseph Bancroft found leaf extracts useful in ophthalmic surgery, mainly in connection with its pupil-dilating properties.[10]

At present, the dried leaves are used as a source of scopolamine (hyoscine), a drug useful in the prevention of air- and sea-sickness[122] and in the treatment of stomach ulcers.

ACTIVE CONSTITUENTS: Apart from scopolamine, the leaves contain a variety of other alkaloids, some of which may become dominant in certain areas. So for instance, hyoscyamine and norhyoscyamine replace scopolamine as the climate becomes cooler (e.g. Sydney district) and some of the highest scopolamine contents are found on the north coast of New South Wales in the Lismore–Grafton area. An exception is the high anabasine content of plants growing on the Acacia Plateau near Killarney in south-eastern Queensland. In New Guinea nicotine is the chief alkaloid of the leaves.[14]

Eriostemon trachyphyllus

FAMILY: Rutaceae

VERNACULAR NAMES: 'Rough eriostemon'

DESCRIPTION: A shrub or small tree, 2–7 m high, with characteristic warty, green, and hairless branchlets. Its stalkless alternate leaves are oblong-elliptic to elliptic, sometimes slightly broadened near the tip, flat with slightly recurved margins, pointed or rounded at the tip and 3–10 cm long. Small white flowers occur either singly or in groups of three in leaf forks; petals are 5-9 mm long. The fruit is a somewhat spherical capsule, 5 mm in diameter and containing a small black seed. Crushed leaves are very aromatic; also, the leaves are dotted with oil glands. Flowers in spring and early summer.

HABITAT AND DISTRIBUTION: Prefers moist and dark gullies; mainly in southern coastal New South Wales and south-eastern Victoria.

MEDICINAL USES: None as such.

ACTIVE CONSTITUENTS: Leaves contain up to 1 per cent of the coumarin bergapten.[123] Bergapten is a skin sensitizer and has been used in cases of insufficient skin pigmentation such as leucoderma.[49] It may cause **serious blistering of the skin.**

Eucalyptus citriodora

FAMILY: Myrtaceae

VERNACULAR NAMES: 'Lemon-scented gum', 'lemon-scented spotted gum', 'citron-scented gum tree', 'boabo'.

DESCRIPTION: A straight, moderately tall tree with a smooth and deciduous bark, greyish in colour. Its juvenile leaves are opposite, fairly broad, tapered at both ends and rough to the touch. Mature leaves are alternate, smooth, fairly narrow and tapered at both ends, 10-16 cm long and 1-2 cm broad; strongly lemon-scented when crushed. Flower clusters at the end of branchlets; fruits are urn-shaped contracted into a short, thick neck. Flowers in winter.

HABITAT AND DISTRIBUTION: Coastal regions of Queensland

MEDICINAL USES: None as such.

ACTIVE CONSTITUENTS: The essential oil contained in the leaves appears to have bacteriostatic activity towards *Staphylococcus aureus;* this is due to synergism between citronellol and citronellal present in the oil.[124] The kino contains the antibiotic substance citriodorol.[16]

Eucalyptus dives

FAMILY: Myrtaceae

VERNACULAR NAMES: 'Broadleaf peppermint'

DESCRIPTION: A medium-sized tree with a short trunk and spreading branches. Its bark is rough and fibrous but not stringy, persistent on the trunk and main branches. Juvenile leaves are opposite, stem-clasping, broad, heart-shaped, thick and leathery, with a pronouced bluish colour. Mature leaves are alternate, 10-15 cm long and 2-5 cm broad, thick and tapered at both ends. Crushed leaves are very aromatic. Blossoms in 7- to 15-flowered bunches in leaf forks; petioles are flattened or angular. Flowers in spring.

HABITAT AND DISTRIBUTION: At higher elevations; northern Victoria, southern coastal New South Wales and adjacent tablelands and as far north as Niangala near Walcha.

MEDICINAL USES: The Aborigines smoked people with burning leaves for the relief of fever: 'heat went out of sick man and went into the fire'.[20]

The leaf oils are used medicinally.

ACTIVE CONSTITUENTS: This species exists in several chemical forms yielding different essential oils on steam distillation.[39] The cineole-rich strain yields medicinal eucalyptus oil (used in the same way as *Eucalyptus globulus* subspecies *globulus* oil); the piperitone-rich strain is used in the manufacture of menthol (used in liniments and mouth washes) and thymol (a fungicide). The piperitone-rich oil is very similar to the piperitone variety of *Eucalyptus piperita* as far as oil composition is concerned.

Eucalyptus globulus subspecies *globulus*

FAMILY: Myrtaceae

VERNACULAR NAMES: 'Tasmanian blue gum', 'blue gum'.

DESCRIPTION: A medium-sized to large tree with a smooth, bluish and deciduous bark. Its bluish white, powdery looking juvenile leaves are opposite, heart- to egg-shaped, broad and quite large, 7-16 cm by 4-9 cm. Mature leaves are alternate, dark glossy green, tapered at both ends, somewhat sickle-shaped and quite pointed, 10-30 cm long and 3-4 cm wide. Buds are single in leaf forks; they are top-shaped quadrangular, up to 20-30 mm in size. Fruits are stalkless, broadly top-shaped, 4-ribbed, often covered with a powdery coating of wax, 10-15 mm by 15-30 mm. Crushed foliage is very aromatic.

HABITAT AND DISTRIBUTION: Loamy soils near the sea in Tasmania; also in southern-most Victoria.

MEDICINAL USES: None as such; source of medicinal eucalyptus oil. It is cultivated for this purpose in Portugal, Spain and China.

ACTIVE CONSTITUENTS: The leaf oil is rich in 1,8-cineole and is extensively used in the manufacture of cough medicines, liniments and the like for the relief of colds, muscular pain, rheumatism, and similar complaints.[49] A drop of oil put into hot water will facilitate breathing when the steam is inhaled.

NOTE: *Eucalyptus globulus* subsp. *bicostata* and *Eucalyptus globulus* subsp. *pseudoglobulus* (synonym: *E. st johnii*) give very similar volatile leaf oils on steam distillation and are used for the same purposes.

Other species distilled for their medicinally used oil include *Eucalyptus leucoxylon*, *E. sideroxylon* and the cineole form of *E. radiata* subsp. *radiata* often referred to by the trade as 'Eucalyptus australiana'. *Eucalyptus oleosa* and *E. kochii* have also been occasionally distilled.

Eucalyptus macrorhyncha subspecies *macrorhyncha*

FAMILY: Myrtaceae *(See colour plate facing page 209)*

VERNACULAR NAMES: 'Red stringybark', 'mountain stringybark' in Gippsland.

DESCRIPTION: A tall, up to 25 m high tree, with usually a straight trunk. Its bark is dense and fibrous, often blackish on the outside, and covers the entire trunk. Its juvenile leaves are elliptical with wavy and irregularly toothed margins. Mature leaves are alternate, tapered at both ends, 7-12 cm long and 1.5-2 cm wide, rather leathery and equally green on both sides. Twigs and stalks are angular. The hemi-spherical to globular fruit (7-10 mm by 10-12 mm) is characterized by long stalks, a prominent edge of the rim, a domed top and projecting valves. During flowering in summer nectar may often be seen dripping from the blossoms.

HABITAT AND DISTRIBUTION: Prefers granite and the poorer white, acid soils. Extends from South Australia (rare) to Victoria (Gippsland, Healesville, Dandenong Ranges) and to northern New South Wales (western slopes, Great Dividing Range).

MEDICINAL USES: Kino is astringent;[99] leaves not as such but as a source of rutin.

ACTIVE CONSTITUENTS: Leaves contain between 6 and 24 per cent of the drug rutin.[125] Rutin has the ability to strengthen the walls of small blood vessels and capillaries and is thus useful for the prevention of nose bleeding during headcolds.[49] It is often used in combination with vitamin C.

Eucalyptus polybractea *(See colour plate facing page 209)*

FAMILY: Myrtaceae

SYNONYMS: The name *Eucalyptus fruticetorum* has been wrongly but commonly applied to this species.

VERNACULAR NAMES: 'Blue mallee'

DESCRIPTION: Generally a small mallee (multi-stemmed shrub growing from a ligno-tuber), up to 8 m high, with 4-angled branchlets. Juvenile leaves are opposite, whereas mature leaves are alternate, tapered at both ends and usually quite narrow, 5–10 cm long and 0.8–1.3 cm wide, dull green with a pronounced bluish grey lustre. Blossoms occur in 8- to 12-flowered clusters in leaf forks. The short-stalked fruits are hemispherical to pear-shaped, 4–5 mm in diameter. Flowers from March to June; sometimes in September.

The crushed leaves exude a powerful camphoraceous ('eucalyptus-like') aroma.

HABITAT AND DISTRIBUTION: Prefers poor clayey–sandy soils of the semi-arid interior. Common around West Wyalong in New South Wales and Bendigo in Victoria.

MEDICINAL USES: None as such; leaves are a source of medicinal eucalyptus oil used, for example, for the relief of headcolds, rheumatism, muscular pain (in the form of liniments), and as expectorant in cases of bronchitis (added to cough syrups).[110]

ACTIVE CONSTITUENTS: 1,8-cineole present in the steam distilled oil (70 to 90 per cent of oil).[110]

Eucalyptus smithii

FAMILY: Myrtaceae

VERNACULAR NAMES: 'Gully gum', 'gully ash', 'white top', 'white ironbark', 'blackbutt peppermint'; also 'Smith's gum' after H.G. Smith, Australia's foremost pioneer of essential oil and natural product chemistry; 'Jimmy Green' is probably a corruption of 'jerrigree' used by the Aborigines of the Bungendore district.

DESCRIPTION: A medium-sized to large tree, up to 45 m high and 1.5 m in diameter. Its dark grey to blackish bark is rough and deeply furrowed (particularly in old trees) and is intermediate between stringybark and ironbark. It covers the lower portion of the tree, the upper trunk and branches being smooth. The distinctive appearance of the bark as well as its peculiarly strong pleasant odour help differentiate it from the similar *E. viminalis*. Its juvenile leaves are opposite, stem-clasping, narrow and tapered at both ends and exhibit a dull bluish haze. Adult leaves are alternate, dark green, narrow and tapered at both ends, 10–16 cm long and 1–1.7 cm wide, exhibiting numerous oil glands. The tree flowers in summer. The fruit is hemispherical to conical, long-stalked and about 6 mm in diameter.

HABITAT AND DISTRIBUTION: Prefers deep soils in gullies and alluvial flats; also on volcanic hills.

MEDICINAL USES: None as such; steam distillation of the foliage yields a medicinal oil similar to *Eucalyptus globulus* subsp. *globulus* oil (see that species).

ACTIVE CONSTITUENTS: 1,8-cineole, the main component of the oil.

Eucalyptus youmanii

FAMILY: Myrtaceae

VERNACULAR NAMES: 'Youman's stringybark'

DESCRIPTION: A sturdy stringybark, 7–15 m high, invariably spreading in habit. The strongly fibrous reddish brown bark is thick and markedly furrowed. Its juvenile leaves are opposite for three to four pairs, thick, slightly hairy, oblong-ovate to tapered at both ends with a blunt or rounded apex, about 3–6 cm long and 2–5 cm wide. Adult leaves are alternate, tapered at both ends, thick, dark green and glossy (duller in more western forms), and 8–14 cm long and 2–3 cm wide. Buds and fruits are stalkless, the fruits being somewhat spherical to top-shaped, 10–12 mm by 12–15 mm. Flowers in winter.

HABITAT AND DISTRIBUTION: Prefers white, acid soils and damp spots. It is found only rarely on red, basaltic soils. Throughout the New England district of New South Wales as far north as Stanthorpe in southern Queensland.

MEDICINAL USES: None as such.

ACTIVE CONSTITUENTS: Leaves contain 7 to 11 per cent rutin used pharmaceutically (see *Eucalyptus macrorhyncha* subsp. *macrorhyncha*).[125]

Melaleuca linariifolia

FAMILY: Myrtaceae

SYNONYMS: *Metrosideros hyssopifolia*

DESCRIPTION: A shrub to small tree, rarely up to 18 m high, with slender branches and hairy young shoots; its bark is papery. Its mostly opposite leaves are quite narrow, often keeled, 12–35 mm long and up to 3 mm wide. Creamy white flowers occur in dense spikes, 3–5 cm long, around the end of stems which grow later into leafy branches. Woody fruit capsules are about 3 mm in diameter and occur in dense elongated clusters around branchlets. Flowers in spring and summer. Crushed leaves are quite aromatic.

HABITAT AND DISTRIBUTION: Wet and swampy places near the coast and coastal plateaux, often on shales; New South Wales and southern Queensland.

MEDICINAL USES: None as such; the terpinen-4-ol rich variety may be used for the production of a bactericidal oil similar in usefulness to that of *Melaleuca alternifolia*. The more common cineole-rich variety could be used in the same way as *Melaleuca symphyocarpa* for the relief of headache.[58]

ACTIVE CONSTITUENTS: Terpinen-4-ol in the essential oil of one chemical form and 1,8-cineole in the oil of the other chemical form of the species.[39]

Nicotiana debneyi

FAMILY: Solanaceae

SYNONYMS: Some references to *Nicotiana suaveolens* var. *parviflora* may apply to *N. debneyi*; once included under *Nicotiana suaveolens*.

DESCRIPTION: A green erect herb or a tall straggling shrub with branched stems. Leaves are alternate, soft, dull green, large and broad, tapered at both ends, long-petioled near the base and stem-clasping near the top of branches. Flowering stems are covered with sticky hairs. Flowers are whitish, tubular, in branched bunches at the end of branchlets. The most distinctive feature of this plant are the stamens affixed in the lower half of the corolla.

HABITAT AND DISTRIBUTION: On deep alluvial soils in softwood scrub near the coast; extends from Sydney in New South Wales to northern New South Wales and Queensland.

MEDICINAL USES: None as such; possible source of alkaloids.

ACTIVE CONSTITUENTS: Contains about 0.4 per cent of anabasine.[21]

Nicotiana megalosiphon

FAMILY: Solanaceae

SYNONYMS: Once included with *Nicotiana suaveolens*.

DESCRIPTION: A herbaceous plant with a rosette of thin and broad leaves at the base of slender, upright and branched stems. Flowers are white with a long slender tube, 4–7 cm long, and a 5-lobed tip emerging from a conspicuously narrow-lobed green calyx. The fruit is a capsule.

HABITAT AND DISTRIBUTION: On clayey soils in open forest and mulga scrub. Abundant in northern New South Wales and Queensland and extending into Central Australia.

MEDICINAL USES: None as such; possibly a source of alkaloids.

ACTIVE CONSTITUENTS: Contains about 0.22 per cent nornicotine; no other alkaloids are present.[21]

Ochrosia moorei

FAMILY: Apocynaceae

DESCRIPTION: A hairless slender tree with narrow-bladed, opposite leaves, tapered at both ends and terminating in a long blunt point; leaves are 7–15 cm long. Bark exudes a milky juice when cut. Flowers are pale yellow. The fruit is a scarlet berry, 4–7 cm long and 2.5 cm broad. The fruit's flatter appearance distinguishes it from *Ochrosia elliptica*. The bark is intensely bitter.

HABITAT AND DISTRIBUTION: Coastal rainforests of far northern New South Wales and southern Queensland.

MEDICINAL USES: The intensely bitter timber and bark are reputed to be pharmacologically active,[19] but their particular activity has not been stated. Could become the source of tumour inhibitory alkaloids.[126]

ACTIVE CONSTITUENTS: The bark contains triterpenes[43] and alkaloids;[31] two of the latter, ellipticine and 9-methoxyellipticine exhibit tumour inhibitory properties.[126]

Solanum aviculare

FAMILY: Solanaceae

VERNACULAR NAMES: 'Kangaroo apple', 'weakich'.

DESCRIPTION: A tall perennial and hairless shrub, up to 2 m tall. Its alternate leaves are dark green, 10–30 cm long on purplish or green stems up to 3 cm long. Leaves on young plants or lower leaves on larger plants are very deeply divided into narrow segments, each segment or lobe is tapered to a point. Upper leaves may be irregularly lobed or not divided at all. Flowers are blue, violet, or purple and occur in open bunches in leaf forks on smooth stalks. The corolla is up to 3.5 cm in diameter with petals fused so as to resemble a wheel; the corolla lobes are sharply pointed. The fruit is a smooth egg-shaped, orange-red to yellow berry, about

2.5 cm long and containing numerous seeds in a soft pulp. The fruiting period is in late autumn.

HABITAT AND DISTRIBUTION: Widespread in wet sclerophyll forest and near rainforest margins of eastern New South Wales, Victoria and South Australia; also in southern Queensland.

MEDICINAL USES: None as such.

ACTIVE CONSTITUENTS: Berries are a source of the steroidal alkaloid solasodine,[127] the starting material for the synthesis of steroidal hormones. Unripe berries have the highest solasodine content.

Solanum capsiciforme

FAMILY: Solanaceae

VERNACULAR NAMES: 'Native pepper'

DESCRIPTION: Belongs to the *Solanum aviculare* group. Its adult leaves are narrow with their margins bent downwards. Lobes, if present, are more shallow and blunt. Flowers are pale violet, 2.5 cm in diameter with blunt and slightly notched lobes. Fruits are conical, pointed at the top, resembling a small capsicum. They are green when ripe, never red, and up to 2.5 cm long.

HABITAT AND DISTRIBUTION: Also prefers more arid environments than *Solanum aviculare*. It is found mainly in South Australia and Western Australia.

MEDICINAL USES: None as such.

ACTIVE CONSTITUENTS: Potential source of solasodine.[127]

Solanum laciniatum

FAMILY: Solanaceae

VERNACULAR NAMES: 'Kangaroo apple'

DESCRIPTION: Very similar to *Solanum aviculare* except for the following: leaf stems are always purplish; corolla tube is larger, up to 5 cm in diameter with rounded lobes, notched at the tip; the fruits are slightly larger, that is longer than 2.5 cm, and usually slightly paler; seeds are also slightly larger, about 2 mm in diameter. Flowers from summer to autumn.

HABITAT AND DISTRIBUTION: Widespread; extends from Western Australia to South Australia, Victoria, Tasmania and New South Wales, mainly along rainforest margins or in other moist sheltered sites.

MEDICINAL PROPERTIES: None as such.

ACTIVE CONSTITUENTS: Unripe berries are a source of solasodine for the pharmaceutical industry.[127]

Solanum linearifolium *(See colour plate facing page 209)*

FAMILY: Solanaceae

VERNACULAR NAMES: 'Mountain kangaroo apple'

DESCRIPTION: A shrub with alternate, narrow and tapered leaves, up to 10 cm long and less than 1 cm wide. Purple bell-shaped flowers occur in leaf forks. Fruits are yellow to brown, shiny, globular and up to 2 cm in diameter; seeds are straw coloured and are marked with close parallel longitudinal lines. Flowers in summer.

HABITAT AND DISTRIBUTION: Mountainous areas of Victoria and New South Wales (including Australian Capital Territory).

MEDICINAL USES: None as such.

ACTIVE CONSTITUENTS: Potential source of the steroidal alkaloid solasodine.[127]

Solanum simile

FAMILY: Solanaceae

DESCRIPTION: The species also belongs to the *Solanum aviculare* group. Its dark green and narrow leaves have straight margins and its violet flowers are relatively small, only 1–2.5 cm in diameter. The fruit is a round berry about 1 cm across, green to ivory and even purple in colour when ripe.

HABITAT AND DISTRIBUTION: Prefers a more arid environment than others of the group. Extends from western New South Wales through north-western Victoria and South Australia to the coastal sands of Western Australia.

MEDICINAL USES: None as such.

ACTIVE CONSTITUENTS: A source of solasodine for the manufacture of steroidal drugs.[127]

Solanum symonii

FAMILY: Solanaceae

SYNONYMS: Has been referred to *Solanum fasciculatum*.

DESCRIPTION: Belongs to the *Solanum aviculare* group. Its leaf margins are rolled downwards; its flowers are 2.5–4 cm in diameter with rounded and very slightly notched petal lobes. Fruits are egg-shaped, less than 2.5 cm long, green to ivory coloured when ripe; rarely purplish black.

HABITAT AND DISTRIBUTION: Prefers more arid conditions. Extends from Kangaroo Island in South Australia to the Fremantle area in Western Australia.

MEDICINAL USES: None as such.

ACTIVE CONSTITUENTS: A potential commerical source of solasodine.[127]

Solanum vescum (See colour plate facing page 209)

FAMILY: Solanaceae

DESCRIPTION: A tall perennial shrub similar to *Solanum aviculare* in general appearance. It differs by having stalkless leaves; also, the corolla has wavy margins, scarcely lobed at all and is paler in colour than either *S. aviculare* or *S. laciniatum*. The fruit is egg-shaped to globular, greenish or purple, sometimes ivory coloured and 3–4 cm in diameter.

HABITAT AND DISTRIBUTION: Mainly in open forest from south-eastern Queensland through New South Wales to Victoria, Tasmania and the Bass Strait islands; it is a coastal species.

MEDICINAL USES: None as such.

ACTIVE CONSTITUENTS: Potential source of solasodine.[127]

Strychnos lucida

FAMILY: Loganiaceae

VERNACULAR NAMES: 'Strychnine bush'

DESCRIPTION: A straggling shrub to small tree up to 4.5 m high. Its bark is smooth, greyish yellow to grey. Its leaves are opposite, thin, mostly ovate and tapered at both ends, with a bright green and shining upper surface and a paler and duller underside, 4–8 cm long with three or five prominent veins starting from the base. Its white flowers are about 2 cm long and tubular and occur in groups of three or five near the end of branchlets. The fruit is a round orange-brown berry, 2.5–5 cm in diameter. The fruit pulp harbours several flat and round, densely silky hairy seeds, almost 1 cm across. All parts of the plant are very bitter.

HABITAT AND DISTRIBUTION: Usually on rocky outcrops from Cape York Peninsula through to northern Western Australia.

MEDICINAL USES: None as such.

ACTIVE CONSTITUENTS: The seed contains up to 1.3 per cent of the alkaloid brucine as well as smaller amounts of strychnine. The fruit pulp contains around 1 per cent loganine.[68,128] The two first named compounds are used by the pharmaceutical industry.[36]

Templetonia egena

FAMILY: Fabaceae

VERNACULAR NAMES: 'Broombush', 'round templetonia'.

DESCRIPTION: A rather tall erect and leafless shrub with slender almost cylindrical branches. Leaves are reduced to broad scales. Flowers occur in elongated clusters on very short stalks; they are brownish yellow and quite small. The pod is oblong to egg-shaped, compressed with tough and leathery valves, black or brown, 12–20 mm long and mostly with one large seed. Flowers in spring.

HABITAT AND DISTRIBUTION: None as such.

ACTIVE CONSTITUENTS: The major alkaloid of the whole plant is sparteine;[129] it has been used, in the form of its sulphate, in cardiac arhythmia and in the early stages of labour.[49]

Duboisia myoporoides (see page 200)

Eucalyptus leucoxylon (see page 202)

Eucalyptus macrorhyncha (see page 202)

Eucalyptus polybractea (see page 203)

Solanum linearifolium (see page 206)

Solanum vescum (see page 207)

Table of plant uses

1. Narcotics
2. Sedatives and antispasmodics
3. Tonics; vitamin deficiencies; blood purifiers
4. Emolients
5. Toothache
6. Headache
7. Other analgesics; earache
8. Rheumatism; swellings; inflammations
9. Coughs and colds
10. Treatment of fever; diaphoretics
11. Bactericides; wounds, sores and ulcers; styptics
12. Eye disease; treatment of sore eyes
13. Skin disease; scabies, tinea, ringworm; itches; leprosy
14. Stomach disorders; emetics
15. Diarrhoea; dysentery
16. Laxatives
17. Diuretics
18. Anthelmintics; treatment of internal parasites
19. Snake bite; insect bites
20. Marine stings
21. Menstrual disorders
22. Lactagogues
23. Contraceptives
24. Venereal disease
25. Aphrodisiacs
26. Plants used industrially or those having industrial potential, including plants with anti-tumour activity
27. Miscellaneous: asthma; tuberculosis; rabies; cancer; deafness; diabetes; infectious diseases; warts; etc.

Australian Medicinal Plants

	1	2	3	4	5	6	7	8	9	10	11	12	13	14	15	16	17	18	19	20	21	22	23	24	25	26	27
Abrus precatorius								×	×			×															
Acacia ancistrocarpa					×	×	×				×																
A. beauverdiana	×																										
A. bivenosa subsp. *wayi*.								×																			
A. cuthbertsonii			×			×																					
A. decurrens															×												
A. falcata													×														
A. holosericea								×																			×
A. implexa													×														
A. inaequilatera										×	×																
A. ixiophylla																											×
A. leptocarpa		×								×																	
A. melanoxylon						×																					
A. monticola								×																			
A. pyrifolia									×																		
A. tetragonophylla								×		×			×														×
A. trachycarpa				×	×	×				×																	
A. translucens					×					×																	
Acalypha wilkesiana	×									×																	
Achyranthes aspera	×						×	×			×	×				×		×									×
Adiantum aethiopicum							×							×													
Aegiceras corniculatum						×										×											
Ageratum conyzoides									×										×								×
Ailanthus triphysa		×						×	×	×			×	×													
Ajuga australis									×																		
Aleurites moluccana						×								×								×					
Allophylus serratus														×													
Alocasia macrorrhizos		×				×	×		×																		
Alphitonia excelsa	×	×	×	×		×					×	×															
A. petriei						×																					
Alstonia actinophylla																					×						
A. constricta		×							×	×																×	
A. scholaris		×	×	×	×			×				×	×		×												×
Alyxia buxifolia														×													
A. spicata																											×
Ammannia baccifera						×	×																				
Amorphophallus variabilis	×																										
Ampelocissus acetosa																	×										

Table of plant uses

	1	2	3	4	5	6	7	8	9	10	11	12	13	14	15	16	17	18	19	20	21	22	23	24	25	26	27
Amyema maidenii subsp. *maidenii*					×																						
A. quandang								×																			
Angophora costata														×													
A. floribunda														×													
A. subvelutina														×													
A. woodsiana														×													
Antidesma dallachyanum									×																		
Araucaria cunninghamii																×											
Asparagus racemosus											×		×														×
Atherosperma moschatum				×	×				×	×	×				×	×							×				×
Atriplex nummularia				×																							
Bacopa monniera				×			×								×	×											
Barringtonia acutangula											×	×	×	×													
B. asiatica																											×
B. calyptrata							×	×																			
B. racemosa								×					×			×		×									
Basilicum polystachyon									×																		
Bauerella simplicifolia																									×		
Beyeria leschenaultii										×																	×
Boerhavia diffusa														×			×										×
Brasenia schreberi															×												×
Breynia cernua														×													
B. stipitata						×					×																
Brucea javanica								×		×			×														
Buchanania arborescens					×																						
B. obovata					×	×					×																
Bursaria spinosa																									×		
Caesalpinia bonduc				×	×				×				×						×			×					×
C. nuga																	×										
Calamus caryotoides						×																					
Callicarpa longifolia		×																									
Callitris columellaris																								×			
C. endlicheri																			×								×
Calophyllum inophyllum								×						×	×		×										

211

Australian Medicinal Plants

Species	1	2	3	4	5	6	7	8	9	10	11	12	13	14	15	16	17	18	19	20	21	22	23	24	25	26	27
Canarium australianum														×	×												
C. muelleri										×																	
Canavalia rosea						×	×	×			×																×
Capparis lasiantha							×	×								×											
C. uberiflora											×																
Carissa lanceolata				×				×	×																		
Cassia absus												×															
C. artemisioides			×																								
C. barclayana													×		×												
C. odorata															×												
C. pleurocarpa															×												
Cassytha filiformis				×				×			×	×															
C. glabella						×		×																			
Casuarina decaisneana																										×	
C. equisetifolia								×						×													
Cayratia trifolia																×											
Centaurium spicatum				×		×		×					×														
Centella asiatica	×		×	×							×		×											×			×
Centipeda cunninghamii				×					×		×	×															×
C. minima									×		×					×											
C. thespidioides					×				×		×																×
Cerbera manghas	×													×													
Chenopodium cristatum							×		×																		
C. rhadinostachyum					×		×																				
Cinnamomum laubatii			×				×	×					×		×												
C. oliveri														×													
Cissampelos pareira															×												×
Cissus hypoglauca							×																				
Clematis glycinoides					×																						
C. microphylla						×																					
Cleome viscosa						×		×	×	×	×				×			×									×
Clerodendrum floribundum						×																					
C. inerme									×	×																	
C. ovalifolium		×																									
Codonocarpus cotinifolius			×		×		×																				×

Table of plant uses

Species	1	2	3	4	5	6	7	8	9	10	11	12	13	14	15	16	17	18	19	20	21	22	23	24	25	26	27
Coelospermum decipiens																								×			
Convolvulus erubescens													×	×													
Crinum asiaticum										×											×						
C. pedunculatum																	×										
C. uniflorum										×																	
Crotalaria cunninghamii				×		×	×	×				×															
Croton insularis			×																								
C. phebalioides			×																								
Curcuma australasica																					×						
Cyanotis axillaris																											×
Cyathea australis			×																								
Cycas media									×																		
Cymbidium canaliculatum														×													
C. madidum													×														
Cymbonotus lawsonianus									×																		
Cymbopogon bombycinus					×					×																	
C. procerus								×																			
Cynanchum floribundum									×																		
Cynometra ramiflora var. *bijuga*														×		×											
Cyperus bifax																							×				
C. rotundus																					×						×
Daphnandra micrantha			×																								×
Daviesia latifolia			×					×																			×
Deeringia amaranthoides																											×
Dendrobium teretifolium					×	×																					
Dendrocnide excelsa							×					×															
Dianella ensifolia				×		×																					×
Dioscorea transversa																											×
Diplocyclos palmatus																×											
Dodonaea attenuata								×																			
D. lanceolata						×											×										
D. viscosa			×		×					×	×		×					×									
Doryphora aromatica			×																								

213

Australian Medicinal Plants

	1	2	3	4	5	6	7	8	9	10	11	12	13	14	15	16	17	18	19	20	21	22	23	24	25	26	27
D. sassafras				×																							
Duboisia hopwoodii	×	×																									
D. leichhardtii																										×	
D. myoporoides	×											×														×	
Eclipta prostrata			×											×	×												×
Ehretia saligna						×																					
Eleocharis dulcis										×																	
Elephantopus scaber			×			×	×																			×	
Entada phaseoloides			×			×		×				×	×														
Eremophila bignoniiflora															×												
E. cuneifolia								×																			
E. fraseri				×		×	×																				
E. freelingii					×																						
E. longifolia									×	×																	
E. maculata								×																			
Eriostemon brucei								×																			
E. trachyphyllus																										×	
Ervatamia angustisepala								×	×																		
E. orientalis										×																	
Erythrina vespertilio	×	×	×								×																
Erythrophleum chlorostachyum											×																
Eucalyptus acmenioides														×													
E. camaldulensis							×	×					×														
E. citriodora																										×	
E. crebra													×														
E. dichromophloia			×	×			×					×															×
E. dives									×																	×	
E. drepanophylla									×																		
E. eugenioides													×														
E. globulus subsp. bicostata																										×	
E. globulus subsp. globulus																										×	
E. globulus subsp. pseudoglobulus																										×	
E. gummifera									×	×	×												×				
E. haemastoma									×		×																

Table of plant uses

	1	2	3	4	5	6	7	8	9	10	11	12	13	14	15	16	17	18	19	20	21	22	23	24	25	26	27
E. kochii																										×	
E. leucoxylon																										×	
E. macrorhyncha														×												×	
E. maculata											×																
E. microcorys														×													
E. microtheca																		×									
E. oleosa																										×	
E. papuana				×				×		×																	
E. pilularis														×													
E. piperita													×														
E. polybractea																									×		
E. polycarpa														×													
E. pruinosa							×																				
E. racemosa														×													
E. radiata																									×		
E. resinifera														×							×						
E. saligna														×													
E. siderophloia														×													
E. sideroxylon																										×	
E. smithii																										×	
E. tereticornis														×													
E. terminalis								×						×													
E. tesselaris														×													
E. tetrodonta						×				×	×			×													
E. viminalis																×											
E. youmanii																									×		
Eucryphia lucida											×																
Euodia vitiflora				×	×																						
Euphorbia alsiniflora									×				×														
E. atoto								×	×																		
E. australis							×			×												×					×
E. coghlanii										×												×					×
E. drummondii								×		×	×	×	×		×			×				×					
E. hirta		×							×				×				×										×
E. mitchelliana														×													
Evolvulus alsinoides			×						×				×														
Exallage auricularia																											×
Excoecaria agallocha							×				×		×				×			×							
E. parvifolia						×																					
Exocarpos aphyllus								×	×																		×

	1	2	3	4	5	6	7	8	9	10	11	12	13	14	15	16	17	18	19	20	21	22	23	24	25	26	27
E. cupressiformis				×											×												
Ficus coronata									×																		
F. opposita										×	×		×														
F. racemosa			×			×																		×		×	
Flagellaria indica					×						×	×									×						
Flindersia maculosa															×												
Geijera parviflora	×			×	×																						
Gnaphalium luteoalbum					×																						
Goodenia ovata																									×		
G. scaevolina								×																			
G. varia			×																								
Gratiola pedunculata																									×		
Grevillea pyramidalis											×							×									
G. striata											×																×
Grewia latifolia														×													
G. retusifolia				×	×		×				×	×		×													
Gyrocarpus americanus							×		×																		
Haemodorum corymbosum																			×								
H. spicatum														×													
Hakea macrocarpa										×																	
Helichrysum apiculatum																		×									
Heliotropium ovalifolium		×																									
Hernandia peltata																×											×
Heteropogon contortus	×							×																			
Hibiscus diversifolius																											×
H. tiliaceus subsp. tiliaceus											×																
H. vitifolius											×																
Hybanthus enneaspermus																											×
Hydrolea zeylanica											×																
Indigofera linnaei									×	×						×											
Ipomoea brasiliensis						×	×		×			×					×							×		×	
I. mauritiana														×													
Isopogon ceratophyllus	×																										
Isotoma petraea	×					×	×																				
Jacksonia dilatata														×													

Table of plant uses

	1	2	3	4	5	6	7	8	9	10	11	12	13	14	15	16	17	18	19	20	21	22	23	24	25	26	27
Lavatera plebeia										×																	
Leichhardtia australis																						×					
Litsea glutinosa					×						×	×	×														
Lycopodium phlegmaria																									×		
Lysiphyllum carronii											×																
Lythrum salicaria														×				×									×
Mallotus mollissimus														×													
M. philippensis													×														×
Melaleuca alternifolia										×															×		
M. cajuputi			×		×			×	×	×	×							×								×	×
M. species aff. cajuputi						×	×																				
M. hypericifolia						×																					
M. linariifolia						×						×													×		
M. quinquenervia						×		×	×								×										
M. symphyocarpa						×	×	×	×																		
M. uncinata								×																			
Melia azedarach var. australasica								×		×			×		×	×											
Mentha australis						×			×																		×
M. diemenica							×			×				×			×		×								
M. satureioides				×				×											×								×
Merremia tridentata											×																
Mimulus gracilis			×																×								
Morinda citrifolia			×					×		×	×															×	
Mucuna gigantea							×																				
Musa banksii							×																				
Myoporum debile																								×			
M. platycarpum															×												
Myristica insipida											×																
Nauclea orientalis			×				×	×					×					×									
Nelumbo nucifera													×														
Nicotiana benthamiana	×																										
N. cavicola	×																										
N. debneyi																										×	
N. excelsior	×																										
N. gossei	×																										
N. megalosiphon																										×	
Orchrosia elliptica								×																			

Australian Medicinal Plants

	1	2	3	4	5	6	7	8	9	10	11	12	13	14	15	16	17	18	19	20	21	22	23	24	25	26	27
O. moorei																										×	
Ocimum sanctum var. angustifolium		×							×	×	×		×														
Oldenlandia galioides																	×										
Omalanthus populifolius									×																		
Operculina turpethum													×														
Ottelia alismoides																		×									
Owenia acidula				×					×	×																	
O. reticulata																		×									
Pagetia medicinalis																											×
Pandanus spiralis						×						×															
Persoonia falcata			×						×	×																	
Petalostigma pubescens	×	×								×	×	×							×								×
P. quadriloculare	×	×								×	×	×							×								
Phyllanthus virgatus												×										×					
Pimelea microcephala				×		×																					
Piper novae-hollandiae	×		×																			×					
Pittosporum phillyraeoides						×	×	×	×											×							
P. venulosum																						×					
Planchonella laurifolia							· ×																				
P. pohlmanniana									×																		
Planchonia careya									×	×																	
Plectranthus congestus													×														
Plumbago zeylanica									×	×		×	×														×
Polygonum barbatum					×							×		×													
P. hydropiper	×									×					×		×										
Pongamia pinnata							×		×		×	×															
Portulaca oleracea	×															×											×
Pratia purpurascens																				×							
Prostanthera cineolifera					•		×																				
P. rotundifolia														×													
Prunella vulgaris	×								×	×	×	×															
Psilotum nudum																										×	
Pteridium esculentum							×										×	×									
Pterigeron odorus				×	×																						
Pterocaulon serrulatum					×				×	×	×																
Raphidophora australasica						×																					

Table of plant uses

Species	1	2	3	4	5	6	7	8	9	10	11	12	13	14	15	16	17	18	19	20	21	22	23	24	25	26	27
Remirea maritima								×								×											
Rhizophora mucronata														×													
Rhyncharrhena linearis																						×					
Rhynchosia minima																											×
Ripogonum papuanum																			×								
Rorippa islandica			×																								
Rubus hillii														×													
R. parvifolius														×													
Santalum acuminatum							×		×													×					
S. lanceolatum				×	×			×	×		×		×		×							×					
S. obtusifolium						×								×													
S. spicatum								×	×																		
Sarcostemma australe									×	×	×											×					×
Scaevola spinescens					×		×		×		×	×															×
S. taccada									×	×																	
Scirpus validus															×		×										
Scleria lithosperma																	×										
Scoparia dulcis					×			×	×	×			×														×
Sebaea ovata			×																								
Securinega melanthesoides						×					×	×															
Semecarpus australiensis								×										×									×
Sesbania sesban								×																			
Sida rhombifolia						×	×						×	×			×										×
Smilax australis			×																								
S. glyciphylla			×					×								×											
Solanum aviculare																										×	
S. capsciforme																										×	
S. laciniatum																										×	
S. lasiophyllum						×																					
S. linearifolium																										×	
S. simile																										×	
S. symonii																										×	
S. vescum																										×	
Sophora tomentosa														×													
Spartothamnella juncea							×	×																			
Spilanthes grandiflora				×																							
Spinifex longifolius				×					×																		

Australian Medicinal Plants

Species	1	2	3	4	5	6	7	8	9	10	11	12	13	14	15	16	17	18	19	20	21	22	23	24	25	26	27
Stemodia grossa						×		×	×																		
S. lythrifolia						×																					
S. viscosa							×	×		×																	
Sterculia quadrifida					×					×	×																
Striga curviflora										×		×															
Strychnos lucida																										×	
Swainsona galegifolia								×																			
S. pterostylis								×																			
Syncarpia hillii											×																
Syzygium suborbiculare							×		×				×														
Tasmannia lanceolata				×																							
Templetonia egena																										×	
Tephrosia varians								×																			
Thespesia populnea												×															
Timonius timon									×	×		×															
Tinospora smilacina							×	×	×				×	×					×	×							
Toona australis										×				×						×							
Trachymene hemicarpa							×	×																			
Tribulus cistoides					×																						
Trichodesma zeylanicum var. *zeylanicum*											×					×	×										
Trichosanthes palmata											×																×
Tricoryne platyptera											×																
Tylophora erecta																								×			
Ventilago viminalis		×			×		×			×																	×
Verbena officinalis								×		×	×		×										×				×
Vigna vexillata															×												
Vitex trifolia																											×
Wedelia calendulacea			×																								
Wikstroemia indica								×		×																	
Ximenia americana																×											
Xylomelum scottianum							×																				
Zieria smithii						×																					
Ziziphus oenoplia											×																

Bibliography and references

1. D. Levitt, *personal communication*.
2. W.E. Roth, 'Superstition, Magic and Medicine'. *North Queensland Ethnography Bulletin No. 5;* Government Printer, Brisbane, 1903.
3. J.H. Maiden, *The Useful Native Plants of Australia.* Turner & Henderson, Sydney, 1889.
4. Ethel Shaw, *Early Days Among the Aborigines,* W. & J. Barr, Melbourne N.D.
5. P. Latz, *personal communication*.
6. R. Travers, *The Tasmanians,* Cassell Australia, Melbourne, 1968.
7. P. Trezise, *personal communication*.
8. J.H. Maiden, *The Forest Flora of New South Wales,* vol. 4, Government Printer, Sydney, 1911.
9. A. Ross, *N.S.W. Medical Gazette, 2,* 149 (1871/72).
10. J.H. Maiden, *The Forest Flora of New South Wales,* vol. 7, Government Printer, Sydney, 1922.
11. S.T. Blake, *Contributions from the Queensland Herbarium,* No. 1 (1968).
12. T.H. Johnston and J.B. Cleland, *Oceania, 4,* 201, 268 (1933/34).
13. L.J. Webb, *Proceedings of the Royal Society of Queensland, 71,* 103 (1959).
14. R. Hegnauer, *Chemotaxonomie der Pflanzen,* vol. 6, Birkhäuser Verlag, Basel, 1973.
15. *Aboriginal Trail Leaflet,* National Botanic Gardens, Canberra, 1977.
16. R. Hegnauer, *Chemotaxonomie der Pflanzen,* vol. 5, Birkhäuser Verlag, Basel, 1969.
17. D.R. Baigent and K.G. Lewis, *Australian Journal of Chemistry, 31,* 1375 (1978).
18. E. Reid and T.J. Betts, *The Records of Western Australian Plants Used by Aboriginals as Medicinal Agents;* Western Australian Institute of Technology, Pharmacy Department, 1977.
19. L.J. Webb, *Guide to the Medicinal and Poisonous Plants of Queensland, CSIRO Bulletin No. 232;* Government Printer, Melbourne, 1948.
20. L.J. Webb, *Mankind, 7,* 137 (1969).
21. S.L. Everist, *Poisonous Plants of Australia;* Angus & Robertson, Sydney, 1974.
22. R. Hegnauer, *Chemotaxonomie der Pflanzen,* vol. 2, Birkhäuser Verlag, Basel, 1963.
23. F.M. Bailey, *A Comprehensive Catalogue of Queensland Plants;* Government Printer, Brisbane, 1909.
24. K.-H. Lee *et al., Journal of Organic Chemistry, 44,* 2180 (1979).
25. D. Levitt, *Hemisphere, 23,* 244 (1979).
26. E.J. Reid and T.J. Betts, *Planta Medica, 36,* 164 (1979).
27. J.H. Maiden, *Agricultural Gazette of N.S.W., 10,* 131 (1899).
28. For references see list given in the article by R.M. Dawson *et al., Australian Journal of Chemistry, 19,* 2133 (1966).
29. J.B. Cleland and T.H. Johnston, *Transactions and Proceedings of the Royal Society of South Australia, 57,*113 (1933).

30. E.V. Lassak and I.A. Southwell, *Australian Journal of Chemistry*, 25, 2491 (1972).
31. L.J. Webb, *Australian Phytochemical Survey*, Part 2, *CSIRO Bulletin No. 268;* Government Printer, Melbourne, 1952.
32. T.H. Johnston and J.B. Cleland, *Transactions and Proceedings of the Royal Society of South Australia*, 67, 149 (1943).
33. R. Hegnauer, *Chemotaxonomie der Pflanzen*, vol. 3, Birkhäuser Verlag, Basel, 1964.
34. R.H. Cambage, *Journal and Proceedings of the Royal Society of New South Wales*, 49, 389 (1915).
35. L.J. Webb, 'Australian Plants and Chemical Research', *The Last of Lands;* Jacaranda Press, 1969.
36. *Hager's Handbuch der Pharmazeutischen Praxis*, J. Springer Verlag, Berlin, 1930.
37. J.B. Cleland and T.H. Johnston, *Transactions and Proceedings of the Royal Society of South Australia*, 63, 22 (1939).
38. J.B. Cleland and T.H. Johnston, *Transactions and Proceedings of the Royal Society of South Australia*, 63, 172 (1939).
39. *A. Phytochemical Register of Australian Plants*, vol. 1, Melbourne, 1959.
40. F.M. Bailey, *Proceedings of the Linnean Society of N.S.W.*, 5, 1 (1881).
41. F.M. Bailey, *The Queensland Flora*, Government Printer, Brisbane, 1883.
42. L.J. Webb, 'Australian Phytochemical Survey', Part 1, *CSIRO Bulletin No. 241*, Government Printer, Melbourne, 1949.
43. J.J.H. Simes, J.G. Tracey, L.J. Webb and W.J. Dunstan, 'Australian Phytochemical Survey', Part 3, *CSIRO Bulletin No. 281*, Government Printer, Melbourne, 1959.
44. I.A. Southwell, Museum of Applied Arts and Sciences, *Year Book 1978.*
45. J. Lauterer, *Proceedings of the Royal Society of Queensland*, 12, 92 (1896).
46. J.H. Maiden, *The Forest Flora of New South Wales*, vol. 8, Government Printer, Sydney, 1925.
47. G. Althofer, *personal communication.*
48. J.S. Fitzgerald, *Australian Journal of Chemistry*, 17, 160 (1964).
49. *The Merck Index*, 7th edition, Merck & Co. Inc., Rahway, N.J., 1960.
50. A. Campbell, *Australian Journal of Pharmacy*, 894 (1973).
51. G.V. Baddeley, A.J. Bealing, P.R. Jefferies and R.W. Retallack, *Australian Journal of Chemistry*, 17, 908 (1964).
52. S.R. Johns, J.A. Lamberton and A.A. Sioumis, *Australian Journal of Chemistry*, 17, 908 (1964).
53. J. McPherson, *Australasian Nurses' Journal*, 28, 1 (1930).
54. R.K. Baslas and R. Agarwal, *Current Science*, 49, 311 (1980).
55. E. Hurst, *The Poison Plants of N.S.W.;* The Snelling Printing Works Pty. Ltd., Sydney, 1942.
56. W. Woolls, *A Contribution to the Flora of Australia;* F. White, Sydney, 1867.
57. J.S. Chauhan and S.K. Srivastava, *Chemistry and Science*, 13, 24 (1979).
58. Museum of Applied Arts and Sciences, unpublished data.
59. J.H. Maiden, *The Forest Flora of New South Wales*, vol. 1, Government Printer, Sydney, 1904.
60. A.J. Ewart, *Flora of Victoria;* Melbourne University Press, Melbourne, 1930.
61. M. Koch, *Transactions of the Royal Society of South Australia*, 22, 101 (1897/98).
62. R.T. Baker and H.G. Smith, *Journal and Proceedings of the Royal Society of New South Wales*, 46, 103 (1912).

63. T.W. Shepherd, *N.S.W. Medical Gazette,* 2, 71 (1871/72).
64. T.W. Shepherd, *N.S.W. Medical Gazette,* 2, 129 (1871/72).
65. B.S. Joshi, V.N. Kamat and D.H. Gawad, *Heterocycles,* 7, 193 (1977).
66. S.G. Brooker and R.C. Cooper, *New Zealand Medicinal Plants.* A handbook of the Auckland War Memorial Museum; Unity Press Ltd., Auckland, 1961.
67. K.-I. Kawai, T. Akiyama, Y. Ogihara and S. Shibata, *Phytochemistry,* 13, 2829 (1974).
68. R. Hegnauer, *Chemotaxonomie der Pflanzen,* vol. 4, Birkhäuser Verlag, Basel, 1966.
69. S.R. Johns and J.A. Lamberton, *Australian Journal of Chemistry,* 19, 297 (1966).
70. W. Woolls, *Victorian Naturalist,* 4, 103 (1887).
71. T.G.H. Jones and F. Berry-Smith, *Proceedings of the Royal Society of Queensland,* 40, 27 (1928).
72. J. Ellis, E. Gellert and R.E. Summons, *Australian Journal of Chemistry,* 25, 1829 (1972).
73. J.M. Petrie, *Proceedings of the Linnean Society of N.S.W.,* 37, 139 (1912).
74. T.G.H. Jones and F. Berry-Smith, *Proceedings of the Royal Society of Queensland,* 37, 89 (1925).
75. A.R. Penfold and F.R. Morrison, *Bulletin No. 14;* Technological Museum, Sydney, 1946.
76. 'Medical and Dental Data of Ti-Trol and Melasol'; Australian Essential Oils Ltd., Sydney, 1931, revised 1936.
77. A.R. Penfold and R. Grant, *Journal and Proceedings of the Royal Society of New South Wales,* 57, 80 (1923); 58, 117 (1924); 59, 346 (1925); 60, 167 (1926).
78. N. Atkinson, *The Medical Journal of Australia,* 605 (1949);
    N. Atkinson and H. Brice, *The Australian Journal of Experimental Biology and Medical Science,* 33, 547 (1955);
    N. Atkinson, *The Australian Journal of Experimental Biology and Medical Science,* 34, 17 (1956).
79. A. Koedam, *Riechstoffe, Aromen, Kosmetica,* No.1, 6 and No. 2, 36 (1977).
80. M.-F. Beylier, *Proceedings of the 10th I.F.S.C.C. Congress,* Sydney, 1978.
81. J. Lauterer, *Proceedings of the Royal Society of Queensland,* 10, 97 (1892/94).
82. H. Egawa, O. Tsutsui, K. Tatsuyama and T. Hatta, *Experientia,* 33, 889 (1977).
83. C.A. Gardner and H.W. Bennetts, *The Toxic Plants of Western Australia;* West Australian Newspapers Ltd., Periodicals Division, Perth, 1956.
84. I.R.C. Bick, H.-M. Leow and M.J. Richards, *Australian Journal of Chemistry,* 33, 225 (1980).
85. N. Mandava, J.D. Anderson and S.R. Dutky, *Phytochemistry,* 13, 2853 (1974).
86. D.K. Bhardwaj, M.S. Bisht and C.K. Mehta, *Phytochemistry,* 19, 2040 (1980).
87. S. Siddiqui, B.S. Siddiqui and Z. Naim, *Pakistani Journal of Scientific and Industrial Research,* 21, 158 (1978).
88. K. Paijmans, *New Guinea Vegetation,* Elsevier Scientific Publishing Co., Amsterdam, 1976.
89. E.K. Adesogan and A.L. Okunade, *Phytochemistry,* 18, 1863 (1979).
90. E. Gildemeister and F. Hoffmann, *Die Aetherischen Oele,* vol. 7, Akademie Verlag, Berlin, 1961.
91. R.M. Carman and D.E. Cowley, *Tetrahedron Letters,* 627 (1964).
92. R. Hegnauer, *Chemotaxonomie der Pflanzen,* vol. 1, Birkhäuser Verlag, Basel, 1962.

93. R.A. Eade, K. Hunt, J.J.H. Simes and W. Stern, *Australian Journal of Chemistry*, 22, 2703 (1969).
94. P.W. Khong and K.G. Lewis, *Australian Journal of Chemistry*, 30, 1311 (1977).
95. J.H. Maiden, *The Forest Flora of New South Wales*, vol. 5, Government Printer, Sydney, 1913.
96. J.T. Pinhey and I.A. Southwell, *Australian Journal of Chemistry*, 24, 1311 (1971).
97. J.H. Maiden, *The Forest Flora of New South Wales*, vol. 2, Government Printer, Sydney, 1907.
98. W.E. Hillis, *Australian Journal of Scientific Research*, 5A, 379 (1952).
99. J.H. Maiden, *The Forest Flora of New South Wales*, vol. 3, Government Printer, Sydney, 1908.
100. F.M. Dean, *Naturally Occurring Oxygen Ring Compounds*, Butterworths, London, 1963.
101. R.B. Longmore, *Gazette* (Journal of the Western Australian Institute of Technology), 11, (3), 10 (1978).
102. J.F. Morton, *Economic Botany*, 32, 111 (1978).
103. J.S. Fitzgerald, *Australian Journal of Chemistry*, 17, 375 (1964).
104. J.S. Fitzgerald and A.A. Sioumis, *Australian Journal of Chemistry*, 18, 433 (1965).
105. J.H. Maiden, *Transactions of the Royal Society of South Australia*, 16, 1 (1892/96).
106. J. Lauterer, *Australian Association for the Advancement of Science*, 6, 293 (1895).
107. J. Lauterer, *Proceedings of the Royal Society of Queensland*, 11, 20 (1894/95).
108. E. Gildemeister and F. Hoffmann, *Die Aetherischen Oele*, vol. 5, Akademie Verlag, Berlin, 1959.
109. J. Lauterer, *Australasian Association for the Advancement of Science Report*, 6, 298 (1895).
110. R.T. Baker and H.G. Smith, *A Research on the Eucalypts*, 2nd edition, Government Printer, Sydney, 1920.
111. A.R. Penfold and F.R. Morrison, *Journal and Proceedings of the Royal Society of New South Wales*, 58, 124 (1924).
112. S.A. Graham, B.N. Timmermann and T.J. Mabry, *Journal of Natural Products*, 43, 644 (1980).
113. I.C. Torres and J.C. Suarez, *Journal of Natural Products*, 43, 559 (1980).
114. H.H.G. McKern and I.W. Parnell, *Journal of Helminthology*, 38, 223 (1964).
115. R. Mendham, *personal communication*.
116. J. Bosisto, *Proceedings of the 2nd Meeting of the Australasian Association for the Advancement of Science*, 554 (1890).
117. B. Kullenberg and G. Bergström, *Endeavour*, 34, 59 (1975).
118. H.G. Smith, *Proceedings of the Royal Society of New South Wales*, 31, 177, 377 (1897).
119. L.J. Webb, *Journal of the Australian Institute of Agricultural Science*, 144, September 1953.
120. J.W. Clark-Lewis and I. Dainis, *Australian Journal of Chemistry*, 21, 425 (1968).
121. K. Kagei et al., *Yakugaku Zasshi*, 100, 216 (1980).
122. H.J.G. Hines, *Proceedings of the Royal Society of Queensland*, 57, 75 (1945).
123. E.V. Lassak and J.T. Pinhey, *Australian Journal of Chemistry*, 22, 2175 (1969).

124. D. Low, B.D. Rawal and W.J. Griffin, *Planta Medica*, 26, 184 (1974).
125. C.N. Rodwell, *Nature*, 165, 773 (1950).
126. L.K. Dalton, S. Demerac, B.C. Elmes, J.W. Loder, J.M. Swan and T. Teitei, *Australian Journal of Chemistry*, 20, 2715 (1967).
127. V. Bradley, D.J. Collins, P.G. Crabbe, F.W. Eastwood, M.C. Irvine, J.M. Swan and D.E. Symon, *Australian Journal of Botany*, 26, 723 (1978).
128. F.A.L. Anet, G.K. Hughes and E. Ritchie, *Australian Journal of Chemistry*, 6, 58 (1953).
129. J.S. Fitzgerald, *Australian Journal of Chemistry*, 17, 159 (1964).

Glossary

Botanical terms have generally been excluded from the glossary. For these, the reader is referred to N.C.W. Beadle, O.D. Evans, and R.C. Carolin, *Flora of the Sydney Region*, 1972, A.H. and A.W Reed, or any of the many popular introductions to botany.

Abortifacient: agent inducing abortion.
Alkaloid: a basic nitrogenous organic compound found in plants; almost all alkaloids are bitter and poisonous; certain alkaloids, such as quinine, scopolamine, atropine, codeine, are used in medicine.
Alterative: a drug which alters favourably the course of an ailment thus restoring healthy body functions; it is an old term rarely used now.
Alternate leaves: leaves arranged singly at different heights along the stem.
Anodyne: a soothing, pain-easing agent.
Anthelmintic: a drug which destroys or expels intestinal worms.
Antidiabetic: a medicine counteracting or checking diabetes.
Antidote: remedy counteracting the effects of a poison.
Antinephritic: counteracting kidney disease.
Antiperiodic: a medicine preventing the regular recurrence of paroxysma of disease such as fever.
Antipyretic: a fever-reducing drug.
Antiscorbutic: a remedy for scurvy.
Antispasmodic: a remedy preventing or relieving spasms or convulsions.
Antitumour: refers to tumour-growth-inhibiting properties; usually referred to in connection with cancer.
Aperient: laxative.
Aphrodisiac: an agent provoking sexual desire.
Astringent: a substance that checks the discharge of mucus, serum etc., by causing shrinkage of tissue.

Bactericide: anything that destroys bacteria.
Bronchitis: an inflammation of the tubes in the lungs.

Calculous: caused by, or characterized by, solid concretions in the body; for example, kidney stones.

Cardiac glycosides: steroidal glycosides exerting an effect on the heart; in small amounts used in the treatment of heart disease (e.g. digitalis), whilst in larger amounts they act as powerful poisons (e.g. some arrow poisons).

Carminative: relieving colic or expelling gas from the alimentary tract; relieving flatulence.

Cathartic: purgative.

Cholera: a severe disease characterized by profuse and watery diarrhoea; endemic in India and some other neighbouring countries.

Colic: a paroxysm of acute abdominal pain caused by a spasm, obstruction, twisting or distension of any of the hollow organs or tubes, particularly the intestines.

Colloid: in a true solution the particles of dissolved substance are of molecular size, that is, very small; in a suspension the suspended particles are so large that they will eventually settle out. A colloidal solution falls in between a true solution (such as a solution of ordinary salt in water) and a suspension (such as when clay is dispersed in water); its particles are too small to settle out, but too large to allow passage through certain semi-permeable membranes. Gelatine and gum arabic are examples of colloidally soluble substances.

Coma: stupor, abnormally deep sleep.

Contraceptive: preventing conception (by chemical or physical means).

Coumarin: the chemical substance responsible for the odour of freshly mown hay; it is the parent compound of a large class of related substances common in Nature, collectively called coumarins.

Counter-irritant: a treatment or agent applied locally to produce a superficial irritation, thus reducing a deeper seated irritation, for example, plasters on chest.

Cyanogenic: capable of generating hydrocyanic acid; for example prunasin, a cyanogenic glycoside present in some types of eucalyptus leaves, which on acid hydrolysis generates the very toxic hydrocyanic acid (hydrogen cyanide).

Decoction: an extract obtained by boiling plant material in water.

Demulcent: a soothing medicine.

Deobstruant: an agent removing an obstruction, for example by reducing swellings of the urinary passage thus facilitating painless urination.

Depilatory: hair removing.

Diaphoretic: an agent or drug increasing perspiration.

Diarrhoea: abnormal frequency of bowel discharge (usually more or less fluid).

Discutient: an agent capable of dispersing morbid matter.

Diterpene: see terpene.

Diuretic: tending to increase the flow of urine.

Dropsy: disease in which watery fluid collects in cavities or tissues of the body.

Dysentery: disease characterized by severe diarrhoea with passage of mucus or blood; usually associated with abdominal pain.

Dysmenorrhoea: menstrual irregularity.

Dyspepsia: indigestion.

Dysuria: painful urination.

Eczema: an itchy, irritating inflammation of the skin characterized by an outbreak of small spots, either wet and weeping or dry, scaly or crusted, on a surrounding reddened area.

Embrocation: a liquid used for rubbing the affected part of the body.

Emetic: a drug causing vomiting.
Emmenagogue: an agent promoting menstrual flow.
Emmolient: a soothing medicine.
Emphysema: enlargement of air vesicles in the lungs; swelling of connective tissues of the body due to the presence of air.
Epiphytic plant: one which is perched on, but not parasitic on, another plant or object, for example, rock.
Essential oil: the volatile oil obtained by steam-distillation of plant material (leaves, bark, flowers, wood), for example, eucalyptus oil, peppermint oil, lavender oil; essential denotes essence and refers to the odoriferous qualities of most such oils and does not mean indispensable or necessary in this context; so called fixed oils, such as olive oil or peanut oil, do not distil with steam.
Expectorant: a medicine promoting secretion of bronchial mucus and facilitating the ejection of phlegm from the lungs by coughing.

Febrifuge: a drug tending to reduce fever.
Flavonoid: a group of organic compounds responsible for a great number of colours in fruits and flowers. In the past they were often used in conjunction with mordants for the dyeing of fabrics. However, the colours thus obtained were usually not lightfast.
Fumigate: apply odorous smoke or vapour to affected part.

Germicide: a substance that kills germs and micro-organisms in general.
Glycoside: a general term denoting a substance composed of a sugar residue and some other part, such as a flavonoid, coumarine, steroid, terpene, collectively referred to as the aglycone. Glycosides are very common in plants. Some are used in medicine, for example, rutin, strophantin.

Haematuria: presence of blood in urine.
Haemolytic: causing the breaking up of the red blood corpuscles.
Haemoptysis: condition in which one coughs blood.
Haemostatic: agent that stops bleeding.
Hydatid cyst: a larval tapeworm composed of a fluid-filled sac (bag-like cavity) enlarging into a spongy mass invading the host tissue, for example various organs such as the liver.
Hydrocele: an accumulation of fluid in bag-like cavities in the body.
Hydrolysis: the addition of a molecule of water to a chemical compound accompanied by a splitting of that compound into usually two fragments; hydrolysis is normally facilitated by the presence of small amounts of acids; for example, the degradation of starch into simple sugars achieved by prolonged heating of an acidified starch slurry in water.
Hypoglycaemic: reducing the concentration of sugar in the blood.
Hypotensive: lowering blood pressure.

Infusion: the extract obtained from steeping of plant material in water, for example, tea.

Kino: a red or orange exudate of eucalyptus or angophora bark.

Lactagogue: promoter of milk secretion.

Lactation: the secretion and yielding of milk by the mammary gland.
Leprosy: a chronic disease of the skin and nerves resulting in disfigurement.

Menorrhagia: excessive menstrual bleeding.
Metrorrhagia: bleeding between periods.
Micturition: abnormally frequent urination.
Monoterpene: see terpene.
Mucilage: a viscous substance.

Narcotic; a drug which, in modest doses, allays sensibility, relieves pain or produces profound sleep; large doses induce coma and stupor.
Nephritic: pertaining to the kidney.

Ophthalmia: inflammation of the eye.
Opposite leaves: arising at the same level but on opposite sides of the stem.
Ozaena: a chronic nose disease characterized by a foul odour.

Palsy: a condition characterized by uncontrollable quivering of the body.
Parasitic: living on, or in, and deriving nourishment from, a host.
Phthisis: a wasting disease, usually pulmonary tuberculosis.
Polyphenol: a group of organic compounds derived from benzene and containing a number of hydroxyl groups; many flavonoids and tannins belong to this group.
Poultice: a mass of material applied to sore or inflamed part of body.
Prolapse: the falling down of an internal part of the body.
Proteolytic: substance that breaks down proteins.
Pruritus: localized or generalized itching due to the irritation of sensory nerve endings.
Pulmonary: relating to the lungs.

Quinones: are organic compounds based on benzene where two hydrogen atoms have been replaced in the same ring by two oxygen atoms. Quinones are usually highly coloured and are often responsible for the yellow and red colours of some seeds, barks, woods. etc.

Rheumatism: painful inflammation of muscles and joints.
Ringworm: a fungal disease of the skin.
Rubefacient: a mild counter-irritant that causes a reddening of the skin.

Saponin: a group of steroidal or triterpenoid glycosides which froth when shaken with water.
Scabies: itch caused by mites burrowing into the skin.
Scrofula: a morbid condition with glandular swellings and a tendency to consumption.
Sedative: an agent that quiets nervous excitement.
Sesquiterpene: see terpene.
Steam-distillation: the process of isolating the volatile principles from a material (often of plant origin) by passing steam through it (or boiling it with water) and condensing the steam to recover the usually insoluble volatile substance.
Steroid: see terpene.
Stomachic: stimulant or tonic for the stomach.
Stricture: abnormal narrowing of a tubular organ; sometimes due to inflammation.

Glossary

Styptic: an agent having an astringent, constricting effect; for example, which stops bleeding.
Sudorific: an agent causing sweating.

Tannin: astringent principle of many plants.
Terpene: this name was originally applied to substances made up of two 5-carbon units, the so-called isoprene units. Nowadays applied collectively to compounds made up of several such units: monoterpenes (two units), sesquiterpenes (three units), diterpenes (four units), triterpenes (six units), tetraterpenes or carotenoids (eight units); steroids are related to triterpenes from which they often derive in living organisms. Most essential oils are mixtures of monoterpenoid and sesquiterpenoid compounds; the latex of certain species of *Euphorbia* often contains triterpenes whereas the orange-red pigment of carrots and tomatoes is the tetraterpene carotene.
Terpenoid: terpene-like.
Tincture: an alcoholic solution of some medicinal principle.
Tinea: a fungal disease of the skin.
Tonic: a drug or agent that invigorates, restores, refreshes or stimulates.
Triglyceride: a compound embodying one molecule of glycerol and three molecules of an organic acid; most fatty oils and fats are triglycerides, for example, peanut oil, olive oil, as well as butter, lard.
Turbid: forming a cloudy liquid.
Tympanites: distension of the abdomen caused by an accumulation of air or gas in the intestines or the abdominal cavity.

Uraemia: condition of the blood caused by retention of urinary matter normally eliminated by the kidneys.

Vermifuge: a drug which expels parasitic worms.
Vesicant: agent inducing blistering.
Vesicatory: agent raising blisters.
Visceral: dealing with the internal organs of the body.

Index

The index includes genus, species and common names; family, subspecies and variety names have not been indexed.

Number in *italics* indicates colour photograph opposite that page; *glos.* indicates that the word is defined in the glossary (pages 226 to 230).

abortifacient, *glos.*, 66, 88, 136, 167, 175
abrasions *see* cuts and abrasions
abrectorin, 100
abricin, 100
abridin, 100
abrine, 100
abscesses, 115, 136; breast, 106; rectal, 186
Abrus pauciflorus, 99
A. precatorius, 81, 99-100
A. squamulosus, 99
Abutilon albescens, 18
A. indicum, 18
Acacia, 17, 23, 33, 39, 47, 101-2, 142, 144, 145
A. ancistrocarpa, 101
A. aneura, 37
A. beauverdiana, 25
A. bivenosa, 49-50
A. cuthbertsonii, 25, 185
A. dealbata, 17
A. deanii, 142
A. decurrens, 17, 142, 146-7
A. falcata, 126
A. holosericea, 49, 145
A. implexa, 112, 126
A. inaequilatera, 102
A. ixiophylla, 193, 197
A. leiophylla, 146
A. leptocarpa, 100
A. ligulata, 49
A. maidenii, 145
A. melanoxylon, 50
A. monticola, 50
A. parramattensis, 146
A. parvipinnula, 146
A. polystacha, 145
A. pyrifolia, 102
A. salicina, 49
A. tetragonophylla, 112, 124, 127
A. trachycarpa, 101
A. translucens, 101-2
Acalypha wilkesiana, 102
acetylcholine, 131
acetylenic acids, 164
acetylenic pigments, 87
aches and pains *see* analgesics; pain
Achras laurifolia, 67
A. pohlmanniana, 116
Achronychia baueri, 197

A. simplicifolia, 197
Achyranthes aspera, 182, 183-4
achyranthine, 184
acronycine, 197
acutagenic acid, 127
ada-a, 169
Adiantum aethiopicum, 49, 51
A. capillus-veneris, 51
A. peltatum, 51
adikalyikba, 13, 185
Aegiceras corniculatum, 25, 26, 32, 166
A. fragrans, 26
A. majus, 26
Aeschynomene sesban, 118
aesculin, 17, 198
ageratochromen, 102
Ageratum conyzoides, 102
agnuside, 180
Agonis linearis, 99
ague, 89
ah-pill, 109
Ailanthus imberbiflora, 77
A. malabarica, 77
A. triphysa, 77-8
Ajuga australis, 81, 102-3
Aleurites moluccana, 184
A. triloba, 184
algoori, 155
alizarin, 89, 187
alkaloids, *glos.*, 17, 23, 31, 34, 35, 37, 43, 49, 55, 60, 66, 68, 69, 70, 75, 79, 81, 89, 90, 100, 104, 105, 109, 111, 113, 117, 120, 125, 129, 134, 135, 139, 151, 158, 159, 168, 169, 172, 174, 177, 183, 184, 185, 187, 189, 196, 197, 199, 200, 204, 205
Allophylus serratus, 147
A. ternatus, 147
Alocasia macrorrhizos, 26, 48, 130-1
alpha-cyperone, 171
alpha-phellandrene, 166
alpha-pinene, 104
alpha-santalol, 69
alpha-terpineol, 38, 65, 98, 104, 166
alphitolic acid, 52
Alphitonia excelsa, 27-8, 32
A. petriei, 51-2
alphitonin, 28, 52
Alsophila australis, 84
Alstonia actinophylla, 167-8
A. constricta, 14, 16, 49, 75, 76, 78-9, 80
A. cuneata, 79
A. scholaris, 49, 79-80
A. verticillosa, 167
alstonidine, 79
alstonilidine, 79
alstonine, 76, 79
alterative, *glos.*, 88, 91, 92
Althofer, George, 48, 75-6
alworn-angka-ina, 68

Alyxia buxifolia, 147
A. capitellata, 147
A. spicata, 49, 52
amellin, 179
Ammania baccifera, 52
A. indica, 52
A. vesicatoria, 52
Amorphophallus variabilis, 28
Ampelocissus acetosa, 168
amulla, 189
Amyema maidenii, 103
A. quandang, 49, 52-3
anabasine, 19, 200, 205
anaesthetics, 24, 25, 42
analgesics, 24-5, 26, 28, 30, 32, 37, 43, 167, 188
anbamar, 139
andan, 170
Andropogon bombycinus, 107
A. exaltatus, 57
A. procerus, 57
anethole, 98, 196
angee, river, 152
Angophora, 18
A. costata, 144, 147-8
A. floribunda, 148
A. intermedia, 148
A. lanceolata, 147
angophoras, 142, 144
A. subvelutina, 148
A. woodsiana, 148
aniseed oil, 196
an-na, 27
ant bush, 129
anthelmintics, *glos.*, 25, 26, 38, 79, 81, 9(105, 128, 135, 166, 174, 178, 199
anthocyanins, 162
anthraquinones, 43, 89, 125
anthrarobine, 125
anticoagulins, 166
Antidesma dallachyanum, 53
antibiotics, 94, 99, 107, 108, 138
antihaemorrhagic, 158; *see also* haemostatic substances
antihistamines, 62, 131
antiperiodic, *glos.*, 78, 79, 136, 179
antiscorbutics, *glos.*, 77, 80, 90, 91, 92, 182
antiseptics, 12-13, 41, 65, 89, 94-7, 98, 99, 104, 106, 109, 110, 113, 115, 117, 127, 128, 132, 133, 186; *see also* bactericides
antispasmodics, *glos.*, 38, 62, 118, 183
antiuraemic, 92
anto, 173
aphrodisiacs, *glos.*, 183, 184, 189, 191
apoatropine, 199
aposcopolamine, 199
apple: cockatoo, 177; cocky, 12-13, 94, 117, emu, 66; kangaroo, 205, 206;

230

Index

mooley, 66; mountain kangaroo, 206; red wild, 163; smoothbark, 147; tree, mountain, 147; wild, 163; winter, 189
aquaie, 159
arabin, 157
aranyi, 34
arlian, 117
Araucaria cunninghamii, 144, 148
Arid Zone Research Institute, 13, 14
aromadendrin, 132, 144
aromoline, 85
aroo-in, 173
arriga, 109
ascaridole, 166
ash: gully, 203; Moreton Bay, 155; mountain, 27; red, 27; scrub, 197
asiaticoside, 126, 185
Asparagopsis brownei, 103
A. decaisnei, 103
A. floribunda, 103
Asparagus fasciculatus, 103
A. racemosus, 103
aspirin, 17, 37
Astragalus, 142
asthma, 38, 54, 62, 78, 121, 139
asthma: herb, 62; plant, 62; plant, Queensland, 62
astringents, *glos.,* 14, 41, 42, 47, 51, 81, 86, 112, 128, 132, 142, 143, 144, 147, 150, 151, 153, 154, 158, 159, 161, 162, 167, 172, 178, 179, 182, 187, 188, 202
atheroline, 80
Atherosperma micranthum, 84
A. moschatum, 80
atherospermidine, 80
atherosperminine, 80
Atkinson, Nancy, 98-9
Atriplex nummularia, 80
Australian Essential Oil Ltd, 96
Australian Phytochemical Survey, 17
australol, 98

Backhousia citriodora, 98
Bacopa monniera, 81
bacoside A, 81
bacoside B, 81
bactericides, *glos.,* 43, 65, 66, 68, 69, 94, 96, 97, 98, 99, 115, 120, 125, 132, 137, 195, 199, 201, 204; *see also* antiseptics
balandu, 39
baldness, 124-5
balemo, 111
balgarda, 169
balm, sacred, 89
banana, native, 38
Bancroft, J. and T.L., 23, 41, 75, 77, 82, 84, 132, 190, 200
banganga, 26
Banks, Sir Joseph, 15
banmung, 101
baobo, 201
barbaddah, 131
barndaragu, 43
barringtogenic acid, 127, 128
barringtogenols, 127, 128
Barringtonia asiatica, 168, *176*
B. acutangula, 113, 127
B. calyptrata, 28
B. careya, 117
B. gracilis, 127

B. racemosa, 127-8
barrinya, 158
barror, 117
Basilicum polystachyon, 53
Bauerella simplicifolia, 197
bauhinia, red, 114
Bauhinia carronii, 114
balavola karping, 132
bead tree, 134
bean: black, 109; jequirity, 99; Leichhardt, 131; McKenzie, 128; matchbox, 131; Molucca, 81; prayer, 99; precatory, 99; Queensland, 131; velvet, 66; white, 77; wild Jack, 128; wood, tonga, 147
beantree, Northern, 114
bear's ear, 107
bedgery, 33
bed-yew-rie, 164
beech: brown, 83, Indian, 136
beefwood, 150, 173
Beilschmiedia obtusifolia, 151
belbowrie, 64
beleam, 117
bell fruit, 185
benaroon, 154
benzoic acid, 166
benzyl cyanide, 185
berbamine, 80
bergapten, 196, 201
bergenin, 134
berrigan, 18, 58
beta-amyrin, 100
beta-carboline alkaloids, 78
beta-nitropropionic acid, 63
beta-santalol, 69
beta-sitosterol, 100
betulic acid, 52, 122, 147
Beyeria leschenaultii, 53-4
biall, 153
bilbun, 31
biliousness, 82, 103, 163
billygoat: plant, 102; weed, 102
binaroley, 160
bindweed: Australian, 151, blushing, 151
birmingal, 137
birrba, 79
bites and stings: insect, 169, 176, 178; marine, 133, 167, 170, 176; scorpion, 184; sea dog, 176; stingray, 178; *see also* snakebite
bitterbark, 60, 78, 109
bitter principle, 41, 74-5, 78, 81, 84, 86, 88, 89, 91, 105, 106, 128, 130, 138, 171, 185
bitter tonic *see* bitter principle
biwil, 81
blackbutt, 154; great, 154
black sally, 50
blackthorn, 195, 197
blackwood, 50
bladder: diseases, 151; inflammation, 99, 110; *see also* urinary
bleeding *see* haemostatic substances
bleeding heart, native, 116
blindesss, 94-5
blind-your-eyes, 132
blisters, 112
blood: diluent, 80, 185; diseases, 88, 185; purifiers, 88, 90, 92

bloodwood, 132; gum topped, 86; longfruit, 155; long-fruited, 34; mountain, 34; red, 125, 132; red barked, 86; variable barked, 86
boan, 99
Boerhavia diffusa, 54
B. procumbens, 54
B. pubescens, 54
boils, 37, 96, 103, 114, 115, 117, 118, 137, 138, 188, 191
bolan, 137
bonducin, 81
bones, broken, 129
booah, 186
boobin, 85
boo-gar-oo, 38
booral, 116
Bosisto, Joseph, 166, 194
bowel complaints, 62, 79
box: flooded, 172; heath, 147; native, 197; Queensland yellow, 117, sea, 147; silver, 61; silverleaf, 61; silver-leaved, 61; thorn, 197
boxwood, yellow, 117
Brachyspatha variabilis, 28
bracken, common, 177
braggain, 130
brahmi, 185
bramble: Queensland, 161; small leaf, 161
Bramia indica, 81
Brasenia peltata, 168
B. purpurea, 168
B. schreberi, 168-9
breathlessness, 52; *see also* asthma; respiratory disorders
Breynia cernua, 148
B. stipitata, 103-4
bronchitis, *glos.,* 62, 78, 80, 203
brooklime, stalked, 173
broombush, 65, 208
Brucea amarissima, 28
B. javanica, 28
B. Sumatrana, 28
bruceins, 29
bruceol, 60
brucine, 196, 208
Brunella see *Prunella*
bruises, 120
Bryonia laciniosa, 152
Bryonopsis laciniosa, 152
bryony, native, 152
Buchanania arborescens, 29
B. muelleri, 29
B. oblongifolia, 29
B. obovata, 29, 94-5
bugle, 102; Australian, 102
bul-bocra, 89
bulla-bulla, 89
buna, 34
bunara, 34
bungkiam, 152
bunu-bunu, 71
burns, 26, 117
burro, 33
Bursaria spinosa, 193, 196-7
bursaria, sweet, 197
butterbush, 135

caalang, 85

cabbage, native, 90, 138
Cabomba peltata, 168
Caesalpinia bonduc, 81, 179
C. bonducella, 81
C. nuga, 149
Ceasaria esculenta, 19
C. multinervosa, 18
cajuput oil, 38, 65, 166
Caladium macrorrhizon, 26
Calamus caryotoides, 12, 54
calcium oxalate, 27, 90
calculous disorders, *glos.,* 149
Callicarpa longifolia, 29, 32
Callitris calcarata, 198
C. columellaris, 143, *193,* 196, 198
C. endlicheri, 143, 196, 198
C. glauca, 198
C. hugelii, 198
calool, 119
calophyllic acid, 128
calophyllolide, 128
Calophyllum inophyllum, 128, *128,* 145
Calyptrostegia microcephela, 67
camel: bush, 147, 179; poison, 33, 109
campesterol, 100
camphor, 118, 151
camphorwood, 83, 150
canaric acid, 104
Canarium australianum, 149
C. muelleri, 104
Canavalia maritima, 128
C. obtusifolia, 128
C. rosea, 128-9, *128*
cancer, 62, 138, 185; skin, 111, 124, 186
candlenut tree, 184
Cape York Ecology Transect Project (CAYET), 14
Capparis lasiantha, 167, 169
C. uberiflora, 104
carbeen, 155
Careya arborescens, 117
C. australis, 117
Carissa lanceolata, 81-2
carissone, 82
carminatives, *glos.,* 42, 83, 160
Carpobrotus, 14
carvacrol, 68
cassaine, 109
cascarilla, 83; native, 83; Queensland, 83
Cassia; 23, 30
C. absus, 104-5
C. artemisioides, 30
C. australis, 149
C. barclayana, 129
C. odorata, 144, 145, 149
C. pleurocarpa, 145, 149
C. schultesii, 149
C. sophera, 129
cassia: blue bush, 30; hairy, 104; silver, 30
Casuarina, 32
C. decaisneana, 199
C. equisetifolia, 150
cassyfiline, 82
Cassytha filiformis, 82
C. glabella, 54-5
cassythicine, 55
cassythidine, 82
catarrh, 65, 83, 88, 100
catechol, 144, 153
cattle bush, 135

caustic: bush, 137; creeper 187; creeping, 187; pencil, 137; plant, 137; tree, 112; vine, 137; weed, 187
Cayratia trifolia, 169
ceanothic acid, 52
cedar, 179; bastard, 134; false, 33; red, 179; white, 134
Cedrela australis, 179
C. toona, 179
Centaurium australe, 82
C. spicatum, 75, 82-3, 145
centaury, 82, 145; Australian, 82; native, 82; yellow, 91
Centella asiatica, 125-6, 184-5
Centipeda cunninghamii, 17, 46, 95, 105, 129-30
C. minima, 46, 95, 105
C. orbicularis, 105
C. thespidioides, 95, 105
Cerbera manghas, 30
C. odollam, 30
cerberoside, 30
Chaemaesyce hirta, 62
chaff flower, 183
Chamaelaucium uncinatum, 99
cheedningnan, 85
cheesewood: canary, 89; white, 79
Chenopodium cristatum, 106
C. rhadinostachyum, 106
cherry: ballart, 86; Herbert River, 53; native, 86
chest: complaints, 51, 67, 70, 92; congestion, 163; pain, 28, 34
chestnut: Chinese water, 108; water, 108
chills, 183
chinaberry, 134
Chisolm, J.R., 22
cholera, *glos.,* 171
cholesterol, 100
choline, 100
chrysophanic acid, 124
chrysophanol, 43
cinchonidine, 78
cineole *see* 1,8-cineole
1,8-cineole, 12, 17, 19, 38, 46-7, 49, 60, 64, 65, 68, 95, 97, 98, 115, 160, 166, 194, 202, 203, 204
cinnamic acid, 109, 151
Cinnamomum laubatii, 83
C. oliveri, 150-1
C. tamala, 83
cis-anethole, 196
cis-chrysanthenyl acetate, 130
Cissampelos pareira, 151
Cissus australasica, 55
C. hypoglauca, 55
citral, 98
citriodorol, 99, 201
citronellal, 97, 98, 201
citronellol, 97, 98, 201
Cleland, J.B., 22
Clematis aristata, 55
C. glycinoides, 55-6
C. microphylla, 56, 64
clematis small, *56;* small leaf, 56
Cleome viscosa, 56, 64
Clerodendron, 30
Clerodendrum floribundum, 30
C. inerme, 106
C. ovalifolium, 30
clerodin, 106

clover, currawinya, 187
cloves, oil of, 98; *see also* eugenol
club-moss, tasselled, 189
clubrush, river, 162
cochlearin, 185
Codonocarpus cotinifolius, 25, 74, 138, 185
Coelospermum decipiens, 169-70, *192*
cogola bush, 175
colds, 29, 33, 38, 46-8, 49, 51, 55, 56, 57, 58, 59, 60, 61, 62, 64, 66, 67, 68, 69, 70, 71, 82, 86, 88, 97, 105, 116, 120, 129, 130, 136, 138, 153, 202, 203; *see also* coughs
colic, *glos.,* 38, 42, 62, 188
Colocasia macrorrhiza, 26
concle berry, 81
conebush, horny, 87
conkerberry, 81
Considen, Denis, 15, 195
constipation, 164
consumption, 192
contagious disease, 71
contraceptives, *glos.,* 29, 112, 167, 170; oral, 170, 175, 178
convolvulus, goatsfoot, 188
convulsions, 81
Convolvulus erubescens, 145, 151
conyzorigin, 102
cooba, small, 49
coobiaby, 89
coolbidgi, 60
coolibah, 172
coolooli, 198
coonam, 148
coondoo, 67
coonta, 33
cooreenyan, 174
coorong, 148
coorung-coorung, 198
Coopers wood, 27
coral tree, bat's wing, 34
Cordia myxa, 19
cork: tree, 34, 200; wood, 34, 195-6, 199
corns, 137
coroglaucigenin, 134
corotoxigenin, 134
cortisone, 17, 196
corwora, 169
cotton tree, 113
coughs, 38, 51, 63, 64, 66, 69, 70, 86, 88, 92, 100, 121, 127, 169; *see also* colds
cough syrups, 194, 202, 203
p-coumaric acid, 166
coumarins, *glos.,* 35, 36, 60, 86, 102
counter-irritant, 56
cow itch, 66
cowpea, wild, 163
crab's eye, 99
cramps, 72, 136; intestinal, 88, 175; stomach, 88, 175
cress, yellow, 90
Crinum asiaticum, 13, 94, 106, 185-6, *192*
C. pedunculatum, 167, 170, *176*
C. uniflorum, 13, 106
Crotalaria cunninghamii, 31
C. sturtii, 31
Croton insularis, 83
C. phebalioides, 74, 83-4
C. stigmatosus, 84

Index

crumbweed: crested, 106; green, 55
Cryptocarya pleurosperma, 196
CSIRO, 14, 17
cuccurdie, 185
cudweed, Jersey, 87
culgera-culgera, 27
culgum, 26
cumburtu, 148
cundilyong, 185
cunjevoi, 26, 48, 130–1
curara, 127
Curcuma australasica, 170, *176*
currant: bush, 138; plain, 37; tree, black, 137
curtain vine, 190
cuts and abrasions, 43, 96, 102, 104, 109, 113, 115, 121, 154, 176, 179
cyanogenic compounds, *glos.,* 27, 32, 57, 59, 112
Cyanotis axillaris, 170–1
Cyathea australis, 74, *80,* 84
cycas, 106
Cycas media, 81, 106–7
cycloartenol, 100
Cymbidium albuciflorum, 152
C. canaliculatum, 145, 151–2
C. leai, 151
C. madidum, 145, 152
C. sparkesii, 151
Cymbonotus lawsonianus, 96, 107
Cymbopogon, 107–8
C. bombycinus, 107–8
C. exaltatus, 57
C. procerus, 46, 57
Cynanchum floribundum, 57
Cynometra bijuga, 130
C, ramiflora, 125, 130
Cyperus bifax, 186
C. retzii, 186
C. rotundus, 171
cypress pines: black, 196, 198; white, 196, 198
cytisine, 163
cytolysins, 167

dalgan, 150
dampy-dampy, 152
Daphnandra aromatica, 85
D. micrantha, 75, 84–5
D. repandula, 75
daphnandrine, 75, 84, 85
daphnoline, 75, 84, 85
darjen, 69
Darwinia citriodora, 99
Daviesia latifolia, 166, 171, *177*
daviesine, 171
deacetyltanghinin, 30
dead finish, 127
deafness, 182–3, 188
Deeringia amaranthoides, 172
D. celosioides, 172
1,2-dehydroapetaline, 85
dehydrogeijerin, 36
Dendrobium teretifolium, 31, *33*
Dendrocnide, 39
D. excelsa, 26–7, 48–9, *128,* 130–1
deobstruent, *glos.,* 81, 83, 89
depilatory, *glos.,* 174
desmethoxycentaureidin-7-0-rutinoside, 100

devil's: guts, 82; twine, 54, 82
devil tree, 79
dhoo-ee, 26
diabetes, 167, 127, 179
Dianella ensifolia, 108
diaphoretics, *glos.,* 69, 80, 83, 175
diarrhoea, *glos.,* 14, 34, 37, 40, 56, 61, 70, 79, 82, 127, 133, 142, 145, 147, 148, 149, 150, 151, 153, 155, 156, 157, 158, 159, 162, 187; in calves, 164
digestion problems, 142, 144–5; *see also* indigestion
digitalis, 84
3,4-dihydroxyrottlerin, 134
Dioscorea punctata, 186
D. transversa, 186
Diplocyclos palmatus, 152
discharge, mucous, 190
discutient, *glos.,* 180
disinfectant *see* antiseptic
dita bark, 49, 79
ditamine, 79
diterpenoids, *glos.,* 148; acids, 32, 34, 198, 199
diuretics, *glos.,* 42, 54, 63, 69, 80, 81, 83, 90, 92, 146, 162, 175, 180, 184, 188
djumbu, 57
do-anjin-jin, 99
Dodonaea attenuata, 57, *64*
D. lanceolata, 32
D. preissiana, 57
D. viscosa, 32, *33*
dog: bush, 36; nut, 37; wood, 58, 159
dog's balls, 37, 157
doomba oil tree, 128
dopamine, 90
doryafranine, 85
doryanine, 85
Doryphora aromatica, 85
D. sassafras, 16, 85–6, 98
doryphorine, 85
Drimys aromatica, 92
D. lanceolata, 92
dropsy, *glos.,* 86, 183, 188
dtheerah, 134
dthumara, 57
Duboisia, 39
D. hopwoodii, 13, 22, 23, 24, 33, *33,* 50
D. leichhardtii, 196, 199–200
D. myoporoides, 19, 195–6, 200, *208*
dundathic acid, 148
dyaridany, 113
dygal, 134
dyiwididiny, 112
dysentery, glos., 28, 35, 37, 62, 78, 79, 82, 91, 127, 145, 147, 148, 150, 151, 152, 154, 155, 156, 157, 158, 159, 169, 179, 187
dysentery: bush, 147; plant, 37
dysmenorrhoea, *glos.,* 88, 175; *see also* menstrual disorders
dyspepsia, *glos.,* 78, 81, 136
dysuria, *glos.,* 108

ear: ache, 26, 31, 38; disease, 56; sores, 121
ebony, Queensland, 114
echicerine, 80
echiretine, 80
echitamidine, 79

echitamine, 79
echiteine, 80
echitenine, 79
Echites scholaris, 79
echitine, 80
Eclipta alba, 86
E. prostrata, 86
eclipta, white, 86
eczema *glos.,* 83, 136; *see also* rashes; skin
eger, 139
Ehretia saligna, 33
Elaeodendron maculosum, 156
Elder Expedition, 24
elemicin, 72
elemi: resin, 103; tree, 103; tree, Queensland, 103
Eleocharis dulcis, 108
Elephantopus scaber, 108
ellagic acid, 110, 132, 144, 154, 158
ellipticine, 205
emenungkwa, 61
emetics, *glos.,* 43, 51, 54, 86, 89, 127, 128, 136, 146, 167
emmenagogues, *glos.,* 81, 89, 90, 171, 179
emphysema, *glos.,* 62
emu: apple, 66; berries, 37; bush, 18, 59, 152; bush, spotted, 59; plant, 33
endabari, 188
engraver's wood, 117
Entada phaseoloides, 131–2
E. scandens, 131
epoxymalabaricol, 78
epoxyoleic acid, 140
eremolactone, 58
Eremophila bignoniiflora, 152–3
E. cuneifolia, 46, 58
E. fraseri, 33–4, 46
E. freelingii, 46, 58
E. longifolia, 18, 46, 58
E. maculata, 59, *65*
eremophila, wedge-leaved, 58
Eriostemon brucei, 60
eriostemon, rough, 196, 200
E. trachyphyllus, 196, 200–201
Ervatamia, 94
E. angustisepala, 60
E. orientalis, 60, 96, 109
Erythraea, 75
E. australis, 82, 145
Erythrina, 200
E. verspertilio, 34
erythrocentaurin, 83
erythrodiol, 117
erythrophlein, 109
Erythrophleum chlorostachys, 109
E. chlorostachyum, 19, 109
E. laboucheri, 109
esculin, 195
e-sie, 163
essential oils, *glos.,* 17, 36, 46, 57, 58, 60, 64, 65, 66, 68, 71, 72, 77, 88, 90, 95, 96, 97–9, 102, 103, 104, 115, 118, 128, 130, 137, 143, 148, 151, 166, 171, 174, 175, 191, 195, 199, 201
ethanol, 75
eucalyptol, 194; *see* 1,8-cineole
eucalypts, 97, 142, 144, 145; *see also Eucalyptus;* gums
Eucalyptus, 18, 23, 46–7, 95, 99, 194–5

233

E. acmenioides, 153
E. australiana, 202
E. camaldulensis, 153
E. citriodora, 19, 97, 99, 201
E. corymbosa, 132
E. crebra, 153
E. dichromophloia, 86
E. dives, 19, 46, 97, 194, 195, 201-2
E. drepanophylla, 109-10
E. elata, 98
E. fruticetorum, 203
E. globulus, 49, 194, 201, 202, 203
E. gummifera, 125, *128,* 132, 182
E. gunnii, 99
E. haemastoma, 153-4
E. kochii, 202
E. leucoxylon, 46, 194, 202, *209*
E. longirostris, 153
E. macrorhyncha, 195, 202-3, *209*
E. maculata, 99, 110
E. micrantha, 155
E. microtheca, 167, 172
E. mycrocorys, 153
eucalyptus oil, 16, 46-7, 49, 95, 97, 194-5, 201, 202, 203
E. oleosa, 194, 202
E. papuana, 60-1, *80*
E. pilularis, 154
E. piperita, 15, 154-5, 195, 202
E. polybractea, 98, 194, 203, *209*
E. polycarpa, 34, 155
E. pruinosa, 61
E. racemosa, 154, 155
E. radiata, 46, 194, 202
E. resinifera, 186-7
E. rostrata, 153
E. saligna, 153, *160*
E. sclerophylla, 154, 155
E. siderophloia, 142, 187
E. sideroxylon, 194, 202
E. signata, 154, 155
E. smithii, 203
E. tereticornis, 153
E. terminalis, 34, 155
E. tessellaris, 155-6
E. tetrodonta, 61
E. viminalis, 145, 156
E. youmanii, 195, 204
Eucarya acuminata, 191
E. spicata, 69
Eucryphia billardieri, 110
E. lucida, 96, 110
eudesmin, 144
Eugenia suborbicularis, 163
eugenol, 83, 90, 98, 151
Euodia vitiflora, 14, 35
Euphorbia, 94, 124
E. alsinaeflora, 61
E. alsiniflora, 61-2
E. atoto, 110-11
E. australis, 111, 124
E. coghlanii, 111, 124
E. drummondii, 182, 187
E. heterodoxa, 124
E. hirta, 62
E. mitchelliana, 156
E. peplus, 124
E. pilulifera, 62
everlasting, common, 174
Evodia see *Euodia*
evolvine, 35

Evolvulus alsinoides, 35
Exallage auricularia, 182-3, 187-8
Exacum ovatum, 91
Excaecaria see *Excoecaria*
Excoecaria, 94, 95
E. agallocha, 132-3
E. parvifolia, 12, 35
exocarpic acid, 87
Exocarpos aphyllus, 62
E. cupressiformis, 81, 86-7
expectorant, *glos.,* 54, 64, 118, 203
eyes: infected, 134; inflamed, 82, 94-5, 129; sore, 28, 29, 31, 34, 41, 61, 67, 94-5, 100, 104, 105, 112, 116, 118, 119, 120, 137, 187; *see also* ophthalmia; sandy blight
eyewashes, 37, 94-5

fanflower, prickly, 138
fatty: acids, 128; oil, 128
febrifuges, *glos.,* 49, 78, 81, 132
fenchol, 118
fenchone, 118
fennel seed oil, 196
fever, 14, 28, 35, 41, 49, 52, 53, 56, 57, 60, 61, 62, 63, 69, 70, 79, 81, 89, 106, 118, 120, 153, 179
fever: bark, 78; tree, 49
fibrewood, 130
Ficus, 94
F. aspera, 111
F. coronata, 12, 94, 111-2
F. glomerata, 188
F. opposita, 125, *129,* 133
F. racemosa, 188
F. scabra, 11, 111
F. stephanocarpa, 111
F. vesca, 188
fig: cluster, 188; creek, 111; purple, 111; rough, 111; sandpaper, 111, 133
firebrush, 150, 185
fixed oil, 191
Flagellaria indica, 112
flannel bush, 118
flavans, 144
flavone, 34
flavonoids, *glos.,* 32, 56, 62, 87, 90, 100, 102, 108, 110, 136, 140, 144, 159, 161, 177, 179, 180
flax, native, 23
flavourings, 96, 98, 194, 195
Flindersia maculata, 156
F. maculosa, 156-7
flower oils, 99
Flueggia microcarpa, 138
F. virosa, 138
3-formyl-4-hydroxy-alpha-pyrone, 81
Fraxinus ornus, 146-7
freckles, 134
freelingyine, 58
Frenela calcarata, 198
F. endlicheri, 198
Fusanus acuminatus, 191
F. spicatus, 69
fungicides, 68, 99, 125, 155, 202
furocoumarins, 138
fuchsia: bush, 59; limestone, 58, native, 59; spotted, 59; wild, 59

Galactia varins, 47-8, 71
galdjal, 31
gallic acid, 99, 144, 154, 158, 168, 169
gamma-terpinene, 115
gangrene, diabetic, 96
gaoloowurrah, 137
gardgu, 86
gargles and mouth washes, 195, 202
geapga, 197
Geijera parviflora, 14, 25, *33,* 36
G. pendula, 36
G. salicifolia, 74
geiparvarin, 36
genital inflammations, 83, 103
gentian, 145
Geraldton wax, 99
geraniol, 98
geranyl acetate, 199
germicides, *glos.; see* antiseptics; bactericides
gidgee-gidgee, 99
giggle-giggle, 48, 130
gingerah, 36
glucuronic acid, 47, 169
glucuronides, 16
glutamic acid, 42
glyciphyllin, 92
glycosides, *glos.,* 41, 83, 90, 107, 118, 138; cardiac, *glos.,* 30; cyanogenic, 27, 59; flavonoid, 87, 159
glycyrrhizin, 67
Gnaphalium luteoalbum, 87
gogo vine, 131
goitcho, 54
golden chain, 163
gonorrhoea, 96, 115, 137, 182, 186, 187, 188, 190, 191; *see also* veneral diseases
Goodenia ovata, 172, *177*
G. scaevolina, 63
G. varia, 36, *48*
goodenia, sticky, 36
goo-mao-mah, 130
go-onje, 117
goomurrie, 34
goonooru, 60
gooramurra, 152
gooroombah, 135
goosefoot, crested, 106
gorarbar, 119
gotoobah, 164
grape: Gippsland, 55; native, 55, 168, 169
grass, scented, 57
Gratiola latifolia, 18
G. officinalis, 173
G. pedunculata, 173
G. peruviana, 19
G. pubescens, 19
green bird flower, 31
Grevillea lineata, 173
G. pyramidalis, 112
G. striata, 173
Grewia, 94, 112
G. helicterifolia, 37
G. latifolia, 157
G. polygama, 37
G. retusifolia, 37
gruie, 66
guaiac resin, 48
guilandina bonduc, 81
G. bonducella, 81

Index

guilandinin, 81
gukwonderuk, 105, 129
gulay, 117
gum: blue, 202; citron-scented, 201; desert, 60; drooping white, 60; ghost, 60; gully, 203; lemon-scented, 201; lemon-scented spotted, 201; manna, 156; Murray red, 153; orange, 147; ribbon, 156; river red, 153; roughbark ribbon, 156; rusty, 147; scribbly, 153, 155; Smith's, 203; snappy, 155; spotted, 110; Tasmanian blue, 49, 194; white, 153, 172; *see also* eucalypts
gumamu, 137
gums: bleeding, 128; sore, 190
gung gara, 81
gunthamarrah, 117
gutchu, 191
guttapercha tree, 35
guwal, 139
gwiyarbi, 117
gympie, 130
Gyrocarpus americanus, 112–13, 196
g. jacquinii, 112
Gyrostemon acaciiformis, 185
G. cotinifolius, 185
G. pungens, 185

haematuria, *glos.,* 188
haemocorin, 174
Haemodorum coccineum, 173
H. corymbosum, 173, *177*
H. spicatum, 157
haemolysins, 167
haemoptysis, *glos.,* 188
haemorrhagins, 167
haemostatic, *glos.,* 90, 116, 137, 158; *see also* bleeding
hair restorers, 43, 124–5
Hakea, 39, 200
H. macrocarpa, 113
hakkin, 26
hautriwaic acid, 57
headache, 27, 31, 32, 34, 38, 43, 46, 54, 55, 56, 61, 64, 65, 66, 67, 68, 69, 70, 71, 72, 82, 101–2, 204
headache vine, 55
heart, 113; arrhythmia, 208; disease, 80, 84, 86, 196; pain, 34
heartsease, 173
hedyotine, 188
Hedyotis auricularia, 187
H. galioides, 175
heilaman tree, 34
Heleocharis see *Eleocharis*
Helichrysum apiculatum, 174, *177*
Heliotropium ovalifolium, 87
helminthosporin, 43
Helms, R., 24, 146
hemp, Queensland, 70
Hernandia peltata, 174
herpes, 136
Herpestis monniera, 185
Heteropogon contortus, 63
Hibiscus diversifolius, 174–5, *177*
H. ficulneus, 174
H. populneus, 140
H. tiliaceus, 113
H. vitifolius, 113–14

hibiscus, yellow, 113
hickory, 50, 126
histamine, 131; *see also* antihistamine
hollyhock, Australian, 114
Homalanthus see *Omalanthus*
homoaromoline, 85
honeysuckle, silvery, 173
hop: bitter-pea, 171; goodenia, 172
hopbush, 32, 57; giant, 32; narrowleaf, 57; slender, 57; sticky, 32
hordenine, 50
horseradish tree, 185
Howitt, A.W., 18, 22
humbug, 27
Hybanthus enneaspermus, 152
hydatid cysts, *glos.,* 171
hydrocele, *glos.,* 81
Hydrocharis dubia, 18
H. morsusranae, 18
Hydrocotyle asiatica, 184
H. cordifolia, 184
H. repanda, 184
hydrocotyline, 185
hydrocyanic acid, 106, 168
Hydrolea zeylanica, 114
Hydropeltis purpurea, 168
hydrophobia *see* rabies
hydroxyproline, 42
4-hydroxyrottlerin, 134
5-hydroxytryptamine, 131
5-hydroxyverbenalin, 192
hyoscyamine, 199, 200
hyoscine, 17, 19, 196, 200
hypaphorine, 100
hyperoside, 118
hypoglycaemic agent, *glos.,* 62, 158
hypotensives, *glos.,* 79, 89

indigestion, 34, 70, 151
indigo: Birdsville, 63; nine-leaved, 63; plant, 119
Indigofera dominii, 63
I. enneaphylla, 63
I. linnaei, 63
infections, 96
inflammations, 94, 106, 188
influenza, 61, 68, 76, 78, 120, 179
ingulba, 40
inhalant, 194, 202
inophyllic acid, 128
inophyllolide, 128
insect repellents, 38, 49, 68, 175
internal complaints, 160, 177
intoxicant, 63, 76
invigorators, 82, 88, 137
iodine plant, 109
Ionidium suffruticosum, 157
ipi-ipi, 137
Ipomoea angustifolia, 115
I. biloba, 188
I. brasiliensis, 188, *192*
I. mauritiana, 157–8
I. paniculata, 157
I. pes-caprae, 188
I. turpethum, 159
ironbark: Bowen, 109; Queensland, 109; white, 203
ironwood, 109; Cooktown, 20, 109
irtaie, 130
islandicin, 43

isobutyroyl tropine, 199
isocorydine, 80, 85
isoorientin, 100
Isopogon ceratophyllus, 87–8
isorhamnetin, 26
isorottlerin, 134
isotetrandine, 80, 85
Isotoma petraea, 24, 37, *49*
isovaleric aldehyde, 46
itching, 117, 124, 125, 137, 139, 187, 190
i-wa-wal, 100

Jack's joy, 37
Jacksonia dilatata, 158
ja-jow-erong, 50
jaln-ba, 139
Jatropha moluccana, 184
je-jo, 53
jelly-boys, 37
jelly leaf, 70
jerrigree, 203
jil-leer, 35
jimbul, 172
Jimmy Green, 203
Jimmy Low, 186
Johnston, T.H., 22
jundal, 117
Justicia procumbens, 19

kabil-kabil, 150
kaempferol, 132
kai-kai, 87, 160
kal-boo-roon-ga, 115
kamala tree, 134
kame, 149
kandurangu, 185
kandjirkalara, 105
kanjirralaa, 105
karkar, 87
kar-kor, 159
karoo, 117
karoom, 37
karum, 136
kelango, 191
Khata edulis, 24
kidney complaints, 148, 149, 163
kilvain, 134
kinos, *glos.,* 142–4
kinotannic acid, 144, 153
kinyamurra, 18
kirni, 32
koo-badg-aroo, 89
kooline, 37
koombi, 26
koona puturku, 129
ko-on-je-rung, 88
koorool, 79
ko-po, 138
ko-ral-ba, 119
kou-nung, 37
kowar, 186
kuiperi, 117
kukula, 175
kulcha, 34
kullingal, 61
ku-man, 119
kumbalin, 179
kumbiji, 170
kunan, 31

kungsberry bush, 81
kuntan, 34
kunyamurra, 18
kura, 112
kurleah, 172
kurrajong, 119; redfruit, 119; scrub, 67
kurroonbah, 135
kurwan, 197
kwatjinga-unbunamba, 71
Kyllinga, brevifolia, 19

Laboucheria chlorostachys, 109
laburnum, sea coast, 163
lacambie, 78
lactagogues, *glos.,* 83, 111, 112, 136, 137, 167, 168
lactones, 57, 58
lanceol, 137
lanoline bush, 72
Laportea gigas, 27, 48, 130
larvicides, 166
laryngitis, 50
latex, 95, 109, 112, 124, 133, 188
Latz, Peter, 13, 14, 24
laurel: Alexandrian, 128; dodder, 54, 82
laurotetanine, 82
Lauterer, Joseph, 48, 103, 142, 144
Lavatera plebeia, 114, 97
lavender oil, 98
lawyer vine, 54, 112
laxatives, 30, 34, 80, 81, 127, 128, 145–6, 149, 150, 151, 152, 153, 156, 159, 174, 184
leather jacket, 27
leatherwood, 110
lecambil, 78
Lechhardtia australis, 175
Leichhardt tree, 89, 167
lenn, 169
leopard tree, 156
leopardwood, 156
leprosy, *glos.,* 43, 126, 128, 129, 130, 133, 134, 135, 136, 139, 185
Leptospermum, 18
L. petersonii, 19, 98
lettuce tree, sea, 138
leucodelphinidin, 154
leucoderma, 201
Levitt, Dulcie, 12–13, 13–4, 19, 94–5
lightwood, 126
lignum vitae, 126
lilac, Cape, 134
lily: crinum, 94, 185; pink water, 159, spoon, 26; swamp, 170; water, 168
limonene, 166
linalool, 36, 98, 160
liniments, 27, 38, 65, 191, 194, 195, 201, 202, 203
liniment tree, 65
linolenic acid, 184
liquorice: Indian, 99; wild, 91
liringgin, 50
liriodenine, 85
Litsea chinensis, 133
L. glutinosa, 125, 133–4
liver complaints, 86, 173
Lobelia purpurascens, 177
lobeline, 37, 177
loganine, 208
lollybush, 30

loosestrife: purple, 158; willow-like, 158
Loranthus maidenii, 103
L. quandang, 52
lotus, sacred, 159
loya vine, 54
lucerne: native, 70; Paddy's, 70
lungs: congestion of, 68; disease, 70, 80, 86
lupus, 198
luteolin, 100, 109
luteolin-7-glucoside, 108
Luzula campestris, 19
L. meridionalis, 19
Lycopodium phlegmaria, 183, 189
lycorine, 167, 170, 186
Lysiphyllum carronii, 114–15
Lythrum salicaria, 158

maband, 113
macrozamin, 107
maculosidine, 60
magnocurarine, 113, 196
mahogany: forest, 186; red, 186
maidenhair fern: common, 51; small, 51
Maiden, J.H., 13, 15, 18, 22, 24, 25, 48, 74–5, 76, 103, 107, 146, 175
malabaricandiol, 78
malabaricol, 78
malaise, 109
malanthin, 78
malaria, 28, 41, 49, 66, 67, 78, 79, 81, 89, 135, 179
mallee, blue, 194, 203
Mallotus mollissimus, 158–9
M. philippensis, 134
M. ricinoides, 158
mamilyaburna, 65
mamurrinya, 37
mangarr, 112
mange, 130
manggar manggal, 100
mangkarrba, 29, 95
mangkurrkwa, 40
mangrove: black, 160; freshwater, 127; milky, 132; river, 26, 166
manna, 145–6, 156, 159; ash tree, 145–6; gum, 156
mannitol, 34, 87, 145–6, 156, 159
mao-wararg, 190
mapoon, 169
mardaudhu, 86
marking: nut, 139; tree, 139
marnuwiji, 81
marrankangu, 57
Marsdenia australis, 175
marshcress, yellow, 90
mat spurge, 187
mbau-nu, 168
measles, 172
medicine tree, 185
mee-a-mee, 27
meemeei, 135
meeninya, 137
Melaleuca, 12, 18, 46
M. alternifolia, 96–7, 97, 99, 115, 195, 204
M. cajuputi, 37, 46, 64, 166
M. hypericifolia, 46, 63–4, *80*
M. lancifolia, 37

M. leucadendron, 18, 37, 64
M. linariifolia, 97, 115, 204 ,
M. maidenii, 64
M. minor, 37
melaleuca oil, 49, 96–7
M. quinquenervia, 18, 19, 37, 38, 46, 49, 64–5, 76, 97, 166
M. smithii, 64
M. symphyocarpa, 46, 65, 204
M. trinervis, 37
M. uncinata, 46, 65
M. viridiflora, 18, 64
Melastoma malabathricum, 19
Melia australasica, 134
M. azedarach, 125, *129,* 134–5
M. composita, 134
M. dubia, 134
menorrhagia, *glos.,* 188; *see also* menstrual
menstrual: disorders, 102, 116, 167, 175, 188; flow, reduction of, 158; *see also* dysmenorrhea
Mentha australis, 46, 65–6
M. diemenica, 15, 88, 175
M. gracilis, 175
M. piperita, 19, 88, 175
M. satureioides, 15, 77, 88, 175
menthol, 15, 19, 88, 98, 155, 195
menthone, 15, 88
methyl acetate, 88
Merremia tridentata, 115
methoxyatherosperminine, 80
7-methoxy-2,2,-dimethylchromen, 102
9-methoxyellipticine, 205
5'-methoxynobiletin, 102
methyleugenol, 58, 72, 98, 151
methyl mercaptan, 104
methyl salicylate, 52
metrorrhagia, *glos.,* 102; *see also* menstrual
Metrosideros gummifera, 132
M. hyssopifolia, 204
micranthine, 75, 84
mida, 112
migirra, 108
migraine, 155
milk: bush, 137; plant, 187; vine, 137
millewah, 126
Mimulus gracilis, 115–16
Mimosa scandens, 131
mindharri, 70
mindjaarra, 70
mindijulu, 118
mingulba, 22, 40
mingkulpa, 39
minjakara, 71
mint: Australian, 65; bush, 68; bush, round-leaf, 160; native, 65; river, 65; slender, 175; *see also* peppermint
miri-miri, 110
mistletoe, grey, 52
moinjal, 133
monoterpenoids, *glos.,* 36, 98
moochai, 188
mooda, 89
moolar, 172
moolerr, 153
mootchong, 50
moradiol, 117
morgogaba, 38
morinda, 88; great, 88

Index

Morinda citrifolia, 88–9
M. quadrangularis, 88
M. reticulata, 169
morindin, 89
morolic acid, 61
Morton, J.F., 145
moschatoline, 80
Moschosma polystachyum, 53
mucilage, *glos.,* 37, 70, 161
Mucuna gigantea, 66
mugurpul, 179
mugwara, 117
mulberry, Indian, 88
mulka wertibi, 103
mumin, 179
mumps, 188
muntju, 39
munya-munya, 187
munyeroo, 90
munyun, 69
murgan, 26
murl-kue-kee, 163
murlun, 31
murn-tyul, 133
murr-rung, 27
Musa banksii, 38–9
Museum of Applied Arts and Sciences, Sydney (formerly Technological Museum, Sydney), 19, 47, 95, 195
mustard tree, 185
muwarraga, 150
Myoporum debile, 189-90, *193*
M. diffusum, 189
M. platycarpum, 146, 159
myriogenin, 130
Myriogyne minuta, 105
Myristica cimicifera, 135
M. insipida, 125, 135
M. muelleri, 135
myrtle, broom honey, 65
Myrtus saligna, 37

na-gobar, 131
namana, 111
nanchee, 116
nanmuta, 109
nappalla, 184
napum-napum, 136
narcotics, *glos.,* 13, 21–4, 25, 28, 29, 30, 33, 35, 36, 37, 39–40, 137, 185, 200
nargan, 26
Nasturtium palustre, 90
N. semipinnatifidum, 90
N. terrestre, 90
nateha, 55
Nauclea orientalis, 89, 167
ndilo tree, 128
nectarine, native, 66
Nelumbium speciosum, 159
Nelumbo nucifera, 159, *160*
neriifolin, 30
nerolidol, 97
nervous system, diseases of, 185
Nesodaphne obtusifolia, 151
nettle: native, 48; tree, giant, 130
neuralgia, 38, 64, 79
neurotoxins, 166
ngama-ngama, 187
ngamul-ngamul, 137
ngean-jerry, 118

ngurbi, 63
ngurubi, 63
niaouli, 64; oil, 166
Nicotiana, 13, 22
N. benthamiana, 39
N. cavicola, 39
N. debneyi, 204–5
N. excelsior, 22, 23, 24, 39
N. gossei, 22, 23, 40
N. megalosiphon, 205
N. sauveolens, 39, 204, 205
nicotine, 19, 23, 24, 33, 37, 39, 40, 81, 86, 200
nilura, 101
nipan, 169
nono-groyinandie, 27
noolburra, 60
noomaie, 111
noradrenaline, 90
noreugenin, 89
norhyoscyamine, 199, 200
nor-nicotine, 23, 24, 33, 39
nornuciferine, 159
nose: bleeding, 203; infections, 89
nuciferine, 159
numbah, 64
nutgrass, 171; downs, 186
nutmeg: oil, 96; Queensland, 135
nuts: bonduc, 81; nicker, 81

oak: beach, 150; coast, 150; desert, 199; swamp, 150
Ochrosia elliptica, 66
O. moorei, 205
Ocimum anisodorum, 89
O. caryophyllinum, 89
O. sanctum, 89
oestrogenic activity, 171
oilgrass, silky, 107
Oldenlandia auricularia, 187
O. galioides, 175–6
oldman's beard, 56
old man weed, 129
oleanolic acid, 87, 118, 147
oleoresins, 143, 171
olive, native, 197
doorgo, 163
Omalanthus populifolius, 116
onion vine, 159
on-tho, 173
oolpanje, 89
oondundo, 42
ootcho, 117
Operculina turpethum, 159–60
opium, antidote for, 41
ophthalmia, *glos.,* 100, 183, purulent, 17, 95, 105, 129
ophthalmic surgery, 200
orchid: arrowroot, 152; curry, 152; pencil, 31
ori, 155
orientin, 100, 158
Ottelia alismoides, 176
ouraie, 37
Owenia acidula, 66–7
O. reticulata, 176
Oxalis corniculata, 19
ozaena, *glos.,* 121, 185

padjapadja, 179
Pagetia medicinalis, 176
pain: abdominal, 79, 89, 149; alimentary, 138; body, 33, 35, 36, 38, 51, 55, 61, 65, 67, 88, 128, 129, 133, 136; internal, 44, 139; joints, 192; loins, 132; muscular, 52, 202, 203
pain-ki, 112
painkillers *see* analgesics
palgarri, 86
pallabara, 60, 109
palsy, 81
pam-mo, 37
panaryle, 18, 65
Pandanus odoratissimus, 40
P. spiralis, 40
paperbark, 64, 71; broad-leaved, 64
parasite infestations, *glos.,* 166; *see also* taenia; worms
pardan, 179
parde-bardette, 137
pareira brava, 151
parka, 30
parpa, 188
parpangata, 131
pea: Darling, 119; parrot, 31; rosary, 99; smooth Darling, 119
peach, native, 66, 191
peanut tree, 119
pedgery, 33
peebeen, 120
Penfold, A.R., 95, 97, 98, 99
penja-penja, 68, 71
pennyroyal, 18, 65; Brisbane, 88; native, 77, 88, 175; wild, 88
pennywort, Indian, 184
5-(10-pentadecenyl)-resorcinol, 112
Pentatropis linearis, 178
pepper: climbing, 190; native, 190, 206; vine, Australian 190; vine, native, 77, 190; water, 90
pepperberry, 83
peppermint, 88, 175, 195; blackbutt, 203; broad-leaf, 194, 201–2; broad-leaved, 19; native, 65; oils, 19, 38; Sydney, 15, 154; *see also* mint
pepperwood, 83
perfumes, 98, 99
pergunny, 114
persicarin, 90
Persoonia falcata, 97, 116
Peruvian bark, 78
Petalostigma, 41
P. cookii, 40
P. pubescens, 40–1
P. quadriloculare, 41
P. solms-laubachii, 40
P. triloculare, 41
Petit, A., 23
phenols, 68, 90, 97, 98, 99, 144
phenylcoumarins, 128
pheromones, 183
phillyrigenin, 136
phlobaphene, 144
phloracetophenone dimethyl ether, 36
phthisis, *glos.,* 70, 169
Phyllanthus baccatus, 138
P. reticulatus, 138
P. simplex, 125, 190
P. virgatus, 190
piban, 31

237

Pigea banksiana, 157
pigface, 14
pigweed, 90
pigurga, 179
piles, 82, 83, 139, 167
Pimelea distinctissima, 67
P. microcephala, 67
pine: black, 198; colonial, 148; hoop, 148; milky, 79; Moreton Bay, 148; Murray, 198, oil, 98; Queensland, 148; red, 198; Richmond river, 148; scrub, 198; white, 79, 198
pinkaraangu, 39
Pinus, 142
P. palustris, 98
Piper methysticum, 77
P. novae-hollandiae, 77, 190
peperitol, 97, 98
piperitone, 15, 97, 98, 154-5, 166, 195, 201, 202
pirrungu, 32
pitcha, 26
pitcheri, 33
pitula, 59
pittosapogenin, 136
pittosporum, weeping, 135
Pittosporum phillyraeoides, 135-6
P. venulosum 183, 190-1
pituri, 13, 18, 22-4, 33, 35, 37, 39; preparation of, 22
piturine, 23
piturr, 39
piturrba, 39
piwi, 111, 187
Planchonella laurifolia, 67
P. pohlmanniana, 116-17
Planchonia careyra, 12-13, 94, 97, 117
P. crenata, 117
Plectranthus congestus, 160
plumbagin, 136
plum: bush, 81, 137; ochrosia, 66; Pohlmann's jungle, 117; sour, 66; wild, 29, 94-5; wood, 137; yellow, 164
Plumbago zeylanica, 136
poison: berry tree, 135; bush, 33; tree, 109; tree, river, 132
polai, 179
polak, 153
Polanisia viscosa, 56
Pollichia zeylanica, 179
Polygonum barbatum, 42
P. hydropiper, 90
polyphenols, *glos.,* 120, 125, 135
Pongamia glabra, 136
P. pinnata, 136
pongamol, 136
poodgee-poodgee, 134
poodgee-poodgera, 134
pooragri, 198
poplar: desert, 185; native, 185; Queensland, 116; western, 185
Portulaca oleracea, 90
potassium nitrate, 90
Pouteria pohlmanniana, 116
poxplant, 187
Pratia purpurascens, 177
precatorine, 100
prickly heat, 139, 185
prolapsus ani, 102
proline, 42

propeller tree, 112, 196
Prostanthera, 46
P. cineolifera, 46, 68
P. cotinifolia, 160
P. retusa, 160
P. rotundifolia, 160, *160*
proteolysins, 167
proteolytic, *glos.,* enzymes, 94, 138; latex, 109, 112, 133, 188; substances, 60
prunasin, 59
Prunella vulgaris, 118
pruritus, *glos.,* 136
Psilotum nudum, 177
P. triquetrum, 177
Psoralea, 23
pteridin, 178
Pteridium aquilinum, 177
P. esculentum, 177-8
Pterigon odorus, 68
Pterocarpus, 142, 144
Pterocaulon glandulosum, 68
P. serrulatum, 46, 68-9
puchiin, 108
pudginjacker, 163
pukati, 25
pulandu, 39
pulantu, 39
pulegone, 88
pulgatura, 118
pulkun, 169
punaangu, 86
punarnavine, 54
pundir-pundir, 99
purgative, 14, 30, 86, 130, 133, 135, 137, 145, 146, 158, 159, 184
purslane, 90
pustules, 134
Pycnonia, 116
pyorrhoea, 96
pyrocatechol, 153

quandong, sweet, 191
quassinoids: anti-leucemic, 29; esters, 29
quercetin, 159
quercitol, 151
quinine, 66, 78, 135; bark, 78; berry, 40, 41; bush, 41; tree, 40, 78, 185
quinones, *glos.,* 25, 26, 166

rabies, 182, 183-4
raisin, white, 139
rancooran, 66
rapanone, 25, 26, 166
Raphidophora australasica, 69
rashes, 137, 138; heat, 139, 185; *see also* eczema; skin
raspberry: native, 161, small leaf, 161; wild, 161
rattlepod, 31
Remirea maritima, 69
relaxant, intestinal, 50
reserpine, 79
respiratory disorders, 62, 65, 86; *see also* asthma; bronchitis; lungs
reticuline, 83
rhamnosides, 134
Rhaphidophora see *Raphidophora*
rheumatic fever, 52

rheumatism, *glos.,* 25, 26, 33, 38, 43, 47, 48, 49, 50, 52, 56, 61, 64, 66, 69, 70, 71, 80, 81, 82, 89, 113, 118, 128, 129, 130, 136, 137, 139, 178, 184, 185, 187, 188, 192, 202, 203
Rhipogonum see *Ripogonum*
Rhizophora candelaria, 160
R. mucronata, 160-1
Rhyncharrhena linearis, 178
Rhynchosia minima, 178
riceflower: Mallee, 67; small-head, 67
ringworm, *glos.,* 115, 125, 132, 133, 135
Ripogonum papuanum, 178
roangga, 186
roemerine, 159
Rorippa islandica, 90-1
rosemary oil, 38
Rostellularia pogonanthera, 19
R. procumbens, 19
Roth, W., 12, 22, 25, 94, 139, 167
rottlerin, 134
rubefacient, *glos.,* 26, 192
Rubus, 161
R. hillii, 160, 161
R. moluccanus, 161
R. parviflorus, 161
R. parvifolius, 161
rubusinic acid, 162
rubitinic acid, 162
rutin, 118, 166, 195, 202-3, 204
rutta, 58

safrole, 58, 72, 80, 83, 85, 86, 98, 151
salicylic acid, 166
sally, 126
salt, 80
saltbush: cabbage, 80; oldman, 80
sandalwood, 69, 137, 195; fragrant, 69; oil, 99; northern, 137; red, 159
sandarac, 143, 196, 198, 199
sandfly: bush, 72; zieria, 72
sandy blight, 95, 105, 129
Santalum acuminatum, 191, 193
S. album, 99
S. angustifolium, 137
S. cognatum, 191
S. cygnorum, 69
S. lanceolatum, 129, 136-7
S. oblongatum, 136
S. obtusifolium, 42
S. preissianum, 191
S. spicatum, 69, 99, 195
santonin, 166
saponin, *glos.,* 28, 67, 81, 87, 103, 117, 127, 128, 135, 138, 169, 178; haemolytic, 26, 136; steroidal, 138; triterpenoid, 28, 81, 117, 127, 128, 168, 184, 188
Sarcocephalus coadunatus, 89
S. cordatus, 89, 167
Sarcostemma, 94
S. australe, 137-8, *144*
sarsaparilla 91, 92; native, 76, 91
sassafras, 80, 84, 85, 150; black, 80; grey, 85; native, 80; net, 85; New South Wales, 85; northern grey, 85; Oliver's, 150; southern, 80; Victorian, 80
satinwood, 84
scabies, *glos.,* 125, 130, 134, 136, 140, 187

238

Index

Scaevola frutescens, 138
S. koenigii, 138
S. spinescens, 138, *144*, 185
S. taccada, 138
scaevolin, 138
scentgrass, 57
scentwood, 129
Schoenoplectus validus, 162
sciatica, 111
Scirpus lacustris, 162
S. validus, 162
Scleria lithosperma, 163
scoparia, 179
Scoparia dulcis, 179
scopolamine, 19, 196, 199, 200
scrofulous complaints, *glos.*, 48, 135, 139, 188
scurvy *see* antiscorbutics
sea sickness, 196, 200
Sebaea ovata, 16, 75, 91, 145
Securinega melanthesoides, 138-9
S. obovata, 138
S. virosa, 138
sedatives, *glos.*, 34, 80, 102
selenium, 170
self heal, 118
Semecarpus australiensis, 139
senna, 149, 150; Australian, 149; native, 150; pepperleaf, 129; ribfruit, 150
Sesbania aegyptiaca, 118
S. grandiflora, 19
S. sesban, 118
sesquiterpenoids, *glos.*, 83, 137
Sharp, J. Gordon, 76
Shaw, Ethel, 13-14
sheep bush, 36
sheoak, coast, 150
Shepherd, T.W., 16, 76-7, 145
shitwood, 112
sickness, 36, 64, 82, 87, 89, 117, 128, 133, 139, 159
sida, common, 70
Sida retusa, 69
S. rhombifolia, 69-70
Sideroxylon laurifolium, 67
S. pohlmannianum, 116
S. richardii, 67
sidratusa, 70
silicic acid, 44
siris, white, 77
sitosterol, 102
skin: cancer, 111, 124, 186; disorders, 48, 89, 115, 124-6, 127, 128, 129, 130, 132, 134, 136, 139, 140, 183, 185; *see also* ringworm; sores
smartweed, 42, 90; water, 90
smallpox, 103, 137, 188
smelly bush, 68
Smilax australis, 91
S. glyciphylla, 16, 76-7, *81*, 91-2, 182
S. officinalis, 92
Smith, H.G., 203
snake: vine, 42; weed, 62
snakebite, 166-7, 169, 172, 174, 180, 183, 187; antidote, 43, 70, 89, 168, 169, 176, 177
sneezeweed, 95, 105; common, 129; desert, 105; spreading, 105
socketwood, 84
Solanum, 17
S. aviculare, 205-6

S. capsiciforme, 206
S. fasciculatum, 207
s. laciniatum, 206
S. lasiophyllum, 97, 118
S. linearifolium, 206-7, *209*
S. simile, 207
S. symonii, 207
S. vescum, 207, *209*
solasodine, 17, 196, 206, 207
Sophora tomentosa, *161*, 163
sores, 20, 26, 43, 56, 58, 60, 62, 79, 90, 101-2, 103, 104, 106, 107, 109, 110, 111, 112, 113, 115, 117, 120, 121, 133, 137, 138, 139, 153, 176, 180, 182, 185, 187, 191; venereal, 132, 185, 187
spade: flower, 157; yellow, 157
sparteine, 208
Spartothamnella juncea, 70, *80*
Spartothamnus junceus, 70
speargrass: black, 63; bunch, 63
speedwell, tropical, 35
spermatheridine, 80
spike rush, 108
Spilanthes, 25
S. acmella, 42
S. grandiflora, 25, 42, *49*
spilanthol, 42
Spinifex longifolius, 112, 119
spleen, enlarged, 180
split Jack(s), 169
sprains, 105, 137, 139
squalene, 100
Staphylococcus aureus, 99, 196, 199, 201
starch, 152
Stemodia grossa, 70
S. lythrifolia, 71
S. viscosa, 71
Stenochilus longifolius, 58
S. maculatus, 59
Stephania hernandifolia, 196
Sterculia quadrifida, 112, 119
steroids, *glos.*, 100, 196, 206, 207
stiffness, 69
stigmasterol, 100, 102
stilbenes, 61
stimulants, 26, 31, 33, 37, 83, 90; cerebro-spinal, 78; heart, 69; intestinal, 50; myocardial, 50
stinging tree, 130; antidote, 26-7, 39, 48-9, 130-1; giant, 26-7, 130
stings *see* bites and stings
stomach, 192; ache, 138; cramps, 38, 175; pains, 40, 55, 108, 149, 151, 163, 179; ulcers, 196, 200; upsets, 28, 158, 162
stomachic, *glos.*, 92
stone fish, antidote for sting, 43
stricture, *glos.*; non-venereal, 128
Striga curviflora, 139
S. curvifolia, 139
stringybark: Darwin, 61; mountain, 202; red, 186, 202; white, 154; Youman's 203
strychnine, 208; bush, 208
Strychnos lucida, 196, 208
sudorifics, *glos.*, 38, 136
sugars, 62, 142, 144, 169, 177, 185
sulphonamides, 17
sunburn, 26
sugarwood, 159
suntan lotions, 198

supinine, 180
supple Jack, 43
supplejack, 43, 112
Swainsona galegifolia, 119-20
S. occidentalis, 120
S. pterostylis, 120
Swainsona *see* Swainsona
swampcress, yellow, 90
sweet: bark, 67; pea, 77
swellings, 43, 56, 100, 108, 120, 167, 169; abdomen, 171; limbs, 31, 37, 65, 118
sycamore, 67
Syncarpia hillii, 120
syphilis, 48, 80, 92, 182, 185, 187; *see also* venereal diseases
syringic acid, 26
Syzygium jambolanum, 19
S. moorei, 20
S. suborbiculare, 163

ta-anji, 106
Tabernaemontana orientalis, 60, 109
tacamahac tree, 128
taenia, 134, 178
tah vine, 54
takking, 169
talara, 39
taliwanti, 31
taliyintiri, 31
Tamarix mannifera, 146
tampara, 169
tandi, 173
tang-gul, 90
tangran, 173
tangungnu, 39
tannins, *glos.*, 28, 32, 34, 47, 50, 51, 58, 86, 87, 90, 101, 110, 126, 127, 128, 133, 143-4, 145, 147, 151, 154, 155, 158, 159, 161, 178, 179, 197
tapeworm *see* taenia
tape vine, 196
tarkal, 184
tarpoon, 116
tar tree, 139
tarvine, 54
Tasmannia aromatica, 92
T. lanceolata, 92
taura, 118
tawalpin, 113
tchaln-ji, 149
tcheergun, 154
tchuldani, 59
tchunba, 155
tdjeundegong, 85
tdun-dambie, 84
tea, sweet, 91
tea tree, 18, 76, 97; broad-leaved, 64, 97; medicinal, 115, 195; oil, 96-7; paperbark, 38, 97; swamp, 38, tecan, 32
Technological Museum, Sydney (later Museum of Applied Arts and Sciences), 95-6
temperature, raising body, 57
Templetonia egena, 208
templetonia, round, 208
Tephrosia brachyodon, 19
T. purpurea, 19
T. varians, 47-8, 71
terpinen-4-ol, 97, 98, 99, 115, 204

terpenoid, *glos.*, acids, 143; hydrocarbons, 143
Tetranthera laurifolia, 133
thalmera, 114
tharragibberah, 137
Thespesia populnea, 140
thespesin, 140
thevobioside, 30
thooromia, 57
thowan, 121
throat: cleanser, 111; complaints, 67; lozenges, 67; sore, 55, 105, 116
thrombase, 167
thujone, 98
thukouro, 90
thurkoo, 30
thymol, 68, 98, 155, 202
tickweed, 56
tiebush, 121
tigloidine, 199
Timonius timon, 120
tinea, *glos.*, 13, 19, 96, 99, 138
Tinospora smilacina, 42-3, 167
t'iranju, 58
tiredness, 72, 137
Ti-trol, 96 *see also* melaleuca oil
tjarin, 120
tjiinngu, 112
tjilkaru, 127
tjinduwadhu, 56
tjipa, 57
tjungarai, 68
tjungu, 112
tjuntiwari, 39
tobacco, native, 43
toi, 154
toka, 89
tonics, *glos.*, 28, 41, 74-7, 78, 79, 80, 81, 82, 83, 84, 85, 86, 87, 88, 89, 91, 92, 171, 188; cardiac, 81; nerve, 81; stomach-strengthening, 82
toolookar, 147
Toona australis, 179
toothache, 14, 25, 28, 29, 33, 35, 36, 37, 38, 41, 42, 43, 79, 86, 185
toothache tree, 35
top-kie, 53
torumba, 186
trachoma, 100
Trachymene hemicarpa, 72
tragacanth, gum, 142
trans-anethole, 196
traveller's joy, 55
treefern, 84; rough, 74, 84
Trezise, Percy, 14
Tribulus cistoides, 43, 49
Trichodesma zeylanicum, 179-80, *192*
Trichosanthes palmata, 121
Tricoryne platyptera, 121
triglycerides, *glos.*, 87
trigonelline, 100
O-3,4,5-trimethoxycinnamoylamajine, 79
triterpenoids, 26, 43, 52, 53, 56, 60, 62, 78, 81, 82, 87, 89, 104, 109, 117, 127, 135, 138, 149, 157, 168, 179, 185, 188, 205
tuberculosis, 70, 130, 169
tulip tree, 140
tumours, 197, 205
turpentine, 120; bush, 33, 112; bush,
pale, 53; plant, 33; scrub, 103
turraie, 173
Tylophora erecta, 191
tympanitis, *glos.*, 171
typhoid fever, 78

ulcers, 56, 78, 82, 89, 103, 109, 111, 114, 117, 120, 128, 133, 136, 154, 182, 185
ulee-ree, 128
ultraviolet radiation screen, 198
umbrella bush, 49
uraemia, *glos.*, 92
urinary: organs, diseases of, 151, 157; problems, 138; *see also* bladder
urine retention, 148
urnarnda, 42
urrgula, 155
ursolic acid, 118, 147, 172
Urtica incisa, 48
urushenols, 139

vanillic acid, 135
vellarin, 185
velvet leaf, 151
venereal diseases, 182, 187, 188, 190, 192; *see also* gonorrhoea; sores, venereal; syphilis
ventilagone, 43
Ventilago viminalis, 43, 124-5
ventimalin, 43
verbena, common, 191
Verbena officinalis, 191-2
verbenalin, 192
vermifuge, *glos.*, 56, 64, 139, 166; horse, 41
vervain, common, 191
vesicatory substances, *glos.*, 136
Vigna vexillata, 163-4
viminalin, 43
vincamajine, 79
vine tree, 43
vitexin, 158
Vitex trifolia, 180
Vitis trifolia, 169
V. acetosa, 168
vitricine, 180
volatile oils, 41, 46, 64, 65, 69, 83, 95, 105, 118, 160, 185; *see also* essential oils

wadura, 57
wakalpuka, 127
walgalu. 86
waljno-jo, 188
walnut: desert, 176; poison, 196
wanna-wuurarumpa, 150
waramburr, 42
warrel, 83, 84
warrongan, 66
warts, 62, 124, 127, 137, 139
wasting diseases, 62
watarka, 49
watchupga, 32
water: shicld, 168; target, 168
watercress, marsh, 90
wattle, 144; fish, 126; kino, 143, 144
wax bush, 33
weakich, 205
Webb, L., 196
Wedelia calendulacea, 92
wedelolactone, 86, 92
wedgerra, 59
weetjellan, 126
whistling tree, 150
white: leaf, 27; root, 177; top, 203; twin heads, 86
White, John, 15
whitewood, 78, 79
widda pooloo, 187
wideerba, 69
Wikstroemia indica, 121
wilawanggan, 72
wilga, 14, 24, 36; creek, 152
wilgar, 42
willer, 173
willow: Australian, 36; native, 135
willparee, 67
windi, 128
wine jujube, 121
wira, 175
wirri-pirri, 67
wondai, 67
wondari, 67
wonkara, 155
woolia, 179
Woolls, William, 145, 146, 200
woonara, 155
woota, 179
worms, 134, 166, 178
wounds, 68, 89, 94, 97, 102, 106, 107, 108, 109, 110, 112, 113, 117, 119, 121, 122, 127, 137, 154, 173, 179, 186; *see also* cuts and abrasions
wurri, 128
wurruwarduwarda, 119

Ximenia americana, 164
X. elliptica, 164
X. exarmata, 164
X. laurina, 164
Xylomelum salicinum, 43
X. scottianum, 43-4

yackahber, 67
yakooro, 127
yambal, 55
yam, long, 186
yarnguli, 137
yarr-warrah, 154
yarrah, 153
yellow: buttons, 174, wood, 84; wood, light, 84
yerroll, 112
yinumaninga, 163
yugam, 128
yumburra, 159
yurol, 112
yuwara, 42

zamia, tree, 106
ziziphine, 122
ziziphinine, 122
Ziziphus celtidifolia, 121
Z. oenoplia, 121-2